A BIRDER'S GUIDE TO MAINE

Elizabeth C. Pierson, Jan Erik Pierson,
and Peter D. Vickery

Maps by Ruth Ann Hill

Down East Books
Camden, Maine

Copyright © 1996 by Elizabeth Cary Pierson, Jan Erik Pierson,
and Peter Douglas Vickery
ISBN 0-89272-365-3
Cover photograph by Bill Silliker, Jr.
Design and typography by Pentagöet Design
Color separation by Roxmont Graphics

Printed and bound at BookCrafters, Inc., Chelsea, Mich.

5 4 3 2 1

Down East Books, P.O. Box 679, Camden, ME 04843

Library of Congress Cataloging-in-Publication Data

Pierson, Elizabeth Cary, 1953–.
    A birder's guide to Maine / Elizabeth C. Pierson, Jan Erik Pierson, and
Peter D. Vickery.
        p.   cm.
    Includes bibliographical references (p.383) and index.
    ISBN 0-89272-365-3 (paper)
        1. Bird watching—Maine—Guidebooks. 2. Birding sites—Maine—Guide-
books. 3. Maine—Guidebooks. I. Pierson, Jan Erik, 1954–.
II. Vickery, Peter D., 1949– . III. Title.
QL684.M2P566 1966
598'.07234741—dc20   96-5728
                                                               CIP

A
BIRDER'S
GUIDE
TO
MAINE

Contents

Acknowledgments

One of the great pleasures in preparing this book has been interacting with the many birders, naturalists, and friends who have assisted us. Some have shared special localities with us, some have taken early drafts and checked to make sure they could actually find the places we described, and some have been brave enough to review entire sections. Others have cared for our children so we could spend a weekend fieldchecking, or have housed us for the night and fed us. Our warmest gratitude goes to everyone involved, because in a very real sense, this book is the product of all these individuals.

Jody Dupres, who in his role as editor of *Maine Bird Notes* has long been a conduit and repository for information on the status of Maine birds, coauthored the checklist that makes up Appendix A in this book and devoted countless hours to the task. We are particularly grateful for his assistance. Bob Berman, of the American Birding Association, generously agreed to format the bar graphs for the checklist and greatly simplified the process of producing camera-ready copy. Lysle Brinker, Charlie Duncan, Rich Eakin, June Ficker, Bill Hancock, David Ladd, Judy Markowsky, Bill Sheehan, and Tom Skaling all reviewed major portions of the text and were immensely generous with their time. Special thanks also go to Dennis Abbott, Paul Adamus, Ann Bacon, Paul Baicich, Dick Banks, Dan Bell, Gorden Bell, Jim Berry, Phil Bozenhart, Greg Butcher, Bobbie Cary, Bill Cleave, Garrett Conover, Rena Cote, Bridget Coullon, the Curtis Memorial Library staff, Gary Donovan, Joan Dow, Norm Famous, Gale and Stan Flagg, Steve Flatling, Kay Gammons, Bill Glanz, Sue and Tom Hayward, Gwen Hazelton, Jim Hinds, Bill Hoadley, Jean Hoekwater, Wendy Howes, Bob Humphreys, Chuck Huntington, Steve Kress, Mark Libby, Colin MacKinnon, Don Mairs, Tom and Josephine Martin, Ken Mattingly, Bob Mauck, Nancy McReel, Jennifer Megyesi, Robert Milardo, Maurry Mills, Mark Murray, Steve Oliveri, Wayne Petersen, Anna and Elspeth Pierson (your parents think you're the greatest!), Don Reimer, Sally Rooney, John Scott, Nancy Sferra, Laurie Sheehan, Rebecca Stanley, Allen Starr, Kyle Stockwell, Wally Sumner, Barbara and Harold Surtees, Fred and Amy Thurber, Bill Townsend, Barbara Vickery, Gabe and Simon Vickery, Steve Weston, Nat and Genie Wheelwright, Ralph Widrig, Herb Wilson, and Bryant Woods. We are grateful to the many people who provided corrections and feedback on the Piersons' 1981 book, *A Birder's Guide to the Coast of Maine*.

We also thank the American Birding Association, the Maine Chapter of The Nature Conservancy, the Maine Audubon Society,

Maine's Departments of Conservation and Inland Fisheries and Wildlife, and our colleagues at Field Guides, Inc., in Austin, Texas, for their assistance and cooperation.

Finally, our thanks to Barbara Feller-Roth, who copyedited the book with great skill; to Ruth Ann Hill, who performed the miracle of turning sketches into maps; and to the editorial staff at Down East Books, who handled the manuscript with such care. In the last department, we are especially grateful to Karin Womer, who never once blew her top when we called to say, "About that deadline, Karin. . . ."

Foreword

I spent all the summers of the 1960s at New England Music Camp on Messalonskee Lake in south-central Maine. My most vivid memories of the first summer are of the wails of the loons and the whistles of the freight trains from the other side of the lake. A few summers later, while being dive-bombed by an Eastern Kingbird, I climbed an apple tree to take a look into the first nest I ever really noticed. A summer or two after that, I canoed to the south end of the lake and encountered my first Black Terns and heard the *oog-a-chuk-a* of the American Bitterns (little did I know I was at a well-known birding spot). A year or two later, I canoed through a number of the Belgrade Lakes and encountered my first Gray Jays, realizing for the first time how far north Maine really is. (The point was driven home during "the summer that never was," when I took daily swimming lessons in the lake even though the temperature never reached 70 degrees.)

Every summer we took a day trip to Reid State Park, where there were always Ospreys, gulls, and assorted migrant shorebirds. During one of my last summers, we discovered a wooded bog across the road from camp and enjoyed Alder Flycatchers, among other typical Maine forest birds. Needless to say, my Maine summers were instrumental in my birth as a birder. If only I'd had this book, I would have discovered the Sidney Grasslands and other nearby birding locations and learned more, faster.

Since those boyhood summers, I have returned to Maine several times to enjoy its birds. Along the way, I picked up a copy of the Piersons' first birding book and used it to guide my journeys. I was lucky enough to take a ride on the old *Bluenose* ferry to Nova Scotia and to tour Mount Desert Island near the ferry terminal. I will never forget staring straight up into the tops of the spruces trying to find the songbird that was capable of producing that incredibly loud and complex song. Here in Colorado, I get phone calls about the same song every spring. It was, of course, a Ruby-crowned Kinglet—unbelievable until you experience it for yourself, preferably in the Maine woods.

One of my favorite recent Maine birding experiences occurred while I was helping to teach a course in late June at the Institute for Field Ornithology in Machias. I was looking forward to seeing all the boreal specialty birds, but I left much more impressed by the breeding and singing warblers and thrushes. Never have I been so impressed with either a dawn or a dusk chorus as during that June in Machias. Be sure to add it to your schedule (and bring this book along as your guide)! During the Machias course, we had two incredible trips to seabird nesting colonies, one to Petit Manan, with its huge tern colony, and another to Machias Seal Island, for its terns, puffins, and Razorbills.

Maine is a fantastic place for a birder, with its mountains, its lakes, its forests, its blueberry barrens, and its incomparable seacoast. I have many more places still to visit, such as Monhegan Island, Baxter State Park, and the North Maine Woods of Aroostook County. I still have never seen a Spruce Grouse, a Manx Shearwater, or a Great Skua. When I return to Maine with this book in hand, I should be able to find all three, and many more besides.

Even my ten summers at a Maine camp, my love of lobster and "Bert and I" stories, and my willingness to swim in 50-degree ocean waters will not make me a native Down-Easter. But *A Birder's Guide to Maine* will enable me to bird like a Down-Easter. I look forward to many trips, in all seasons, when I can do just that. And I thank Liz and Jan Pierson and Peter Vickery for providing in this book all the information I will need to find birds just as efficiently as the native Down-Easters do.

Greg Butcher, Executive Director
AMERICAN BIRDING ASSOCIATION

Code of Ethics

The American Birding Association believes that all birders have an obligation at all times to protect wildlife, the natural environment, and the rights of others. Wherever you bird, we urge you to adhere to the ABA's general guidelines of good birding behavior. They are printed here with the permission of the ABA. (For more information on the ABA, see page 400.)

I. **Birders must always act in ways that do not endanger the welfare of birds or other wildlife.**
In keeping with this principle, we will
   - Observe and photograph birds without knowingly disturbing them in any significant way.
   - Avoid chasing or repeatedly flushing birds.
   - Only sparingly use recordings and similar methods of attracting birds and not use these methods in heavily birded areas.
   - Keep an appropriate distance from nests and nesting colonies so as not to disturb them or expose them to danger.
   - Refrain from handling birds or eggs unless engaged in recognized research activities.

II. **Birders must always act in ways that do not harm the natural environment.**
In keeping with this principle, we will
   - Stay on existing roads, trails, and pathways whenever possible to avoid trampling or otherwise disturbing fragile habitat.
   - Leave all habitat as we found it.

III. **Birders must always respect the rights of others.**
In keeping with this principle, we will
   - Respect the privacy and property of others by observing "No Trespassing" signs and by asking permission to enter private or posted lands.
   - Observe all laws and the rules and regulations which govern public use of birding areas.

- Practice common courtesy in our contacts with others. For example, we will limit our requests for information, and we will make them at reasonable hours of the day.
- Always behave in a manner that will enhance the image of the birding community in the eyes of the public.

IV. Birders in groups should assume special responsibilities.
As group members, we will
- Take special care to alleviate the problems and disturbances that are multiplied when more people are present.
- Act in consideration of the group's interest, as well as our own.
- Support by our actions the responsibility of the group leader(s) for the conduct of the group.

As group leaders, we will
- Assume responsibility for the conduct of the group.
- Learn and inform the group of any special rules, regulations, or conduct applicable to the area or habitat being visited.
- Limit groups to a size that does not threaten the environment or the peace and tranquillity of others.
- Teach others birding ethics by our words and example.

INTRODUCTION

Maine has long been a magnet for birders. This beautiful state supports a variety of boreal and coastal birds, many of which do not occur regularly elsewhere in the eastern United States. It is also a transition zone in which many species approach their southern or northern limits. Of the 419 species of birds recorded in Maine as of 1995, approximately 330 occur annually or near annually. More than 210 species nest in the state. In general you will find the greatest variety of birds during the breeding season and migration, whereas winter is often a good time to find northern landbirds and waterbirds. Seasonal highlights depend to some extent, of course, on what you are interested in seeing. From our perspective, they are as follows: waterfowl and breeding-plumage warblers in spring; boreal specialties (particularly warblers), breeding and nonbreeding seabirds (the latter being primarily Southern Hemisphere breeders "wintering" in the Gulf of Maine), and southbound shorebirds in summer; southbound hawks and landbirds in fall; and sea ducks, gulls, alcids, and irruptive species (owls, Bohemian Waxwings, and finches) in winter.

Whether you live in Maine or are "from away," the purpose of this book is to help you find the best birding sites in Maine. In some cases this means sites where you can find species that are locally distributed, hard to find, or otherwise of special interest. In other cases it means sites where you can see an unusually good variety of birds, or a particular group of birds, such as waterfowl or shorebirds. Some of the sites we describe offer unusual birding opportunities during a specific season; others offer interesting possibilities at any time of year.

Except in a few instances where we have the explicit permission of the landowner, we have included only sites that are accessible to the public. We have also confined our selection to sites that can accommodate visiting birders. We have made every effort not to direct birders onto private property or into vulnerable habitats, even if the latter are on public property.

Maine is blessed with a myriad of delightful and productive birding sites. Having just spent the past two years birding intensively all over the state, we are more aware than ever of just how true this is. Even in a state where some 95 percent of the land is privately owned (one of the highest percentages in the United States), it has been no chore to come up with a broad array of fine birding sites. They range in diversity from seabird-nesting islands many miles offshore to the summits of Maine's highest mountains, from extensive salt marshes to small harbors, from distant woodlands to city parks, and from commercial blueberry barrens to remote inland waterways. Sometimes just getting to these sites is half the fun, which to our minds is yet another attraction of birding in Maine.

Six introductory sections follow: The Face of Maine, Habitats and Associated Breeding Birds, Migration, Pelagic Birding, Winter Birding, and Practical Information. You may find these helpful, especially if you are visiting Maine for the first time or are new to birding. Together they provide a concise overview of the state's physical features and discuss important topics related to birding throughout the state. You should also be sure to consult the appendixes, where you will find a checklist of Maine birds; information on birds of special interest; a list of the algae, lichens, fungi, plants, and animals mentioned in the text; and a list of resources for birders in Maine.

The Face of Maine

Maine comprises about 33,000 square miles and is the largest of the six New England states—almost as large as the other five combined. Eighty percent of it is forested, but the landscape is far from monotonous. The coast—which measures 230 miles from Kittery to Eastport as the crow flies but more than 7,000 miles if measured to include islands, inlets, bays, and peninsulas—looks seaward to the Gulf of Maine, which extends from Cape Cod north to Cape Sable Island and east to Georges Bank. Scattered offshore are more than 2,000 islands, as dense a concentration as anywhere in the world. Maine is also distinguished by mountains that constitute a northeast extension of the Appalachians and that rise from a few hundred feet to 5,267-foot Katahdin; more than 5,000 lakes and ponds; and approximately 32,000 miles of flowing waters. The most prominent rivers, from west to east, are the Saco, Androscoggin, Kennebec, Penobscot, St. Croix, and St. John.

With a population of about 1.2 million, Maine is the most sparsely populated state east of the Mississippi. About half the people live on the coast (mostly in the southwest), whereas much of northern and western Maine is uninhabited. Portland, with a population of about 65,000, is the largest city, followed by Lewiston and then Bangor. Paper and wood products, manufacturing, service industries, and tourism form the backbone of the economy.

Maine owes many of its topographical features to the effects of glaciation, and nowhere is this more apparent than on the coast. During the most recent Ice Age, which began about a million years ago, Maine was covered by glaciers a mile or more thick. This immense weight depressed both land and sea, perhaps as much as several hundred feet in some areas. Then, as the ice began to melt about 10,000 to 15,000 years ago, the sea level rose and flooded the still-depressed land. Although the land has been slowly rising, the glaciers left in their wake what is known as a drowned coast. River valleys once miles from the sea now are offshore fishing grounds, and the tops of former mountains now submerged form the multitude of Maine's islands.

The landscape of Maine today reflects the geologic youthfulness of a region scoured and sculpted by ice. From Kittery to the mouth of the Kennebec River in Bath, the coast is low-lying, with sand beaches and salt marshes typical of the Atlantic Coast farther south. East of the Kennebec, the coast is characterized by bold, rocky headlands and promontories that the sea has not yet had time to erode. The sediments needed to seal off drowned valleys are yielded slowly, and the marshes and beaches seen farther south become smaller and more infrequent as you move east up the coast. Inland, the effects of glaciation can be seen in glacier-carved valleys, rounded-off and glacially polished mountaintops, an abundance of lakes and peatlands, and an extensive series of prominent eskers (or "horsebacks," as they are called in Maine), which are ridges of sand and gravel deposited by melting glaciers.

Habitats & Associated Breeding Birds

This section outlines Maine's major habitats and the characteristic (which does not always mean common) breeding birds associated with them. In many of the sites we describe in this book, we focus on breeding species that are locally distributed, hard to find, or otherwise of special interest. We do not mean to neglect the more widespread and conspicuous species; we simply assume that you do not need a special guide to help you find them. Instead, you will find most of them listed here.

Although the best time to see breeding species in Maine can vary considerably from south to north, it is generally between about mid-May and mid- to late July.

Islands.   Numbering more than 2,000, Maine's islands range in size from 13,000-acre Mount Desert to innumerable ledges of less than an acre or two. Many of the outer islands are small and treeless, typically covered with grasses, herbs, ragweeds, goldenrods, and often impenetrable thickets of Bayberry and Red Raspberry. Like the mainland coast, many of the inner islands are covered with dense stands of Red and White spruces, Balsam Fir, and scattered birches.

Characteristic breeders on Maine islands are Leach's Storm-Petrel, Double-crested Cormorant, Common Eider, Great Black-backed and Herring gulls, Common and Arctic terns, Razorbill, Black Guillemot, and Atlantic Puffin. On treeless islands you may also find nesting Spotted Sandpipers, American Tree Sparrows, Savannah Sparrows, and if there is a lighthouse or some other building, Barn or Cliff swallows. On wooded islands Great Blue Herons, Ospreys, and Common Ravens may nest, in addition to many of the passerines you would expect to see on the mainland.

Sand Beaches.   Maine has only 75 miles of sand beaches, almost all of which are found west of the Kennebec River. American Beach Grass vegetates the foredunes. Behind it grow such typical beach plants as Dusty Miller, Beach Pea, Seaside Goldenrod, Bayberry, Rugosa Rose, and beyond the backdune, Pitch Pine.

Small numbers of Least Terns and Piping Plovers nest along some of Maine's larger beaches, and Spotted Sandpipers may nest along nearby tidal inlets. Savannah Sparrows often nest in the dune grass, and Yellow Warblers, Common Yellowthroats, and Song Sparrows nest in nearby thickets. Pine Warblers sometimes nest in the Pitch Pines.

Salt Marshes.   Maine's salt-marsh acreage is small compared with that of other states along the Atlantic Coast. Like the sand beaches, most of the salt marshes are found west of the Kennebec River. Scarborough Marsh, with about 3,000 acres, is the largest in the state. Like all salt marshes, those in Maine are a meeting place for land and sea. The predominant plant in the lower marsh is Salt-meadow Cord Grass. In the upper marsh, which is flooded only on a very high tide, grows the finer and much shorter Salt-meadow Grass, along with glassworts, Sea Lavender, Seaside Goldenrod, and Orach. In salt pans, the small depressions that trap and hold water on a high tide, grow glassworts, Orach, and Seaside Plantain. Black and Spike grasses are found along the highest edges of the marsh.

Although many birds feed in salt marshes, only a few actually nest in them. Nelson's Sharp-tailed and Saltmarsh Sharp-tailed sparrows typically nest in the Salt-meadow Cord Grass, and Willets may nest there, too. In the upper marsh, where it is drier, you may find

Northern Harriers, Savannah Sparrows, Bobolinks, and occasionally Eastern Meadowlarks nesting. In thickets that border the marsh are Green Herons, Common Yellowthroats, and Song Sparrows.

White Pine and/or Deciduous Woods.   White Pines and deciduous trees are the predominant forest cover on the well-drained, sandy soils of southern and central Maine. Mixed with the White Pine, or sometimes bordering it, are Eastern Hemlock, maples, birches, oaks, aspens, and American Beech. Mountain Ash, viburnums, cherries, and Witch Hazel are typical of the understory; species such as Clintonia, Common Wood Sorrel, Star Flower, Goldthread, Twinflower, and Bunchberry are found on the ground. You can also find stands of mixed deciduous woods scattered throughout some areas of western and northern Maine.

Characteristic breeders in this habitat include the following.

Northern Goshawk	Sharp-shinned Hawk
Cooper's Hawk	Red-tailed Hawk
Red-shouldered Hawk	Broad-winged Hawk
Ruffed Grouse	Great Horned Owl
Barred Owl	Northern Saw-whet Owl
Northern Flicker	Yellow-bellied Sapsucker
Pileated Woodpecker	Hairy Woodpecker
Downy Woodpecker	Great Crested Flycatcher
Least Flycatcher	Eastern Wood-Pewee
Blue Jay	American Crow
Black-capped Chickadee	White-breasted Nuthatch
Wood Thrush	Hermit Thrush
Veery	Red-eyed Vireo
Black-and-white Warbler	Chestnut-sided Warbler
Pine Warbler	American Redstart
Ovenbird	Scarlet Tanager
Rose-breasted Grosbeak	

Boreal Forest.   Maine's boreal forest covers the upper two-thirds of the state as well as much of Hancock and Washington counties along the coast. Dense stands of Red and White spruces, Balsam Fir, and Eastern Hemlock, typically intermixed with Tamarack, maples, birches, willows, poplars, and sometimes Atlantic White Cedar, create a world of stillness, dampness, and shade. The needle-strewn forest floor contributes to a highly acidic, nutrient-poor soil which supports a variety of ferns, mosses, mushrooms, and lichens.

Permanent residents in Maine's boreal forest include the following.

Spruce Grouse	Black-backed Woodpecker
Three-toed Woodpecker	Common Raven
Gray Jay	Black-capped Chickadee
Boreal Chickadee	Red-breasted Nuthatch
Golden-crowned Kinglet	Brown Creeper
Evening Grosbeak	Purple Finch
Pine Grosbeak	Pine Siskin
American Goldfinch	Red Crossbill
White-winged Crossbill	

Several migratory species also nest in boreal forests.

Yellow-bellied Flycatcher	Olive-sided Flycatcher
Brown Creeper	Winter Wren
Swainson's Thrush	Ruby-crowned Kinglet
Solitary Vireo	Northern Parula
Magnolia Warbler	Cape May Warbler
Yellow-rumped Warbler	Black-throated Green Warbler
Blackburnian Warbler	Bay-breasted Warbler
Blackpoll Warbler	Dark-eyed Junco
White-throated Sparrow	

Peatlands.   Maine has more than 750,000 acres of peatlands. They range in size and diversity from the 4,000-acre Great Heath, which is actually a series of coalesced domed peatlands (see "Additional Sites of Interest" in the Washington County section), to tiny alpine bogs of less than an acre. These freshwater wetland ecosystems occur throughout Maine, although along the coast they are noticeably more common east of Mount Desert Island.

Peatlands are typical of areas where the underlying bedrock is granite, which yields few nutrients for plants. Characterized by a layer of sphagnum moss, high acidity, and slow-moving or stagnant water, they are specialized, self-contained environments. Sheep Laurel, Labrador Tea, Leatherleaf, Pitcher Plant, sundews, and lovely bog orchids are common ground plants; Black Spruce, Tamarack, Balsam Fir, and Atlantic White Cedar are common trees.

Ring-necked Duck, Yellow-bellied Flycatcher, Palm Warbler, and Lincoln's and Savannah sparrows are characteristic peatland nesters. Particularly in the northern half of Maine, Olive-sided Flycatcher, Boreal Chickadee, Ruby-crowned Kinglet, and a variety of other boreal species may nest around the edges of peatlands.

Inland Waters and Freshwater Marshes. Maine has an abundance of inland waters and freshwater marshes. Included within the state are an estimated 32,000 miles of flowing water (much of it undeveloped), more than 5,000 lakes and ponds, and several hundred acres of freshwater marshes. The shores of Maine's rivers, lakes, and ponds are generally bordered by woodlands typical of the local area. Freshwater marshes are usually characterized by sedges, shrubs, or extensive stands of cattails and bulrushes, and they are often bordered by dense stands of one or more species of alders.

You can see an interesting assemblage of breeding birds in and around any of these areas, although exactly what you see will depend on just where you are. An early morning canoe across an undisturbed lake or pond, a day-long river trip, and a walk around a cattail-bordered marsh will all yield a different cross section of birds. Although you will not see all of the species mentioned below at any one site, all the species are characteristic of inland waters and freshwater marshes and their respective borders.

Common Loon	Pied-billed Grebe
American Bittern	Least Bittern
Great Blue Heron	Green Heron
Canada Goose	Wood Duck
Green-winged Teal	American Black Duck
Mallard	Blue-winged Teal
Ring-necked Duck	Common Goldeneye
Hooded Merganser	Common Merganser
Red-breasted Merganser	Northern Harrier
Osprey	Bald Eagle
Virginia Rail	Sora
Spotted Sandpiper	Common Snipe
American Woodcock	Belted Kingfisher
Alder Flycatcher	Willow Flycatcher
Marsh Wren	Veery
Yellow Warbler	American Redstart
Northern Waterthrush	Common Yellowthroat
Wilson's Warbler	Swamp Sparrow
Red-winged Blackbird	Rusty Blackbird
Common Grackle	

Mountains. Maine's mountains form a northeast extension of the Appalachian Mountains and run in a southwest–northeast line from the New Hampshire border in the south well into northern and central Maine. Elevations average between 1,500 and 2,000 feet, with 5,267-foot Katahdin in central Maine being the highest point in the state. Many of Maine's summits are accessible from the Appalachian Trail, which runs 276 miles between Katahdin and the New Hampshire border. The habitat on most of these mountains is generally quite similar. Mature deciduous woodlands occur at the base and lower elevations and gradually blend into a mixed spruce-fir forest, which in turn yields to a stunted, thick spruce forest (krummholz, or literally "crooked wood") near the peak. Some of the summits are forested, but many are not.

In the mixed woods at lower elevations, look and listen for the same species listed above under "White Pine and/or Deciduous Woods," as well as for Red-breasted Nuthatch, Winter Wren (all the way above treeline and singing vigorously almost all day), Solitary and Philadelphia vireos, Nashville, Magnolia, Black-throated Blue, Yellow-rumped, Black-throated Green, Mourning (often common in regenerating areas), and Canada warblers, and Northern Parula.

Climbing higher, look and listen for such boreal nesters as Black-backed Woodpecker, Olive-sided and Yellow-bellied flycatchers, Gray Jay, Common Raven, Boreal Chickadee, Golden-crowned and Ruby-crowned kinglets, Brown Creeper, Swainson's Thrush, several species of warblers (among them Tennessee, Cape May, Blackburnian, Bay-breasted, and Blackpoll), White-throated Sparrow, Dark-eyed Junco, and Purple Finch. Spruce Grouse are common anywhere above about 3,000 feet (and are especially conspicuous when their young have fledged in late July and August), and Bicknell's (formerly Gray-cheeked) Thrushes occur (usually not until late May) in the thick vegetation near treeline. Pine Siskin, Red and White-winged crossbills, and Evening and Pine grosbeaks are irregular breeders but are always possible.

Open Land. Wherever you go in Maine, you will find fields, meadows, farmlands, orchards, and backyards, collectively referred to here as open land. Breeding birds in and around these areas include the following.

Northern Harrier	American Kestrel
Killdeer	American Woodcock
Mourning Dove	Common Nighthawk
Ruby-throated Hummingbird	Eastern Phoebe
Eastern Kingbird	Purple Martin
Tree Swallow	Cliff Swallow
Barn Swallow	House Wren
Eastern Bluebird	American Robin

Gray Catbird	Cedar Waxwing
European Starling	Yellow Warbler
Indigo Bunting	Chipping Sparrow
Field Sparrow	Vesper Sparrow
Savannah Sparrow	Song Sparrow
Bobolink	Eastern Meadowlark
Common Grackle	Brown-headed Cowbird
Baltimore Oriole	House Finch
House Sparrow	

Northern Mockingbird (southern Maine)
Northern Cardinal (southern Maine)

Migration

Many of Maine's birds are migratory because the climate is so severe. Of 214 species known to nest in the state, only about 83 typically winter over. Even among these, many individuals within a species may undertake a true migration; those that don't may undertake a limited migration, moving from northern to southern Maine, for example. And just as Maine is the summering ground for many species that migrate south for the winter, it likewise is the southern wintering ground for some species that nest farther north. Spring migration, when birds are en route to their breeding grounds, usually is more urgent and concentrated than fall migration, which by contrast is quite protracted. With numbers augmented by first-year birds, fall migration can be especially impressive. On both migrations the coast and, to a lesser extent, major river valleys are important flyways.

Given the widely varying dates during which different groups of birds migrate, you can observe some type of migration in Maine over at least eight months of the year. The following chart outlines the important migration periods for most of Maine's major migrant groups.

GROUP	SPRING MIGRATION	FALL MIGRATION
Loons & Grebes	Apr–May	Sep–Nov
Wading Birds	Apr–May	Sep–Oct
Waterfowl	Late Feb–early May	Aug–Nov
Diurnal Raptors	Mid-Mar–early May	Sep–Oct
Shorebirds	Late Mar–early Jun	Early Jul–Oct
Terns	May	Aug–mid-Sep
Alcids	Mar–early Apr	Oct–Nov
Flycatchers & Swallows	Late Apr–May	Aug–mid-Sep
Thrushes	Late Apr–late May	Late Aug–Oct
Vireos & Warblers	Mid-Apr–early Jun	Aug–Sept
Sparrows	Late Mar–May	Sep–early Nov

Below we discuss in more detail the migration of three of the groups listed above as well as a fourth, landbirds, which includes the flycatchers, swallows, thrushes, vireos, warblers, and sparrows mentioned above. The specific sites mentioned under each group are all included in the Contents and/or Index.

Waterfowl. Waterfowl are usually the earliest migrants in spring and the latest in fall. Every species (which is not to say every individual) that occurs in Maine is migratory. Along the coast, spring migration extends from late February (Brant and the first diving ducks) through late April or early May. Some of the more unusual species, such as Gadwall, often don't appear until May. Fall migration begins in late August, when Blue-winged Teal begin to concentrate in favorite areas, and extends through November. Regular coastal migrants, many of which winter in Maine, include Snow Goose, Brant (primarily spring), Canada Goose, Wood Duck, Green-winged Teal, American Black Duck, Mallard, Northern Pintail, Blue-winged Teal, American Wigeon, Ring-necked Duck, Greater Scaup, Common Eider, Oldsquaw, Black, Surf, and White-winged scoters, Common Goldeneye, Bufflehead, and Hooded, Common, and Red-breasted mergansers. Northern Shoveler, Gadwall, Lesser Scaup, and Ruddy Duck tend to be uncommon and locally distributed, and Canvasback and Redhead are rare. Harlequin Ducks, which migrate to Maine's coast for the winter, are unlikely to be seen in passage away from their few favored wintering sites (see Appendix B, "Birds of Special Interest," for more information). Often migrating in association with waterfowl along the coast are Common and Red-throated loons, Red-necked and Horned grebes, and Double-crested and Great cormorants.

At inland sites, the spring waterfowl migration begins as soon as the first patches of open water begin to appear with ice-out (which can vary from mid-March in southern Maine to late April in Aroostook County) and continues into May. Fall migration dates are similar to those along the coast. Although you will generally find more dabbling ducks than diving ducks, the variety of species stopping over at many inland sites can be quite impressive, including the occasional Common Eider, Oldsquaw, Bufflehead, or scoter.

Some of the best places to look for migrating waterfowl are Scarborough Marsh, Back Cove, Sabattus Pond, Cobbosseecontee Lake watershed, Messalonskee Lake, Bigelow Preserve (Flagstaff Lake), Merrymeeting Bay, Sebasticook Lake, Moosehorn National Wildlife Refuge, and Christina Reservoir.

Shorebirds. Shorebirds are especially well known for their extensive migrations. Many species nest in the far north and winter in southern South America. In Maine this group is represented almost entirely by migrants; only 8 of the 36 species that regularly (meaning at least annually) occur in Maine nest here.

Although the first Greater Yellowlegs can arrive in southern Maine by late March, the peak of the spring shorebird migration is brief and quite late. Most birds pass through in the last two weeks of May and the first week of June. Despite the brevity of the passage, savoring the beauty of shorebirds in full, crisply clean breeding plumage is always a delight. The fall migration, by contrast, is wonderfully protracted. Since many prebreeding birds summer south of the nesting grounds, it is not unusual to see some southbound migrants by late June. The first Short-billed Dowitchers and Lesser Yellowlegs are back by late June or early July, for example, and from this point on things only get better. By mid-July you can usually find a wide variety of birds, with numbers building through August. By mid-September most of the shorebirds have moved south, but White-rumped Sandpipers, Dunlin, and some of the unusual species such as Long-Billed Dowitcher and Baird's and Buff-breasted sandpipers can still be found. Sanderlings may linger into December at some sites.

Common species that pass through are Black-bellied and Semi-palmated plovers, Killdeer, Greater and Lesser yellowlegs, Spotted Sandpiper, Whimbrel, Ruddy Turnstone, Sanderling, Semipalmated and Least sandpipers, Dunlin, Short-billed Dowitcher, Common Snipe (wet meadows and fields), American Woodcock (see Appendix B, "Birds of Special Interest"), and Red-necked and Red phalaropes (both pelagic; see Appendix B). Species regularly reported in smaller numbers are American Golden-Plover, Piping Plover, Solitary Sandpiper, Willet, Upland Sandpiper, Hudsonian Godwit, Red Knot, Western, White-rumped, Pectoral, and Stilt sandpipers, Long-billed Dowitcher, and Wilson's Phalarope.

One of the keys to successful shorebirding is knowing the preferred habitats of the different species. For example, Piping Plovers and Sanderlings prefer sandy beaches, Upland Sandpipers and Whimbrels are often found on barrens, and Pectoral Sandpipers inhabit salt-marsh pools and wrack lines. It is also important to keep close track of the tide (check the tide tables in a local newspaper, or purchase an inexpensive tide table). Depending on the site, we generally prefer to watch birds on an incoming tide or just as the tide is dropping from high tide. In both circumstances, birds are concentrated, which generally allows for better viewing. The best times to bird individual sites are noted in the text. Finally, shorebirding invariably requires a good telescope and a good field guide. As for the latter, we recommend *Shorebirds: An Identification Guide to the Waders of the World* by Hayman, Marchant, and Prater, and the National Geographic Society's *Field Guide to the Birds of North America* edited by Scott (excellent, but the shapes are not always correct). See Appendix D for full information on both books.

With its convoluted coastline, Maine provides extensive shorebird habitat. Large numbers of birds can be found along much of the coast, especially between mid-July and late September, and smaller numbers can also be found at some inland sites. Among our favorite coastal sites south of Mount Desert Island are Webhannet Marsh in Wells, Biddeford Pool, Scarborough Marsh, Popham Beach State Park, and Weskeag Marsh in Thomaston. From Mount Desert east, you can find shorebirds in nearly every cove; the Beals Island Flats, Homes Bay, Little Machias Bay, and the Lubec Flats are just a few of our favorite spots. Several inland sites can also provide some surprisingly good shorebirding. Although you will see fewer numbers of birds at inland sites than along the coast, there is often an intriguing variety of species. Sabattus Pond, the Cobbosseecontee Lake watershed, and Flagstaff Lake in the western mountains and lakes region, and Christina Reservoir and Lake Josephine in Aroostook County are all worth checking for shorebirds in late summer and fall.

Wherever you watch shorebirds, please remember that these long-distance migrants depend heavily on traditional roosting and feeding sites, where they rest and put on the fat needed to fuel their migrations. They cannot afford to expend energy unnecessarily (and once flushed, they generally disappear). Instead of flushing the birds, use patience and a telescope, both of which are essential ingredients for successful shorebirding.

Diurnal Raptors (Hawks and Others).

The spring "hawk" migration can begin in southern Maine as early as March, when the first Turkey Vultures and Red-tailed Hawks begin to move north, but the majority of birds pass through the state between mid-April and early May. Fall migration, by contrast, is more protracted. It usually extends from early September through October, with the number of birds peaking about the third week in September. For sheer numbers of birds, fall migration is more spectacular than spring.

At least 14 species of hawks regularly migrate through Maine. Accipiters and falcons tend to be more common along the coast, whereas buteos (which use thermal updrafts for soaring and thus tend to avoid open water) are more common inland. Sharp-shinned and Broad-winged hawks and American Kestrel are usually the most abundant species, followed by Osprey, Northern Harrier, and Red-tailed Hawk. Other species regularly reported in smaller numbers include Turkey Vulture, Bald Eagle, Cooper's Hawk, Northern Goshawk, Red-shouldered, Red-tailed, and Rough-legged hawks, and Peregrine Falcon.

The best hawk-watching is invariably linked to the weather, which means brisk northwest or westerly winds in fall and south winds in spring. Pick your day accordingly. Even on what looks like a beautiful sunny day, be sure to bring plenty of warm clothing. An exposed mountaintop or beach can be a chilly spot, especially if you plan to spend the day.

Maine's best-known hawk lookout is Mt. Agamenticus in southern Maine, but there are many other places where you can also get spectacular views of migrating hawks. Since the coast acts as a funnel for many hawks, it is here that you will usually see the most birds. On the right day, almost any exposed site along the coast can provide good hawk-watching. Some of our favorite spots are Fort Foster and Seapoint Beach in Kittery, Laudholm Farm in Wells, Popham Beach State Park, Clarry Hill in Union, Camden Hills State Park, Mount Desert Island, and Schoodic Peninsula. If you have a chance to get out to any of the islands, particularly Monhegan or Matinicus, and you hit the weather just right, you may be in for a real treat. These offshore islands are the haunts of Sharp-shinned Hawks, Peregrine Falcons, and Merlins, as many unfortunate passerines have discovered. It is an unforgettable experience to watch these raptors chase bewildered grosbeaks and flickers—and to realize that the challenge is to identify the prey rather than the predator. The Peregrine migration usually peaks during the last 10 days of September and the first week of October.

A good field guide can be a great help when hawk-watching. The one we usually use is *Hawks in Flight* by Dunne, Sibley, and Sutton (see Appendix D for full information).

Landbirds.   By "landbirds" we mean the passerines, or perching birds, which account for nearly half the bird species that occur in Maine. The most obvious groups that pass through the state are the flycatchers, swallows, thrushes, vireos, warblers, sparrows, and blackbirds. Their spring migration begins as early as March, when the first Red-winged Blackbirds and Common Grackles appear in southern Maine, and continues through late May or early June, when the last of the flycatchers and warblers pass through. In general, however, most of the landbirds pass through between late April and late May, with warblers—a highlight for many birders—peaking in the latter half of May.

Fall migration begins as early as mid-August, builds to a peak in September, and then continues into November, when the last of the sparrows move through. The fall warbler diversity usually peaks between late August and early September; the sparrow diversity peaks in late September and early October. Most birds seen along the coast in fall are young birds, many of which get swept off course and land on offshore islands or the tips of peninsulas. This is one reason why strays and vagrants are so often seen in fall—and also why peninsulas and offshore islands tend to provide such good migration birding.

Most landbirds migrate at night, when they are less vulnerable to predators, and rest and feed by day. Conditions are usually best for migration on a clear night, with southwest winds in spring and northwest winds in fall. Some of our favorite migration sites are Fort Foster in Kittery, Laudholm Farm in Wells, Biddeford Pool, Evergreen and Calvary cemeteries in Portland, Monhegan Island, Isle au Haut, Mount Desert Island, Schoodic Peninsula, University Forest in Orono, Petit Manan Point, Campobello Island, and Moosehorn National Wildlife Refuge.

Pelagic Birding

One of the great attractions of birding in Maine is the opportunity to see several species of seabirds. A few species, such as Common Terns and Black Guillemots, are common nesters in the Gulf of Maine and can readily be seen from many points along the mainland. Other species are occasionally blown inshore during severe storms and can also be seen from the mainland at such times. But to see the majority of seabirds that occur in the Gulf of Maine—be they breeding species, summer visitors, or migrants—you will have to venture out to sea. Many birders are particularly interested in the truly pelagic species: the shearwaters, storm-petrels, phalaropes, jaegers, skuas, certain gulls (Black-legged Kittiwakes and the rare Sabine's Gull), and alcids.

The Gulf of Maine has long been known for its diversity of seabirds. Birds are abundant year-round, but given the often severe conditions at sea between November and March, getting out to them is not always practical. Many birders find the period between mid-June and late September to be the best time to take a pelagic trip in Maine. Breeding species as well as summering visitors typically are abundant, marine mammals are likely to be encountered along with the birds, and the options for getting out to sea are at their greatest. The most commonly seen birds during this period are Greater, Sooty, and Manx shearwaters (these three in order of decreasing likelihood), Leach's and Wilson's storm-petrels (the latter far more abundant), Northern Gannet, Common Eider, Red-necked and Red phalaropes (primarily late summer and early fall), Parasitic and Pomarine jaegers (both in small numbers), South Polar and Great skuas (also in small numbers), Great Black-backed, Herring, Laughing, and Bonaparte's gulls, Common and Arctic terns, Black Guillemot, and Atlantic Puffin. The more southerly Cory's Shearwater, usually rare in the Gulf of Maine, sometimes occurs in late summer when surface-water temperatures are unusually warm. Species less likely to be encountered but nonetheless occasional are Razorbill, Common Murre, and Black-legged Kittiwake.

From September through mid-October look for good numbers of Northern Gannets, Bonaparte's Gulls, and Black-legged Kittiwakes and for smaller numbers of Northern Fulmars (October onward), Greater Shearwaters, and possibly Leach's Storm-Petrels, Red Phalaropes, a Pomarine or Parasitic jaeger, and a South Polar or Great Skua. From November through March it is possible to see all six species of alcids that occur in the Gulf of Maine as well as Northern Fulmars, Northern Gannets (rare in midwinter), Glaucous and Iceland gulls, Black-legged Kittiwakes, and possibly a skua (presumably Great, but be careful; don't rely on the calendar to identify skuas). Remember that it is a challenge to see alcids, especially from the deck of a large boat. Most of the time they simply sit on the water, and they can be devilishly hard to find (let alone identify) among the waves.

There are basically three ways to see pelagic species in Maine: by taking a scheduled ferry, by joining a seabird cruise or whale-watching trip, or by chartering a fishing boat. In the first category you have two outstanding options: the M.V. *Bluenose* and the M.V. *Scotia Prince*, the Canadian-operated car ferries that travel between Bar Harbor (*Bluenose*) or Portland (*Scotia Prince*) and Yarmouth, Nova Scotia. Both ferries cross the entire Gulf of Maine and generally offer a chance to see more species than do whale-watching or chartered seabird trips. See the chapters "M.V. *Bluenose*" and "Greater Portland Area" for detailed information on these trips. Several small ferries, such as those to Monhegan or Matinicus islands (see those chapters), can also offer good pelagic birding, but these are relatively short trips of only an hour or two.

During the summer months, whale-watching trips depart from several points along the coast. These trips are certainly convenient for birders. Indian Whale Watch out of Kennebunkport (see "Additional Sites of Interest" in the Southern Maine section) takes passengers about 25 miles offshore to Jeffrey's Ledge, a well-known area for seabirds as well as whales. Other whale watches that go several miles offshore leave from Mount Desert Island, Campobello, and Eastport (see these chapters for more information). Although the primary purpose of these trips is to see marine mammals, you can often see a good variety of seabirds as well. It never hurts to have a word with the captain when you get on board and let him or her know of your interest in birds.

If you have a chance to join a chartered pelagic trip, so much the better. Unfortunately, however, there are not many options in Maine. A few commercial pelagic trips currently operate out of Mount Desert Island (see "Boat Trips" in that chapter), and the Maine Audubon Society runs a few each year out of southern Maine. Call or write Maine Audubon at P.O. Box 6009, Falmouth, ME 04105-6009, telephone 207-781-2330 for information. You can also consult the annual January issue of *Winging It* (the newsletter of the American Birding Association; see "Periodicals" in Appendix D), which publishes a list of pelagic trips scheduled for both the Atlantic and Pacific coasts.

Finally, you can always try chartering a fishing boat yourself. This is usually an expensive proposition, however, and many captains are not especially keen on chasing seabirds. Local chambers of commerce can provide you with possible contacts.

Remember that whichever option you choose for a pelagic trip, the success of sightings can vary widely. Much of your success (or lack of it) will depend on factors over which you have no control, such as the weather, currents, water temperature, and local food supplies. But part of your success will depend on factors over which you do have control. For example, it pays to stay on deck as much as possible; as alluring as a warm cabin may be, you won't see many birds from it. Coming well prepared for a day on deck will also increase your likelihood of seeing more birds—and will certainly make the trip more fun. Warm clothes, including hat and gloves, are essential. We cannot overstate this. Water temperatures in the Gulf of Maine rarely get above 60°F even in August (the warmest month), which means that the breeze is chilly. Other items you should bring with you are sunscreen, lip screen, sunglasses, plenty of food and drink, and plastic bags to protect your binoculars from spray. If you are prone to seasickness, consult with your physician about the best remedy. As Liz knows all too well, it is a miserable experience to be sick on an all-day trip. It is only slightly less miserable to be so dopey with an anti-nausea drug that you can't get your eyes to focus on any birds. Liz has found that the prescription drug Phernergan works wonders and doesn't make her sleepy; ask your physician what she or he suggests.

Seabirds can often be a challenge to identify, particularly when the boat is rocking or visibility is poor. A good field guide can help. We recommend *Seabirds: An Identification Guide* by Harrison (see Appendix D). Familiarizing yourself beforehand with the various plumages of species you are likely to see can also be immensely helpful.

Winter Birding

Birders from away often seem to be under the impression that winter birding in Maine is akin to winter birding in the Arctic. We can assure you that this really is not the case (besides, we have seen a ptarmigan in Maine only once). Although it is certainly true that you will not find the diversity of winter birds here that you would in many parts of the country, Maine is not dull at this season. Several groups of winter birds are of special interest, and many of them are uncommon south of Maine. Loons and grebes, Great Cormorants, northern waterfowl (including Harlequin Ducks, King Eiders, and Barrow's Goldeneyes), Purple Sandpipers, white-winged gulls, six species of alcids, northern owls, Bohemian Waxwings, and several species of winter finches are all enticing possibilities. All of these species or groups are discussed in more detail in Appendix B, "Birds of Special Interest."

In general, you are likely to see the greatest variety of birds in winter along the coast or not far from it. Each year we participate in several Christmas Bird Counts in southern and midcoast Maine, and although we have to work for it, it is not unusual to see 80-plus species on a good count. Inland counts typically record fewer species.

Many of Maine's winter specialties are unpredictable and irregular in their occurrence and distribution. A call to one of Maine's bird alerts (see Appendix D, "Resources") or to a friend knowledgeable about Maine birding can be particularly helpful at this time of year.

See the sections below on "Clothes" and "Winter Travel Tips" for practical information on winter birding in Maine.

Practical Information

Maps. The maps in this book are designed to give you a visual overview of an area, not to help you get there (although in many cases they can do that, too). We recommend that you use this book with *The Maine Atlas and Gazetteer* by DeLorme (listed in Appendix D and referred to in the text simply as the *Maine Atlas*). Just about everyone in Maine owns at least one dog-eared copy of this invaluable and widely available reference. In the title of each site we describe, you will find a reference to the appropriate map in the atlas.

Birders who desire greater topographical detail may want to get copies of the U.S. Geological Survey maps for certain areas. These are especially helpful if you are planning a trip to some of the more remote sections of western or northern Maine. USGS maps are available in Maine at L.L. Bean and many hardware, outdoor-supply, art, and stationery stores, as well as from the Maine Geological Survey (State House Station #22, Augusta, ME 04333, telephone 207-287-2801).

Weather. Mainers will tell you that they have two seasons, July and winter. There is an element of truth to that, but don't let it scare you off. After all, many of us actually like the weather here. It can vary considerably from one corner of the state to another. In January, the average high and low temperatures in Portland are 32.4 and 14.4°F, respectively; in Caribou they are 16.9 and 2.8°F. In July, the average high and low temperatures are 81.0 and 59.1°F in Portland and 77.0 and 54.5°F in Caribou. Portland averages about 70 inches of snow a year, Caribou about 110 inches. But those are just averages. If there is one thing you can expect of Maine weather, it is the unexpected. Generally speaking, though, the weather from May through October is quite pleasant; from late November through at least February, it is cold. Remember that in any season, and especially in winter, strong winds can make it feel colder than the thermometer reads. Fog is characteristic of the coast; the farther east you go, the more of it you will see, especially in summer.

You can get information on current weather conditions from many sources. This can be very helpful, especially if you will be going far afield. For a good overview of weather-prediction resources for birders, see the article entitled "To Go . . . Weather or Not?" in the August 1995 issue of *Birding* (see "Periodicals" in Appendix D).

Tides. A tidal day lasts 24 hours and 50 minutes and includes two low and two high tides. The average difference between high and low tide is 9 feet in Portland and 20 feet in Eastport. Each month there are two particularly high (spring) tides on the new and full moons and two particularly low (neap) tides on the quarter moons. Local newspapers carry tide tables, and most bookstores and outdoor-supply stores carry inexpensive yearly tide calendars.

Ferries. Many ferries offer not only transportation but good birding opportunities. Some, such as those to Isle au Haut or Monhegan, are described in individual chapters, but many are not. Local chambers of commerce can provide schedules.

Clothes. In summer you will want warm-weather clothes such as T-shirt, shorts, and sandals, but you will also need a heavy sweater, long pants, and warmer (and sturdier) footwear. Come prepared for cool and foggy weather even in mid-July.

In winter get out the warmest clothes you have, and dress in layers. You will need thermal underwear, heavy wool socks, down parka, wool hat, gloves or mittens, scarf or other face protector, and warm (preferably felt-lined or otherwise insulated) boots. Frostbite is no joking matter. Unfortunately, we speak from experience.

At any time of year bring rain gear and waterproof boots.

Pests. The most notorious Maine pests are black flies (Simuliidae), several species of which appear in late spring and early summer, particularly in wooded areas and around bodies of water. Female black flies are tiny but voracious biters, and although they don't hurt when they bite, they certainly are obnoxious. It is hard to hold a pair of binoculars steady and shoo away black flies at the same time. Fortunately, a good head net can go a long way toward protecting you from these insects. You can buy head nets at many hardware and outdoor-supply stores in Maine.

Mosquitoes can also be bothersome, especially around salt marshes, where they tend to be active all day rather than just in the early morning and evening. You may well find a head net handy for salt-marsh birding, too.

Unfortunately, Maine now has Deer Ticks—and with them, Lyme disease. Presently, this is problematic only in southernmost and coastal Maine, but in all likelihood the problem will continue to spread. You can help protect yourself by wearing long pants and a long-sleeved shirt whenever you go birding in grassy and shrubby areas, and by checking yourself carefully afterward. (Deer Ticks are about the size of a pinhead.) We use a pyrethrum-based insect repellent on our socks, pants, and shirts.

Hunting. Hunting is a time-honored tradition in Maine, popular with residents and nonresidents alike. Particularly in fall, hunters and birders often turn up in the same places. If you are from away, you should familiarize yourself with a few precautions that should be taken at this time of year.

Maine has what is called a nonpermissive trespass law, which means that hunting is allowed on any land, public or private, that is not posted. Most of Maine's state parks, wildlife management areas, and national wildlife refuges are open to hunting. You should be particularly cautious during the deer season, which runs for four weeks from late October or early November through the Saturday after Thanksgiving Day.

Forget blending in with the woods at this time of year; wear at least one item of blaze-orange clothing (preferably a jacket and hat) that is visible from all directions. Avoid being out at dawn and dusk when the light is poor, and don't be afraid to make a bit of noise to let people know you are around. **DO NOT WEAR ANY WHITE CLOTHING, INCLUDING HAT OR MITTENS; IT CAN BE MISTAKEN FOR THE TAIL OF A DEER.**

Maine's duck season usually begins in early October and is split into two periods with a hiatus of about two weeks, typically in late October and early November. The exact dates of this hiatus may be different in the northern and southern halves of the state.

For more detailed information on Maine's hunting seasons, write or call the Maine Department of Inland Fisheries and Wildlife, 284 State Street, Station #41, Augusta, ME 04333, telephone 207-287-8000 (ask for the Division of Information and Education).

Winter Travel Tips. You will enjoy winter birding in Maine a lot more if you are well prepared for it. And part of that means having your car well prepared. We can laugh now about some of the winter birding predicaments we have found ourselves in, but at the time they didn't seem particularly hilarious. (One of the more memorable was the morning of the 1980 Jonesport Christmas Bird Count, when it was so cold that Jan built a small fire under the oil pan of his diesel VW Rabbit to get the car started.)

Make sure your car has a well-charged battery, plenty of gasoline antifreeze, and an ample supply of windshield-washer fluid with antifreeze. In addition, it is a good idea to carry the following items in your car: windshield scraper, flashlight (with good batteries), bag of sand or kitty litter (for traction), compact snow shovel, jumper cables, and warm blanket.

You can get information on winter road conditions by calling the Maine AAA at 800-482-7497 or the Maine Turnpike Authority at 800-675-PIKE.

Accommodations.   Accommodations in Maine run the gamut from five-star hotels to rustic walk-in campsites; in between are motels, sporting camps, bed-and-breakfasts, and "full-service" campgrounds. Except in the most remote parts of western and northern Maine, where camping may be your only option, you shouldn't have any trouble finding a place to stay. Bear in mind, however, that many places are open only between late May and mid- to late October. It is always a good idea to call ahead and make reservations.

Local chambers of commerce can be excellent sources of information on accommodations (and much more). At the end of each chapter in this book, you will find the address and phone number for the chamber of commerce in each area mentioned. Guidebooks can also be a good source of information, and there are certainly plenty to choose from for Maine. One that we especially like is *Maine: An Explorer's Guide* by Tree and Roundy (see Appendix D).

The Maine Atlas and Gazetteer (see the previous section "Maps") has a partial list of municipal, state, and national parks and private campgrounds. You can get a complete list of state-owned campgrounds from the Maine Department of Conservation, Bureau of Public Lands, State House Station #22, Augusta, ME 04333, telephone 207-287-3061. Be sure to ask for the list of public-lands as well as state-park campgrounds. For a list of private campgrounds, write or call the Maine Campground Owners' Association, 655 Main Street, Lewiston, ME 04240, telephone 207-782-5874.

If you will be staying in northern or western Maine, you may want to consider a sporting camp. These typically consist of a main dining lodge and several private cabins, often situated on a quiet lakeshore. In many cases, the only access is by boat or floatplane. For a list, write the Maine Sporting Camp Association, P.O. Box 89, Jay, ME 04239 (no telephone).

Another good source of information is the Maine Publicity Bureau, P.O. Box 2300, Hallowell, ME 04347, telephone 800-533-9595 or 207-623-0363. The bureau publishes a wide variety of resources, including lists of campgrounds, bed-and-breakfasts, and cottage rentals.

Resources for Birders. See Appendix D for information on resources, including books, periodicals, bird alerts, workshops and courses, and natural history and conservation organizations.

A Note to the Reader

We hope that this book will guide you well on many pleasurable birding expeditions. Having made every effort to ensure the accuracy of mileages and many other details, we also hope that you will find no major errors. The book will almost certainly be revised in the future, however, and when it is, it will be the better for your feedback. If you have any corrections or suggestions on how we can improve this guide, please let us know. We will be grateful for your help. Send your comments to Elizabeth Pierson, c/o Down East Books, P.O. Box 679, Camden, ME 04843.

Finally, it is always with some concern that anyone shares their favorite birding spots with others, even in a book like this where many of the sites are well known. We do so with the fervent plea that wherever you bird, you will keep the health of Maine's environment and the welfare of its birds foremost in mind. We want to be sure that your grandchildren (and ours!) will derive as much pleasure from these sites as we hope you will.

Elizabeth C. Pierson
Jan Erik Pierson
Peter D. Vickery

SOUTHERN MAINE

The area we refer to as southern Maine stretches from Kittery north to Portland and west to the New Hampshire border. Few other regions in Maine include as great a variety of landscapes and habitats as this region does. The shoreline varies from barrier beaches and salt marshes to rocky coves and headlands and generally is low-lying, gently sloping, and at least by Maine standards, relatively straight. Inland the topography is low and flat, with 692-foot Mt. Agamenticus being the highest point of land. Distinctive habitats in the region include the southern deciduous forests of the Berwick-Eliot-York area (where several tree and shrub species reach the northern extremes of their ranges), the 1,000-plus-acre Saco Heath in Saco, and the extensive grasslands of the Kennebunk Plains in Kennebunk.

Whatever the season, you can find some excellent birding in southern Maine. Some of the sites we mention—such as the Kennebunk Plains, where you can find nesting Grasshopper Sparrows and Upland Sandpipers, or the Cliff House in Ogunquit, where you can find wintering Harlequin Ducks—offer unusual birding opportunities during a specific season. Far more sites, however, offer interesting possibilities at any time of year. Seasonal highlights include an excellent variety of migrating hawks, shorebirds, and landbirds (particularly warblers), winter waterbirds, and breeding wading birds and landbirds. Among Maine's unusual or locally distributed breeding species that occur in this region are Piping Plover, Upland Sandpiper, Roseate and Least terns, Horned Lark, Blue-winged, Prairie, and Palm warblers, Louisiana Waterthrush, and Vesper, Grasshopper, Saltmarsh Sharp-tailed, Nelson's Sharp-tailed, and Seaside sparrows (see Appendix B for information on the taxonomic split of the two salt-marsh sparrows).

Much of the birding we do throughout the year is in southern Maine, and we never tire of the diversity it offers. This may not be the wildest or most unspoiled part of the state, but it certainly has plenty to offer even the most avid birder.

Kittery

Fort Foster
Seapoint Beach

Kittery overlooks the Piscataqua River and Atlantic Ocean and offers two fine birding sites just a few miles apart. Fort Foster and Seapoint Beach lie on opposite ends of Gerrish Island and are both worth checking at any time of year. Highlights include an excellent cross section of migrants in spring and fall, nesting marsh birds (freshwater and salt-marsh) in summer, and a good variety of waterbirds in winter. As one local birder says, "There is almost always a surprise bird on Gerrish Island." Allow at least three to four hours to bird both the fort and the beach. In summer you will want to get here early in the day, as both sites are popular with beachgoers.

Fort Foster (*MAINE ATLAS* map 1, C-4)

Fort Foster sits on the southwest side of Gerrish Island and commands a wide, spectacular view of open ocean, the Piscataqua River, and across the river, New Castle, New Hampshire. The fort, originally constructed in the early 1900s and an important defense installation during World War II, has since closed, but the town of Kittery now manages this attractive area as an 88-acre town park. Its diverse habitats—which include mature hardwood forests, spruce-hemlock-fir forests, shrub edges, freshwater marsh, river, cobble beaches, and ocean—make this an excellent birding locale at any time of year.

Like many headlands projecting out to sea, Fort Foster acts as a migrant trap and often concentrates large numbers of birds. On

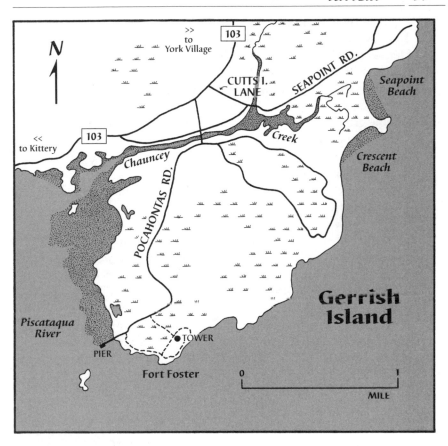

spring and fall migration, warblers and other landbirds can build up in impressive numbers, and the open vegetation affords excellent visibility. Birding tends to be most exciting in the early morning before the birds start to disperse inland. All of Maine's regularly occurring migrant landbirds—more than 110 species, including thrushes, flycatchers, warblers, sparrows, and other passerines—have been reported in the park. Blue-gray Gnatcatchers, White-eyed Vireos, and Prairie Warblers are uncommon but regular migrants. Rarities have included Fork-tailed and Acadian flycatchers, Golden-winged Warbler, Dickcissel, and Lark and Henslow's sparrows. Be sure to scan the shore for shorebirds. Black-bellied and Semipalmated plovers, Greater and Lesser yellowlegs, Ruddy Turnstones, Semipalmated Sandpipers, and Dunlin (primarily September and October) are all regular.

The varied habitats at Fort Foster also support a nice variety of breeding species. Some of the more interesting nesters that can be found here from late May through July include American Black

Duck, Virginia Rail, American Woodcock, Least Flycatcher, Tufted Titmouse, Brown Creeper, House and Marsh wrens, Brown Thrasher, Hermit and Wood thrushes, Yellow and Black-and-white warblers, Northern Waterthrush, and Swamp Sparrow. "Wintering" Great Cormorants roost on the rocks offshore until early June, and a few sometimes linger throughout the summer alongside the more common Double-crested Cormorants. You can generally see Common Eiders offshore, too. Be sure to get here early in the morning, when the breeding birds will still be vocal and before the swimmers and windsurfers arrive for the day.

In winter you may well have the park to yourself, and the birding can be delightful. Great Cormorants are abundant at this time of year and are easily observed roosting on the rocky outcroppings just offshore. Red-throated and Common loons, Horned and Red-necked grebes, American Black Ducks, Common Eiders, Oldsquaws, all three scoters, Common Goldeneyes, Buffleheads, Red-breasted Mergansers, Black Guillemots, and Purple Sandpipers are also regular through the winter. Other noteworthy winter species include Northern Gannet (December through mid-January), Mute Swan (rare), King Eider (rare), Barrow's Goldeneye (rare), Northern Goshawk, Rough-legged Hawk, Black-legged Kittiwake (most likely with east or northeast winds), Dovekie (irregular), Barred and Long-eared owls (the latter rare), Boreal Chickadee (irregular), Snow Bunting, Pine Grosbeak (irregular), White-winged Crossbill (irregular), and Evening Grosbeak. We almost always find unusual lingering migrants here on the Christmas Bird Count; in 1994, for example, we saw a small flock of Eastern Bluebirds.

The best way to bird Fort Foster is to park your car along the roadside before the entrance and walk in. Bird down the paved road to the mouth of the Piscataqua River (about a quarter-mile walk), checking the shrubs and trees for warblers and other migrants and the open areas for sparrows. Straight ahead you will see the old concrete fort and a long pier extending into the river. The pier offers a good (though, in winter, chilly) vantage point. After scanning the beach and river, take the path left (east) toward the ocean and the main part of the park. This path soon borders a large freshwater marsh where Least Bitterns, Virginia Rails, and Marsh Wrens nest. Migrants invariably collect in the shrubs along the edge of the marsh, so it is worth lingering in this area. Continue to the southern tip of the park, investigating the various small paths that crisscross through the shrubs. When you see the old concrete tower and pavilion, you can turn left and follow the path that cuts across the marsh and back to the entrance road; or you can continue along to the cobble beach and then turn left through the hemlock and spruce woods, following signs to join the path across the marsh.

Fort Foster is open seven days a week from Memorial Day through Labor Day and on weekends in May and September. Hours are 10:00 a.m. to 8:00 p.m. or sunset (whichever is earlier), and there is a small fee. Between Labor Day and Memorial Day and on weekdays in May and September, the park is open to pedestrians from 8:00 a.m. to dusk, free of charge. There are picnic and, in season, rest-room facilities.

DIRECTIONS

At the intersection of Rts. 1 and 103 in Kittery, take Rt. 103 east for 3.5 miles and turn right onto Chauncey Creek Rd. (Rt. 103 winds around a lot, so watch the signs carefully; the one spot where the road is not well marked is at the first T intersection, where you turn left). Go 0.5 mile down Chauncey Creek Rd., turn right onto Pocohontas Rd., cross the Gerrish Island bridge, and immediately turn right again (this is still Pocohantas Rd.). Fort Foster is 1.2 miles ahead.

FROM SEAPOINT BEACH: Go 1.2 miles back up Seapoint Rd. (which turns into Chauncy Creek Rd.), turn left, and cross the Gerrish Island bridge. Continue as above.

(Note that these directions differ slightly from what you see in the *Maine Atlas*, which is incorrect.)

Seapoint Beach (*MAINE ATLAS* map 1, B 5)

Less than 2 miles north of Fort Foster, on the north side of Gerrish Island, is Seapoint Beach—a small (550 yard) crescent sand beach that is bordered to the south by a low headland and to the west by a salt marsh. Seapoint is not an extensive area, but it usually offers some fine birding, especially in fall and winter.

The low headland at the southern end of Seapoint Beach is a particularly good vantage point for viewing coastal waterbirds at close range. October through March is when you will find the greatest variety. Regularly occurring species at this time of year include Red-throated and Common loons, Horned and Red-necked grebes, Northern Gannet, Common Eider, Oldsquaw, scoters, Common Goldeneye, Bufflehead, Red-breasted Merganser, Black-legged Kittiwake, and Black Guillemot. King Eider and Barrow's Goldeneye are rare, and Dovekie is irregular. Be sure to check all loons closely, as single Pacific Loons have been found here a few times. Walking along the beach near the edge of the grass, also look in winter for Horned Larks, Lapland Longspurs, Snow Buntings, and the occasional Snowy or Short-eared Owl or Northern Shrike.

Fall can also be a fine season at Seapoint. On a brisk September or October day with northwest winds, Sharp-shinned Hawks, American Kestrels, and Merlins generally pass down the coast, and Peregrine Falcons are occasional. Caspian Terns have also been seen here on several occasions in September and October. The headland is a particularly good spot to look for fall sparrows, and "Ipswich" Savannah Sparrows (*Passerculus sandwichensis princeps,* formerly considered a separate species, Ipswich Sparrow) are regular in October and November. Migrating American Pipits can also be seen here. Be sure to scan Crescent Beach, the small pebble and seaweed-strewn beach to the south, which attracts shorebirds. At low tide the birds tend to feed along the exposed flats, whereas at high tide they feed in the wrack or roost along the upper beach. Look particularly for Black-bellied Plovers, American Golden-Plovers, and a variety of sandpipers, including an occasional Baird's or Buff-breasted Sandpiper.

During spring and fall migration and in summer, scan the marsh at Seapoint for herons, egrets, Glossy Ibis, American Bittern, and shorebirds (Spotted Sandpiper is a common nester). In June and July listen for Saltmarsh Sharp-tailed Sparrows singing their quiet, whispering songs from the tall *Spartina* grass that grows along the inlets in the marsh. *Please do not enter the salt marsh in any season.* The town of Kittery has posted it as off-limits in order to protect it.

Seapoint Beach is a town park administered by the town of Kittery. It is open year-round, free of charge, and has no facilities. The small parking area immediately adjacent to the beach is reserved for Kittery residents from April 1 to October 1, but there is a parking spot for nonresidents just up the road from the beach.

DIRECTIONS

FROM THE SOUTH: At the intersection of Rts. 1 and 103 in Kittery, take Rt. 103 east for 3.5 miles and turn right onto Chauncey Creek Rd. (Rt. 103 winds around a lot, so watch the signs carefully; the one spot where the road is not well marked is at the first T intersection, where you turn left). Continue 1.7 miles down this road (which will become Seapoint Rd.) to Seapoint Beach.

FROM THE NORTH: At the intersection of Rts. 1A and 103 in York Village, follow Rt. 103 south for 4.1 miles and turn left onto Cutts Island Lane. Continue 1.2 miles down the road (which will become Seapoint Rd.) to Seapoint Beach.

FROM FORT FOSTER: After you come back across the Gerrish Island bridge, turn right and continue 1.2 miles to the end of Seapoint Rd.

(Note that these directions differ slightly from what you see in the *Maine Atlas*, which is incorrect.)

LOCAL ACCOMMODATIONS

For information on local accommodations and services, write or call the Kittery–Eliot Chamber of Commerce, P.O. Box 526, Kittery, ME 03904, telephone 207-439-7545.

Cape Neddick Light & Prebbles Point   (*MAINE ATLAS* map 1, B-5)

On a tiny island just off Cape Neddick stands one of Maine's most famous and most frequently photographed lighthouses—Cape Neddick Light. Tourists from far and near may know Cape Neddick, or "the Nubble," for its lighthouse and view, but birders know it for its birds. This is a wonderful spot to look for waterbirds, particularly Harlequin Ducks and King Eiders, from late fall through spring and for migrating sparrows and sometimes warblers in fall. The town of York's 3-acre Sohier Park looks out at the lighthouse and provides an ideal place to park and scan the shore and surrounding grassy areas. There is virtually no walking involved here, so you can usually see all of the birds in half an hour or less. You should also check Prebbles Point, about 2 miles south, where large flocks of gulls often roost at low tide.

The birding at Cape Neddick is most exciting in winter, when you can sometimes see up to 20 Harlequin Ducks diving in the heavy surf along the rocky shoreline. Whether seen on a sparkling blue day or through the spray of a wild and tumultuous storm, these ducks are always a spectacular sight. But even if you don't see Harlequins, you are likely to see a good variety of other ducks and waterbirds: Great Cormorants, Red-throated and Common loons, Horned and Red-necked grebes, Common Eiders, Oldsquaws, scoters, Common Goldeneyes, and Black Guillemots are all regular here. Look, too, for Purple Sandpipers, which often forage on the rocks exposed offshore at low tide. One or two King Eiders are uncommon but regular among the numerous Common Eiders, and it is always worth checking the Common Goldeneyes for the occasional Barrow's. Glaucous and Iceland

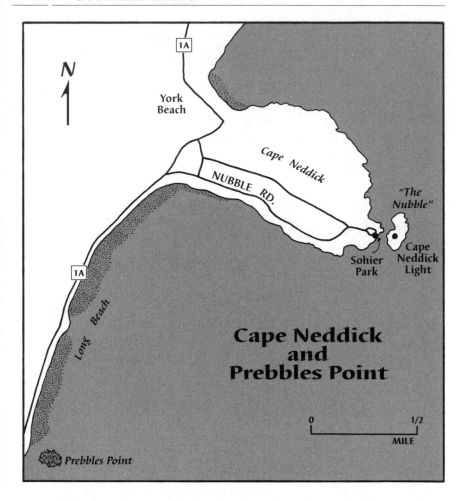

N

York
Beach

Cape Neddick

NUBBLE RD.

"The
Nubble"

Cape
Neddick
Light

Sohier
Park

1A

Long Beach

Cape Neddick
and
Prebbles Point

0   1/2
MILE

Prebbles Point

gulls can sometimes be found among the Herring and Great Black-backed gulls. Gyrfalcon has been seen here on several occasions in winter, and Northern Gannets, Dovekies, Thick-billed Murres, and Razorbills are sometimes found after northeast storms; take the time to scope the offshore waters. Rarities at Cape Neddick have included Common Black-headed, Lesser Black-backed, and Ivory gulls.

It is also worth looking for landbirds at Cape Neddick in winter. Both Long-eared and Short-eared owls have been seen at dusk hunting over the brushy areas just north of the parking lot; an occasional Snowy Owl perches on a nearby rooftop; and Horned Larks, Lapland Longspurs, and Snow Buntings can sometimes be seen around the parking lot.

In fall, the parking lot, grassy edges, and nearby rocks at Cape Neddick often attract sparrows (rarities have included Dickcissel and

Lark and Grasshopper sparrows), and migrant warblers frequently collect in the sparse shrubbery.

If you have an eye for geological features, you may notice that the rocky shore at Cape Neddick and the Nubble is distinctly different from what you see elsewhere in southern Maine; it is gabbro, an unusual igneous rock in the basalt family, and it is characterized by its high iron and magnesium content.

Take time before or after visiting Cape Neddick to check Prebbles Point. A large rocky point is exposed here at low tide, and from late fall through spring you may see several hundred gulls roosting here at low water. Park along the roadside on Route 1A and scan for white-winged gulls or other unusual species. It is worth checking a tide table for nearby York Harbor so you can be at Prebbles Point at the right time.

Sohier Park is open year-round, free of charge. It has a seasonal information center, with rest rooms.

DIRECTIONS

FROM THE SOUTH: At the intersection of Rts. 1 and 1A in York Village, take Rt. 1A north. In 3.4 miles, across from the York Harbor Motel, you will see Prebbles Point (exposed only at low tide). Continue another 1.6 miles, turn right onto Nubble Rd., and in 0.9 mile bear right onto Sohier Park Rd.; you will see the lighthouse directly ahead.

FROM THE NORTH: At the intersection of Rts. 1 and 1A in Cape Neddick, take Rt. 1A south for 2.1 miles and turn left onto Nubble Rd. Proceed as from the south to the lighthouse. To get to Prebbles Point, follow Rt. 1A another 1.6 miles south from Nubble Rd.

LOCAL ACCOMMODATIONS

For information on local accommodations and services, write or call the York Chamber of Commerce, P.O. Box 417, York, ME 03909, telephone 207-363-4422.

Mt. Agamenticus   (*MAINE ATLAS* map 1, A-4)

Mt. Agamenticus is Maine's premier hawk-watching lookout. Situated 5 miles from the coast and rising 692 feet above sea level in an otherwise low and relatively flat area, this small monadnock (meaning a mountain or other rocky mass that has not succumbed to erosion and thus lies isolated on a plain or valley) commands a broad, spectacular view of southern Maine and adjacent New Hampshire. On a clear day Mt. Washington, at 6,288 feet the highest mountain in the northeastern United States, looms to the west in the Presidential Range; to the east the coast stretches north toward Cape Elizabeth.

Strategically perched between the coast and the Presidential Range, Mt. Agamenticus lies along an especially attractive route for migrating hawks. Since 1981 an average of nearly 4,000 hawks has been recorded passing by this spot each fall, and in 1988 (the most productive year in recent history), more than 10,000 birds were recorded. You can spend anywhere from 30 minutes to the better part of a day here hawk-watching. Mt. Agamenticus is also worth a visit in the breeding season, when a fine variety of woodland species nest in the area; the best time to visit is on an early morning between late May and late June, when you can cover the area thoroughly in a few hours or less.

A comprehensive hawk watch has been coordinated at Mt. Agamenticus for many years. Birders monitor the summit in both spring and fall on almost every day in suitable weather, so you are likely to find yourself in good company. A large open area (cleared many years ago for a ski area that has since gone out of business) affords excellent visibility, especially to the north and east. You can also climb partway up an old fire tower, although the platform itself is inaccessible.

As elsewhere in North America, it is the fall migration—far more protracted than the spring migration and featuring much higher numbers of birds—that is most exciting at Mt. Agamenticus. Although the first Broad-winged Hawks may fly over as early as mid-August and a few Turkey Vultures and Red-tailed Hawks may still be straggling through in November, overall numbers of migrants typically peak in mid-September. It is not at all uncommon to see several hundred hawks on a good day. Sharp-shinned and Broad-winged hawks and American Kestrel are usually the most common species. Broad-wings tend to be most numerous in early and mid-September. Sharpies and kestrels fly south throughout the fall, with maximum numbers in late September and early October. Turkey Vultures, Ospreys, Northern Harriers, Red-tailed Hawks, and Merlins are all common. Less common but also regular are Cooper's Hawk, Northern Goshawk (October), Red-shouldered Hawk, and Peregrine Falcon; downright uncommon are Bald Eagle and Rough-legged Hawk (the latter more likely in late fall). Rarities in recent years include Black Vulture and Golden Eagle.

The spring migration is more concentrated and less spectacular, but on the right day you can still see a wide variety of birds. The earliest migrants—often Turkey Vultures, Northern Harriers, and Redtails—may move through in mid-March, and the latest in mid- to late May, but overall numbers generally peak in mid- to late April. In general you can expect to see the same species here in spring that you do in fall, although numbers are much fewer.

Although Mt. Agamenticus does not offer the diversity of species or spectacular numbers of birds found at more famous hawk-watching sites along the East Coast, it does offer unusually good views of the birds. Remember that on either migration the best hawk-watching is invariably linked to the weather—brisk northwest or westerly winds in fall and south winds in spring. Pick your day accordingly. Even on what seems like a beautiful sunny day, be sure you have warm clothing; we usually bring gloves, a warm hat, a windproof jacket, and a thermos of hot coffee or tea. For more information on hawk-watching in Maine, see the section entitled "Diurnal Raptors (Hawks and Others)" in the Introduction.

Mt. Agamenticus is also of interest during the breeding season. The extensive woodlands that surround the area support a good variety of species, and the many trails that wind about the slopes provide excellent access. A trail guide is posted in front of the lodge at the summit. The area is notable as Maine's southernmost breeding site for Common Raven and Dark-eyed Junco and is a reliable place to find nesting Prairie Warblers. Other breeding species include Wild Turkey, Mourning Dove, Black-billed Cuckoo, Pileated Woodpecker, Eastern Wood-Pewee, Eastern Phoebe, Great Crested Flycatcher, Eastern Kingbird, Tree Swallow, Blue Jay, Black-capped Chickadee, Tufted Titmouse, Red-breasted Nuthatch, Veery, Hermit and Wood thrushes, American Robin, Cedar Waxwing, Red-eyed Vireo, Chestnut-sided, Magnolia, Black-throated Blue, Black-throated Green, and Black-and-white warblers, Ovenbird, Canada Warbler, Scarlet Tanager, Rose-breasted Grosbeak, Indigo Bunting, Eastern Towhee, Purple and House finches, and Chipping and Song sparrows.

Mt. Agamenticus is noteworthy in other ways as well. Botanically this is one of the best places in Maine to see the transition between southern hardwood and northern evergreen forests. Two tree species—Flowering Dogwood and Chestnut Oak—reach their northern limits here and occur nowhere else in Maine. This is also one of the few places in Maine where the threatened Blanding's and Spotted turtles are known to occur.

Fortunately, much of the land around Mt. Agamenticus (more than 1,100 acres) has been preserved, thanks to the Maine Department of Inland Fisheries and Wildlife, Land For Maine's Future Board, The Nature Conservancy, the town of York, and concerned citizens.

The only feasible public access to the land currently is from the summit, where the town of York maintains a small park.

Mt. Agamenticus is open year-round, free of charge. A parking lot, horse stable, former ski lodge, picnic tables, and seasonal outhouse are located at the summit. Most birders simply drive to the summit and park, but you can also park along the road at the bottom of the hill and walk the road or half-mile trail to the top; during the breeding season this can be a productive as well as very pleasant short walk.

DIRECTIONS

At the intersection of Rt. 1 and Clay Hill Rd. (also called Agamenticus Rd.) in Ogunquit, turn south onto Clay Hill Rd. Drive 3.9 miles, turn right at the T, and follow the road another 1.6 miles. The access road up Mt. Agamenticus will be on the right. You can park along the roadside here and walk the road or trail up to the summit; or you can drive 0.6 mile up the hill to the summit. There is ample parking at the top.

LOCAL ACCOMMODATIONS

For information on local accommodations and services, write or call the York Chamber of Commerce, P.O. Box 417, York, ME 03909, telephone 207-363-4422.

Ogunquit

Cliff House
Marginal Way

Ogunquit is one of Maine's oldest resort towns, as famous today for its motel strip, boutiques, and art galleries as it is for its beautiful sand beach. In summer and early fall the town bustles with tourists, especially on weekends, but from November through April it is nearly deserted and is a fine birding spot. The two best areas to check are Cliff House and Marginal Way. Allow about two to three hours to bird both sites.

Cliff House (*MAINE ATLAS* map 1, A-5)

Cliff House is a 70-acre resort that sits atop Bald Head, a spectacular promontory just south of Ogunquit. The dramatic ocean views from Cliff House are unbeatable, and the winter birding is consistently good. From November through March this is one of the most reliable

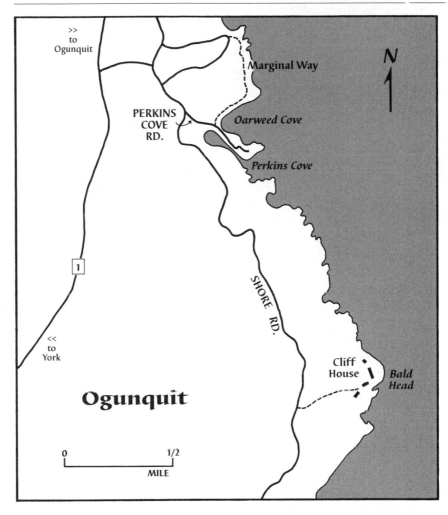

places in southern Maine to look for Harlequin Ducks, King Eiders, alcids, and Purple Sandpipers. Although this is private property, the owner generously welcomes birders. Allow at least half an hour to scan the water below the cliffs and to scope the offshore waters. Even on what seems like a sunny, mild day in early or late winter, you will want a warm coat, hat, and gloves.

Regular winter sightings from Cliff House include Red-throated and Common loons, Horned and Red-necked grebes, Common Eider, Oldsquaw, scoters, and Black Guillemot. What really makes Cliff House worth a stop, however, is the better-than-average chance of finding something really special. A small raft of Harlequin Ducks (20 to 40 birds) can usually be found in winter, diving in the surf near shore, and at least four or five King Eiders seem to turn up annually among the numerous Common Eiders. Some days you can look down and watch the eiders swimming underwater almost at your feet—a rare treat indeed. Look, too, for Northern Gannets, alcids (Dovekies, Thick-billed Murres, and Razorbills are all possible), and Purple Sandpipers (often foraging on the seaweed-covered rocks along the shore). Rarities seen here in recent years include Pacific Loon.

Cliff House is open from April through November, but the owner welcomes birders year-round, free of charge. The gates are open in winter on weekdays (and often weekends) from 8:00 a.m. to 5:00 p.m. and in season from sunrise to sunset; you can always call ahead to verify the hours (207-361-1000). Park in the "sight-seeing" parking lot, on the left side at the head of the driveway, and walk up to scan the ocean from the cliff side of the buildings.

DIRECTIONS

FROM THE SOUTH: At the intersection of Rts. 1 and 1A in Cape Neddick, take Rt. 1A south for 0.9 mile and turn left onto Shore Rd. In 2.9 miles you will see the entrance to Cliff House on the right.

FROM THE NORTH: At the intersection of Rt. 1 and Shore Rd. in Ogunquit, take Shore Rd. 2.5 miles south. The entrance to Cliff House is on the left.

FROM MARGINAL WAY: At the intersection of Shore Rd. and Perkins Cove Rd., follow Shore Rd. 1.7 miles south to Cliff House.

Marginal Way (MAINE ATLAS map 1, A-5)

Just north of Cliff House is Marginal Way, a mile-long public foot-path—paved and much used—that winds along the rocky shore of Oarweed Cove. The path was given to the town in 1923 by a local farmer who used to drive his cattle over this land. In many places the path almost hugs the shoreline, providing birders with a terrific overview of the cove and, beyond it, open ocean. Several benches along the way make ideal spots to stop and scan. The best time to bird Marginal Way is in winter, when ducks and waterbirds are abundant (and people aren't, at least during the week). Allow about an hour to walk and bird the path at leisure.

From November through March the real highlight to look for at Marginal Way is Harlequin Duck. Flocks of 20 or more "squeakers" (an old name that refers to this species' voice) often feed right along the shore here, particularly on an incoming tide. This can be a spec-tacular sight, especially with the afternoon sun highlighting the males' beautiful chestnut flanks and "eyebrows." You can also expect to see all of southern Maine's regularly occurring winter ducks and waterbirds along this route: Red-throated and Common loons, Horned and Red-necked grebes, Common Eiders, Oldsquaws, scoters, Common Goldeneyes, Buffleheads, Red-breasted Mergansers, and Black Guillemots. King Eiders are rare but regular enough to make scanning all the Common Eiders worth your time.

Marginal Way can be walked in a loop (it connects to Shore Road at the north and to Perkins Cove Road at the south), but the most productive birding is along its southern side. The path is open year-round, free of charge.

DIRECTIONS

FROM THE SOUTH: At the intersection of Rts. 1 and 1A in Cape Neddick, take Rt. 1A south for 0.9 mile and turn left onto Shore Rd. Follow Shore Rd. north for 4.6 miles and then bear right onto Perkins Cove Rd. In 0.2 mile you will see a parking area on the left and signs for Marginal Way, which begins about 100 feet to the left of the parking area.

FROM THE NORTH: At the intersection of Rt. 1 and Shore Rd. in Ogunquit, follow Shore Rd. 0.8 mile south to Perkins Cove Rd. and bear left. Proceed as above.

FROM CLIFF HOUSE: Follow Shore Rd. 1.7 miles north to Perkins Cove Rd.

LOCAL ACCOMMODATIONS

For information on local accommodations and services, write or call the Ogunquit Chamber of Commerce, Box 2289, Ogunquit, ME 03907, telephone 207-646-2939 or 646-5533.

Wells

Laudholm Farm
Webhannet Marsh
Wells Beach & Harbor
Rachel Carson National Wildlife Refuge Headquarters

The town of Wells is situated on a rich estuary—where the Webhannet, Little, and Merriland rivers meet the Atlantic Ocean—and is a fine birding site at any time of year. More than 200 species of birds have been recorded in Wells, with highlights including a wide variety of waterbirds year-round, wading birds in summer, and shorebirds,

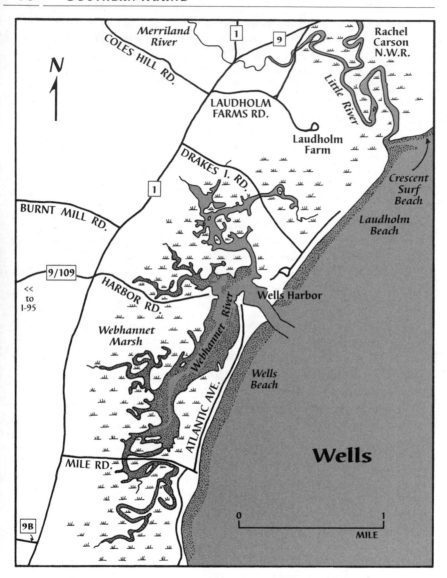

hawks, and landbirds on spring and fall migration. The area is characterized by extensive salt marshes, sand beaches, mixed woods, fields,
and a sheltered harbor; fortunately, much of the area is protected.
The focal points for birders are Laudholm Farm, Webhannet Marsh,
and Wells Beach and Harbor. Allow at least half a day to bird all three
sites. You can bird Webhannet Marsh and Wells Beach and Harbor
from the roadside (without straying far from your car), but at Laudholm Farm you will want plenty of time to explore the trails and sim-

ply enjoy the views. Time permitting, you may also want to visit the Rachel Carson National Wildlife Refuge (NWR) headquarters. Remember that in summer Wells is full of people, so it is a good idea to get here early in the day, especially if you want to walk the beach.

Laudholm Farm (MAINE ATLAS map 3, E-1)

Laudholm Farm is the site of the Wells National Estuarine Research Reserve, established in 1986 to protect 1,600 acres of estuarine waters, wetlands, and adjacent uplands. As longtime local birder June Ficker aptly says, "This is a gem of a spot at any time of year." More than 200 species of birds have been recorded on the reserve, and more than 45 have been documented nesting. Seven miles of trails (some of them handicapped accessible) provide access to a rich variety of habitats, including open fields, salt marsh, mixed woods, sand and pebbly beaches, extensive areas of low deciduous scrub, abandoned orchards, and a Red Maple swamp. Particularly at the height of spring or fall migration, you can easily spend three to four hours exploring this spectacular spot. Be sure to get a trail map and bird list at the headquarters; you can also ask here about recent sightings or species of special interest.

Given its variety of habitats, it is not surprising that Laudholm Farm is such a good birding spot. On the right day during spring and fall migration (typically peaking in the latter half of May and between late August and late September, respectively), you can usually see an excellent cross section of birds here, especially landbirds. Flycatchers, thrushes, warblers, sparrows, blackbirds, and finches often pass through in impressive numbers, and frequently you can get very good looks at the birds as they congregate to feed and rest in low thickets of Bayberry, barberry, honeysuckle, and Chokecherry. The reserve can also be a good place to observe migrating hawks, particularly in September and October; Ospreys, Northern Harriers, Sharp-shinned Hawks, American Kestrels (also nesting here), Merlins, and Peregrine Falcons (in small numbers) are all seen regularly. Between mid-July and late October, also look for southbound shorebirds. Black-bellied and Semipalmated plovers, Greater and Lesser yellowlegs, Solitary Sandpiper, Willet, Spotted Sandpiper, Whimbrel, Semipalmated Sandpiper, Dunlin, and Short-billed Dowitcher are the most commonly seen species. At high tide, when shorebirds are roosting in the marsh, the two overlooks along the Laird Norton Trail (noted on the reserve map) are often productive spots to scan. On a receding tide you can sometimes see good numbers of shorebirds along the edge of Laudholm Beach and, across the Little River, on Crescent Surf Beach.

During the breeding season, Laudholm Farm offers an opportunity to see and hear a broad array of common southern Maine nesters. Some of the breeding species you are most likely to observe include American Kestrel, Downy Woodpecker, Northern Flicker, Eastern Phoebe, Eastern Kingbird, Tree and Barn swallows, Black-capped Chickadee, Red-breasted and White-breasted nuthatches, Veery, Gray Catbird, Northern Mockingbird, Brown Thrasher, Red-eyed Vireo, Yellow, Chestnut-sided, Black-throated Green, and Black-and-white warblers, Ovenbird, American Redstart, Common Yellowthroat, Eastern Towhee, Chipping, Savannah, Song, and Swamp sparrows, Bobolink, Red-winged Blackbird, Eastern Meadowlark, Purple and House finches, and American Goldfinch. Pine and Prairie warblers may well be nesting here, too, but to date neither species has been confirmed.

Great Blue Herons and Snowy Egrets feed and roost in the marshes of the Webhannet and Little rivers in spring and summer; occasionally you may also see an American Bittern, Little Blue or Green Heron, or Glossy Ibis. Also look for Bonaparte's Gulls and Common Terns feeding here and for nesting Canada Geese, American Black Ducks, and Willets. Small numbers of Piping Plovers and Least Terns nest on the beach on the north side of the Little River, and sometimes you can see the birds on or from Laudholm Beach. Common Eiders and Black Guillemots are usually regular offshore all year.

Between November and April you will be hard-pressed to find a lovelier birding spot than Laudholm Farm. Although you can certainly find more accessible vantage points from which to scan for offshore birds (Wells Beach and Harbor, for example), the trails at Laudholm are delightful at this time of year. Occasionally you will get lucky and see a Snowy or Short-eared Owl hunting over the fields or marsh, or in late winter you might hear a Great Horned or Barred Owl calling. Keep your eyes open for late-lingering migrants and for overwintering passerines.

Whatever the time of year, Laudholm Farm may well provide a surprise bird or two. Among the unexpected species that have been seen here in recent years are Sooty Shearwater, Golden Eagle, Wilson's Plover, American Avocet, Ruff, Caspian, Royal, Forster's, and Sandwich terns, Black Skimmer, Scissor-tailed Flycatcher, and Lark Sparrow.

Keep your eyes open for mammals at Laudholm Farm, too. White-tailed Deer, Red Fox, Coyote, River Otter, Raccoon, Mink, Varying Hare, and Muskrat are all resident.

The Wells National Estuarine Research Reserve at Laudholm Farm is a well-equipped and active facility that is engaged in a variety of research topics involving the estuarine environment. From May through October, the reserve offers tours, banding demonstrations, bird walks, special events, and several educational activities. For more information, write or call the Wells National Estuarine Research Reserve at Laudholm Farm, RR 2 Box 806, Wells, ME 04090, telephone 207-646-1555.

Laudholm Farm is open year-round, every day, from 8:00 a.m. to 5:00 p.m. (If you arrive before 8:00 a.m., pull off and park on the side of the road by the entrance to the parking lot, making sure that your vehicle does not obstruct the road or gate.) A parking fee is charged in summer. Facilities include a visitor center and rest rooms.

DIRECTIONS

FROM THE SOUTH: On Rt. 1 at the blinking light 1.5 miles north of the intersection of Rts. 1 and 109/9 in Wells, turn right onto Laudholm Farms Rd. (called "Laudholm Rd." in the *Maine Atlas;* you will see a small sign for the Wells National Estuarine Research Reserve). Continue 0.5 mile, fork left, and in another 0.1 mile turn right at the reserve entrance.

FROM THE NORTH: At the blinking light 0.3 mile south of the intersection of Rts. 1 and 9, turn left off Rt. 1 onto Laudholm Farms Rd. Continue as from the south.

Webhannet Marsh (*MAINE ATLAS* map 3, E-1)

Webhannet Marsh, on the Webhannet River, is a large salt marsh measuring about 3 miles long and 0.5 mile wide. As you will quickly realize from the many signs posted in the marsh, Webhannet is part of the Rachel Carson National Wildlife Refuge, a string of nine preserves between Kittery and Cape Elizabeth that were established in 1970 to protect long-neglected and often abused wetlands. Although well worth a visit at any time of year, Webhannet is especially interesting between early April and late October, when you can see migrant waterfowl and shorebirds, nesting marsh birds (including Willet, Saltmarsh Sharp-tailed Sparrow, and a few Nelson's Sharp-tailed Sparrows), and feeding and roosting wading birds. Three roads running between Route 1 and the shore—Mile Road, Harbor Road, and Drakes Island Road (see "Directions," below)—provide excellent vantage points from which to scan this area. Although there are no trails into the marsh, you can do some fine birding right along the roadside.

Webhannet Marsh is best known for its shorebirding. The marsh is notable not only for its size but also for its large salt pans, several of which lie right along the roadside, especially on Harbor Road. About two hours either side of high tide, these pools can offer some of the most diverse shorebirding in Maine, and they often provide intimately close studies of birds. At least 22 species of shorebirds have been observed roosting and feeding in Wells. Regularly occurring species in spring as well as fall include Black-bellied and Semipalmated plovers, Killdeer, Greater and Lesser yellowlegs, Willet (nesting), Solitary, Spotted, Semipalmated, Least, and Pectoral sandpipers, Dunlin, Short-billed Dowitcher, and Common Snipe. Some of the more unusual species to look for, especially in fall, include Hudsonian and possibly Marbled godwits (the latter rare), Red Knot, Western, White-rumped, and Stilt sandpipers, Ruff (rare), Long-billed Dowitcher, and Wilson's Phalarope. In fall, the shorebirds often attract migrating hawks; look for Northern Harriers, Merlins, Peregrine Falcons, and other hawks hunting over the marsh in September and October.

Between early May and late September, Webhannet Marsh is also a good place to see wading birds. Great Blue and Little Blue herons, Snowy Egrets, and Glossy Ibis are all regular, and Tricolored and Green herons, Great and Cattle egrets, and Black-crowned Night-Herons are occasional. Like the shorebirds, the wading birds are often close to the road; scan from your vehicle before stepping out. Salt-marsh Sharp-tailed Sparrows and possibly a few Nelson's Sharp-tailed Sparrows nest in the marsh in the *Spartina* grass, and Savannah Sparrows nest in the uplands around the edges of the marsh. Purple Martins nest nearby and often hunt over the marsh. A few Horned Larks, local and uncommon breeders in southern Maine, sometimes nest in the sparse grass separating Webhannet Marsh and Wells Harbor at the end of Harbor Road.

During spring and fall migration on the Webhannet River (and on the Little River to the north), you may see Snow and Canada geese (both species more common in spring), American Black Ducks (year-round), Mallards, Green-winged and Blue-winged teal, and Common and Red-breasted mergansers. Occasionally you may also see Northern Pintails, American Wigeons, Ring-necked Ducks, Hooded Mergansers, and perhaps a few Gadwalls.

Although Webhannet Marsh typically is fairly quiet in winter, it warrants at least a quick check. Oftentimes you can see mixed flocks of Horned Larks, Snow Buntings, and sometimes Lapland Longspurs, and you never know when you will get lucky and see a Rough-legged Hawk, Snowy or Short-eared Owl, or Northern Shrike.

Webhannet Marsh is accessible year-round, free of charge. There are no facilities.

DIRECTIONS

Three roads running between Rt. 1 and the shore provide good vantage points over Webhannet Marsh. From south to north, these are Mile Rd., Harbor Rd., and Drakes Island Rd. The most productive of the three is Harbor Rd., which cuts through the heart of the marsh.

MILE RD. See the directions under Wells Beach and Harbor, below. Mile Rd. provides an excellent overview to the north and south of the Webhannet River as well as the marsh. From the end of Mile Rd., you also have access to Wells Beach and Harbor.

HARBOR RD. This road turns east off Rt. 1 immediately north of the intersection of Rts. 1 and 109/9 in Wells and provides access to the center of Webhannet Marsh. You will see the marsh on either side of the road in 0.4 mile, and in another 0.6 mile you will see Wells Harbor (see below). Scan each marsh pool carefully, as well as the harbor.

DRAKES ISLAND RD. This road turns east off Rt. 1 at the blinking light 1.1 miles north of Harbor Rd. and 0.4 mile south of Laudholm Farms Rd. (called "Laudholm Rd." in the *Maine Atlas*). In 0.4 mile you will see the marsh on either side of the road. Continue another 0.9 mile to a T intersection, where you can go straight ahead to a small parking lot on the beach (where a fee is charged to park) or turn right. (Turning left takes you down a dead-end road with Private Property and No Parking signs). If you go right, bear left at the fork and continue to a parking lot overlooking Wells Harbor from the north. This is another good spot from which to scan the harbor and open water.

Wells Beach & Harbor (*MAINE ATLAS* map 3, E-1)

Wells Beach is a long sand beach (about 4,000 yards) that runs between the Webhannet River and the Atlantic Ocean. The north end of the beach overlooks Wells Harbor. Particularly in fall, winter, and early spring, the beach and offshore waters here can be quite interesting. Look especially for Red-throated and Common loons, Horned and Red-necked grebes, Great Cormorants, Northern Gannets (absent in midwinter), all three scoters, and feeding on the kelp-covered rocks just offshore, Purple Sandpipers. Thick-billed Murres are irregular, and Common Murres are rare. Along the beach look for Horned Larks, Snow Buntings, and occasionally Lapland Longspurs, for Piping Plovers on fall and spring migration, and for Sanderlings well into December. Be sure to check the harbor, too. Ducks often seek shelter here, especially during and just after storms, and occasionally you can find something out of the ordinary, such as a King Eider, Barrow's Goldeneye, or a few Harlequin Ducks. Regular species include American Black Duck, Common Eider, Oldsquaw, Common Goldeneye, Bufflehead, and Red-breasted Merganser. Check the inlet behind the parking lot at the end of Atlantic Avenue (see "Directions," below) for white-winged or other unusual gulls; there are often good numbers of gulls here, especially when a fishing boat comes in. Looking directly north over the harbor, scan the Drakes Island jetty across the water for Purple Sandpipers.

Although Wells Beach typically is quite crowded in summer, you can often see Common Eiders and Black Guillemots offshore, and occasionally you can see a few Piping Plovers or Least Terns on the beach or flying overhead. In summer and early fall, the harbor is often a good place to see Laughing, Ring-billed, Bonaparte's, and possibly Common Black-headed gulls. Dozens of Common Terns are usually in the harbor diving for fish, and occasionally there are a few Least Terns among them. Shorebirds, primarily Black-bellied and Semipalmated plovers, feed in the harbor at low tide.

On a crisp fall day with northwest winds, scan the beach for migrating hawks, especially Peregrine Falcons.

Rarities seen at Wells Beach and Harbor in recent years include Western Grebe, Black Skimmer, and Royal Tern.

Wells Beach and Harbor are accessible year-round; a parking fee is charged at the beach in summer. There are no facilities.

DIRECTIONS

The best access to the beach and harbor is from Mile Rd., which turns east off Rt. 1 at the stoplight halfway between the intersection of Rts. 1 and 9B to the south and Rts. 1 and 109/9 to the north; the turn is well marked by a sign for Wells Beach. Follow Mile Rd. to the end, stopping to scan Webhannet Marsh along the way. At the shore is a large parking lot (expensive in summer but free in winter) with access to Wells Beach. You can scan from here or walk the beach. As you come out of the parking lot, turn right onto Atlantic Ave. and drive 1.3 miles to the end for an overview of Wells Harbor. You will see Harbor Rd. to the west, Drakes Island Rd. to the north, and open ocean to the east.

Rachel Carson National Wildlife Refuge Headquarters (*MAINE ATLAS* map 3, D-1)

Time permitting, there is one other birding spot in Wells you might want to visit: the headquarters for the Rachel Carson National Wildlife Refuge. The headquarters is located on the north side of Wells, where a mile-long trail (handicapped accessible) loops through a White Pine forest along the Little River and opens onto an extensive salt marsh with an overview of a barrier beach and, beyond it, open ocean. This is a pleasant spot to look for nesting Pine Warblers between mid-April and late July (they are easiest to find in early spring, when they are the most vocal); for wading birds and nesting Saltmarsh Sharp-tailed Sparrows and possibly a few Nelson's Sharp-tailed Sparrows in spring and summer; and for migrant shorebirds and waterfowl (including Hooded Mergansers on occasion) in spring and fall. You usually won't find many landbirds here, however.

The refuge headquarters is open every day, year-round, from sunrise to sunset. There is no fee. Facilities include picnic tables and seasonal rest rooms.

DIRECTIONS

The headquarters is located on the east side of Rt. 9, 0.7 mile north of the intersection of Rts. 9 and 1, and is well marked with a sign

LOCAL ACCOMMODATIONS

For information on local accommodations and services, write the Wells Chamber of Commerce, P.O. Box 356, Wells, ME 04090, telephone 207-646-2451.

Kennebunk Plains
(*MAINE ATLAS* map 2, D-5)

The Kennebunk Plains is an extensive glacial marine delta that was formed by the most recent glacier some 12,000 years ago. Today this 1,600-acre site, which includes a 600-acre open grassland and adjacent Pitch Pine/Scrub Oak woodlands, comprises a unique habitat in Maine and supports an assemblage of birds and plants that are not found anywhere else in the state. Here you can find Maine's largest colony of Grasshopper Sparrows (a rare and local nester in New England) as well as healthy populations of Upland Sandpipers and Vesper Sparrows (both uncommon and local nesters in New England). A few pairs of Horned Larks nest here as well. For many years the Plains was intensively managed for commercial blueberries, but since 1989 it has been jointly owned by the Maine Department of Inland Fisheries and Wildlife and The Nature Conservancy and has been managed to protect the rare birds and plants.

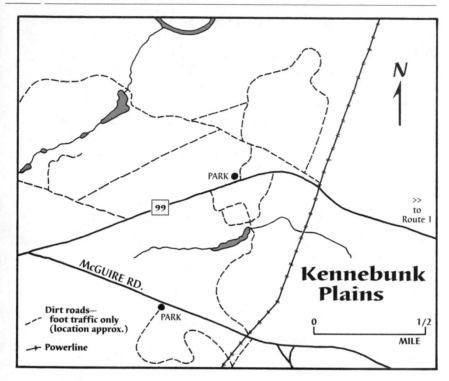

The best time to visit the Plains for birds is between June 1 and mid-July. About 20-plus pairs of Grasshopper Sparrows currently (mid-1990s) nest on the blueberry barrens here, making this one of the largest known colonies in New England and one of only four in Maine. The males are usually in song until mid-July, typically delivering their soft, buzzing notes from astride a grassy stem or other low perch. Upland Sandpipers circle about and call vociferously, Horned Larks hover overhead giving their delicate flight songs, and Vesper Sparrows sing from the telephone wires. Indigo Buntings, Savannah Sparrows, and Bobolinks are abundant, and Eastern Meadowlarks, though less common than they once were, are still regular.

The brushy margins bordering the barrens and the Pitch Pine/ Scrub Oak woodland beyond also support an interesting variety of breeding species. Look and listen for Red-tailed Hawk, American Kestrel, Black-billed and Yellow-billed cuckoos, Least and Great Crested flycatchers, Eastern Bluebird, Wood Thrush, Brown Thrasher, Nashville, Pine, Prairie (abundant), and Black-and-white warblers, American Redstart, Scarlet Tanager, Eastern Towhee, and Field Sparrow. Great Horned Owls often call at night, and Whip-poor-wills, generally uncommon in the Northeast, are surprisingly loud in May, June, and July. Small numbers of Wild Turkeys are resident in the area and sometimes feed on the barrens, especially in spring. In total, more than 87 bird species have been recorded nesting at the Plains, and another 50 species have been recorded on migration (including, on one occasion, a Sandhill Crane).

You can hear and see the birds at the Plains simply by walking the designated dirt roads. The Maine Department of Inland Fisheries and Wildlife (MDIFW) maintains two parking lots, one on Route 99 and another on the McGuire Road (see "Directions," below), and you are welcome to walk along these roads or the dirt roads that cross the Plains. Because the barrens are systematically burned and mowed to preserve the habitat (with the treatment of different sections rotating annually), the concentration of Grasshopper Sparrows and other grassland nesters changes from year to year. Be patient, and by listening and watching carefully you should eventually find all the birds. Most years the Grasshopper Sparrows are easier to find along the McGuire Road than along Route 99. On the McGuire Road, also take the time to bird along the path under the power lines, where you will find an area of brushy habitat. Just south of the power lines, check the dirt road that swings off to the east for woodland species and for Blue-winged Warbler. One or two pairs of these warblers, which reach the northern extreme of their breeding range in southern Maine, have nested here in recent years.

The Plains is also unusual in other ways. In August and September this area turns a brilliant magenta purple with Northern Blazing Star, a fiery and spectacular wildflower that is threatened throughout its restricted range. It is estimated that more than 80 percent of this plant's world population occurs on the Plains. Toothed White-topped Aster, once thought to have been extirpated from Maine, also occurs here. Several rare moths depend on the Pitch Pine/Scrub Oak woodland, and the open pine woods support one of Maine's few known populations of the endangered Northern Black Racer snake.

Today the Kennebunk Plains is one of the last large open spaces remaining in southern Maine. Please remember that this site is managed to protect the rare birds, plants, and other species. *It is critical that you not disturb the Plains in any way.* Please stay on the dirt roads, park only in designated areas, and pick blueberries (they are unsprayed) only in areas posted for picking.

The Plains is open year-round, free of charge. There are no facilities.

DIRECTIONS

At the intersection of Rts. 1 and 9A in Kennebunk, take Rt. 9A (High St.) west. In 0.3 mile turn right onto Rt. 99 and continue for 4.2 miles, where the barrens emerge on both sides of the road. You are on the northern side of the Plains here; there is a small MDIFW parking lot on the north side of the road, marked with a sign. To bird the southern side of the Plains, continue west on Rt. 99 for 1 mile, then take a sharp left onto McGuire Rd. (a good dirt road). This road quickly opens onto more blueberry barrens, and in 0.5 mile you will see another MDIFW parking lot on the south side of the road.

LOCAL ACCOMMODATIONS

For information on local accommodations and services, write or call the Kennebunk-Kennebunkport Chamber of Commerce, P.O. Box 740, Kennebunk, ME 04043, telephone 207-967-0857.

Biddeford Pool   (*MAINE ATLAS* map 3, C-3)

The Pool   **East Point Sanctuary**
Fortunes Rocks Beach Hills Beach

Biddeford Pool is one of southern Maine's best-known birding localities, and with good reason. Distinguished by a vast enclosed tidal pool and by an eastern arm that extends well into open ocean, this area provides a variety of habitats for shorebirds, wading birds, and ducks. It is also a trap for migrant landbirds and storm-tossed vagrants and is a fine vantage point from which to scan for seabirds. Although it can be particularly good for shorebirds on spring and fall migration, Biddeford Pool is also known as an exceptionally productive place where just about anything can turn up at any time of year—and often does. A Variegated Flycatcher from South America in November 1977 provided a first North American record, and a Red-necked Stint in July of the same year provided a first state record. Other unusual species seen here in more recent years include Black Vulture, Gyrfalcon, Curlew Sandpiper, Ruff, Franklin's Gull, Royal Tern, Fork-tailed Flycatcher, Green-tailed Towhee, Boat-tailed Grackle, and Black-headed Grosbeak. Not a bad collection of birds for a small peninsula.

Biddeford Pool is worth a visit at any time of year. There are four areas you should check: the pool itself, East Point Sanctuary, Fortunes Rocks Beach, and Hills Beach. Allow at least half a day to cover all these sites thoroughly; in summer, avoid weekends if you want to see more birds than people. Even during the week in summer, Biddeford Pool can be quite crowded, especially on a good beach day.

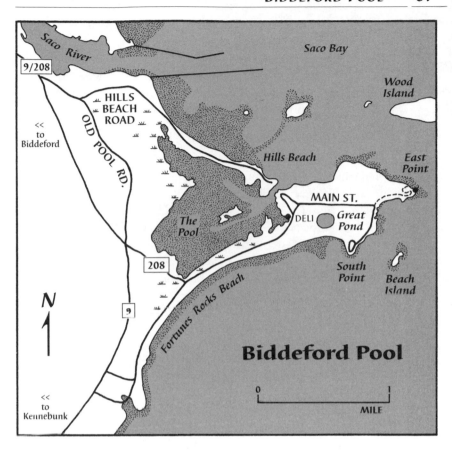

The Pool

Biddeford Pool is a shallow basin that measures about 1 mile in diameter and empties into the sea through a narrow channel at its northeast corner. It is a fine spot to see a variety of shorebirds (an astounding 34 species have been recorded here) and wading birds. Bird it on a rising or falling tide, but not at high tide (when the flats are covered) or at dead low tide (when the birds are too dispersed to scan easily). Feeding generally is most fervid on the falling tide, when the high tide has replenished the food supply and the birds have not fed for several hours. Bear in mind that the pool tends to fill early—the higher the tide, the earlier it fills. Depending on the height of the tide, the pool can be full anywhere from one to three hours before high tide. If you are unfamiliar with the tide here, it is best to arrive well before high tide and bird other sites around the pool first. That way you can come back to check the pool at regular intervals and catch it at just the right time. It is worth the effort.

The best way to bird the pool is to work the southern shore—from west to east on a rising tide and from east to west on a falling tide. The best access is by Hattie's Deli on the left side of the road, 1 mile after you turn left on Route 208 at the southwest corner of the pool (see "Directions," below). You can park at Hattie's or in the public lot directly across the road; there is a fee at both places in summer, although if you arrive before 7:00 a.m. you can usually avoid it. Behind the deli is a path that has been used by birders for years. This is private property, so please ask at Hattie's before you go tramping out there. (If you're smart, you'll fieldcheck Hattie's first anyway; the soups, sandwiches, and desserts are wonderful.) This path brings you out by the pool's easternmost flats, which are the last to be covered on a rising tide and the first to be exposed on a falling tide. Large numbers of shorebirds congregate here on either side of the full tide and can be studied at close range. They are especially numerous on fall migration (mid-July though early October) but are also present in spring (mid-May to early June). *Please take care not to flush the birds, especially on a rising tide when they may be settling down to roost.* About an hour before high tide, birds begin congregating here from all over the pool, and if you wait patiently in one spot, the birds will pour in to you as the tide rises.

Common species at the pool include Black-bellied and Semipalmated plovers, Killdeer, Greater and Lesser yellowlegs, Willet (especially in fall), Spotted Sandpiper, Ruddy Turnstone, Semipalmated and Least sandpipers, Dunlin (primarily in fall), and Short-billed Dowitcher. Less common but fairly regular are Pectoral Sandpiper and, in fall, American Golden-Plover, Whimbrel, Hudsonian Godwit, Red Knot, and White-rumped Sandpiper (the last in small numbers in September and October). Occasional birds include Marbled Godwit, Western Sandpiper (September), Baird's and Buff-breasted sandpipers, Long-billed Dowitcher, and Wilson's Phalarope. The large flocks of shorebirds often attract migrating hawks, particularly Sharp-shinned Hawks, Merlins, and small but regular numbers of Peregrine Falcons.

In spring and summer, Great Blue, Green, and Little Blue herons, Snowy Egrets, Black-crowned Night-Herons, and Glossy Ibis frequent the pool, and occasionally a Great or Cattle Egret or a Tri-colored Heron appears. Several of these species nest some years just north of the pool on Wood Island, which is owned by the Maine Audubon Society and is one of Maine's few mixed-species heronries. (Having once canoed out to Wood, we can assure you that it really is easier to see the birds from the mainland.) Common Terns are numerous around the pool in summer, Arctic and Roseate terns are present in smaller numbers, and Laughing Gulls are occasional. Bonaparte's Gulls generally are common in spring and from midsummer well into fall. American Black Ducks, Saltmarsh Sharp-tailed and possibly a few Nelson's Sharp-tailed sparrows, and Savannah Sparrows nest around the pool, and House Finches are year-round residents.

In late summer and fall, Forster's and Caspian terns are sometimes seen around the pool, and Western Kingbirds occasionally perch on the telephone wires. The nearby grasses and shrubs are good places to look for migrating American Pipits, sparrows (most notably Saltmarsh Sharp-tailed, Savannah, "Ipswich" Savannah, and rarely Seaside), and other songbirds. From November through March look for Horned Larks, Snow Buntings, and perhaps Lapland Longspurs (the last occasionally in more-or-less single-species flocks of 50+). Sometimes a Snowy or Short-eared Owl hunts along the marsh, too. Christmas Bird Count participants often find late lingering migrants in this area. Where open water remains in winter, you are likely to see American Black Ducks, Common Goldeneyes, Buffleheads, and Red-breasted Mergansers. Gulls often roost on the ice, and it is always worth scanning them for a Glaucous or an Iceland Gull. Canada Geese and a few Snow Geese are regular in early spring, and Brant are occasional.

The pool is accessible year-round; in summer there is a parking fee. There are no facilities.

East Point Sanctuary

From the pool, follow Main Street around to the right and out toward Ocean Avenue. On the left, about 20 yards before Main Street runs into Ocean Avenue, is the inconspicuous entrance to East Point Sanctuary. There is room for a few cars to park along the roadside here. (If you park on Ocean Avenue, you may get a parking ticket.) The entrance is marked by a chain-link gate and, inside, a small Maine Audubon Society sign. Follow the path out around the golf course to East Point and then west along the shore, which is heavily vegetated with Rugosa Rose, Bayberry, and Red Raspberry. This is about a 1-mile walk round-trip. Please remember that the golf course is private property.

The 30 acres that make up East Point Sanctuary were given to the Maine Audubon Society in 1976 by a group of Biddeford Pool landowners. With the mix of large open areas, abundant shrubs, rocky shore, and a fine vantage point, the birding here is consistently good all year. In early morning during migration, the path along the golf course is one of the best places in southern Maine to look for grassland shorebirds such as American Golden-Plover and Upland, Buff-breasted (scarce), and Baird's sandpipers. (It is also where the Variegated and Fork-tailed flycatchers were seen.) The shrubs that border the path are sometimes full of warblers and sparrows; in October and November this is excellent habitat for Orange-crowned Warblers and Yellow-breasted Chats. It can also be a good place to look for migrating hawks, including Northern Harriers, Merlins, and Peregrine Falcons, and at high tide for plovers and sandpipers roosting along the shore or on nearby rocks. In late fall and winter, look also for a Rough-legged Hawk, Snowy or Short-eared Owl, or Northern Shrike and for Horned Larks, Snow Buntings, and Lapland Longspurs.

From November through April, East Point is also a good place to look for a variety of waterbirds, notably Brant (February to April), Great Cormorants, Common Eiders, scoters, Red-breasted Mergansers, Black Guillemots, and on the rocks offshore, Purple Sandpipers. A few King Eiders and Black-legged Kittiwakes are usually reported each winter, and Dovekies, Atlantic Puffins, Razorbills, and Common and Thick-billed murres are irregular, especially after northeast storms. Snowy Owls are surprisingly regular near the lighthouse on Wood Island, just north of the sanctuary. With persistent scanning you may find a Northern Gannet at any time of year (except the dead of winter), and after a good strong easterly wind you may even find a shearwater, jaeger, or some other seabird normally not seen from the mainland. Yellow-rumped Warblers spend the winter here feeding on the abundant Bayberries.

In summer, swallows hawk overhead at East Point (Bank Swallows sometimes nest in the bank at the end of the point), and Gray Catbirds and Yellow Warblers nest in the surrounding shrubs. Offshore you are likely to see Common Eiders (often with ducklings), Arctic and Common terns, and Black Guillemots, all of which nest nearby. In years when wading birds nest on Wood Island, East Point is an excellent spot from which to observe their comings and goings early and late in the day.

East Point Sanctuary is open year-round, free of charge. There are no facilities.

Fortunes Rocks Beach

Fortunes Rocks Beach is the long, narrow sand beach (interspersed with patches of rocky shoreline) that runs along the southern shore of Biddeford Pool. To scan the northern half of the beach, drive south down Ocean Avenue from East Point and go past the old Coast Guard station to the loop around South Point. This can be a good place to look in spring and fall for roosting shorebirds at high tide, in winter for ducks, and in summer for Piping Plovers and Least Terns, which sometimes nest along this beach. At the Coast Guard station, be sure to scan over Beach Island, directly offshore, where Roseate Terns have nested irregularly in the past. The rocks directly offshore can also be an excellent place to observe roosting shorebirds at high tide. Interestingly, Ruddy Turnstones reach the northern limit of their winter range here.

To scan the southern half of the beach, trace your way back past Hattie's, and at the southwest corner of the pool, go straight instead of turning right. (In 1.8 miles this road joins Route 9.) In winter this stretch of open water is often a very good place to observe seabirds, and Purple Sandpipers can usually be found along the rocky shore. During migration, shorebirds sometimes roost along this beach at high tide. (If you miss the tide at the pool, it is especially worth a look here.) In late fall and early winter you can sometimes find "Ipswich" Savannah Sparrows here, particularly on the southernmost part of the beach. The freshwater pond on the opposite side of the road is also worth a check; on migration it may yield a good variety of ducks and gulls.

Fortunes Rocks Beach is open year-round. A city parking sticker is required from mid-June through Labor Day, but the rest of the year parking is free and readily available. There are no facilities.

Hills Beach

Hills Beach is the small sand spit that forms the northern shore of the pool. From the southwest corner of the pool, head back toward Biddeford and take the first right turn off Route 208 onto Old Pool Road. Continue slightly more than 1 mile and turn right at the T intersection onto Hills Beach Road. The road will dead-end at the northeast corner of the pool in 1.5 miles. (When you turn around, turn right at the T intersection to get back on Route 208/9 toward Biddeford.)

Hills Beach overlooks the mouth of the Saco River and is a good place from which to scan for gulls, terns, and other waterbirds. Common, Arctic, and Roseate terns feed here in summer, and Caspian Terns are possible in September. Royal and Sandwich terns, both rare in Maine, have each occurred at least twice along this beach, and on one occasion a Gull-billed Tern was seen. Many gulls and terns roost on the sandbar at low tide in summer. This is also a good place to look for wintering waterbirds; Brant (50+) can be seen here each spring (late February into April). Bonaparte's Gulls are numerous in fall, Little Gulls are occasional, Iceland and Glaucous gulls are sometimes present in winter, and Common Black-headed Gulls are probably more regular than the few records suggest.

Hills Beach is open year-round. There is little parking space, especially in summer, but no fee is charged. There are no facilities.

DIRECTIONS

At the intersection of Rts. 208/9 and 208 in Biddeford, turn south onto Rt. 208. In 0.5 mile you will see the southwest corner of the pool on the left.

LOCAL ACCOMMODATIONS

For information on local accommodations and services, write or call the Biddeford-Saco Chamber of Commerce, 180 Main St., Biddeford, ME 04005, telephone 207-282-1567.

Saco Heath   (*MAINE ATLAS* map 3, B-2)

Situated within the city limits of Saco is a vast peatland known as Saco Heath. Most of this unusual 1,000-acre peatland, once considered a "worthless" wetland and later the site of a small peat-mining operation, is now owned and managed by The Nature Conservancy. As one of the last large tracts of undeveloped land in southeastern Maine, the heath is a haven for naturalists. Birders are likely to find it most interesting during the nesting season, when several peatland-associated species, including Palm Warbler, can be found. Anytime between early May and late August, you can easily spend a peaceful few hours exploring this distinctive ecosystem. The nesting species are easiest to see in May and June in the early morning.

Saco Heath is a raised coalesced bog, which means that the heath's domed surface has grown above the influence of the local water table; as a result, the peatland plants must depend entirely on precipitation for nutrients. Scattered throughout the open heath are many of Maine's common peatland plants, including Black Spruce, Tamarack, Sheep Laurel, Labrador Tea, sedges, Pitcher Plant, sundews, Cotton Grass, and several species of sphagnum moss. Interestingly, Atlantic White Cedar, which approaches the northern extreme of its range here, also grows on the heath; this is the only known location where this species grows on a northern raised peatland. Around the edges of the heath is a forest community consisting pri-

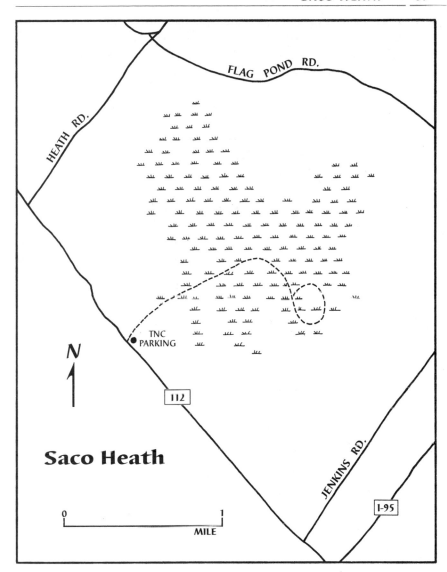

FLAG POND RD.

HEATH RD.

TNC
PARKING

N

112

Saco Heath

JENKINS RD.

I-95

0   1

MILE

marily of Red Maples, White Pines, and Eastern Hemlock. A half-mile-long trail leads through the woods and then to a 2,000-foot boardwalk across the heath. As you start down the boardwalk and into the heart of the heath, you suddenly feel as though you are entering an entirely different world.

The highlight for many birders at Saco Heath is undoubtedly the presence of nesting Palm Warblers. This species typically arrives in southern Maine by mid-April, and small numbers begin breeding at the heath by early May. You will have to watch carefully for these tiny, active sprites, as their song is not easily heard. By the end of May, they are joined by nesting Prairie Warblers. Other species you are likely to see during the nesting season include Black-capped Chickadee, Brown Creeper, Veery, Hermit Thrush, American Robin, Cedar Waxwing, Yellow and Black-throated Green warblers, Ovenbird, Common Yellowthroat, Scarlet Tanager, Rose-breasted Grosbeak, and White-throated and Swamp sparrows. A pair of Northern Goshawks may also be nesting in the area.

Mammals you might encounter at the heath include Moose and White-tailed Deer, both of which are seen regularly (the deer especially in winter).

Saco Heath is open to visitors daily, free of charge, from sunrise to sunset. There are no facilities. Please remember that this is a very valuable and fragile natural area, and observe the few guidelines posted at the preserve entrance. Access is limited to the trail and boardwalk.

DIRECTIONS

Take I-95 to exit 5 (Saco, Old Orchard Beach) and follow signs to Rt. 112. Turn right onto Rt. 112 North, and in 2.3 miles turn right into the dirt parking lot at the entrance to the preserve. It is marked by a small sign.

LOCAL ACCOMMODATIONS

For information on local accommodations and services, write or call the Biddeford-Saco Chamber of Commerce, 180 Main St., Biddeford, ME 04005, telephone 207-282-1567.

Scarborough

Scarborough Marsh   Pine Point Narrows
Scarborough Beach Park

One of the best places in Maine to see an excellent variety of waterbirds, wading birds, and migrating shorebirds and waterfowl is in the town of Scarborough, just south of Portland. Most birders probably know this area best for Scarborough Marsh, the largest salt marsh in the state. Nearby, however, are two other good birding spots: Pine Point Narrows and Scarborough Beach Park. The marsh and narrows are usually most productive between late March and late October, whereas the park is primarily a winter birding spot. At any time of year you can easily spend at least a half day exploring the Scarborough area.

Scarborough Marsh   (*MAINE ATLAS* map 3, B-3 & -4)

Acre for acre, the *Spartina* grass of a salt marsh produces more food for wildlife than does any other natural habitat on earth. With 3,100 acres traversed by five tidal rivers and several creeks and streams, Scarborough Marsh is the largest salt marsh in Maine. Within its boundaries are an estimated 220 acres of mudflats, 400 acres of brackish marsh, and more than 2,400 acres of salt meadow. The marsh is owned by the Maine Department of Inland Fisheries and Wildlife (MDIFW) and is managed primarily for waterfowl. The birding generally is most productive from mid- or late March through at least October, with highlights including waterfowl (especially Snow Geese) on spring and fall migration, several species of wading birds and breeding Saltmarsh Sharp-tailed, Nelson's Sharp-tailed, and Seaside sparrows (the last local and uncommon) during the nesting season, and migrating shorebirds in spring and between late July and mid-October. There are three main access points into the marsh, and at all of them you can often get good looks at birds out in the marsh. If you want to experience the excitement of salt-marsh birding, it is hard to beat Scarborough Marsh.

The first spring migrants to arrive at Scarborough are Canada Geese, which usually begin stopping over to feed in the marsh and surrounding upland fields by early March. Several thousand birds sometimes gather in one field. Snow Geese, starkly white against the still-brown vegetation, appear by mid-April, although in smaller numbers than the Canadas. Both species of geese can usually be seen in fall, too, although usually in smaller numbers. American Black Ducks, Mallards, Northern Pintails, Blue-winged and Green-winged teal, and Common and Red-breasted mergansers are also regular on spring and fall migration, along with smaller numbers of Wood and Ring-necked ducks, American Wigeons, and Hooded Mergansers. Occasionally you can find a few Northern Shovelers or Gadwalls.

By late April or early May you can usually see several species of wading birds at the marsh. Great Blue, Green, and Little Blue herons, Snowy Egrets, and Glossy Ibis come in to feed regularly, and occasionally they are joined by a few Black-crowned Night-Herons, Cattle or Great Egrets (the latter are more common in late summer), or Tricolored Herons. Most of these wading birds nest about a mile and a half offshore on Stratton Island, which is owned and managed by the National Audubon Society. Small numbers of Wood and American Black ducks, Mallards, Green-winged Teal, and Hooded Mergansers nest in the marsh, as do American Bitterns, Virginia Rails,

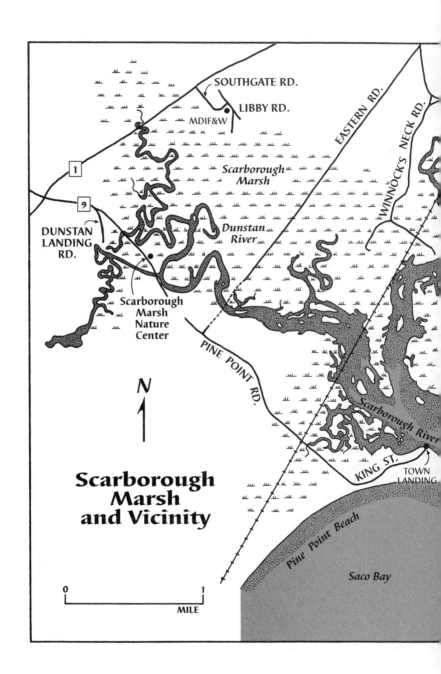

SOUTHGATE RD.

LIBBY RD.

MDIF&W

EASTERN RD.

WINNOCK'S NECK RD.

Scarborough Marsh

1

9

DUNSTAN LANDING RD.

Dunstan River

Scarborough Marsh Nature Center

PINE POINT RD.

Scarborough River

KING ST.

TOWN LANDING

N

Scarborough Marsh and Vicinity

Pine Point Beach

Saco Bay

0   1

MILE

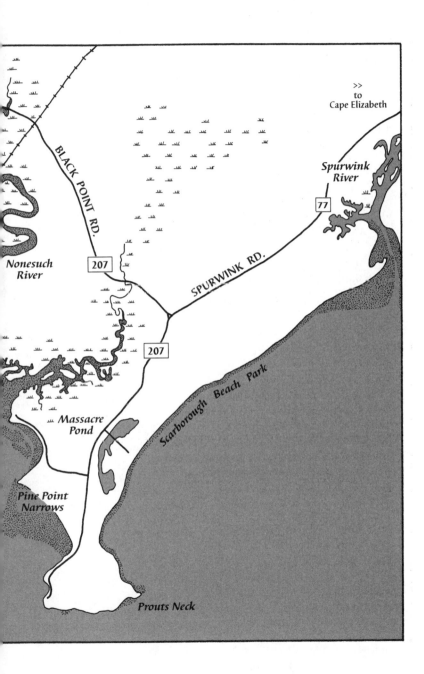

>>
to
Cape Elizabeth

Spurwink
River

BLACK POINT RD.

Nonesuch
River

207

SPURWINK RD.

77

207

Scarborough Beach Park

Massacre
Pond

Pine Point
Narrows

Prouts Neck

Willets, and Saltmarsh Sharp-tailed, Nelson's Sharp-tailed, and Savannah sparrows. Marsh Wrens, Red-winged Blackbirds, and Swamp Sparrows nest in the many cattail stands scattered around the edges. Small numbers of Seaside Sparrows have been seen in the marsh every summer since the early 1980s, and in 1995 they were documented nesting—the first state nesting record for this species. Bonaparte's Gulls generally are common in spring and from midsummer into fall, and Laughing Gulls are occasional throughout the summer. Common Terns feed in the marsh in summer, as do a few Least Terns occasionally. Overhead look for an Osprey or a Northern Harrier. Interestingly, Cooper's Hawk is also surprisingly regular here.

In spring and again in late summer and fall, Scarborough Marsh can be a wonderful place to see an impressive variety of shorebirds. For us, this is what really makes the marsh special. As elsewhere along the Maine coast, the spring shorebird migration is relatively brief and peaks between mid-May and early June, whereas the fall migration is quite protracted (mid-July though early October) and features much larger numbers of birds. August is typically an exceptional month for shorebirds at Scarborough. Regular species you can expect to see, particularly on fall migration, include Black-bellied and Semipalmated plovers, Killdeer, Greater and Lesser yellowlegs, Willet, Hudsonian Godwit, Least, Semipalmated, Pectoral, White-rumped, and Stilt sandpipers, Dunlin, and Short-billed Dowitcher. American Golden-Plover, Solitary Sandpiper, Whimbrel, Red Knot, Western Sandpiper, Long-billed Dowitcher, and Wilson's Phalarope (look for this species in shallow pools actively pursuing prey) usually occur in small numbers. Marbled Godwit, Baird's Sandpiper, and Ruff are all uncommon to rare but are certainly seen from time to time. Another species worth looking for is American Oystercatcher, which was documented nesting for the first time in Maine in 1994 on Stratton Island. *A note of caution: please remember that shorebirds expend a great deal of valuable energy if they are flushed from their roosts. Please do not get so close to the birds that you disturb them.*

In winter Scarborough Marsh is a good place to look for a Rough-legged Hawk, Snowy Owl, or Northern Shrike. You should also look over the gulls that roost on the marsh for an Iceland or a Glaucous Gull. Horned Larks and Snow Buntings flock in the marsh grass, and you can often find Lapland Longspurs among them (the last occasionally occurring in more-or-less single-species flocks of 50+). Where open water remains you are likely to see American Black Ducks, Buffleheads, Common Goldeneyes, and Common and Red-breasted mergansers.

Among the most unusual species that have been seen at the marsh in recent years are Gyrfalcon, Sandhill Crane, Yellow and King rails, American Avocet, Black-necked Stilt, Curlew Sandpiper, Caspian Tern, Northern Wheatear, and Loggerhead Shrike.

Below we describe the three main birding sites at the marsh. Although we usually try to bird all three, Eastern Road is by far our favorite and almost always the most productive. At any of these sites, rubber boots, a telescope, and a healthy supply of mosquito repellent will make your visit more enjoyable.

Eastern Road.   Eastern Road cuts through the middle of Scarborough Marsh from the north and provides a wonderful opportunity to explore a large, central portion of this vast wetland. The road is 2.2 miles long (only the first 0.4 mile of which is paved) and ends at a footbridge over the Dunstan River, from which you can see Route 9 and the Scarborough Marsh Nature Center (see below). As you come down the road into the heart of the marsh, you will pass a golf course and two ponds on the right, all of which can be worth checking for birds. You will get your first open views of the marsh, on the left, 1 mile down the road. In another 0.7 mile, where the marsh really opens up on both sides of the road, you will see a series of good-sized salt pans on the left side of the road and, on the right side, room for one vehicle to pull off and park. We like to park here, scan both sides of the marsh carefully, and then walk out into the marsh to the left.

There is an extensive series of pools here that can be outstanding for shorebirds, especially at high tide, but many of them are invisible from the roadside. If you are adventurous enough to walk out to them, however, you may be well rewarded (just watch for old drainage ditches and holes overgrown with *Spartina* grasses). Saltmarsh Sharp-tailed and Nelson's Sharp-tailed sparrows are both common breeders in this part of the marsh, making it the best place we know to observe these two species together. Willets are also common breeders here. Hudsonian Godwits, Red Knots, Stilt and White-rumped sandpipers, and Wilson's Phalaropes are all regular in small numbers on fall migration (primarily August and September), and Ruff are rare but regular enough that you should look carefully for them. Several species of wading birds are usually present in this area, too.

If you walk out into the marsh at Eastern Road, by all means wear rubber boots. Even if you stay on the road, you should still see plenty of birds. From the parking spot mentioned above, you can walk another half mile down the road and cross the footbridge over to Route 9. This is often a productive walk.

We should mention that in exceptionally dry years, many of the salt pans visible or accessible from Eastern Road may be dry and thus not used by shorebirds (which are restricted to regularly flooded pans). Fortunately, this is not a common occurrence. There have been years, however, when the marsh here was so dry that we felt as though we were birding on the moon rather than in a salt marsh.

It is also worth checking Winnock's Neck Road, just south of Eastern Road. There are several pools here (easily scanned from the car window) that attract shorebirds and wading birds, particularly at high tide.

DIRECTIONS

Eastern Rd. runs south off Rt. 207 (also called Black Point Rd.) in Scarborough. At the intersection of Rts. 1 and 207, turn south onto Rt. 207, and in 0.4 mile turn right onto Eastern Rd. In 0.4 mile the road turns to dirt, and from this point it continues another 1.8 miles to the footbridge over the Dunstan River. You can also get to Eastern Rd. from Rt. 9, via the parking area just south of the Scarborough Marsh Nature Center (see below).

To get to Winnock's Neck Rd., come back out Eastern Rd. to Rt. 207, turn right, go 0.2 mile farther south on Rt. 207, and turn right onto Winnock's Neck Rd. Follow it 1.2 miles to the railroad tracks that cut across the marsh. Just ahead, you will see several small pools on either side of the road.

Libby Road.   This road provides access into the northwesternmost section of the marsh. Park before the gate, where you see the MDIFW sign, then follow the trail on the other side of the gate through a stand of White Pines and out to the marsh (it's about a quarter-mile walk).

In summer, Snowy and Great egrets (the latter more common in late summer) and Little Blue and Tricolored herons frequently roost in the dead trees scattered throughout this part of the marsh. In July, August, and September, the many small pools attract a wide assortment of shorebirds. It was in this section of the marsh that Seaside Sparrows were first documented breeding in Maine in 1995.

In winter, a Short-eared Owl can sometimes be flushed from the field bordering the marsh, and Long-eared Owls sometimes roost in the pines.

DIRECTIONS

Libby Road is located off Southgate Rd., which turns south off Rt. 1 in Scarborough—1.3 miles north of Rt. 9 if you are coming from Scarborough Marsh Nature Center, or 1.7 miles south of Rt. 207 if you are coming from Eastern Rd. (You will see a large sign for Scarborough Industrial Park.) After turning south onto Southgate Rd., continue 0.3 mile to the stop sign and turn right onto Libby Rd. In another 0.4 mile turn right onto an unmarked paved road (a sign reads "Dead End") and then immediately right into a short dirt driveway. You will see an MDIFW sign and a small wooden building. The path out to the marsh is straight ahead, beyond the gate.

Scarborough Marsh Nature Center. Scarborough Marsh Nature Center lies along the Dunstan River on the southwest side of the marsh and is operated by the Maine Audubon Society under a cooperative agreement with the Maine Department of Inland Fisheries and Wildlife. The small visitors' building, open only in summer, includes interpretive displays and a gift shop. Recent bird sightings are usually posted on a chalkboard near the entrance. Directly across the road is a short trail along the edge of the marsh, and 0.2 mile south of this is a half-mile-long trail (actually an old roadbed) into the marsh (you will see an MDIFW sign here).

Some years ago you could get an excellent overview of the marsh from atop an observation platform at the nature center, but unfortunately the platform fell apart and (at least as of 1996) has not been rebuilt. If it ever is rebuilt, this will become a much more productive birding site. In the meantime, scan the pools behind the visitors' building, and be sure to walk the path across the road. Marsh Wrens, Saltmarsh Sharp-tailed Sparrows, and a few Nelson's Sharp-tailed Sparrows breed at the latter spot, which can be an excellent place to study shorebirds at close range, particularly at high tide. Pectoral and Stilt sandpipers, Wilson's Phalaropes (uncommon), and a wide assortment of more common shorebirds all occur here. Long-billed Dowitchers, uncommon in Maine, have been found in these pools from mid-September through October.

One of the nicest things about the nature center is that you can put in a canoe right behind the visitors' building. This is a lovely way to explore the marsh, as you can sometimes drift within a few feet of egrets, shorebirds, and Saltmarsh Sharp-tailed and Nelson's Sharp-tailed sparrows. You can bring your own canoe or, in summer, rent one here. (It's a good idea to time your visit so you can paddle with the tide rather than against it.)

A few other sites near the nature center are also worth checking. The Dunstan Landing Road, just north of the nature center, provides another overview of marshland. Just south of the nature center, you can park and take the footbridge over the Dunstan River to Eastern Road. South of this, you can pull over next to a large abandoned canning factory and scan a portion of the marsh from the edge of the parking lot. The pans at this last spot are above the influence of the daily tides and thus are used by shorebirds throughout the tidal cycle for roosting and feeding.

Scarborough Marsh Nature Center is open daily, free of charge, from Memorial Day through Labor Day from 9:30 a.m. until 5:30 p.m. For information on canoe rentals, call the nature center at 207-883-5100 or the Maine Audubon Society at 207-781-2330.

DIRECTIONS

The nature center is located on Rt. 9 (also called Pine Point Rd.) in Scarborough. At the intersection of Rts. 1 and 9, turn south onto Rt. 9, and you will see the nature center on the left in 0.8 mile.

If you continue 0.3 mile farther south, you will see the small parking area on the left (marked by an MDIFW sign) from which you can walk over to Eastern Rd. In another 1.7 miles, on the right, you will see the large parking lot next to the abandoned canning factory. Coming back north up Rt. 9, Dunstan Landing Rd. is 0.5 mile past the nature center, on the opposite side of the road; drive the 0.3 mile to the end for another overview of marshland (you will be at the northern end of the old roadbed that is also accessible from south of the nature center).

Scarborough Marsh is open to the public daily from sunrise to sunset, free of charge. Except for rest rooms at the seasonally operated nature center, there are no facilities. Bear in mind that this is a wildlife management area and not a refuge; trapping and duck hunting are allowed in season. If you are unfamiliar with what precautions should be taken during this season in Maine, see the section entitled "Hunting" in the Introduction.

Pine Point Narrows (*MAINE ATLAS* map 3, B-4)

Just beyond Scarborough Marsh at the mouth of the Scarborough (sometimes spelled Scarboro) River, Pine Point peninsula stretches east toward Prouts Neck and forms Pine Point Narrows. The protected basin that results is a fine place to see a variety of waterbirds year-round, and the extensive sand- and mudflats that are exposed at low tide make it an excellent shorebirding area in spring and from midsummer well into fall. This area is worth a stop at any time of year, and the town landing makes an ideal parking and birding spot. There is very little walking involved, so you can usually bird the narrows in a half hour or so. Particularly in winter, this is often a good place to check after a storm, when ducks and other waterbirds seek refuge in the protected harbor. After birding the narrows, you can drive up to Pine Point Beach and scan the beach and offshore waters of Saco Bay (this is usually most productive between late September and late March).

From November through March check the narrows and Saco Bay for Red-throated and Common loons, Horned Grebes, Great Cormorants, Brant (small numbers from February through April), several species of sea and bay ducks (Oldsquaws, Black Scoters, Common Goldeneyes, and Buffleheads are all regular), and Sanderlings (usually present through December). Scan the dunes and upper beach, too; Horned Larks, American Pipits, Lapland Longspurs, Snow Buntings, and "Ipswich" Savannah Sparrows can sometimes be found in the grass in fall and winter.

In summer look for Piping Plovers and Least Terns (the plovers nest on Prouts Neck most years, and the terns nest not too far south) and for Common, Arctic, and Roseate terns feeding offshore at the mouth of the Scarborough River. In recent years, as many as 100 Roseates have been seen here in late summer. Bonaparte's Gulls usually are common in spring and from midsummer well into fall, and Laughing Gulls are occasional. One or two Little Gulls seem to be an annual occurrence, usually foraging with the large flocks of Bonaparte's Gulls in September. In August and September, Forster's and Black terns are sometimes seen here in small numbers. At the height of the breeding season, the narrows can often be a good spot to observe the evening flight of wading birds going out to Stratton Island.

During the spring and fall shorebird migrations, look at the narrows for most of the same shorebirds you would expect to see at Scarborough Marsh, as well as for Piping Plovers, Sanderlings, and Ruddy Turnstones. Particularly between mid-July and mid-September, hundreds of southbound birds feed on the sand- and mudflats here. Activity is usually most pronounced on a mid- to low tide, with birds beginning to arrive in good numbers about two hours after high tide. Be sure to scan both sides of the town landing. The somewhat local Whimbrel and Red Knot can usually be found feeding with a wide variety of more common shorebirds, and Hudsonian Godwits are often present, too. This is also a good place to keep your eyes out for something unusual. Pine Point Narrows provided Maine with its first state record for Bar-tailed Godwit. American Avocet and American Oystercatcher (one pair of the latter has nested on Stratton Island) have also been seen here. Other recent rarities include Sabine's, Franklin's, and Mew gulls and Royal Tern.

Northern Mockingbirds are numerous at all seasons, and Orchard Orioles (uncommon) have sometimes nested in nearby trees.

The parking lot at the town landing is accessible year-round, free of charge. There are no facilities.

DIRECTIONS

From the Scarborough Marsh Nature Center (see above), continue another 2.4 miles south down Rt. 9, and instead of bearing right at the stop sign here, turn left onto East Grand Ave. In another 0.5 mile turn left onto King St., which soon opens onto the large municipal town landing parking lot. To scan Saco Bay, follow King St. back up to the beach, where you can park. There is a hefty fee in summer, but in winter—which is when this spot is most interesting— you can park for free.

Scarborough Beach Park
(*MAINE ATLAS* map 3, B-4)

Scarborough Beach Park lies along the eastern shore of Prouts Neck, the long peninsula that protrudes like a fist into Saco Bay. This beach system comprises about 135 acres and includes a closed barrier beach that protects a freshwater marsh with extensive stands of cattails. The marsh is called Massacre Pond because in 1713 twenty settlers were slaughtered here by Indians. Geologists speculate that perhaps 4,000 years ago this same beach system was an open barrier beach with a salt marsh and mudflats. As the sea level has risen, the dunes have retreated up and over the old salt marsh, creating what you see today. There are a few low-relief parabolic dunes with healthy stands of American Beach Grass, a narrow band of dry, semiopen dunes, and good stands of Pitch Pine forest. The area is notable for the high diversity of its vegetational cover, which includes stands of the very fragile Beach Heather and patches of Earth Star Puffball and Tall Wormwood, which are uncommon in Maine.

Scarborough Beach Park is primarily a winter birding spot. Between November and late March, you can almost always find several species of common waterbirds here, and sometimes you can also find Harlequin Ducks and a King Eider. Common Loons, Red-necked Grebes, Common Eiders, and all three scoters are usually present, and in many winters one or two King Eiders are surprisingly consistent among the large rafts of Common Eiders. The Harlequin Ducks seem to prefer the rocky point at the north end of the beach, which is an easy and enjoyable walk. Sometimes the birds are hidden from view, so if you don't see them along the beach, round the point and look there. A small flock of these strikingly handsome ducks has wintered offshore here for as long as anyone can remember. Sanderlings often feed along the beach well into December, and Purple Sandpipers sometimes fly by. Look for Horned Larks, Snow Buntings, and possibly Lapland Longspurs along the beach, and check the Pitch Pines and shrubs around Massacre Pond for overwintering passerines.

In spring look for Piping Plovers along the beach and for Marsh Wrens nesting in the cattails at Massacre Pond. Sometimes there are a few ducks on the pond, too, including Ring-necked Ducks and an occasional Gadwall. Look for nesting Pine Warblers in the Pitch Pines. We rarely visit the park after mid-June because the beach is crowded and the birdlife decidedly less interesting.

Scarborough Beach Park is open every day, year-round, from 9:00 a.m. until half an hour before sunset. Between April 1 and early November there is a small parking fee. Facilities include picnic tables, outhouses, and in summer, a snack bar.

DIRECTIONS
Scarborough Beach Park lies on the east side of Rt. 207 (also called Black Point Rd.) in Scarborough. At the intersection of Rts. 1 and 207, turn south onto Rt. 207, and in 4 miles you will see the park on the left.

LOCAL ACCOMMODATIONS
For information on local accommodations and services, write or call the Greater Portland Chamber of Commerce, 145 Middle St., Portland, ME 04101, telephone 207-772-2811.

Cape Elizabeth

Spurwink Marsh	Crescent Beach State Park
Two Lights State Park & Dyer Point	Kettle Cove

The small town of Cape Elizabeth sits on one of southern Maine's outermost headlands, overlooking the entrance to Portland Harbor and open ocean. Four good birding spots are located within easy distance of one another, and together they offer a good cross section of birds year-round. Two Lights State Park is a particularly productive spot, especially in winter. At any time of year, allow about three to four hours to visit all four sites.

Spurwink Marsh (*MAINE ATLAS* map 3, A-4)

Situated due east of Scarborough Marsh (see the preceding chapter) on the Spurwink River is a lovely, small salt-marsh complex known as Spurwink Marsh. Although Spurwink may not rival nearby Scarborough Marsh in size or diversity, it still has much to offer—and you can check it quickly, primarily from your vehicle. Spurwink also has the advantage of easy accessibility to its salt pans, and it is often possible to observe waterfowl, shorebirds, and wading birds at close range. Unfortunately, new homes are springing up in every direction around the marsh, and we wonder if development will eventually take a toll on the birdlife. For the present, however, a drive around the marsh at any time of year is likely to yield something of interest. Although the marsh is private property, you can scan it from the roadside.

Look for essentially the same species of birds at Spurwink Marsh as you would at Scarborough Marsh. Snow and Canada geese often feed here in early spring, and dabbling ducks—particularly American Black Ducks, Mallards, Northern Pintails, and Blue-winged and Green-winged teal—are common in spring as well as fall. Great Blue, Green, and Little Blue herons, Snowy and Great egrets, and Glossy Ibis all frequent the marsh in summer, and shorebirds stop over on their spring and fall migrations. The pools at Spurwink seem to be especially attractive to Greater and Lesser yellowlegs, Willets (almost certainly nesting here), Solitary and Pectoral sandpipers, and occasionally a Wilson's Phalarope or two. Saltmarsh Sharp-tailed and Nelson's Sharp-tailed sparrows nest in the *Spartina* grass in the marsh, and Marsh Wrens and Swamp Sparrows nest in the scattered cattails. Although we have not seen Seaside Sparrows here, they are undoubtedly worth looking for, especially since this species was first confirmed nesting in Maine in 1995 at nearby Scarborough Marsh.

In summer, several pairs of Willow Flycatchers nest in the alders bordering the marsh, and Ring-necked Pheasants, Eastern Meadowlarks, Bobolinks, and Savannah Sparrows nest in the upland meadows.

The best way to work Spurwink Marsh is simply to drive around it, scanning the marsh from the roadside. The directions below will take you in a loop.

Spurwink Marsh is accessible year-round, free of charge. There are no facilities.

DIRECTIONS

Traveling between Scarborough and Cape Elizabeth on Rt. 77 (also called Spurwink Rd. in Scarborough and Bowery Beach Rd. in

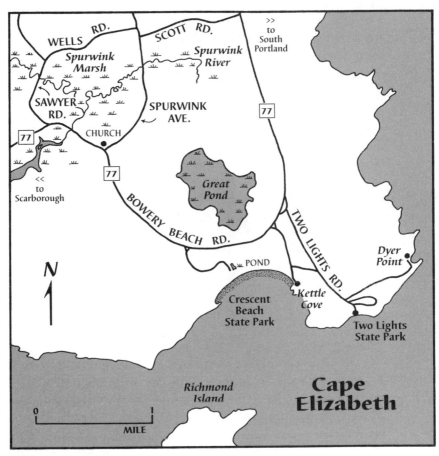

Cape Elizabeth), look for the intersection of Rt. 77 and Spurwink Ave. (which is distinct from Spurwink Rd.). You will see a conspicuous white church at the corner on the north side of the road. Turn north onto Spurwink Ave., and just behind the church turn into the small cemetery. This lovely spot affords a good overview of the marsh below, and you can park and scan the nearby pools.

Continue 0.5 mile north on Spurwink Ave. and park on the left side of the road (across from the Cape Elizabeth dump). This is a good place to scan across a large meadow to the edge of the marsh and over several pools.

To make a full loop around the marsh, continue 0.7 mile farther north on Spurwink Ave., turn left onto Wells Rd., and in 0.9 mile turn left again onto Sawyer Rd. Many of the pools in this portion of the marsh are quite close to the road, so in shorebird season it is a good idea to scan carefully before stepping out of your vehicle.

Crescent Beach State Park
(MAINE ATLAS map 3, B-5)

Crescent Beach State Park, just off Route 77 in Cape Elizabeth, is popular with beachgoers in summer and with cross-country skiers in winter. It can also offer some pleasant birding, especially in June. The park is relatively small (244 acres), so you can cover it quite thoroughly in an hour or two. Especially in summer, it is a good idea to arrive early in the day, before the swimmers and sunbathers.

Although known primarily for its lovely mile-long sand beach, Crescent Beach State Park also includes a spruce-fir forest and an interesting freshwater pond. As you might expect, the beach itself is crowded in summer and not especially noteworthy for its birdlife. However, the spruce-fir forest, more typical of the boreal forests farther north and east, provides breeding habitat for Golden-crowned Kinglet, Solitary Vireo, Hermit Thrush, Northern Parula, Magnolia, Yellow-rumped, Black-throated Green, Blackburnian, and Canada warblers, Purple Finch, and White-throated Sparrow. More ubiquitous breeders include Least Flycatcher, Veery, Northern Mockingbird, American Redstart, Scarlet Tanager, and Rose-breasted Grosbeak. Pileated Woodpecker occurs irregularly.

Just west of the large parking lot by the beach is a freshwater pond bordered by cattails. This is not an easy spot to bird, unfortunately, but if you don't mind wet feet (or better yet, if you have a pair of boots), you can work your way to the edge. Marsh Wrens, Red-winged Blackbirds, and Song and Swamp sparrows nest around the pond, and American Black Ducks and Blue-winged Teal are regular throughout the summer. Look patiently for a Mink at any time of year; a friend of ours surprised one on the ice here one winter.

Between late September and April, check the beach for Horned Larks, Lapland Longspurs, Snow Buntings, and sparrows, and in October and November look along the dune edges for migrating "Ipswich" Savannah Sparrows. The dunes are more extensive on the western half of the beach than on the eastern half. A Smith's Longspur was an unexpected discovery here one January. At any time of year, scan offshore for waterbirds.

The best way to bird the park is to proceed past the entrance gate and park in the main (large) lot by the beach. From here you can walk the main road back toward the entrance gate (it's only 0.2 mile), detouring into the woods as interesting birdcalls attract your attention. Just before the entrance gate, follow the wide trail on the left into the woods. This winds through the spruce-fir forest, passes across a lovely meadow (fork left after the meadow), then comes out at the western end of the beach. You can then walk up the beach and back to your vehicle. Don't forget to check the pond.

Crescent Beach State Park is open from Memorial Day through Columbus Day weekend from 9:00 a.m. to 8:00 p.m. (until Labor Day) or dusk (after Labor Day). There is a small entrance fee. Facilities include a beach house, snack bar, and toilets. If you are here before 9:00 a.m. or during the off-season when the entrance gate is closed, you may park outside it (making sure that your vehicle does not block the gate or road) and walk in. Better yet, however, park at Kettle Cove (see below), which overlooks the north end of the beach.

DIRECTIONS

FROM THE NORTH: From the south end of the Fore River bridge at the northern end of Rt. 77 in South Portland, drive 6.4 miles south on Rt. 77 (also called Ocean House Rd.) and turn left into the park, which is well marked.

FROM THE SOUTH: From the intersection of Rts. 207 and 77 in Scarborough, drive 4.5 miles north on Rt. 77 and turn right into the park.

FROM TWO LIGHTS STATE PARK: From the intersection of Two Lights Rd. and Rt. 77, drive 1 mile south and turn left into the park.

Two Lights State Park & Dyer Point
(*MAINE ATLAS* map 3, B-5)

Two Lights State Park, which lies less than 10 miles southeast of the center of Portland, marks the southern entrance to Casco Bay. Situated on the southern tip of the Cape Elizabeth headland, this lovely spot offers a spectacular vantage point from which to scan for seabirds year-round (November through March is generally most productive), and in spring and fall it often attracts large numbers of migrant landbirds. There is not much walking involved here, so you can easily bird the park in an hour or so. Even on the best of days, you will want to dress extra warmly—and be prepared for some salt spray. A half mile northeast of the park is Dyer Point, which is also worth checking, as many birds move back and forth between Two Lights and Dyer Point.

Named for two nearby lighthouses, Two Lights consists of 41 acres of steep, rocky shoreline and associated uplands. With extensive conifers, shrubs, and protected brushy pockets, it is just the kind of habitat that is often so attractive to migrant songbirds. In spring, particularly throughout the month of May and after strong southerly winds, this is a good place to look for flycatchers and warblers en route to nesting areas farther north. In fall, the best birding is immediately after northwest winds. From mid-August through October, you can often find impressive numbers of migrants here, especially sparrows. White-eyed Vireo, Blue Grosbeak, and Le Conte's Sparrow are a few of the more interesting vagrants that have been reported. Explore the grassy area around the parking lot and the narrow paths that wind through the vegetation above the shore.

Two Lights is also a good place to look for many of Maine's regularly occurring waterbirds. As elsewhere along the southern Maine coast, you will usually find the greatest variety from November through March. Red-throated and Common loons, Horned and Red-necked grebes, Common Eiders, Oldsquaws, all three scoters, Common Goldeneyes, Buffleheads, Red-breasted Mergansers, Black Guillemots, and Herring and Great Black-backed gulls are all regular. Occasionally you can also find a King Eider or a few Harlequin Ducks. Look for Purple Sandpipers, which are quite regular along the surf-bound ledges, and for Great Cormorants and white-winged gulls. Northeast storms, particularly in November and December, can sometimes bring in large flights of Dovekies, Razorbills, and murres—and also a magnificent surf beating over the rocks. This is a spectacular place to witness the power and beauty of a winter storm. Be sure to wear foul-weather gear over your parka, and don't even think about getting close to the shore if the seas are rough. Northern Gannets and Black-legged Kittiwakes are also blown in by strong winds sometimes, so scan carefully offshore.

In summer you generally won't find too much of interest in the park, although Black Guillemots are regular offshore.

If you are a geology buff, you will be interested in the rocks at Two Lights State Park, where the bedrock geology has been dramatically exposed by wave action. The cliffs here are composed of tan quartzite and dark gray phyllite, which originally accumulated in alternating layers that have since folded and twisted into dramatic patterns. In their blocky, steplike formation and woody-looking texture, these metamorphic rocks look remarkably like petrified wood.

Two Lights is also known for its many shallow tide pools, which occur in all four intertidal zones. In summer and fall you can often find a good variety of marine invertebrates in them, including sponges, whelks, sea stars, brittle stars, hermit crabs, and Green Sea Urchins.

After birding the park, you should also check Dyer Point, the easternmost point of land on Cape Elizabeth. Here you will see the two lighthouses and a public parking lot (by the small Lobster Shack Restaurant). Dyer Point provides another elevated vantage point from which to scan the water; like Two Lights, it is especially productive in fall and winter. In fall this can also be a good spot to see migrating hawks crossing outer Casco Bay. Osprey, Northern Harrier, Sharp-shinned Hawk, American Kestrel, and Merlin are the most frequently observed species, and Peregrine Falcon is sometimes seen as well. One winter we were treated to a spectacular sight when an adult Bald Eagle flew by at eye level and put up a flock of 1,000-plus Common Eiders that had been rafting just beyond the shoreline. The area around the parking lot is also a good place to look in fall and winter for Lapland Longspurs, Snow Buntings, and occasionally sparrows, including "Ipswich" Savannah Sparrows.

Two Lights State Park is open every day, year-round, from sunrise to approximately dusk (the closing time, which varies according to the season, is posted on the park gate). A small fee is charged. Facilities include picnic tables and toilets. If you arrive early in the morning and find the park gate closed, you may park outside (provided that your vehicle does not block the gate or road) and walk the short way (about 500 feet) to the parking lot.

The parking lot at Dyer Point is open year-round, free of charge. There are no facilities here.

DIRECTIONS

FROM THE NORTH: From the south end of the Fore River bridge at the northern end of Rt. 77 in South Portland, drive 5.4 miles south on Rt. 77 (also called Ocean House Rd.) and turn left onto Two Lights Rd. The park, well marked, is 1 mile ahead on the right.

FROM THE SOUTH: From the intersection of Rts. 207 and 77 in Scarborough, drive 5.5 miles north on Rt. 77 and turn right onto Two Lights Rd. Proceed as above.

TO DYER'S POINT: Coming out of Two Lights State Park, turn right onto Two Lights Rd. and continue 0.6 mile to the end of the road. You will see the shore directly ahead of you and a parking area on the right. Watch your ears if the foghorn is active!

Kettle Cove (*MAINE ATLAS* map 3, B-5)

Kettle Cove is the small cove that lies between Two Lights State Park and Crescent Beach State Park. Inconspicuous as it may be (it isn't on most maps, including the *Maine Atlas*), it still warrants checking. Especially in winter, you can often find something of interest here. Common Loons, Horned Grebes, Common Eiders, Oldsquaws, Common Goldeneyes, and Buffleheads are usually present offshore, and if you scope the open fields on Richmond Island (the large island to the southwest), you can sometimes turn up a Rough-legged Hawk or

Snowy Owl. During spring and fall migration, the short trail along the shore can be a good area to find migrants, especially in the early morning. You can also scan the eastern end of Crescent Beach from Kettle Cove.

The Kettle Cove parking lot is open every day, free of charge, from sunrise to sunset. The only facilities are toilets.

DIRECTIONS

FROM TWO LIGHTS STATE PARK: Coming out of the park, turn left onto Two Lights Rd., continue 0.2 mile, and take the first left onto Fessenden Rd. Continue 0.2 mile to the end of Fessenden Rd. and turn left onto Ocean House Rd. (which at this point is a side road, not Rt. 77). In 0.1 mile you will see the Kettle Cove parking lot (which overlooks the eastern end of Crescent Beach State Park).

FROM CRESCENT BEACH STATE PARK: Coming out of the park, turn right onto Rt. 77, continue 0.8 mile north, and turn right onto Ocean House Rd. Follow the small sign for "Kettle Cove Area," and in 0.6 mile you will see the parking lot.

LOCAL ACCOMMODATIONS

For information on local accommodations and services, write or call the Greater Portland Chamber of Commerce, 145 Middle St., Portland, ME 04101, telephone 207-772-2811.

Greater Portland Area

Back Cove	Eastern Promenade
Portland Harbor	Evergreen Cemetery
Calvary Cemetery	Capisic Pond Park
Mackworth Island	Gilsland Farm
M.V. *Scotia Prince*	

With a population of about 65,000 people, Portland is the largest city in Maine. It lies on a saddle-shaped peninsula extending into Casco Bay and is surrounded on almost all sides by water—Casco Bay, Back Cove, and the Fore and Presumpscot rivers. Its deep, sheltered harbor has made the city an important seaport since its settlement in the seventeenth century, and today Portland's harbor and waterfront still bustle with activity. This is a delightful small city, and it is full of good birding year-round.

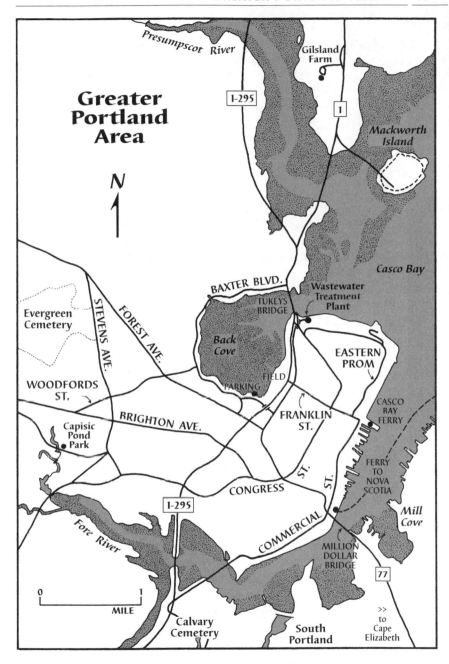

Greater
Portland
Area

N

Presumpscot River

Gilsland
Farm

I-295

1

Mackworth
Island

Casco Bay

BAXTER BLVD.

Evergreen
Cemetery

STEVENS AVE.

FOREST AVE.

TUKEYS
BRIDGE

Wastewater
Treatment
Plant

Back
Cove

EASTERN
PROM

WOODFORDS
ST.

FIELD

PARKING

BRIGHTON AVE.

Capisic
Pond
Park

FRANKLIN
ST.

CASCO
BAY
FERRY

ST.

FERRY
TO
NOVA
SCOTIA

CONGRESS

ST.

I-295

Mill
Cove

Fore River

COMMERCIAL

MILLION
DOLLAR
BRIDGE

77

0   1

MILE

Calvary
Cemetery

South
Portland

>>
to
Cape
Elizabeth

Back Cove (*MAINE ATLAS* map 73, E-3)

Some of the best birding in Portland is right in the heart of the city at Back Cove. Established as a wild bird sanctuary in 1915 and administered by the Maine Department of Inland Fisheries and Wildlife, this shallow bay measures about 1 mile in diameter and includes 33 acres of tidal flats. I-295 runs along its eastern shore, and Baxter Boulevard circles it on the west. Back Cove is a good place to see waterfowl in fall, winter, and spring, shorebirds on spring and fall migration, and gulls year-round. It also attracts rare or unusual birds each year. Whether it is a Snowy Owl, Northern Hawk Owl, Common Black-headed Gull, or Western Sandpiper, there is usually something interesting at Back Cove. Check the cove at any time of year, and plan on spending at least an hour or so to do an adequate job.

You can scan Back Cove from anywhere along Baxter Boulevard, but with the traffic, this is often inconvenient. A better way to bird the cove is from the large parking lot along the southeast shore. If you park here you have direct access to the shore as well as to the athletic field between the east shore and the interstate. This field is an excellent birding spot in its own right (at least when there aren't any soccer players on it), so be sure to scan it carefully, as well as the cove and shore. From the parking lot you also have access to the 3.5-mile-long pedestrian trail that winds around the cove. If you have the time, this is a wonderful way to bird Back Cove.

Our favorite time to bird the cove is between mid-July and late November, when the bulk of the shorebirds and landbirds move south. The fall shorebird migration (mid-July through October) can be especially interesting. We like to be here on a high tide, when roosting birds often concentrate on the shore near the parking lot. (The flats near the southwest corner of the parking lot are the first to be exposed on a falling tide and the last to be covered on a rising tide.) Black-bellied Plovers are abundant, and they are regularly joined by Semipalmated Plovers, Greater and Lesser yellowlegs, Ruddy Turnstones, Least and Semipalmated sandpipers, Dunlin, and Short-billed Dowitchers. American Golden-Plovers usually occur in small numbers each year, and in late August or September a handful of White-rumped and Western sandpipers can often be found among the peep. Willets, Whimbrels, Hudsonian Godwits, Red Knots, Upland, Baird's, and Pectoral sandpipers, and Long-billed Dowitchers are infrequent visitors to the cove; Solitary, Stilt, and Buff-breasted sandpipers are rare. Scan the athletic field for birds before you walk over to the shore, and take care not to approach roosting birds too closely. These long-distance migrants cannot afford to expend energy unnecessarily (and once flushed, they generally disappear). Instead, use patience and a telescope, both of which are essential ingredients for successful shorebirding.

By late August, the shorebirds are joined by good numbers of sparrows and other passerines, and the athletic field and its weedy edges typically harbor many birds. Savannah Sparrows often account for the bulk of the sparrows moving through, but it is worth sorting through them for other species. Vesper, "Ipswich" Savannah, Saltmarsh Sharp-tailed, Nelson's Sharp-tailed, Seaside (rare), Swamp, White-throated, and White-crowned sparrows are all possibilities. Look, too, for other open-country species such as Horned Larks, American Pipits, Bobolinks, Eastern Meadowlarks, Lapland Longspurs, and Snow Buntings. Also be sure to scan the cove; Forster's Terns, which are rare in Maine, have been seen here in August and September. And don't forget all those gulls. Herring, Great Black-backed, and Ring-billed gulls roost along the shore all year; Bonaparte's Gulls are regular in spring and in late summer and fall; and Laughing Gulls are occasional between about mid-April and mid-October. A few Little Gulls have been seen here in September, and Common Black-headed Gulls, which are regular around the cove in small numbers each winter, occasionally show up in late summer and fall. Remember to watch for Merlins and the occasional Peregrine Falcon in fall, too; both species are known to chase shorebird flocks.

From early November through March, Back Cove is an excellent area for duck-watching, particularly at high tide. You are likely to see large numbers of Mallards, American Black Ducks, Buffleheads, and Common Goldeneyes, as well as Common and Red-breasted mergansers and sometimes Northern Pintails (primarily in early fall and spring) and Greater and Lesser scaup. Barrow's Goldeneyes, once regular here, have almost disappeared from the cove in recent years, but on rare occasions you can still find a few (look for them out in the middle of the cove, usually associated with Common Goldeneyes and Buffleheads). At one time or another almost every eastern duck has been seen here, so it pays to look over the waterfowl carefully. Check the gulls carefully, too. A few Common Black-headed Gulls inevitably show up each winter, as do small numbers of Iceland and, less often, Glaucous gulls (these two white-winged gulls are most likely between December and March). "Thayer's" and Lesser Black-backed gulls have also been seen here, both in December. One or two Snowy Owls and sometimes a few Short-eared Owls sometimes winter near the athletic field or along the edge of the cove by the interstate. Look along the weedy edges of the field for Horned Larks, Snow Buntings, and Lapland Longspurs. This is also a good spot to look for late-lingering migrants. Our friend Rich Eakin, who probably knows Back Cove better than anyone else in Maine, says that his two favorite off-season finds are Yellow-breasted Chat and Grasshopper Sparrow, both of which he saw in January.

Spring and summer are typically the "slow" seasons at Back Cove, but you never know what might turn up. Glossy Ibis are occasional in spring, and some interesting ducks sometimes appear then, among them Gadwall, Northern Shoveler, and American Wigeon. Regularly seen species in summer include Double-crested Cormorant, Great Blue Heron, Snowy Egret, American Black Duck, Blue-winged and Green-winged teal (early and late summer), and Common Tern. Killdeer, Spotted Sandpipers, and Savannah Sparrows nest around the cove.

To date, more than 200 species of birds have been recorded at Back Cove. Some of the more intriguing finds in recent years include Tundra Swan, King and Clapper rails, American Oystercatcher, American Avocet, Black Skimmer, Thick-billed Murre, Western King-bird, Rusty and Yellow-headed blackbirds, Loggerhead Shrike, and Grasshopper, Seaside, and Lark sparrows.

You should also check the inlet to Back Cove on the east side of Tukeys Bridge (I-295), especially in fall and winter. See the next write-up, on Eastern Promenade.

Back Cove is accessible year-round, free of charge.

DIRECTIONS

FROM THE SOUTH: Follow I-295 into Portland and take exit 6B to Forest Ave. North (Rt. 100). Turn right at the first light onto Rt. 1/Baxter Blvd.; at the next light turn right again onto Preble St. Ext. You will see the parking lot overlooking the cove on the left and, beyond it, the athletic field.

FROM THE NORTH: Follow I-295 into Portland, and on the north side of the city exit right onto Baxter Blvd. Circle the cove, turn left at the light onto Preble St. Ext., and turn into the parking lot on the left.

Eastern Promenade (*MAINE ATLAS* map 73, E-4)

Eastern Promenade, or Eastern Prom as Portlanders call it, is the wide boulevard that runs the length of Portland's East End. Designed by the famous landscape architect Frederick Law Olmsted in the late

1800s, this historic drive offers a wide, dramatic view of outer Portland Harbor and Casco Bay. It is also a fine winter birding spot.

Casco Bay supports a great many waterbirds, and it is between early November and April that you will find the richest variety. American Black Ducks, Common Eiders, Oldsquaws, Common Goldeneyes, Buffleheads, and Red-breasted Mergansers are all abundant. You can usually find a few Red-throated or Common Loons, Great Cormorants, and Greater Scaup among them. Occasionally a King Eider winters here, and small numbers of Barrow's Goldeneyes are recorded every winter. Iceland Gulls sometimes perch on the railroad bridge or the rocks offshore. Take the time to look over the harbor carefully.

At the eastern end of Eastern Prom, be sure to take Cutter Street down to the water. This short (0.4 mile) street ends up at a public boat landing on the shore. You cannot leave your car here, but you can park and scan the water.

Near the western end of Eastern Prom (but accessible only from Marginal Way), check the Portland Water District's wastewater treatment plant. In winter this is an almost mandatory stop for us whenever we're in Portland. It offers a wonderful overview of the inlet to Back Cove and is a good place to look for gulls. We often turn up something of interest here: Common Black-headed Gulls are regular visitors in winter and are occasional in late summer and fall, and small numbers of Iceland Gulls are usually reported each winter.

Just before the plant gate, you will see a small area on the left where you can pull over and scan the inlet to Back Cove. After doing this, proceed through the gate (it seems to be open all the time, or at least during daylight hours) and ask someone outside or in the main building for permission to scan the gulls that hang around the treatment tanks. As our friend Lysle Brinker says, "Hold your nose!"

DIRECTIONS

Follow I-295 into Portland and take exit 7 (Franklin St.). In 0.1 mile, at the second stoplight, turn left onto Fox St. Continue 0.3 mile to the stop sign at the top of the hill and turn left onto Washington Ave./Rt. 26 (unmarked). In 0.2 mile turn right onto Eastern Prom.

TO REACH THE WASTEWATER TREATMENT PLANT: Get off I-295 at exit 7 and immediately take the first left onto Marginal Way. Continue 0.6 mile to the end of the road, where you will see the plant. If you are coming from Back Cove, simply continue down Preble St. Ext. to Marginal Way, turn left, and proceed as above.

Portland Harbor (MAINE ATLAS map 73, F-4)

The main attraction for birders at Portland Harbor is gulls, particularly winter gulls. Between November and March, thousands of gulls roost along the waterfront, offering an unusual opportunity to study immature and winter-plumage gulls at close range. Herring and Great Black-backed gulls are (of course) by far the most abundant species, with smaller numbers of Ring-billed and sometimes Bonaparte's gulls also present (the latter primarily in spring and fall). This is an excellent area to look for Iceland and Glaucous gulls between early December and late March.

The best way to bird Portland Harbor is via Commercial Street, which runs the length of the waterfront. Start at the Casco Bay Lines Ferry Terminal at the north end of the street and work your way down to the Million Dollar Bridge (a distance of 0.9 mile). All along the way you will find gulls roosting—on the piers, on the roofs of old warehouses, on the fishing boats. This isn't necessarily the easiest birding (especially on a bitter cold day), but it can be a lot of fun. Be sure to check the parking lot at the Portland International Ferry Terminal and the adjacent docks and shorefront near the Million Dollar Bridge.

DIRECTIONS

Follow I-295 into Portland and take exit 7 (Franklin St.). From the first stoplight, continue straight for 0.7 mile and turn right. You are now at the north end of Commercial St. and can begin checking the buildings and piers along the left side of the street.

Evergreen Cemetery
(MAINE ATLAS map 73, E-1 & -2)

Local birders consider Evergreen Cemetery one of the best places in the Portland area to look for migrant landbirds, particularly spring warblers. This 270-acre municipal property includes mixed deciduous trees, conifers, shrubs, open areas, and four small ponds. The coniferous trees and low shrubs that surround the ponds at the west end of the cemetery typically attract the greatest concentrations of birds. In the early morning on a good migration day, you can easily spend two to three hours prowling around the back of the cemetery and exchanging notes with the other birders who are certain to be here. Be sure to walk the trail that circles around behind the large pond.

In spring, virtually every eastern warbler is found regularly at Evergreen, and softwood species such as Cape May, Blackburnian,

Bay-breasted, and Blackpoll warblers can be surprisingly numerous in the nearby Tamarack trees. Rarities that have occurred here include Blue-winged, Golden-winged, Cerulean, Hooded, Kentucky, and Worm-eating warblers and Louisiana Waterthrush. The migration usually peaks in the second to third week in May. Blue-gray Gnatcatchers and Yellow-throated and Philadelphia vireos, unusual species in Maine, seem to show up annually, and Tufted Titmice and Fish Crows, formerly unusual in southern Maine, are now established breeders. Interestingly, Winter Wrens are also confirmed nesters here, and Carolina Wrens are probable nesters. Pileated Woodpeckers nest in the cemetery and can often be heard drumming. Red Crossbills are irregular but are occasionally found feeding on the Tamarack and spruce cones. Waterfowl and gulls sometimes concentrate on the ponds; it is always worth looking them over for something unusual.

The latter half of August and September can also be productive, primarily for southbound warblers and other passerines.

Evergreen Cemetery is open every day, free of charge, from 8:00 a.m. (and sometimes earlier, especially in May) to sunset. There are no facilities.

DIRECTIONS

Follow I-295 into Portland and take exit 6 (Forest Ave. North, Rt. 100). From the first stoplight, which is at the intersection of Forest Ave. and Baxter Blvd., continue 0.8 mile to Woodfords Corner, where five streets meet. Take the soft, not the hard, left onto Woodfords St. and continue 0.5 mile. Turn right onto Stevens Ave., and in 0.5 mile you will see the first cemetery gate on the left. There is a second gate (which is the main entrance) 0.2 mile farther down Stevens Ave. Once through the second gate, drive down the hill to the ponds, thickets, and coniferous trees at the west end of the cemetery.

Calvary Cemetery (MAINE ATLAS map 73, G-2)

Across the Fore River in South Portland is another cemetery that has also become well known as a fine migrant trap. Local birders are divided as to which cemetery is better, Evergreen or Calvary. Fortunately, both are nearby, and on the right morning, especially in spring, both can be full of birds.

Like Evergreen Cemetery, Calvary Cemetery offers a pleasant expanse of mixed deciduous and coniferous woods in the midst of an urban landscape. The highlight here, as at Evergreen, is the spring warbler migration, which typically peaks in the second to third week in May. Most birds seem to congregate near the ponds close to the entrance and along the wooded section to the west; keep forking left after you drive through the entrance gate. The sloping hillside makes it easy to look into the crowns of some of these large trees, improving visibility and easing "warbler neck."

Calvary Cemetery is open seven days a week, free of charge. Weekday hours are 7:00 a.m. to sunset, weekend hours 8:30 a.m. to sunset. There are no facilities.

DIRECTIONS

FROM THE NORTH: Take I-295 south to exit 4 and follow it until it joins Main St. Continue 0.2 mile, and you will see the cemetery entrance gate on the right.

FROM THE SOUTH: Take I-295 north to exit 1. Continue 1.5 miles and turn left (north) onto Rt. 1 (Main St.). In 1.2 miles you will see the entrance gate on the left.

Capisic Pond Park (*MAINE ATLAS* map 73, E-2)

Capisic Pond Park is a small city park that birders have recently discovered is well worth a stop, especially in the spring and early breeding season. Located only a few minutes' drive from Evergreen Cemetery, this unpretentious-looking spot consists of what looks like a small freshwater pond (it's actually a dammed backwater of the Fore River) backed by a large cattail marsh and an overgrown field. The park is often a good place to find a few species you may not see as easily elsewhere in the city. Breeding species on the pond or in the marsh and surrounding uplands include American Black Duck, Blue-winged Teal, Virginia Rail, Sora, Eastern Phoebe, Eastern Kingbird, Marsh Wren, Warbling Vireo, Northern Cardinal, Red-winged Blackbird, and Baltimore Oriole. In 1995, Orchard Orioles also nested here. In spring you can usually see a surprising variety of migrating swallows, flycatchers, vireos, and warblers. Common Moorhens and American Coots are occasional spring migrants.

You can bird Capisic Pond Park in half an hour or less. Park near the pond and walk the path back through the field and then along the edge of the cattail marsh.

The park is open daily, free of charge, from sunrise to sunset. There are no facilities.

DIRECTIONS

FROM THE SOUTH: Follow I-295 into Portland and take exit 5. Immediately move to the left lane and take the first left, following signs for Rt. 22/Congress St. West. At the end of this short connecting road, turn left onto Rt. 22/Congress St. West. In 0.8 mile turn right onto Stevens Ave., and in 0.2 mile turn left onto Frost St. Continue 0.5 mile (bearing right onto Capisic St.) and turn right onto Macy St. Drive in this narrow dirt road several hundred feet and park where you see the small "Capisic Pond Park" sign on the left.

FROM THE NORTH: Follow I-295 into Portland and take exit 5B to Rt. 22/Congress St. West. In 0.5 mile turn right onto Stevens Ave. and continue as above.

FROM EVERGREEN CEMETERY: When you come out of the main gate of the cemetery, turn right onto Stevens Ave. Continue 1.2 miles (crossing Brighton Ave.) and turn right onto Frost St. Continue as above.

Mackworth Island (*MAINE ATLAS* map 72, D-4)

Mackworth Island, just north of Portland, offers good possibilities for seeing a wide variety of birds at any time of year. Situated at the mouth of the Presumpscot River in Falmouth and connected to the mainland by a causeway, the island was given to the state by former governor Percival Baxter and since 1957 has been the home of the Baxter State School for the Deaf. Although comprising only slightly more than 100 acres, this small island has a variety of habitats, including rocky shore, extensive mudflats, coniferous and deciduous woods, low shrubs, and a small field and orchard. In spring and fall you can see a good cross section of migrant landbirds here, and in winter you can see many waterbirds offshore, including Barrow's Goldeneyes. A mile-long, easy walking path circles the island. Allow one to two hours to bird the island at leisure. You will almost certainly find yourself with company, as this is a popular walking spot for Portland residents (and their dogs), particularly on weekends.

Whatever time of year you visit Mackworth, begin your birding by scanning the shore along the causeway for waterfowl, which are usually most numerous and easiest to observe at high tide (don't park on the causeway, however). This is the island's only stretch of sheltered shoreline. Once you cross onto the island, park in the dirt parking lot to the right. A broad and quite level trail begins by the parking lot and follows the perimeter of the island. At several spots, additional trails (never long but sometimes fairly steep) lead down to the shore. We recommend wearing boots in mud season, as both the parking lot and trail can be wet.

In spring and fall, the low shrubs, woodlands, and scattered open areas on Mackworth attract a wide variety of migrant landbirds. On a good spring morning, you might easily observe 12 or more species of warblers here. Migrant shorebirds, particularly Semipalmated Plovers, sometimes roost along the causeway at high tide, and at low tide it is always worth checking the mudflats, especially for Black-bellied

Plovers. Canada Geese are typically abundant along the north side of the causeway from November through April, and in spring and fall you may see an occasional Snow Goose.

Although Mackworth offers a lovely overview of Casco Bay at any time of year, it is from late fall through early spring that birders particularly appreciate this vantage point. With access to 360 degrees of shoreline, you can often see an excellent variety of waterbirds here, especially if you have a telescope. Regular winter sightings include Red-throated and Common loons, Horned and Red-necked grebes, Canada Geese (primarily on the north side of the causeway), American Black Ducks, Oldsquaws, Common Goldeneyes, Buffleheads, and Red-breasted Mergansers. Small numbers of Barrow's Goldeneyes are fairly regular, one or two King Eiders sometimes occur among the hundreds of Common Eiders, and white-winged gulls occasionally roost along the causeway among the Herring, Great Black-backed, and Ring-billed gulls. Small numbers of Greater Scaup are usually reported around the island each winter, and in one recent winter a flock of approximately 800 rafted offshore for several days. Brant generally appear in early spring (February to April). Rarities reported off Mackworth in recent winters include Tundra Swan (four lingered for several weeks one December and January) and Ruddy Duck.

In winter check the trees along the trail for roosting owls, notably Great Horned, Barred, and Northern Saw-whet. One friend of ours says he often finds feathers and other prey remains along the edge of the soccer field—presumably the work of a resident Great Horned. From October through December, Mackworth is also a good place to look for late-lingering migrants, as Portland Christmas Bird Count participants well know.

In summer you can find many common passerines breeding on the island but nothing that really warrants a special trip. Great Horned Owls usually nest here, and Wild Turkeys were introduced on the island some years ago, although the last we heard, only one male remained.

Mackworth Island is state property. Visitors are welcome free of charge year-round, seven days a week, from sunrise to sunset. Please follow the few rules posted by the parking lot (which is limited to 20 cars). There are no facilities for visitors.

DIRECTIONS

FROM THE SOUTH: Take I-295 north through Portland, and on the north side of the city bear right at exit 9, following signs for Rt. 1 North and Falmouth Foreside. Cross the Presumpscot River, and in

0.2 mile turn right onto Andrews Ave., which will lead to the Mackworth Island causeway. The parking lot is on the right just after you cross onto the island and after the gatehouse.

FROM THE NORTH: Take I-95 south to exit 10 (Bucknam Road, Falmouth Foreside). At the head of the exit ramp, turn left and proceed to the stoplight at the intersection with Rt. 1. Turn right onto Rt. 1, and in 2 miles turn left onto Andrews Ave. Proceed as above.

Gilsland Farm (*MAINE ATLAS* map 72, C-4)

Just a mile north of Mackworth Island is Gilsland Farm, headquarters of the Maine Audubon Society. Overlooking the mouth of the Presumpscot River, this 60-acre sanctuary includes several habitats representative of southern Maine: mixed hardwoods and softwoods, meadows, shrublands, salt marsh, and a small pond. Two miles of trails traverse the property, and at any time of year you can spend a pleasant hour or so looking for birds. More than 140 species have been recorded here.

Gilsland Farm offers an opportunity to see a good cross section of common southern Maine birds. In summer Great Blue Herons and Snowy Egrets frequent the pond and marsh, Tree and Barn swallows hunt for insects overhead, Gray Catbirds "mew" from the thickets, and Bobolinks and Eastern Meadowlarks nest in the meadows. Winter brings a good variety of waterbirds to the mouth of the Presumpscot River and the chance to look for owls; over the years, an impressive seven species—Great Horned, Snowy, Barred, Great Gray, Long-eared, Short-eared, and Northern Saw-whet—have been recorded here. On the right day at the height of spring and fall migration, you can see many of New England's regular migrant hawks, shorebirds, and landbirds.

Maine Audubon is one of Maine's most influential environmental and conservation organizations and is active in many aspects of natural history. The society operates the Maine Rare Bird Alert (see Appendix D) and offers a wide array of field trips (many of them geared to birders) all over Maine year-round. The interpretive building at Gilsland Farm and its small but attractive gift shop (with a variety of books and birding equipment) are well worth a visit. Ask at the front desk about any recent unusual bird sightings in Maine.

The grounds at Gilsland Farm are open daily, free of charge, from sunrise to sunset. The gate is usually open on weekdays from 7:30 a.m. until 5:00 p.m., on Saturday from 9:00 a.m. to 5:00 p.m., and on Sunday from noon to 5:00 p.m. If you arrive during daylight hours and find the gate locked, you are welcome to park outside and walk in, provided that your vehicle does not obstruct the gate or road.

For more information about Gilsland Farm or the Maine Audubon Society, write or call Maine Audubon Society, P.O. Box 6009, Falmouth, ME 04105-6009, telephone 207-781-2330.

DIRECTIONS

FROM THE SOUTH: Take I-295 north through Portland, and on the north side of the city bear right at exit 9, following signs for Rt. 1 North and Falmouth Foreside. Cross the Presumpscot River, and in 0.7 mile bear left onto an unmarked road (look for the "MAS" sign). In 0.1 mile turn left into the sanctuary and continue 0.3 mile to the parking lot and interpretive building.

FROM THE NORTH: Take I-95 south to exit 10 (Bucknam Road, Falmouth Foreside). At the head of the exit ramp, turn left and proceed to the stoplight at the intersection with Rt. 1. Turn right onto Rt. 1, and in 1.2 miles bear right onto an unmarked road (look for the "MAS" sign). Continue 0.3 mile and turn right into the sanctuary.

M.V. Scotia Prince

The M.V. *Scotia Prince* is the 470-foot cruise ship that travels between Portland and Yarmouth, Nova Scotia, between early May and late October. Although increasing numbers of seabird and whale trips are offered every year, the *Scotia Prince* still provides one of the few regular opportunities for true pelagic birding in Maine. The crossing takes 11 hours each way. You can expect to see essentially the same species you would on the M.V. *Bluenose*, which crosses between Bar Harbor and Yarmouth (see the chapter "M.V. *Bluenose*").

The real birding on the *Scotia Prince* begins not when you leave Portland (when it is dark or nearly so, depending on the time of year) but the next morning. If you are on deck as soon as the sun comes up, you will be on hand for what is usually one of the most productive areas along the route—Lurcher Shoal, on the southwest shore of Nova Scotia and about an hour and a half out of Yarmouth. Coming back to Portland, the best birding is usually between the second and sixth hours out of Yarmouth and, depending on whether it is dark or not, during the last two hours before arriving in Portland.

The *Scotia Prince* carries 1,500 passengers and 220 cars. It leaves Portland at 9:00 p.m. every evening between early May and late October, arrives in Yarmouth at 9:00 a.m. the following morning, and returns to Portland at 8:00 p.m. The ticket price includes an economy cabin and four meals. Advance reservations are suggested both for cars and walk-on passengers. We strongly advise that you call ahead to confirm the schedule. For more information, write or call Prince of Fundy Cruise Lines, 468 Commercial St., Portland, ME 04101, telephone 800-774-6233 or (locally) 775-5616.

DIRECTIONS

The Portland International Ferry Terminal is located on the south end of Commercial St. near the Million Dollar Bridge (Rt. 77), which connects Portland and South Portland (see *Maine Atlas* map 73, F-4, and "Directions" for Portland harbor, above).

LOCAL ACCOMMODATIONS

For information on local accommodations and services, write or call the Greater Portland Chamber of Commerce, 145 Middle St., Portland, ME 04101, telephone 207-772-2811.

Additional Sites of Interest

Route 236, Eliot & South Berwick (*MAINE ATLAS* map 1, B-3 & A-3)

One of the best and easiest areas to see some of Maine's "southern" breeding species, such as Willow Flycatcher, Blue-winged and Prairie warblers, Indigo Bunting, and Field Sparrow, is along Route 236 in Eliot and South Berwick. From mid-May through late June or early July, when the males are singing, you can hear and see most of these species right along the roadside. Because the traffic can be heavy, it is best to do your birding early, preferably before 6:00 a.m.

From the intersection of Routes 1 and 236 in Kittery, take Route 236 west. Drive 4.2 miles to a wet meadow and alder swale in Eliot that opens on both sides of the road about 150 yards before the Marshwood High School. Nesting Willow Flycatchers can be heard *"fitz-bew*ing" in the alder thickets from late May through early August, and singing American Bitterns and Virginia Rails are regular in the wet meadow and probably breed there. Swamp Sparrows nest in the thicker vegetation, and Eastern Meadowlarks, Bobolinks, and Savannah Sparrows occupy the drier fields nearby.

Continue west on Route 236 for another 3.9 miles, where the road parallels a high power line (you are now in South Berwick).

Prairie Warblers are abundant in the dense shrubbery below the power lines, and you will be hard-pressed to find a greater concentration of Indigo Buntings and Field Sparrows. Blue-gray Gnatcatcher is also a possibility. The area under this stretch of power line was the first known breeding locality in Maine for Blue-winged Warbler. Golden-winged Warbler, rare in Maine, has also occurred in this area.

Merriland River (*MAINE ATLAS* map 3, D-1)

For several years a pair of Louisiana Waterthrushes have nested in a large hemlock grove underneath the Merriland River bridge on the Coles Hill Road in Wells. The male's sweet song is frequently audible from the bridge, but if not, walk the path along the river both up- and downstream. Louisiana Waterthrushes occupy large territories, and the birds may be as much as a quarter mile in either direction. To date this is one of the easternmost nesting localities for this species in North America, and it is certainly the most accessible in Maine. *Please do not, under any circumstances, use tape playback to attract the birds.* Other breeding species found along the river include Veery, Hermit and Wood thrushes, Red-eyed Vireo, Black-throated Green and Black-and-white warblers, American Redstart, and Chipping Sparrow.

At the intersection of Route 9 and the Coles Hill Road in Wells, turn west onto the Coles Hill Road, and in 1 mile you will see the Merriland River bridge. Park along the road and look for a trail on the north side of the road, just before the river; follow it past the rocky gorge and down to the lower and quieter section of the river. This is Maine Public Reserve Land and is accessible to the public year-round, free of charge.

Kennebunk Beach (*MAINE ATLAS* map 3, D-2)

Kennebunk Beach, a wide sand beach about 800 yards long, is an excellent spot to find Purple Sandpipers from early November through late April. The best time to see these birds, which tend to be very local, is on an outgoing tide, when they feed close to the surf on the rocky outcroppings that are exposed offshore. In midwinter it is not at all uncommon for flocks here to average 150 to 200 birds. You can also see most of southern Maine's common winter ducks and waterbirds here, and from August through October you can usually see good numbers of Bonaparte's Gulls. On rare occasions we have also seen Little and Common Black-headed gulls here. American Pipits occur along the beach in fall, and Sanderlings are usually present through December.

Kennebunk Beach is open year-round. There are no facilities or fees in winter.

At the stoplight at the intersection of Route 9 and Beach Road in Kennebunkport, turn south onto Beach Road. In 0.8 mile the road takes a sharp right, and you will see the east end of Kennebunk Beach. Follow the road another mile along the beach, then turn around or continue another mile to rejoin Route 9.

Indian Whale Watch (KENNEBUNKPORT)

Indian Whale Watch, which operates out of Kennebunkport, offers a chance to see not only marine mammals but several species of seabirds. The 75-foot *Indian* travels about 25 miles offshore to a submerged ledge known as Jeffrey's Ledge. Although the birding can vary significantly according to the weather, you can usually see a good variety of pelagic species. Greater and Sooty shearwaters, Wilson's Storm-Petrels, and Northern Gannets are usually sighted regularly, and occasionally you will also see a few Manx Shearwaters, a Parasitic or Pomarine Jaeger, or alcids. See the section entitled "Pelagic Birding" in the Introduction.

For more information, write or call Indian Whale Watch, P.O. Box 2672, Kennebunkport, ME 04046, telephone 207-967-5912.

Laurel Hill Cemetery (*MAINE ATLAS* map 71, B-3)

Laurel Hill Cemetery, just outside the center of Saco, offers a delightful expanse of greenery in the midst of a small city. Like Evergreen and Calvary cemeteries in Portland, Laurel Hill is also a fine spring migrant trap. The large stands of oak trees are excellent for warblers in May, and you can often see a variety of other migrant landbirds. The cemetery overlooks a large salt marsh and the Saco River, so there are waterfowl and wading birds here as well. From the cemetery entrance, follow the left-hand road through the woods, then work your way to the back of the cemetery and down toward the river.

The cemetery is open daily, free of charge, from 7:30 a.m. to dusk. There are no facilities.

At the intersection of Routes 1 and 9 East in Saco, turn onto Route 9 East. In 0.6 mile you will see the first entrance to the cemetery on the right and, in another 0.1 mile, the second entrance.

Mill Creek Shop 'n Save (SOUTH PORTLAND)
(*MAINE ATLAS* map 73, F-4)

The Mill Creek Shop 'n Save supermarket, which overlooks Mill Cove in South Portland, is one of the best places in southern Maine to look for Glaucous and Iceland gulls in winter. Hundreds of gulls roost on the ice here, and you can usually observe and study them at close range. Between early December and March, it is not at all uncommon to find a few white-winged gulls among the many Herring and Great Black-backed gulls.

Take Route 77 to South Portland and turn east onto Hinckley Drive. Coming from Portland, Hinckley Drive is on the left, just south of the intersection of Route 77 and Cottage Street; coming from Cape Elizabeth it is on the right, just after Route 77 crosses Broadway. Continue just a short way down Hinckley Drive to Cottage Street; the Shop 'n Save is straight ahead.

Sandy Point Beach (*MAINE ATLAS* map 6, D-1)

Sandy Point Beach, on the northwest tip of Cousin's Island in Yarmouth, is one of the best places in the Portland area to see southbound migrant landbirds. In late August and September, the trees and shrubs around the parking area and power line can be dripping with warblers, which often pause here before flying to the mainland. The first two to three hours of daylight are usually the most productive. Good numbers of shorebirds also stop to feed and rest here at this time of year. In winter, the beach is well worth a quick check. Barrow's Goldeneyes are seen on occasion, and in March and April impressive numbers of Common Eiders (approximately 4,500 one March) stage offshore.

Take I-95 to exit 16, and at the end of the exit ramp take Route 1 South. In 1 mile turn left onto Powell Road (unmarked) and proceed 0.2 mile to its intersection with Route 88 (Foreside Road). Turn left onto Route 88 (heading north), continue 1.5 miles, and bear right onto Gilman Road (unmarked, but you will see signs for Cousin's Island). In 0.3 mile, at the stop sign, go straight and continue 1.3 miles to the Cousin's Island bridge. Cross the bridge, and in 0.5 mile turn left into the unpaved parking area that overlooks the beach.

WESTERN MOUNTAINS & LAKES REGION

Maine's western mountains and lakes region extends from the Kennebec River on the east to the New Hampshire border on the west and from Oxford County north into southern Somerset County. This is a distinctive and delightful area, where the pine-oak forests of southern Maine blend into mixed hardwood and spruce-fir forests and where the low hills and many lakes and ponds of the Kennebec Valley gradually give way to the steeper and more rugged contours of the western mountains. The last include the Katahdin group and the Boundary, White, and Longfellow mountains.

Birders who have not explored this region may be surprised to discover how much good birding it has to offer. The highlight is the breeding season, when you can find a good cross section of wetland-associated breeders in the lowlands and boreal breeders at higher elevations. And oftentimes the lowland and high-elevation sites are not all that far apart. You can also find many of Maine's more unusual or locally distributed breeding species here, including Least Bittern, Common Moorhen, Black Tern, Blue-gray Gnatcatcher, and Yellow-throated Vireo. Fall migration brings waterfowl and even, at some sites, shorebirds. Winter birding is usually far less interesting, but depending on the cone crop and other whims of nature, you can get excellent flights of Bohemian Waxwings, Northern Shrikes, Red and White-winged crossbills, and Pine and Evening grosbeaks.

If you like to combine birding with hiking or canoeing, you will particularly enjoy this area—and will have access to even more good birding sites than those we describe here.

Brownfield Bog   (*MAINE ATLAS* map 4, B-2)

Brownfield Bog, which lies nestled near the New Hampshire border on the southern side of Maine's western mountains and lakes region, doesn't seem to be particularly well known among birders. Don't let the fact that you haven't heard much about this unassuming spot deter you, though. Brownfield Bog is well worth a visit. Most notably, it supports Maine's largest known breeding populations of Willow Flycatchers, Blue-gray Gnatcatchers, and Yellow-throated Vireos, the latter two of which reach the northern limits of their breeding range in Maine. It is also a possible nesting site for Golden-winged Warbler, marks the southern breeding limit in eastern North America for Common Goldeneye, and supports eight species of nesting flycatchers. Add to these distinctions several species of nesting waterfowl and a good variety of wetland-associated and woodland breeders, and you have an interesting spot indeed. The birding is best from early or mid-May well into fall, with late May to mid-July being the best time to find breeding species. Spring and fall migration feature a broad variety of migrants, including waterfowl. Whatever the season, you can bird the area thoroughly in a few hours.

Brownfield Bog is officially known as the Brownfield Bog Wildlife Management Area and is owned and managed by the Maine Department of Inland Fisheries and Wildlife (MDIFW). The 5,700-acre parcel is not a bog in the true sense of the word—that is, it is not a peatland—but is a shallow wetland bisected by the meandering Saco River. The area consists of open water, shallow wetlands, seasonally flooded woodlands, old fields, and upland forests and is covered primarily with dense aquatic vegetation, alders, and thickets. Large Silver Maples and oaks overhang the wetlands.

Maine birders should be especially interested in Brownfield's so-called southern breeding birds, several of which are not widely distributed or common in Maine. The maples and oaks along the edges of the wetlands provide ideal habitat for Blue-gray Gnatcatchers and Yellow-throated Vireos; both species are surprisingly common here.

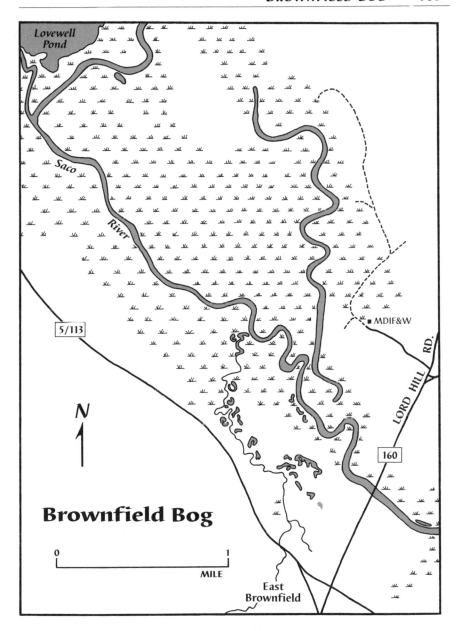

Brownfield Bog

Lovewell Pond

Saco River

5/113

N

MDIF&W

LORD HILL RD.

160

0   MILE   1

East
Brownfield

The gnatcatchers tend to be noisy and conspicuous, if not downright brazen; the vireos tend to remain higher in the canopy and are less active. Willow Flycatchers nest in the extensive alder thickets around the bog. In fact, Brownfield is one of the few places in Maine where the Willow's *fitz-bew* easily outnumbers the Alder Flycatcher's *wee-bee-o*. It is also worth looking at Brownfield for Golden-winged Warblers.

Two males were present and singing in the summer of 1992, but the species has not been confirmed as nesting here.

MDIFW manages Brownfield primarily for waterfowl and has erected more than 100 boxes for such cavity-nesting species as Wood Duck, Common Goldeneye, and Hooded Merganser. Other nesting waterfowl include Canada Goose, Mallard, American Black and Ring-necked ducks, and Blue-winged and Green-winged teal. The bog is also worth checking in spring and fall for migrant waterfowl, although once the fall duck-hunting season opens, you are not likely to see much (see the section entitled "Hunting" in the Introduction).

Also nesting on or around the bog are several other wetland-associated species, among them Pied-billed Grebe, Great Blue and Green herons, American Bittern, Osprey, Virginia Rail, Belted Kingfisher, Northern Waterthrush, Common Yellowthroat, and Swamp Sparrow. Since the early 1990s, Bald Eagles have been occasional throughout the summer, and in the spring of 1994 a Golden Eagle was reported; it is always worth checking any dark eagles you see. Other interesting species include Broad-winged and Red-shouldered hawks, Ruffed Grouse, American Woodcock, Yellow-billed and Black-billed cuckoos, Great Horned and Barred owls, Whip-poor-will, Yellow-bellied Sapsucker, House Wren, Veery, Wood Thrush, Brown Thrasher, Warbling Vireo, Northern Parula, Nashville, Yellow, and Black-and-white warblers, American Redstart, Northern Cardinal, Scarlet Tanager, Rose-breasted Grosbeak, and Indigo Bunting. Brownfield is also notable for supporting eight species of nesting flycatchers: Eastern Kingbird, Great Crested Flycatcher, Eastern Phoebe, Alder, Willow, Least, and Olive-sided flycatchers, and Eastern Wood-Pewee.

Large mammals found at Brownfield Bog include Moose, Beaver, River Otter, Mink, Muskrat, White-tailed Deer, and Varying Hare.

The best way to bird the bog is to park by the small MDIFW building (see "Directions," below) and explore the dirt roads on foot, birding the thickets, open marsh, and large trees. Follow the road around to the right, and in 0.4 mile fork left. In another 0.4 mile fork right. The road enters tall deciduous forest here, and in 0.7 mile it opens out onto a wonderful overview of the marsh. Scope from here for waterfowl. If you have a canoe, so much the better; you will be able to bird the wetlands much more thoroughly. A good place to put in is right next to the MDIFW building. In any case, it is a good idea to bring boots; the walking can be very wet even along the roads, especially in spring. And by all means, don't forget insect repellent.

The Brownfield Bog Wildlife Management Area is open daily from dawn to dusk, free of charge. There are no facilities.

DIRECTIONS

At the intersection of Rts. 5/113 and 160 in East Brownfield, turn north onto Rt. 160. Continue 0.8 mile and cross the Saco River, and in another 0.7 mile fork left onto Lord Hill Rd. In 0.1 mile you will see a dirt road on the left and a sign for Brownfield Bog Wildlife Management Area. Follow the dirt road (it can be extremely muddy in spring) 0.7 mile to a small, white MDIFW building and parking area, to the right, on the edge of the marsh. Park here and explore on foot or by canoe.

LOCAL ACCOMMODATIONS

For information on local accommodations and services, write or call the Bridgton Lakes Region Information Center, P.O. Box 236, Bridgton, ME 04009, telephone 207-647-3472.

Sabattus Pond   (MAINE ATLAS map 12, E-1)

Situated just northeast of Lewiston in the small town of Sabattus is a shallow, eutrophic lake known as Sabattus Pond. Most people probably cruise right by this site on Route 126/9 and don't give it much thought, but among birders it has gained a steady reputation as one of the most intriguing fall birding sites in interior Maine. Measuring about 3.5 miles long and nearly 1 mile wide, Sabattus Pond attracts both a remarkable variety of rare birds and unusual numbers of more common birds—primarily shorebirds, waterfowl, and gulls. The southern end of the pond seems to offer the best birding, and it is easily scanned from a small public park at Martin Point on the southwest shore. The best time to bird the pond is from early September until freeze-up, which is usually in late November. It is also worth checking the pond in spring, beginning with ice-out in early April. There is virtually no walking involved here, so you can scan the pond in half an hour or so.

Fall is generally the most interesting time of year at Sabattus Pond, largely because this is when water levels are lowered annually for phosphorus control, exposing extensive mudflats for migrating shorebirds and roosting gulls. Good numbers of Black-bellied Plovers, Greater Yellowlegs, and Semipalmated, White-rumped, and Least sandpipers are regular. They are often joined by Short-billed Dowitchers and unusually large numbers of Pectoral Sandpipers (100+). Ameri-

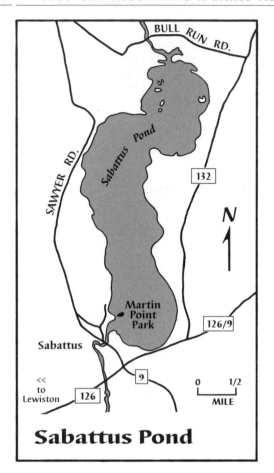

Sabattus Pond

can Golden-Plovers are also seen here on occasion. Bonaparte's and Ring-billed gulls are common in September, and careful examination may produce something exotic, such as the adult Sabine's Gull that graced a flock of Bonaparte's Gulls one September. Large flocks of American Pipits (100+) sometimes feed along the exposed flats.

Waterfowl start arriving in late September or early October, and by mid-October you can typically find a good variety. This is one of the best places in Maine to see Ruddy Ducks (30+ are not uncommon), and it is an excellent place to get good looks at several more regular species, among them Mallard, American Black and Ring-necked ducks, Greater and Lesser scaup (the first far more common), scoters, Common Goldeneye, Bufflehead, and Hooded and Common mergansers. The waterfowl in turn attract Bald Eagles every fall, and these are often seen harassing (and sometimes catching and eating) ducks. Oftentimes it is the sheer numbers of birds that are impressive at Sabattus: the

1,000-plus Common Mergansers that seem to congregate on the south end of the lake every fall, for example, or in fall 1994 the 385-plus American Coots and 150-plus Ruddy Ducks we saw one day.

Sabattus Pond has not attracted much attention in spring, but this is almost certainly the result of inadequate coverage rather than a lack of birds. It is undoubtedly worth a visit anytime between ice-out and late May, primarily for waterfowl. (Like other inland lakes, Sabattus does not offer any shorebirding in spring because the water levels are invariably too high to expose any habitat.) As more birders visit Sabattus Pond both in spring and fall, more interesting records are sure to result.

The best place to scan Sabattus Pond is from Martin Point Park on the southwest shore. (Although it is possible to see the southern end of the pond from Route 126/9—and a map makes this look like the best vantage point—you will see No Trespassing signs all along the roadside.) Scan offshore for ducks, and check the coves on either side of the point for shorebirds and gulls.

Martin Point Park is open daily, free of charge, from sunrise to 10:00 p.m. It has no facilities.

DIRECTIONS

At the blinking light at the intersection of Rts. 126 and 9 on the east side of Lewiston, turn north onto High St. (called Sawyer Rd. in the Maine Atlas). In 0.2 mile, at the stop sign, go straight, and in another 0.2 mile, at the war memorial, bear right. In 0.3 mile turn right onto Lake St. In 0.2 mile you will see Martin Point Park and a public boat launch on the right.

LOCAL ACCOMMODATIONS

For information on local accommodations and services, write or call the Androscoggin County Chamber of Commerce, P.O. Box 59, Lewiston, ME 04243, telephone 207-783-2249.

Cobbosseecontee Lake Watershed (MAINE ATLAS map 12, C-3 & -4)

Few areas of comparable size in Maine have as many lakes and ponds as does western Kennebec County. For birders, one of the most interesting areas in the region is the Cobbosseecontee Lake watershed.

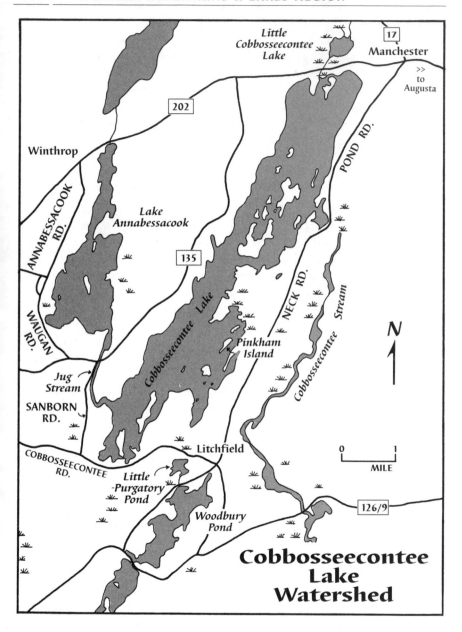

Despite ever-increasing development, the Cobbossee region, as it is
known locally, supports a surprising variety of breeding birds. A large
Great Blue Heron rookery has existed on Pinkham Island at the south
end of Cobbosseecontee Lake for many years, and the lake also supports a healthy Common Loon population. Few birders may realize,
however, that this is also one of the best areas in Maine to find some

unusual or locally distributed breeding birds, among them Least and American bitterns, Virginia Rail, Sora, Common Moorhen, Marsh Wren, Willow Flycatcher, and Yellow-throated and Warbling vireos. It is possible to see and hear all of these species on a tranquil June morning. More widespread species such as Pied-billed Grebe, Wood Duck, Hooded Merganser, Osprey, and Barred Owl are also regular. As impressive as the breeding season is, the Cobbossee watershed is also fascinating in late summer and fall, and to a lesser degree in spring, when a remarkable array of waterfowl and shorebirds—many of them highly unusual for an inland site—congregate at the south end of Cobbosseecontee Lake. The loop we describe below is worth doing anytime between early April and mid- to late November, depending on ice-out and freeze-up. Allow at least a few hours, especially in the breeding season, to cover the area thoroughly.

Situated due west of Augusta, the Cobbossee watershed is dominated by Cobbosseecontee Lake, which measures about 8 miles long and, near its southern end, nearly 2 miles wide. Jug Stream at the southwest end of the lake connects it to Lake Annabessacook; from the eastern shore, Cobbosseecontee Stream feeds into the Kennebec River in Gardiner. Extensive areas of shallow freshwater marsh occur along Cobbosseecontee Lake, especially on its eastern side. Just north of the lake is the aptly named Little Cobbosseecontee Lake. *Cobbosseecontee* is an Abenaki Indian word that means "plenty of sturgeon." We can't attest to the quantity (or quality) of sturgeon in the lakes these days, but we certainly see plenty of people fishing here.

Below we describe a 20-mile loop (actually three-quarters of a loop) around the watershed that begins at the northern end of Cobbosseecontee Lake. Except for a few public boat launches in the area, there is very little public access to the shore, so you will be birding primarily from your car or along the roadside. Don't let that deter you, however; there is plenty to see. Particularly at the height of the breeding season in June, it is imperative to do this loop as early in the morning as possible, when song is at a maximum and traffic at a minimum; even at 6:00 a.m., it can already be quite noisy. Sunday mornings are often ideal.

This is also a delightful area to bird by canoe. You can put in on Annabessacook Lake at the bridge on Annabessacook Road or at Jug Stream (see "Directions," below), or at public boat launches on the south and north ends of Cobbosseecontee Lake (see *Maine Atlas* map 12, C-4 and D-3). The 11-mile trip down Cobbosseecontee Stream is also very pleasant (see the *AMC River Guide: Maine*, by Yates and Phillips, listed in Appendix D). Please make every effort not to disturb breeding or roosting birds.

Although the loop described below is not complicated, it is long; a good map will make following these directions much easier.

Little Cobbosseecontee Lake

Begin the loop at the stoplight at the intersection of Routes 202 and 17 in Manchester (2.7 miles west of exit 30 off I-95 in Augusta). Drive 1.7 miles west on Route 202 and stop on the right-hand side of the road next to a cattail-bordered pond. This is Little Cobbosseecontee Lake. In June look on the lake for Wood Ducks, and in the wet marsh on both sides of the road look and listen for Least and American bitterns, Virginia Rails, Soras, Great Blue and Green herons, Willow Flycatchers, Marsh Wrens, and Swamp Sparrows. Additional species such as Eastern Kingbird, Tree and Barn swallows, Yellow Warbler, Common Yellowthroat, Baltimore Oriole, Red-winged Blackbird, and Song Sparrow are common in the surrounding marsh or uplands. We have also seen Beaver here. Route 202 is a busy, noisy highway; this stop is most enjoyable and productive at dawn, preferably before 5 a.m. Even at that hour, be very careful crossing the road.

Annabessacook Lake

Continue west on Route 202, and in 5 miles, at the top of the hill *after* Winthrop, turn left onto Annabessacook Road (which will become Waugan Road). In 2.8 miles you will see a small bridge bordering Annabessacook Lake and a small cattail marsh. This popular fishing hole is usually pleasantly quiet in the early morning, and a surprising variety of birds nest in the unpretentious little delta here. Common Loons, Pied-billed Grebes, American Bitterns, Common Moorhens, Common Snipe, Marsh Wrens, Alder Flycatchers, and Swamp Sparrows can all be found in or near the marsh. Virginia Rails are common and make curious sights as they occasionally run across the road. Even more amusing are the times when these odd birds linger on the road and start calling loudly, apparently declaring territorial rights to the pavement. American Coots usually appear here every fall, but as yet they are not known to breed at Annabessacook.

Check the roadside trees here and the mixed woods beyond the bridge. Yellow-throated Vireos, uncommon in Maine, usually nest in the Red Maples and Northern Red Oaks bordering the marsh, and several Warbling Vireos can usually be heard singing their slow songs in the more open canopy near the cattails. Least Flycatchers, Eastern Wood-Pewees, Red-eyed Vireos, Yellow Warblers, Ovenbirds, Northern Waterthrushes, Common Yellowthroats, and Baltimore Orioles all occur commonly. Red-shouldered Hawks can sometimes be heard giving their territorial calls over the nearby forest. Barred Owls are also present; they are usually quiet after sunrise, but occasionally you can hear their familiar *who-who-who-cooks-for-you-all* coming from deep within the woods.

Continue south, and in 1.3 miles turn left onto Route 135. Stop to scan the marsh immediately on the right (another good spot to look for Marsh Wrens), then continue 0.5 mile and park at the corner of Sanborn Road and Route 135. The bridge over Jug Stream, which connects Lake Anabessacook and Cobbosseecontee Lake, provides a good vantage point from which to scan for Common Loons and ducks. The large maples and oaks here and farther south on Sanborn Road provide nesting habitat for Yellow-throated and Warbling vireos, Chestnut-sided Warblers, and American Redstarts. Other regular species in the area include Eastern Wood-Pewee, Red-eyed Vireo, Veery, and Rose-breasted Grosbeak. Yellow-billed Cuckoos, Eastern Bluebirds, and Bobolinks sometimes nest nearby, too.

South End of Cobbosseecontee Lake

Go 1.8 miles south on Sanborn Road to the stop sign and turn left onto Cobbosseecontee Road. You are now on the south end of Cobbosseecontee Lake. In 0.4 mile this road dips into a small pocket of Tamarack and Northern White-Cedar trees, where Black-throated Green and Blackburnian warblers breed. Interestingly, Black-backed Woodpecker has been found here in winter.

Continue along this road, and in 0.7 mile pull over and stop along the causeway that crosses the south end of the lake. Breeding species in this area include Common Loon, Pied-billed Grebe, Great Blue Heron, American Bittern, Mallard, American Black Duck, Least and Great Crested flycatchers, Eastern Wood-Pewee, Cliff Swallow, Marsh Wren, Pine, Canada, and Black-and-white warblers, Scarlet Tanager, Rose-breasted Grosbeak, and Swamp Sparrow.

The highlight of the south end of Cobbosseecontee Lake is the fall shorebird or waterfowl migration. From August through November this is a major stopping point for hundreds of ducks and shorebirds migrating south, and the causeway is an excellent place from which to scan them. Whether you see primarily ducks or shorebirds depends on the water levels. When the water level is lowered (irregularly from year to year) between mid-August and mid-November, a wide grassy flat is exposed that attracts an interesting variety of shorebirds. The large numbers of Pectoral Sandpipers (200+) and Common Snipe (30+) are very different from the shorebird concentrations found along the coast. Black-bellied Plovers and American Golden-Plovers are joined by Greater and Lesser yellowlegs, Semipalmated, Least, and White-rumped sandpipers, and Dunlin. Locally rare species that have been found here include Hudsonian Godwit and Long-billed Dowitcher.

In years when the water level is not lowered, the fall highlight is waterfowl. Hundreds of Mallards, American Black Ducks, Greenwinged and Blue-winged teal, American Wigeon, Ring-necked Ducks, Greater and Lesser scaup, Common Goldeneyes, and Hooded Mergansers are usually busy feeding in the shallow water just offshore. Unusual waterbirds (for an inland site) that have been seen here include Red-throated Loon, Brant (in fall), Canvasback (regular), Redhead, Surf Scoter, and even Red-necked Grebe. Rusty Blackbirds can sometimes be found feeding in the wet areas near the cattails in fall.

The spring waterfowl migration here tends to be quite brief but can be equally rewarding. The shallow water is usually free of ice by early April, and it is sometimes possible to observe ducks at very close range. Spring water levels are invariably high, so there is no shorebird habitat available then.

Woodbury Pond

From the causeway, continue east on Cobbosseecontee Road toward Litchfield. In 1.8 miles, just *before* the stop sign, take a sharp right onto an unmarked road that parallels the west shore of Woodbury Pond. Listen in the deciduous and pine woods at the head of the road for singing Veerys, Wood Thrushes, Pine Warblers, and Ovenbirds. In 0.8 mile you will see Little Purgatory Pond on the right and Woodbury Pond on the left. From this point the road soon parallels a high power line, and the shrubby areas beneath the line provide nesting habitat for Eastern Towhees, Indigo Buntings, and Field Sparrows. For several years a pair of Ospreys has nested atop one of the power-line poles (0.7 mile south of the Little Purgatory/Woodbury pond overlook), and you can get a wonderful look at their nest. Chestnut-sided Warblers, American Redstarts, and Baltimore Orioles are common along the wooded margins.

From the Osprey nest, continue south 1 mile to the stop sign at the junction of Route 126/9. The loop concludes here. Turn left to Gardiner, Augusta, and points north, or retrace your steps and return to Manchester via the east side of Cobbosseecontee Lake. To go south toward Lewiston (and Sabattus Pond; see the preceding chapter), turn right onto Route 126/9. Keep alert for Turkey Vultures, which undoubtedly breed on the ridge overlooking this part of the highway.

DIRECTIONS
To begin the loop described above, take I-95 to Augusta and get off at exit 30. Turn west onto Rt. 202 and drive 2.7 miles to the stoplight at the junction of Rts. 202 and 17 in Manchester.

LOCAL ACCOMMODATIONS
For information on local accommodations and services, call or write the Kennebec Valley Chamber of Commerce, P.O. Box E, University Dr., Augusta, ME 04330, telephone 207-623-4559.

Messalonskee Lake & the Sidney Grasslands

Messalonskee Lake and the Sidney Grasslands are two of the most interesting birding sites in the Kennebec Valley. Messalonskee Lake is by far the better known of the two sites, having been a regular haunt of Maine birders since the 1940s when Black Terns were first discovered nesting there. Unbeknownst to many birders, however, there is another fine birding site only 5 miles east of Messalonskee, in the little town of Sidney, where Upland Sandpipers and other open-country species can be found in an extensive stretch of grasslands off Route 104. Both sites, located midway between Augusta and Waterville and easily accessible from I-95, are worth checking at any time of year.

Messalonskee Lake (*MAINE ATLAS* map 12, A-5)

Birders know Messalonskee Lake (also called Snow Pond) primarily for its Black Tern colony. This handsome species reaches the eastern limit of its breeding range in New Brunswick and Nova Scotia and was first discovered nesting in Maine on Messalonskee Lake. Although Black Terns have since been found to nest on several other inland lakes and ponds in Maine, Messalonskee remains one of the largest colonies in the state and a favored site among birders. It is hardly a surprise; the lake also supports several other wetland breeders, is easily accessible, and offers superb views of the birds. The birding can be good anytime between early April and late October, but the real highlight is the breeding season, which is generally at its best in early June. Whatever the season, you can bird the lake thoroughly in an hour or less from the shore, or you can take a few hours and do

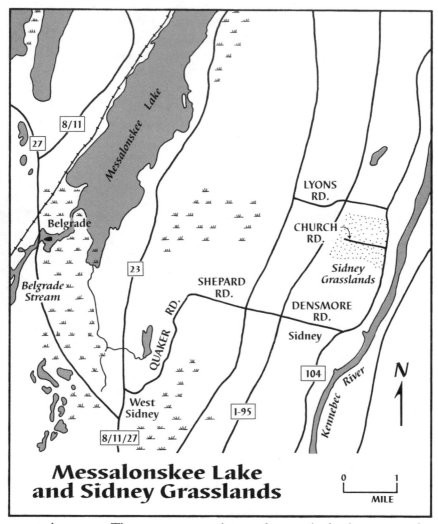

Messalonskee Lake and Sidney Grasslands

0   1
MILE

it by canoe. The area can even be worth a quick check in winter for owls and various open-country species.

Messalonskee is a long, narrow lake bordered by an extensive freshwater marsh to the south. A public boat launch (see "Directions," below) provides access to Belgrade Stream on the west side of the lake and offers the best overview of the area. Park here and scan the marsh and water, preferably with a telescope. The birding can be excellent right around the parking area, but an even better way to bird the lake and surrounding wetlands is by canoe. In fact, it is almost a shame to come to Messalonskee without a canoe. You will probably see most of the birds without one, but you will see them much better with one. It's about a mile-long paddle from the boat launch through Belgrade

Stream to the lake itself. Once there, you can turn right (east) and paddle another mile to the large cattail stand and rice beds in the southeast corner of the lake, or you can turn left (west) and paddle three-quarters of a mile to the west shore, near the railroad tracks. From a canoe, you will also have a better chance of seeing Painted and Snapping turtles, Muskrat, and the occasional River Otter.

Beginning in mid- to late May, Messalonskee begins to attract an excellent variety of breeding species, and by June the lake and marsh are in full swing. Common Loons have chicks, American Bitterns call loudly, Black Terns are conspicuous overhead, and Marsh Wrens are easy to find (primarily in the large cattail stand in the southeast corner of the lake). Pied-billed Grebes are regular, Common Snipe fly high overhead proclaiming their territories with soft winnowing sounds, and Soras and Virginia Rails call frequently but are difficult to observe in the dense vegetation (the west shore, up near the railroad tracks, is especially good for rails). Purple Martins nest nearby and sweep across the marsh, hunting insects among the more numerous Tree, Bank, and Barn swallows. Waterfowl are busy rearing young. Look for Canada Geese, Wood, American Black, and Ring-necked ducks, Mallards, Blue-winged and occasionally Green-winged teal, and Hooded Mergansers. In 1992 a pair of Sandhill Cranes spent most of the summer courting at Messalonskee Lake, and since then, isolated birds have occasionally been seen here and in nearby areas (including the Sidney Grasslands). In the spring of 1995, a King Rail was also seen here.

Other species to look for on or around the lake in the nesting season include Great Blue and Green herons, American Coot (uncommon), Least Bittern (uncommon), Osprey, Northern Harrier (breeding on the upper edges of the marsh), Broad-winged Hawk, Herring, Great Black-backed, and Ring-billed gulls (the last more common on the southern end of the lake), Common Tern, Belted Kingfisher, Eastern Kingbird, Alder and Willow flycatchers (the latter breeding in the thickets near the railroad tracks 0.4 mile north of the parking area), Blue-gray Gnatcatcher (occasional), Warbling Vireo (regular around the parking area), Yellow Warbler, Common Yellowthroat, Northern Waterthrush, Baltimore Oriole, Rose-breasted Grosbeak, Song and Swamp sparrows, Red-winged Blackbird, and Purple Finch. Take the time to walk north along Route 27 to the bridge overlooking Belgrade Stream. Black Terns often feed in the stream and sometimes fly directly overhead, and you can often get good looks at Pied-billed Grebes and ducks here.

The breeding season may be the most exciting time of year for birders at Messalonskee, but the lake is also worth a visit at other times, particularly spring and fall. As soon as Belgrade Stream is open in late March or early April—long before the lake and marsh have lost their ice—waterfowl begin stopping here to feed and rest. Look for Canada Geese, Mallards, American Black and Ring-necked ducks, Northern Pintails (occasional), Greater Scaup, Common Goldeneyes, Buffleheads, and Common and Hooded mergansers. Even an occasional Gadwall and Canvasback have been seen here. Northern Harriers occur around the lake in early spring, as do Great Blue Herons. Fall migration can also be productive for waterfowl (especially the rice beds at the southeast corner of the lake): Black Scoters and Ruddy Ducks can occasionally be seen in addition to the more regular species and, in October, there are large concentrations of Greater Scaup (100+). The lake is hunted quite heavily early in the season, but the pressure usually lets up within a week or so, except on weekends. (See the section entitled "Hunting" in the Introduction.)

For the most intrepid birders, Messalonskee may also be worth checking in late fall and winter. Rough-legged Hawks are occasionally seen here in fall, and the conifers along the southern end of the marsh are worth checking for roosting owls. On the marsh itself, look for Snowy and Short-eared owls and for such open-country species as Horned Lark, Snow Bunting, Lapland Longspur, and Common Redpoll.

The boat launch at Messalonskee Lake is open year-round, free of charge, from dawn to dusk. There are no facilities.

To rent a canoe, write or call Belgrade Canoe and Kayak, Route 27, Belgrade, ME 04918, telephone 207-495-2005 or 800-682-8161; or Great Pond Marina, Route 27, Box 405, Belgrade, ME 04918, telephone 495-2213.

DIRECTIONS

The public boat launch on the west side of Messalonskee Lake is located along Rt. 27 (Belgrade Rd.), about halfway between the intersection of Rts. 27 and 23 in West Sidney to the south and the intersection of Rts. 27 and 11/8 in Belgrade to the north. A conspicuous sign marks the launch from mid-May through early fall, but it is taken down for the winter.

The Sidney Grasslands (*MAINE ATLAS* map 13, A-1)

Wedged between I-95 and the Kennebec River is Route 104, the back road that runs north-south between Augusta and Waterville. Rolling along past farms, open fields, and scattered woodlots, this route looks like just another back road that wouldn't necessarily offer much in the way of birds—until just north of the village of Sidney, between the Densmore and Church roads, when an extensive stretch of hayfields and pastures suddenly appears. The few birders who know this area refer to it as the Sidney Grasslands. Small numbers of Upland Sandpipers have nested here for many years, and it is a good spot to see other open-country species, too. As best we know, the area has not been well explored by birders on a year-round basis.

The Sidney Grasslands are private property, but you can scan them from the roadside. The best access into the grasslands is the Church Road, a narrow, little-traveled, and discontinued town road that runs west off Route 104 (see "Directions," below). The first half mile of Church Road offers excellent views of the hayfields to the north and south, and you can stop to scan them as birds and inclination warrant. The road then leads into a wooded area with a good-sized Beaver flowage where you can see several wetland species.

Beginning in late April or early May, small numbers of Upland Sandpipers usually arrive on the Sidney Grasslands to nest and raise their young, and the adults can frequently be observed sitting on fence posts or circling overhead in territorial display. May and early June are usually the easiest times to see them. American Woodcock and Common Snipe also display over these fields early in the nesting season, and Northern Harriers, American Kestrels, Killdeer, Eastern Kingbirds, Eastern Bluebirds (irregular), Bobolinks, Eastern Meadowlarks, and Savannah Sparrows occur here as well. Indigo Buntings occur along the brushy edges. Herring and Ring-billed gulls can be found almost anytime of year except when there is snow on the ground; they are especially common after haying, when they are attracted by the multitude of prey flushed up by the mowing equipment. It is always worth looking over these gulls in the hopes of finding something unusual.

Beyond the hayfields bordering Church Road is a densely wooded area with a conspicuous Beaver flowage on the right side of the road (the flowage begins about 0.8 mile down the road from Route 104). We usually pull off to the right and park here—partly because this is where the flowage starts, but also because it's where the potholes take a major turn for the worse. From here you can explore the rest of Church Road by foot. Alder Flycatchers, Veerys, Common Yellowthroats, Swamp Sparrows, and Red-winged Blackbirds are all vociferous in the nesting season. Several species of waterfowl go about their jobs more quietly, among them Mallards, Wood Ducks, and Green-winged and Blue-winged teal. Red-shouldered Hawks are also seen here regularly in summer and probably nest nearby.

The Sidney Grasslands are also worth checking outside the nesting season, especially from November through March. Look for such open-country specialties as Rough-legged Hawk, Snowy and Short-eared owls, Northern Shrike, Horned Lark, Snow Bunting, and Lapland Longspur. The fields are also a good place to look for impressive numbers of crows. Our friend David Ladd saw an estimated 550 American Crows here in late fall one year, and as he put it, "You may not think of crows as all that interesting, but five hundred fifty sure are!" Among the more exciting recent records from the grasslands were six Sandhill Cranes in October 1994.

The Sidney Grasslands may not comprise the largest or most diverse birding site in the western mountains and lakes region, but they certainly warrant more extensive investigation than they have received thus far. As birders explore the grasslands more thoroughly, and in all seasons, a better picture of the birdlife will undoubtedly emerge.

The Sidney Grasslands are accessible year-round, free of charge. There are no facilities. *Please remember that the fields are private property and that you must bird from the roadside.*

DIRECTIONS

The Sidney Grasslands lie along Rt. 104 between Augusta and Waterville and are accessible from Church Rd., a narrow gravel road that runs west off Rt. 104 between Densmore Rd. to the south and Lyons Rd. to the north. Look for the small white church at the intersection of Church Rd. and Rt. 104.

FROM LAKE MESSALONSKEE: From the public boat launch, go 3.7 miles south on Rt. 27 to the intersection with Rt. 23. Turn left (north) and in 0.6 mile turn right onto Quaker Rd. Continue 2.4 miles and make a sharp right onto Shepard Rd. (which will turn into Densmore Rd.). In 3 miles turn left onto Rt. 104. Continue 1.8 miles and turn left onto Church Rd.

LOCAL ACCOMMODATIONS

For information on local accommodations or services in the Belgrade/Sidney area, write or call the Kennebec Valley Chamber of Commerce, P.O. Box E, University Dr., Augusta, ME 04330, telephone 207-623-4559.

Grafton Notch State Park
(*MAINE ATLAS* map 18, D-1)

Grafton Notch State Park lies at the northern end of the Mahoosuc Mountains on the Maine–New Hampshire border in a beautiful glacier-sculpted area of cliffs, gorges, and waterfalls. Nine rugged peaks, all higher than 3,500 feet, dominate the Mahoosucs. Best known as a major crossing point on the Appalachian Trail (AT), Grafton Notch State Park is generally considered to be primarily a hiker's park, but it is also a wonderful birding area.

The birdlife in Grafton Notch blends a rich combination of northern boreal species and more southerly deciduous breeders. It is an interesting area where you can find the unlikely combination of Eastern Towhees and Lincoln's Sparrows singing side by side. Although species such as Spruce Grouse, Gray Jay, Blackpoll Warbler, and Bicknell's (formerly Gray-cheeked) Thrush are restricted to the higher elevations (and thus require you to do some moderate to strenuous hiking), almost all of the other nesting species in the park can be found along the road or on lower, flatter sections of the trails. The best time to visit the area is at the height of the breeding season in June, but you are likely to find much of interest anytime between mid-May and late July. You can cover the park in three to four hours if you stay in the lowlands, but you will need a full day or more if you intend to hike to the higher elevations.

The park includes almost 3,200 acres lying along either side of a 5.6-mile stretch of Route 26 in Grafton Township. Old Speck, at 4,180 feet Maine's third highest mountain, rises along the west side of the road. To the east rises Baldpate Mountain with its two open summits, the West Peak at 3,680 feet and the East Peak at 3,812 feet. Both mountains are accessible by trails in the park. Also included in the park are three narrow, twisting gorges and several small waterfalls and caves, all of which are well marked with park signs. These are not exciting stops for birds, but if you have an eye for unusual geological features and the beauty of the landscape, you won't want to miss them.

There are two ways to bird Grafton Notch—by following Route 26 north and stopping along the way to bird the "lowlands" (you will find several well-marked stopping points within the park) and by hiking to the higher elevations of Old Speck or Baldpate. For a full cross section of the area's birdlife, you will want to do both.

Route 26

As Route 26 threads its way north from the Androscoggin River at Newry Corner and begins its steady climb toward Grafton Notch, it provides a dramatic contrast between the pine-oak forests typical of southern Maine and the birch and spruce forests of the north woods. The lower section of the highway is punctuated with farms and open

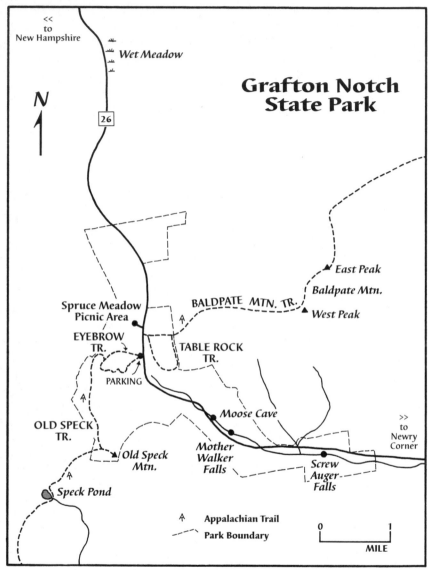

fields, where Eastern Kingbirds, Tree, Barn, and Cliff swallows, Cedar Waxwings, Chipping, Savannah, and Song sparrows, Bobolinks, and American Goldfinches are all regular. You might also find Eastern Bluebirds nesting in some of the roadside boxes, American Kestrels hunting over the fields or perched on telephone wires, or Chimney Swifts hawking for insects overhead. For many years there has been a large, active Bank Swallow colony in the sandpit on the east side of Route 26 just a short distance beyond the intersection of Routes 26 and 2.

Following the shallow, rocky Bear River, Route 26 rises steeply into a narrow valley covered with Yellow and Paper birches, American Beech, Sugar Maple, and poplars. These hardwoods support many of the same breeding birds found farther south, among them Barred Owl, Pileated, Hairy, and Downy woodpeckers, Yellow-bellied Sapsucker, Least and Great Crested flycatchers, Black-capped Chickadee, Blue Jay, American Crow, Eastern Wood-Pewee, Veery, Wood and Hermit thrushes, American Robin, Gray Catbird, Black-and-white Warbler, Ovenbird, Northern Waterthrush, American Redstart, Scarlet Tanager, and Rose-breasted Grosbeak.

One distinctive feature separating these deciduous woods from those to the south, however, is the presence of nesting Philadelphia Vireos. These inconspicuous vireos are fairly common in Grafton Notch but can be frustrating to find and difficult to see well. They are often found in small, open patches of birch, aspen, and White Ash, and they tend to stay up high in the canopy. The song can be maddeningly similar to that of a Red-eyed Vireo, and it is easy to become confused by an odd Red-eyed song. Philadelphia Vireos have a shorter, snappier song that is higher pitched, and they generally don't drone on all day long in the monotonous way typical of Red-eyeds. We have had good luck finding Philadelphia Vireos in the birch-aspen groves right along the roadside near the southern entrance to the park and between Screw Auger and Mother Walker falls.

As Route 26 climbs higher in elevation, the hardwoods give way to spruces. Look along this portion of the highway for a varied cross section of breeding species, among them Ruby-crowned and Golden-crowned kinglets, Brown Creeper, Red-breasted Nuthatch, Winter Wren, Swainson's Thrush, Solitary Vireo, Northern Parula, and Nashville, Bay-breasted, and Cape May warblers. Be sure to check Spruce Meadow Picnic Area, 4.6 miles north of the park's southern boundary on the west side of the road. This open, level area with scattered spruces is an excellent place to see Boreal Chickadees and Tennessee, Magnolia, and Blackburnian warblers. It is often easier to see the birds here than it is when you are looking up a mountainside. Spruce Meadow is also a good place to look for Moose and a lovely vantage point from which to survey the valley below.

At the northern border of the park, continue north on Route 26 another 2.6 miles to a wet meadow on the right (east) side of the highway. The scattered alders here provide nesting habitat for Alder Flycatchers, Chestnut-sided and Wilson's warblers, Common Yellowthroats, and Swamp and Lincoln's sparrows. Curiously, Eastern Towhee, a species more typical of southernmost Maine, also occurs in this meadow. This is private property, but you can scan it from the roadside.

At any point along Route 26, keep an eye on the upper ridges across the valley. The Common Raven's loud, grating croaks are a familiar, pleasant sound frequently heard from the cliffs, and Northern Goshawks and Red-tailed Hawks sometimes soar on the updrafts.

Specific places where you may want to stop within the park, in addition to Spruce Meadow, include Screw Auger and Mother Walker falls, Moose Cave, and the trailhead parking lot (see below). In years with tent-caterpillar infestations, Yellow-billed Cuckoos can sometimes be found in the trees around this parking lot.

Old Speck & Baldpate Mountains

Those who love the solitude of remote mountaintops, who thrill at the delicate, quavering notes of Bicknell's Thrush, who admire diminutive alpine wildflowers, will undoubtedly seek the higher elevations of Old Speck or Baldpate. Both mountains offer a similar birding experience and are accessible from the trailhead parking lot located 3.7 miles north of the park's southern boundary on the west side of Route 26. (This is where the AT crosses Route 26.) A trail map at the parking lot will direct you, but we recommend having a park or an AT map with you as well. (See the AMC *Maine Mountain Guide*, or *Appalachian Trail Guide to Maine* edited by Cilley; both references are listed in Appendix D.) You should be properly equipped and conditioned for strenuous hiking.

Four trails—two on each side of Route 26—start at or near this parking lot. On the west side of the highway, starting at the parking lot, are the Eyebrow Trail, a 2.3-mile loop that ascends about 1,000 feet to the Eyebrow Cliff on Old Speck, and the Old Speck Trail, a 3.9-mile trail to the summit. On the east side of the highway, on Baldpate, are the 2.4-mile Table Rock Trail Loop and the Baldpate Mountain Trail. Following the latter, it is 2.9 miles to the West Peak and 3.8 miles to the East Peak. Of the four hikes, we prefer the two to the summits. Old Speck is the longer of the two hikes, Baldpate the steeper. Either one makes for a full and tiring day, but the birds, and the scenery, make it worth the effort.

Whether you choose Old Speck or Baldpate, you will soon start to climb above the beeches and maples and into the first scattered firs. Winter Wrens (all the way up the mountain and typically singing vigorously much of the day), Hermit and Swainson's thrushes, Yellow-bellied Flycatchers, Black-throated Blue and Canada warblers, White-throated Sparrows, and Dark-eyed Juncos can be seen or heard in the understory. Nashville, Black-throated Green, Blackburnian, and Yellow-rumped warblers occupy the upperstory.

The higher trail sections of both mountains are dominated by spruce forests with breeding Blackpoll (often surprisingly common), Cape May, and Bay-breasted warblers. Spruce Grouse are common at this elevation and can often be found dust-bathing in the trail. Flaking on the spruce trunks indicates that Black-backed Woodpeckers are probably fairly regular (although always hard to find). Yellow-bellied Flycatchers reveal their presence with their subtle *click* note, whereas Purple Finches are more obvious with their rich, warbling songs. Gray Jays, White-winged and Red crossbills, Pine Siskins, and Evening Grosbeaks are irregular but always possible. At and near the summits of both mountains, listen for the slurred *wee-you* call note of Bicknell's Thrush (generally not present until late May). The Bicknell's magical fluting song, typically heard in the early evening or on cloudy days, is one of the pleasures to be found in Maine only near the tops of these isolated mountains.

The summit of Baldpate, as its name implies, is open, with wonderful views in almost all directions. Clumps of alpine wildflowers, rare in a state where treeless mountaintops are uncommon, can be found on this exposed area, especially on East Peak. The summit of Old Speck is covered with spruce, but for many years a fire tower has provided a stunning view in all directions, particularly of the White Mountains.

If you don't have time for an all-day hike, try the Table Rock Trail, which ascends a shoulder of Baldpate; this is the shortest hike that provides both a spectacular view and a change in the avian community. The easiest route is to follow the white (AT) trail about 0.8 mile up Baldpate and then turn right on the blue trail to Table Rock. Another option is to take the very steep orange trail straight up the boulders to the base of the mountain and then return via the blue and white (AT) trails; you will cover more territory this way and will also get some spectacular views. Total round-trip hiking time is two to three hours depending on birding and rest stops.

If you have time for more than a full day's hike, you might want to explore the AT south of Old Speck. The trail continues south another mile to Speck Pond, which at 3,777 feet is the highest pond in Maine. This part of the trail passes through large areas of thick subalpine heathlands, an interesting and uncommon vegetation type found along these ridge tops.

Wherever you are in Grafton Notch, watch for mammals, too. White-tailed Deer, Moose, and Black Bear are all spotted with some regularity.

It is also worth noting here that the White Mountain National Forest in nearby New Hampshire supports many of the same breeding species found in Grafton Notch State Park.

Grafton Notch State Park is open from May 15 to October 15 and has picnic and outhouse facilities. There is a small fee for day use.

DIRECTIONS

Grafton Notch State Park is located along Rt. 26 in Grafton Township. At the intersection of Rts. 26 and 2 in Newry (at the Androscoggin River), bear north on Rt. 26. The southern boundary of the park is 8.6 miles north, and the various trails and scenic spots are well marked.

LOCAL ACCOMMODATIONS

For information on local accommodations and services, write or call the Bethel Area Chamber of Commerce, P.O. Box 439, Bethel, ME 04217-0439, telephone 207-824-2282.

Mt. Blue State Park
(*MAINE ATLAS* map 19, C-3)

Mt. Blue State Park lies in the village of Weld, right in the heart of Maine's western mountains. As anyone familiar with it will attest to, this park is easily one of Maine's loveliest—and surprisingly, also one of its least used. The park comprises approximately 5,000 acres surrounded by stunning mountain scenery and is divided into two separate sections, each with its own set of breeding birds. On the west side of Weld is a fully developed campground on the shore of Webb Lake; on the east side of Weld, in the Center Hill section of the park, is Mt. Blue itself. About a 14-mile drive separates one section from the other. The birding is excellent at both sites, with breeding species being the main attraction. The campground offers a varied mix of southern and northern species. The trail up Mt. Blue (classified in most hiking guides as a beginner to intermediate hike) offers several distinctly boreal species, among them Boreal Chickadee, Bicknell's (formerly Gray-cheeked) Thrush, and Blackpoll Warbler.

Although often busy on summer weekends, Mt. Blue State Park otherwise is a relatively quiet spot, even on a beautiful midsummer

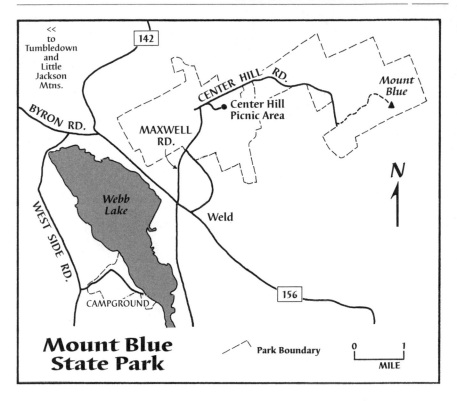

<<
to
Tumbledown
and
Little
Jackson
Mtns.

142

BYRON RD.

CENTER HILL RD.

Center Hill
Picnic Area

Mount
Blue

MAXWELL
RD.

WEST SIDE RD.

Webb
Lake

Weld

N

156

CAMPGROUND

Mount Blue State Park

Park Boundary

0   1
MILE

day. The best time to bird the park is in June, when the breeding season is at its peak. Anytime from mid-May through July or even early August, however, you can easily spend a half-day birding both sections of the park. We like to bird the campground at dawn, start up the mountain by 7:00 a.m. or so, and then come back to the lake for a well-deserved swim. If you have your heart set on finding a Bicknell's Thrush, however, you will probably want to climb the mountain first (or save it for late afternoon). However you do it, there aren't many better ways to spend a summer day.

Webb Lake Campground

The habitat at the Webb Lake campground brings northern and southern breeding birds together in an interesting combination. Whip-poor-wills and Pine Warblers nest around the lake; Yellow-bellied Flycatchers and Cape May and Bay-breasted warblers can be found in the spruce-fir woods around the campsites. Few campers use the campground in June, so birding the park roads and trails is quiet and easy and affords excellent visibility. By July the campground is busier and the song much subdued.

Other species nesting in this area include Common Loon, Osprey, Broad-winged Hawk, Ruffed Grouse, Black-billed Cuckoo, Barred Owl, Ruby-throated Hummingbird, Yellow-bellied Sapsucker, Least Flycatcher, Eastern Wood-Pewee, Eastern Kingbird, Blue Jay, Winter Wren, Golden-crowned and Ruby-crowned kinglets, Veery, Wood and Hermit thrushes, Solitary and Red-eyed vireos, Tennessee, Nashville, Magnolia, Black-throated Green, Blackburnian, Black-and-white, and Canada warblers, Northern Parula, Ovenbird, Northern Waterthrush, American Redstart, Baltimore Oriole, Scarlet Tanager, Rose-breasted and Evening grosbeaks, White-throated Sparrow, Dark-eyed Junco, Purple Finch, and Pine Siskin.

Mt. Blue

Mt. Blue rises 1,800 feet above the village of Weld and, seen from a distance, forms an almost perfect cone on the horizon. This is one of Maine's best-known examples of a monadnock—a mountain or other rocky mass that has not succumbed to erosion and thus lies isolated on a plain or valley. At 3,187 feet, Mt. Blue is not as high as many of the mountains to the north and west, but it still attracts many of the same breeding birds, including six species of thrushes. Perhaps the only boreal species regularly encountered on Maine's higher mountains and not seen on Mt. Blue is Spruce Grouse. In all other respects, this handsome mountain offers much the same birding to be found on Maine's larger, more remote, and steeper mountains.

The trail up Mt. Blue is 1.7 miles long and relatively steep, but even with leisurely stops for birding, it takes less than two hours to reach the peak. The mature deciduous lowlands at the base of the mountain gradually blend into a mixed spruce-fir forest, which in turn yields to a stunted, thick spruce forest near the peak. Although the peak is forested, several ledge outcroppings provide wonderful views in almost all directions.

The bird distribution on Mt. Blue is similar to that of other Maine mountains; as you progress up the mountain, the birds change along with the habitat. As you approach the mountain on the Center Hill Road, look for open-country nesters such as Eastern Kingbirds and Eastern Bluebirds (the bluebirds often occupy nest boxes just a few yards from the road). In the mixed-deciduous lowlands at the base of the mountain, you are likely to encounter such species as Broad-winged Hawk, Ruffed Grouse, Northern Flicker, Pileated, Hairy, and Downy woodpeckers, Eastern Wood-Pewee, Black-capped Chickadee, Red-breasted Nuthatch, Winter Wren (all the way up the mountain and singing vigorously even at midday), Veery, Wood and Hermit thrushes, American Robin, Red-eyed, Solitary, and Philadelphia vireos (the last in the birch-aspen patches near the parking lot), Magnolia, Black-throated Blue, Black-throated Green, Yellow-rumped, and Black-and-white warblers, American Redstart, Ovenbird, and Scarlet Tanager.

Climbing higher, look and listen for Yellow-bellied Flycatchers, Boreal Chickadees, Swainson's Thrushes, Cape May, Blackburnian, and Bay-breasted warblers, and Dark-eyed Juncos, all of which are regular on the mountain. Bicknell's Thrushes (typically not arriving until late May) and Blackpoll Warblers nest on or just below the peak. It is usually quite easy to see and hear the Blackpolls, as they are conspicuous when singing or feeding young, but finding a Bicknell's can be another matter. This shy species is most easily found by voice, and the earlier in the morning you reach the peak (or the later you stay in the early evening), the better your chance of hearing it. Listen for its beautiful, slurred, flutelike song or for its low *wee-you* note.

It is also worth walking the short nature trail at the Center Hill Picnic Area, which is below the Mt. Blue trail (see "Directions," below). In addition to offering wonderful views of the valley below, this is a good spot to find a roosting Northern Saw-whet Owl at almost any time of year.

If you like the combination of hiking and birding, two other nearby hikes offer similar birding opportunities. Tumbledown and Little Jackson mountains, 3,068 and 3,434 feet high, respectively, are just a few miles north of Webb Lake; ask a park ranger at Webb Lake for more information, or check a local map or hiking guide.

Mt. Blue State Park is a well-developed park with camping sites, recreation hall, bath house, rental canoes, and many other amenities available at Webb Lake; there is a modest fee for overnight as well as day use here. This section of the park is open from May 15 to October 15. The Center Hill section of the park, which includes Mt. Blue, is open year-round, free of charge. There are no facilities. For information on camping, write or call Mt. Blue State Park, R.R. 1, Box 610, Weld, ME 04285, telephone 207-585-2347 (summer) or 585-2261 (winter).

DIRECTIONS

TO WEBB LAKE CAMPGROUND: At the intersection of Rts. 142 and 156 in Weld (at the Weld General Store), go north on Rt. 142. In 2.3 miles, bear left onto Byron Rd. (also called West Side or West Rd.), following signs for Webb Lake. Stay on the paved road, and in 4 miles turn left. The park gate is 0.9 mile ahead.

TO MT. BLUE (CENTER HILL AREA): At the intersection of Rts. 142 and 156 in Weld, turn north onto Maxwell Rd., following signs for the Center Hill Area. Bear left in 0.4 mile onto Center Hill Rd., which in another 1.3 miles becomes dirt. In 0.9 mile you will see the road to the Center Hill Ranger Station and Picnic Area on the right. To reach the Mt. Blue trail, go straight here instead of turning, and in another 0.9 mile bear right onto Mt. Blue Rd. In 2.5 miles you will see a small but well-marked parking area on the left, and just beyond it is the trail.

LOCAL ACCOMMODATIONS

For information on local accommodations and services, write or call the Rangeley Lakes Region Chamber of Commerce, P.O. Box 317, Rangeley, ME 04970, telephone 207-864-5364.

Rangeley Lakes Area
(*MAINE ATLAS* map 28, E-4)

Route 16 to Wilsons Mills   **Rangeley Lake State Park**
Rangeley Village   **Saddleback Mountain**
Bemis Mountain

With six major lakes, dozens of ponds, and a mountainous backdrop dominated by one of Maine's premier mountains—4,116-foot Saddleback—the Rangeley Lakes area has long been known for its scenic beauty. It is also one of Maine's oldest resort areas, having attracted anglers, wilderness campers, and other "rusticators" for nearly a century and, more recently, alpine and cross-country skiers. Rangeley village, with a permanent population of just over 1,200, lies on the north side of Rangeley Lake and is a delightful base from which to enjoy the area.

For birders, the main attraction is breeding birds. This region supports nearly all of the northern coniferous warblers, including Tennessee, Cape May, Blackburnian, Bay-breasted, Blackpoll, Mourning, and Wilson's. Other boreal species such as Yellow-bellied Flycatcher, Gray Jay, Boreal Chickadee, Ruby-crowned and Golden-crowned kinglets, Winter Wren, Swainson's Thrush, and Lincoln's Sparrow all occur regularly around the lakes. Spruce Grouse, Pine Grosbeak, and Rusty Blackbird are more locally distributed. Black-backed Woodpeckers, once regular and fairly easy to find, have declined in numbers since the peak of the Spruce Budworm infestation in the 1980s but are still a possibility. Bicknell's (formerly Gray-cheeked) Thrush is common at higher elevations. At the height of the

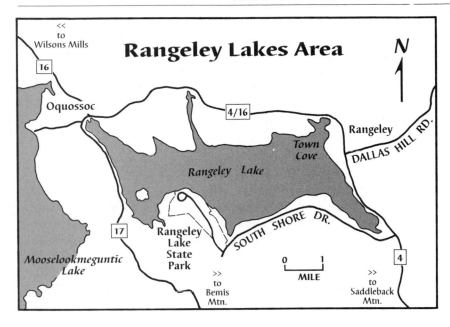

breeding season (late May through mid-July), you can easily spend a day or more birding around the lakes and ponds, alder swales, mountains, and boreal forests of this delightful region. For those birders also interested in hiking or canoeing, the Appalachian Trail (AT) on the south side of the lakes and the lakes themselves provide additional opportunities.

Below we describe the better-known and most accessible birding sites in the Rangeley Lakes area. We also encourage you to explore other sites on your own. This area is full of inviting little streams, trails, interesting patches of spruce-fir woods, perhaps a recent blowdown. Check a map; many places are accessible to the public, including more than 26,000 acres of Maine Public Reserve Land south of Rangeley Lake (the Richardson Unit) and east of Mooselookmeguntic Lake (the Four Ponds Unit). If you are unsure about access, bird from the roadside or ask permission to investigate. The entire Rangeley Lakes area is well used by many outdoorspeople, and chances are your inquiries will be well rewarded.

Route 16 to Wilsons Mills

Some of the best, and certainly the most accessible, birding in the Rangeley Lakes region lies along Route 16 between Rangeley village and Wilsons Mills to the west. There are plenty of places along Route 16 where you can pull over safely or get off the road altogether. Bird this road as early in the morning as possible, when traffic is at a minimum, and at all times be on the lookout for logging trucks. Plan on several hours to bird the road and off-road sites thoroughly.

The most productive stretch of Route 16 usually is the 20 miles between Oquossoc and Wilsons Mills, where there are extensive stands of spruce-fir forest, smaller stands of mixed hardwoods, several good-sized blowdowns, alder swales, and scattered areas of regenerating growth created by logging operations. This route also crosses several streams and boggy areas and overlooks a number of ponds and lakes, oftentimes right from the shore. Stop along the highway every quarter mile or so, or as good parking spots and inclination warrant, and don't forget to look down the many side roads as well. Just be sure to yield the right of way to any Moose you see.

At the height of the breeding season, you should be able to hear or see a dozen or more species of warblers along this road, among them Tennessee, Nashville, Northern Parula, Magnolia, Cape May, Black-throated Blue, Yellow-rumped, Black-throated Green, Blackburnian, Bay-breasted, Blackpoll (common in the short, thick, new-growth spruce so similar in form to the stunted growth found on mountaintops, which are more typical of this species' nesting habitat in Maine), Northern Waterthrush, Mourning (common along this route), Common Yellowthroat, Wilson's, Canada, and American Redstart. Other regularly occurring species include American Kestrel, Northern Flicker, Yellow-bellied Sapsucker, Pileated, Hairy, and Black-backed woodpeckers (the last is difficult to find, but one year it nested right along the roadside), Common Raven, Yellow-bellied and Olive-sided flycatchers, Gray Jay, Boreal Chickadee, Brown Creeper, Golden-crowned and Ruby-crowned kinglets, Veery, Hermit and Swainson's thrushes, Solitary Vireo, Lincoln's and White-throated sparrows, Dark-eyed Junco, and Purple Finch. Pine and Evening grosbeaks, White-winged and Red crossbills, and Pine Siskins occur sporadically; some years they are common, other years absent. Ruffed and Spruce grouse are both present, particularly along the side roads, with Spruce Grouse being more evident later in summer when the young are more mobile. Interestingly, this road is also one of the northernmost known nesting sites for House Wren, a species that typically occurs farther south and seems somewhat out of place in this coniferous setting.

The many wet areas along this route, from open lakes to slightly damp alder swales, harbor still more species. Look for Common Loons, Canada Geese, Mallards, Common Goldeneyes, Common Mergansers, Bald Eagles, Ospreys, Ring-billed Gulls, and Common

Terns on or around the lakes, and look in marshy areas or uplands for American Bitterns, American Woodcocks, and Common Snipe. Rusty Blackbirds can sometimes be found along the alder-bordered streams that cross the road.

The dirt road that leads into the Maine Public Reserve Land bordering Mooselookmeguntic and Upper Richardson lakes provides an ideal opportunity to get off Route 16—and also a chance to bird on foot rather than by car. Located on the east side of Route 16 (see *Maine Atlas* map 28, E-2), this road is 13.9 miles south of the intersection of Routes 16 and 17 in Oquossoc and is marked with a small Bureau of Public Lands and boat launch sign. Follow the right-hand fork in the road, and in 1 mile you will see the boat ramp on Upper Richardson Lake; or follow the left-hand fork about the same distance to the two East Richardson ponds. Either road makes for a lovely— and very productive—walk, especially in the early morning. When the road gates are open (usually from late spring through late June), you can also drive or hike over to the shore of Mooselookmeguntic Lake, which with 25.9 square miles and 17 islands is Maine's fifth-largest lake. (The public lands can also be explored from the south, from dirt roads leading off Route 17. Just be sure you have a good map with you.)

Rangeley Lake State Park

Rangeley Lake State Park, on the south shore of Rangeley Lake, encompasses nearly 700 acres of mixed hardwoods, spruce-fir woods, open areas, and shoreline. It is a good place to see many of the region's birds, and the mountain views and comfortable campsites make it an ideal base for campers. (It is also excellent for fishing, especially for Landlocked Salmon and trout.)

The park is easy to explore and needs no lengthy explanation. In general you can expect to find many of the more common birds described above for Route 16. Be sure to bird the wet areas along the entrance road and also the area around the entrance gate, where a Black-backed Woodpecker can sometimes be found. Certainly one of the park's most enchanting features is the delightful evening chorus of Swainson's Thrushes, which fill the woods with their soft, liquid songs.

Rangeley Lake State Park is located off South Shore Drive, which runs between Routes 17 and 4 south of the lake. The park is open from May 15 to September 30. Facilities include a campground, swimming beach, boat launch, and picnic area; there are modest fees for both day and overnight use. For information on camping, call or write Rangeley Lake State Park, HC 32, Box 5000, Rangeley, ME 04970, telephone 207-864-3858.

Rangeley Village

The open fields around Rangeley village provide nesting habitat for Savannah and Lincoln's sparrows and Bobolinks. It may seem surprising, but in this part of its range, Lincoln's Sparrow is quite common in brushy upland fields, along shrubby roadside borders, and in bramble thickets; it is by no means restricted to peatlands. Cliff Swallows are common in the village itself, especially near the lake. From the public boat launch at Town Cove, which provides a good view of the lake, you can invariably see some Common Loons offshore and often Common Mergansers, Ring-billed Gulls, and Common Terns. A single Chilean Flamingo (of unknown origin) appeared on the lake one September, and needless to say, it caused quite a stir.

Saddleback Mountain

Saddleback Mountain is appropriately named, for it is a long mountain (running east–west) with several peaks separated by saddles (see *Maine Atlas* map 29, E-1). The two highest peaks both reach more than 4,000 feet and offer spectacular views in all directions from their open, rocky summits. The Saddleback Ski Area occupies the northwestern slope of the mountain, and the AT traverses it from the southwest to the northeast.

Although one of the attractions of the Rangeley Lakes area is that you don't have to climb a mountain to see most of the boreal breeders, consider climbing Saddleback if you like the combination of birding and hiking. As inveterate Maine birder and hiker Bill Hancock says, "This is simply an outstanding birding hike." The 4,116-foot summit is 5.1 miles from the crossing of the AT on Route 4 (the vertical rise is 2,450 feet); it is another 1.6 miles to the Horn, the second-highest peak, at 4,023 feet. Along the way you will pass boulder fields, two lovely ponds, and several small streams; at the top you will traverse the long, bare, granite summits. You should be properly equipped and conditioned for strenuous hiking and should plan on devoting a full day just to the mountain. It is a long hike but not all that steep, and if you enjoy the splendor and solitude of the mountains, you will find it delightful. Just remember that even on a calm day in Rangeley village, it can be cold and windy on the mountain, so come prepared.

As with any birding hike, we recommend starting up the mountain as early in the day as possible, when the song is at its peak. As you progress through northern hardwoods and then through thick spruce-fir woods, listen and look for all of the regularly occurring boreal-forest breeders mentioned above for Route 16. This hike is especially good for warblers, with 15 or more breeding species being a solid possibility. Gray Jays and Boreal Chickadees usually are common. Black-backed Woodpeckers sometimes can be found, too, especially in the small stands of deadwood around Ethel and Eddy ponds. Saddleback is also one of the most reliable places we know to see Bicknell's Thrush. This shy denizen of Maine's higher mountains usually arrives on its breeding grounds in late May and is common near treeline on Saddleback—but it is not always easy to find. Bicknell's are often silent for long periods, and they typically spend much of their time under heavy cover. The opportunity to hear this thrush's splendid song, however, is well worth the effort, and the earlier you get up the mountain, the better your chances will be. Look, too, for Spruce Grouse, especially in late July and August. You can often walk right up to these "fool hens" as they stand motionless on or beside the trail.

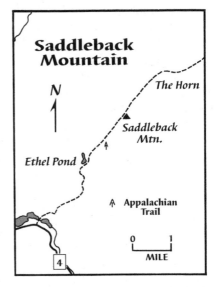

With its extensive treeless areas, Saddleback also supports an unusual array of arctic-alpine vascular plants, among them Diapensia, Mountain Sandwort, Mountain Cranberry, Bigelow's Sedge, and Dwarf and Alpine bilberry. The mountain is also known for its krummholz (literally "crooked wood") communities of Balsam Fir and Black Spruce at treeline.

The Saddleback trail (actually part of the AT) begins on the east side of Route 4, 9.9 miles south of the intersection of Routes 4 and 16 in Rangeley village. Park on the shoulder of the road. We recommend carrying an AT map or hiking guide with you. (See the *AMC Maine Mountain Guide*, or *Appalachian Trail Guide to Maine* edited by Cilley; both references are listed in Appendix D.)

It is also possible to hike Saddleback in summer via the ski trails on the other side of the mountain, but these trails are much steeper and not nearly as interesting for birds. They begin under the chairlifts at the base lodge, which is located 7 miles up the Dallas Hill Road from Route 4; just follow the signs to the ski area. (As of this writing, at least, the chairlifts do not operate in summer.)

Bemis Mountain

Another hike we recommend in the Rangeley Lakes region is Bemis Mountain, located on the south side of Mooselookmeguntic Lake (see *Maine Atlas* map 18, B-3). Bemis runs northeast-southwest and is characterized by a long, open ridge with four distinct peaks, only one of which (the highest) is forested. The views are spectacular and the birding is delightful. Although not as high as Saddleback, 3,592-foot Bemis supports virtually all of the same breeding species, including Bicknell's Thrush.

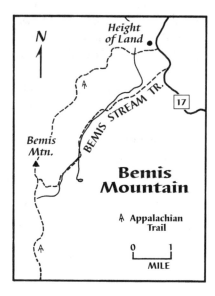

There are two trails up Bemis, one being the AT and the other the Bemis Stream Trail. The AT begins 11 miles south of Oquossoc on Route 17 (just south of the magnificent overview known as Height of Land) and leads 6.3 miles to the highest peak. The Bemis Stream Trail also begins off Route 17, 0.6 mile south of the AT, and is 6.1 miles long. Park for both trails along the roadside by the Bemis Stream Trail. A pleasant loop is to hike in via the AT and return by the Bemis Stream Trail. Be prepared for some wet going; both trails cross Bemis Stream.

Wherever you go in the Rangeley Lakes region, look for mammals as well as birds. Moose and White-tailed Deer are particularly common, and Coyote, Red Fox, Raccoon, Fisher, and Mink are all sighted with some regularity. If you are especially keen to see a Moose, try driving east on Route 16 toward Stratton at dusk. A waitress in Rangeley village gave us this tip a few years ago, and zingo! There were the Moose.

LOCAL ACCOMMODATIONS

For information on local accommodations and services, write or call the Rangeley Lakes Region Chamber of Commerce, P.O. Box 317, Rangeley, ME 04970, telephone 207-864-5364.

Bigelow Preserve (*MAINE ATLAS* map 29, C-4)

Bigelow Preserve is a vast area of beautiful and rugged land that encompasses the entire 12-mile-long Bigelow Range and 21 miles of frontage on the south shore of Flagstaff Lake. The preserve was created in 1976 by public referendum, in response to a ten-year battle by developers to turn this magnificent wilderness into the "Aspen of the East." What we have instead today is one of the largest tracts of public land in Maine—more than 35,000 acres. Thank goodness for the common sense of Mainers. Although much of the land surrounding Bigelow Preserve is commercial forestland (and some harvesting is allowed even within the preserve), there is still a good deal of undeveloped wilderness in this area.

Birders have not explored Bigelow Preserve very thoroughly, probably because of its remoteness. But largely because of its remoteness, and also because of its sheer size, Bigelow has much to offer. As elsewhere in western Maine, the primary attraction is breeding birds. You can find all of Maine's characteristic boreal breeders here, including Spruce Grouse, Black-backed Woodpecker (uncommon), Gray Jay, Boreal Chickadee, Bicknell's (formerly Gray-cheeked) Thrush, and all of the northern coniferous warblers, as well as Osprey, Bald Eagle, and several species of nesting waterfowl. The Bigelow area is also a suspected nesting site for Golden Eagle, a rare nester in Maine. Migrating waterfowl stop on Flagstaff Lake in spring and fall, and migrating shorebirds stop in late summer and fall. Breeding activity and song are at their peak in June, but the birding is likely to be good anytime from mid-April through October. Plan to spend at least a few days to explore the area in any depth. The combination of boreal birds, outstanding mountain scenery, and isolation are hard to beat, especially for those birders interested in really getting off the beaten track.

There are basically two areas to bird at Bigelow, the alpine zone and the "lowlands." Each is described below.

The Alpine Zone

The Bigelow Range runs east-west and includes six major peaks: the twin peaks—Avery Peak at 4,088 feet and West Peak at 4,150 feet, both of which have open, rocky summits; the twin horns—South Horn at 3,831 feet and North Horn at 3,810 feet; Cranberry Peak at 3,213 feet; and Little Bigelow at 3,040 feet. Included in the range are mature hardwood and spruce-fir forests, windswept treeless areas (supporting a small number of common arctic-alpine plants), extensive dwarf shrub-heath communities, alpine krummholtz (literally "crooked wood"), and two mountain tarns (Horns and Cranberry ponds). In short, it is a range of exceptional diversity.

Fortunately, much of Bigelow's alpine zone is accessible via 17 miles of the Appalachian Trail (AT) and several side trails. We recommend hiking any of the major trails in the preserve, which include the following: Bigelow Range Trail (3.2 miles from Route 27 to Cranberry Peak); the AT from the south (3.4 miles from Route 27 to the intersection with the Bigelow Range Trail); the Firewarden's Trail (3.9 miles from Stratton Brook to West Peak); the Horns Pond Trail (4.3 miles from Stratton Brook to Horns Pond, just west of the twin horns); the Safford Brook Trail (4.5 miles from Round Barn to Avery Peak, or 6.3 miles to the summit of Little Bigelow Mountain); and the AT to Little Bigelow (2.8 miles from East Flagstaff Road to the summit of Little Bigelow). For more details, consult the AMC *Maine Mountain Guide*, or *Appalachian Trail Guide to Maine* edited by Cilley (see Appendix D). Carry a good map with you, and be prepared (and conditioned) for moderate to strenuous hiking.

Whichever access you take into the higher elevations of Bigelow, you are likely to see a similar progression of birds. In the mixed woods at lower elevations, look and listen for such species as Ruffed Grouse, Great Horned, Barred, and Northern Saw-whet owls, Northern Flicker, Pileated, Hairy, and Downy woodpeckers, Yellow-bellied Sapsucker, Eastern Wood-Pewee, Blue Jay, American Crow, Black-capped Chickadee, Red-breasted Nuthatch, Winter Wren (all the way up to treeline and singing vigorously almost all day), Veery, Wood and Hermit thrushes, American Robin, Red-eyed, Solitary, and Philadelphia vireos, Nashville, Northern Parula, Magnolia, Black-throated Blue, Chestnut-sided, Yellow-rumped, Black-throated Green, Mourning (common in regenerating areas), Black-and-white, and Canada warblers, American Redstart, Ovenbird, Scarlet Tanager, and Rose-breasted Grosbeak.

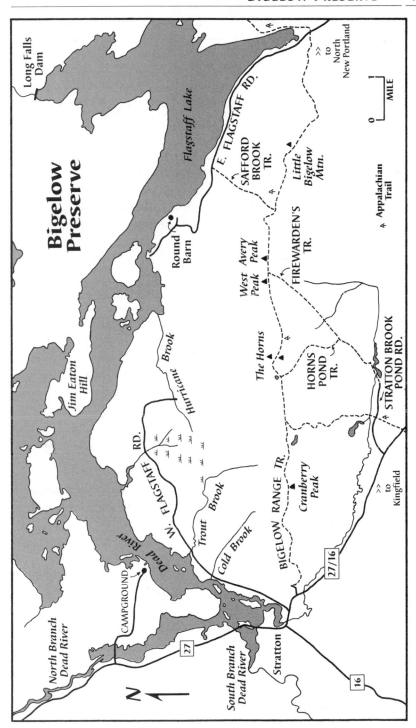

Climbing higher, look and listen for such boreal nesters as Black-backed Woodpecker (uncommon), Olive-sided and Yellow-bellied flycatchers, Gray Jay, Common Raven, Boreal Chickadee, Golden-crowned and Ruby-crowned kinglets, Brown Creeper, Swainson's Thrush, several species of warblers (among them Tennessee, Cape May, Blackburnian, Bay-breasted, and Blackpoll), White-throated Sparrow, Dark-eyed Junco, and Purple Finch. Spruce Grouse are common anywhere above about 3,000 feet, especially when their young have fledged in late July and August. Bicknell's Thrushes occur (usually not until late May) in the thick vegetation near treeline. This shy species is most easily found by voice, so listen carefully for its beautiful, slurred, flutelike song or for its low *wee-you* note. Species such as Pine Siskin, Red and White-winged crossbills, and Evening and Pine grosbeaks are irregular but always possible.

The "Lowlands" (including Flagstaff Lake)

The lower elevations of Bigelow consist of extensive stands of northern hardwoods, mixed hardwood and spruce-fir forests, and hundreds of acres of wetlands, including numerous brooks and flowages, Atlantic White Cedar and alder swamps, sedge meadows, and Beaver ponds. There is also 20,000-acre Flagstaff Lake, Maine's fourth-largest lake, which is actually a flowed reservoir that was created in 1949 when Central Maine Power Company (CMP) constructed the Long Falls Dam on the Dead River. That's a story in itself, which we won't go into here, but suffice it to say that it's a pretty strange sight when you occasionally see some of the infrastructure of two former villages (Flagstaff and Dead River) poking up when the lake is drawn down. Today Flagstaff Lake's varied shoreline provides habitat for several species that otherwise wouldn't be anywhere in the neighborhood—despite the fact that the water level fluctuates more than 20 vertical feet during the year. It is at its highest in early spring and at its lowest by December.

A broad cross section of species can be found in Bigelow's varied wetlands. At least eight species of waterfowl nest on or around Flagstaff Lake (Canada Goose, Mallard, Wood, American Black, and Ring-necked ducks, Common Goldeneye, and Common and Hooded mergansers), and another five species have been sighted on spring and fall migration (Snow Goose, Green-winged Teal, Greater Scaup, and Black and White-winged scoters). Other breeding species on or around the lake or in associated wetlands include Common Loon (as many as 19 pairs one year), Pied-billed Grebe, Double-crested Cormorant, Great Blue Heron, American Bittern, Killdeer, Spotted Sandpiper, American Woodcock, Common Snipe, Ring-billed and Herring gulls, Belted Kingfisher, Chimney Swift, Alder and Least flycatchers, Yellow Warbler, Northern Waterthrush, Common Yellowthroat, Swamp Sparrow, and Rusty and Red-winged blackbirds. Lincoln's Sparrow is regular around Flagstaff Lake in spring and fall and probably breeds in the area.

In late summer and fall, when the lake is drawn down, migrant shorebirds feed on the extensive mudflats exposed along the shore. At least 12 species have been recorded: Black-bellied Plover, Killdeer, Willet (possibly breeding in the area), Greater and Lesser yellowlegs (more than 160 Greaters in late September one year), Spotted and Solitary sandpipers, Semipalmated, Western, and Pectoral sandpipers, Short-billed Dowitcher, and Common Snipe. Sizable flocks of American Pipits (200+), Horned Larks, and Snow Buntings sometimes feed here, too.

Common nesting species you are likely to see in and around Stratton village or along roadsides include American Kestrel, Tree and Barn swallows, Eastern Phoebe, Eastern Bluebird, and Song and Chipping sparrows.

Because of its remoteness and size, Bigelow is a better than average place to look for nesting raptors. Ospreys and Bald Eagles nest around Flagstaff Lake. Possible woodland nesters include any of the accipiters (Sharp-shinned Hawk being the most likely), Red-tailed and Broad-winged hawks, and American Kestrels. Peregrine Falcons are seen occasionally on migration, and Golden Eagles are reported rarely. A good place to scan for raptors is over recently cut areas.

There are several good birding spots to check in the lowlands—some of them within the preserve and some just outside it. Within the preserve, Stratton Brook Pond (accessible from Stratton Brook Pond Road; see "Directions," below) is an excellent place to see waterfowl and other wetland-associated species. From the end of East Flagstaff Road, check the shore and offshore islands at the outlet of Hurricane Brook. In general, however, the lowland birding is not very good on the east side of Flagstaff Lake. There is very little marshland here, and because of the way the mountain range funnels the airflow, it is usually very windy. The west side of the lake, accessible from West Flagstaff Road, is usually more productive. The mouths of Cold and Trout brooks are good places to put in a canoe at high water. (Please note that the wind can blow up very quickly on the lake and that canoeing can be dangerous.) Or during drawdowns you can park here and walk along the shore to look for shorebirds. As long as you have a good pair of waterproof boots, this is quite feasible. Simply walk as far as you can, both north and south.

Two areas just outside the preserve are also worth checking. The first is the bridge and causeway over the south branch of the Dead River just north of Stratton village on Route 27. There is good, easy viewing on both sides of the road for waterfowl and shorebirds. The second place to check is the small piece of Maine Public Reserve Land on the west shore of Flagstaff Lake about 4 miles north of Stratton Village (see *Maine Atlas* map 29, B-2, and "Directions," below). This is a lovely spot, situated in a Red Pine grove with spectacular views of the Bigelow Range. We have known this site for years simply as "the Spruce Grouse place"—it is one of the most reliable (and easiest) places we know to see this species. It is also a good place to see waterfowl and shorebirds. During deep drawdowns, you can walk east along the shore all the way to Jim Eaton Hill, and the shorebirding can be quite interesting. The extensive wetland behind the beach is also worth checking.

Wherever you are in Bigelow, be on the lookout for mammals as well as birds. The Bureau of Public Lands estimates that more than 40 species of mammals occur in the preserve, including Black Bear, Moose, River Otter, Coyote, Red Fox, Bobcat, and Mink.

Bigelow Preserve is owned and managed by the Maine Bureau of Public Lands and is open year-round, free of charge. Facilities include several boat launches, picnic sites, outhouses, and camping sites. For more information, write or call the Maine Bureau of Public Lands, Western Regional Office, P. O. Box 327, Farmington, ME 04938, telephone 207-778-4111.

DIRECTIONS

There are four main access routes into Bigelow Preserve.

EAST FLAGSTAFF RD. provides access to the north and east sides of the preserve and is reached by turning north off Rt. 16 in North New Portland (east of Kingfield) onto Long Falls Dam Rd. Continue 17.4 miles, fork left onto the gravel Bog Brook Rd. (unmarked), continue another 0.7 mile, and then fork left again onto East Flagstaff Rd. This brings you out on the southern shore of Flagstaff Lake and continues past the Round Barn public use area.

WEST FLAGSTAFF RD. provides access to the west side of the preserve. It turns right off Rt. 27 in the center of Stratton (at the Stratton post office) and continues about 7 miles to Hurricane Brook, crossing several streams along the way and providing access to boat launches on the Dead River.

STRATTON BROOK POND RD. provides access to the south side of the preserve. Turn east off Rt. 27, either 4.6 miles south of the intersection of Rts. 27 and 16 in Stratton, or coming from the south, 3.2 miles north of the Sugarloaf Mountain Ski Area access road. In 1.7 miles you will see the parking area for the Firewarden's and Horns Pond trails.

RT. 27 NORTH OF STRATTON VILLAGE. The bridge and causeway over the south branch of the Dead River are located on Rt. 27, 0.7 mile north of the intersection of Rts. 27 and 16 in Stratton village. The access road to the Maine Public Reserve Land on the west shore of Flagstaff Lake is another 3.3 miles north on Rt. 27. Turn right just north of the big cemetery, bear right and then left, and follow the main dirt road down to the beach.

LOCAL ACCOMMODATIONS

For information on local accommodations and services, write or call the Sugarloaf Area Chamber of Commerce, RR 1, Box 2151, Kingfield, ME 04947, telephone 207-235-2500.

Additional Sites of Interest

Pine Tree State Arboretum (AUGUSTA)
(*MAINE ATLAS* map 76, C-3 & -4)

The Pine Tree State Arboretum in Augusta comprises 224 acres of open space within view of the state capitol dome. As our friend Steve Oliveri says, "This is a real gem of a spot—and not well known outside the immediate area." More than 150 species of birds have been recorded on the property, which includes fields, mixed deciduous woods, wetlands, two ponds, and an orchard. A web of trails winds throughout the area, and in the early morning during migration or the breeding season, you can spend a very pleasant hour or two birding here. Be sure to get a trail map at the signboard by the parking lot; it is easy to get confused by the many narrow trails.

Some of the breeding species of interest at the arboretum include Wood Duck, Northern Harrier, Broad-winged Hawk, American Kestrel, Virginia Rail, Sora, Great Horned and Barred owls, Marsh Wren, Red-eyed, Solitary, Warbling, and Yellow-throated vireos, Eastern Bluebird (not present every year), Black-throated Blue, Pine, and Canada warblers, Eastern Meadowlark, Indigo Bunting, and Bobolink. A wide variety of more common species occurs as well, and on the right day during spring and fall migration, you can see many migrant landbirds. If you are a botanist or gardener, you will also appreciate the many labeled plants.

The arboretum is open from dawn to dusk seven days a week, free of charge. There are no facilities. A small visitor center is open weekdays from 7:00 a.m. to 4:00 p.m.; check the bulletin board inside for recent bird sightings.

At the rotary on the east side of Memorial Bridge in Augusta, turn south onto Route 9. You will see the arboretum entrance (well marked) on the left in 1.2 miles. Coming up Route 9 from the south, the entrance is on the right, 5 miles north of the bridge over the Kennebec River in Randolph.

Thorncrag Bird Sanctuary (LEWISTON)
(*MAINE ATLAS* map 75, B-6)

Thorncrag Bird Sanctuary is a 310-acre wildlife preserve on the northeast side of Lewiston that is owned and managed by the Stanton Bird Club. The property is largely forested, primarily with White Pines and large deciduous trees, but it also includes orchards and open meadows and a pond, stream, and series of small pools. Many shrubs have been planted to attract birds. There are 3 miles of groomed trails, and at any time of year they provide an opportunity to do some enjoyable birding. Early May through late August is when you are most likely to see something of interest.

Some of the more conspicuous woodland breeding species in the sanctuary include Barred Owl, Pileated Woodpecker, Eastern Wood-Pewee, Wood and Hermit thrushes, Black-throated Green Warbler, Ovenbird, and Scarlet Tanager. Around the meadows and orchards look for Baltimore Orioles and Eastern Meadowlarks.

Visitors are welcome seven days a week from dawn to dusk, free of charge. There are no facilities.

The sanctuary is located on the east side of Montello Street in Lewiston, 0.3 mile south of the intersection of Montello Street and East Avenue, and just north of the intersection of Montello Street and Highland Spring Road (which runs off Sabattus Street).

MIDCOAST MAINE

Midcoast Maine stretches from Casco Bay north and east to the mouth of the Penobscot River near Bucksport. This extensive and varied coastline is characterized by a series of long, narrow peninsulas separated by equally long, narrow bays—the drowned river valleys left behind by the rise of sea level after the last ice age. In many ways this is a transitional area of Maine's coastline. At the mouth of the Kennebec River in Bath, the sand beaches and salt marshes so characteristic of southern Maine give way to rocky headlands, and spruces and firs begin to replace the White Pines and hardwoods. Offshore are a myriad of islands, many of them small and close to shore, others lying more than 20 miles out to sea. Several rivers flow through the region, and their tidal estuaries are rich in marine and bird life.

The birding in midcoast Maine is delightfully diverse. You won't find any obvious specialties here that you can't find elsewhere in Maine, but you will find a broad mix of birds. The peninsulas, for example, are excellent spots to look for seabirds, waterfowl, and windblown vagrants year-round and for a good mix of hawks and landbirds on spring and fall migration. Small numbers of Piping Plovers and Least Terns nest along the largest sand beaches; Common Eiders, Laughing Gulls, Common, Arctic, and Roseate terns, and Black Guillemots nest on many islands; and Atlantic Puffins and

Razorbills nest on Eastern Egg Rock and Matinicus Rock. Bald Eagles seem to be increasingly numerous each year, nesting as far south as Casco Bay now and occurring in substantial numbers around Merrymeeting Bay from early fall through winter. Nesting landbirds are largely similar to those in southern Maine—which means that boreal species are essentially absent.

Having birded extensively throughout this region for the past 20 years, we can assure you that it is full of good birding sites—from sand beaches to rocky promontories, from small working harbors (with their attendant gulls) to offshore migrant traps, from salt marshes to large tidal estuaries. Wherever you go in midcoast Maine, you are likely to find something of interest at any time of year.

Merrymeeting Bay
(including Swan Island) (*MAINE ATLAS* map 6, B-4)

Merrymeeting Bay is an enormous tidal freshwater estuary—the largest in Maine and indeed the largest on the Atlantic Coast north of Chesapeake Bay. Called "Merrymeeting" by early English explorers because it was a rendezvous point for several Indian tribes, the bay is formed by the confluence of two major rivers—the Kennebec flowing in at the north and the Androscoggin at the south—and four lesser rivers: the Muddy, Cathance, Abagadasset, and Eastern. Not surprisingly, this is one of the best places in Maine to see large numbers and an outstanding variety of waterfowl. From about mid-March, when the ice goes out, through April and from early September through at least October, it is possible to see thousands of Canada Geese, hundreds of Snow Geese, and smaller numbers of nearly every duck regularly found on the East Coast. The bay also supports at least two pairs of nesting Bald Eagles and is the most reliable place in Maine south of Mount Desert for seeing this species. Several more eagles (primarily subadults) winter in the area. A wide variety of wetland-associated and upland nesting birds adds to the attraction. Although you are likely to find something of interest on or around the bay at any time of year, spring and fall migration are the undeniable highlights. The birding usually is best on a midtide. (The bay is about an hour and a half behind—that is, later than—Bath; check a local newspaper for a tide table.) Allow about three to four hours to bird your way around the bay, and if at all possible, bring a scope.

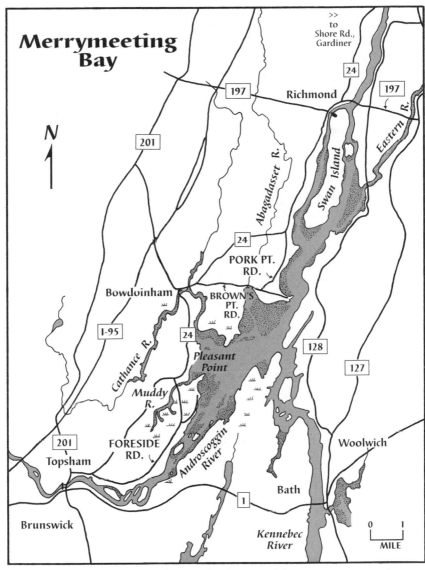

Merrymeeting
Bay

>>
to
Shore Rd.,
Gardiner

24

197   Richmond   197

N

201

Eastern R.

Abagadasset R.

Swan Island

24

PORK PT.
RD.

Bowdoinham   BROWN'S
PT.
RD.

I-95   24

Pleasant
Point

128

127

Cathance R.

Muddy
R.

FORESIDE
RD.

201   Androscoggin River   Woolwich

Topsham

1

Bath

Brunswick

Kennebec
River

0   1
MILE

Measuring approximately 5 miles long and from 0.3 to 0.5 mile wide, Merrymeeting Bay encompasses about 100 miles of shoreline and 4,500 acres of prime waterfowl habitat. There is one large island in the bay—1,700-acre Swan Island in the Kennebec River (see below)—and a handful of small, scattered islands. At the mouths of the rivers are broad, fertile mudflats which produce a lush growth of important food and cover plants and which at high tide provide extensive feeding and resting grounds. Mallards, American Black

Ducks, Blue-winged Teal, Wood Ducks, Common Goldeneyes, and Hooded Mergansers nest along the bay, and many other waterfowl species stop over on migration. Regular migrants include thousands of Canada Geese (primarily spring, peaking in mid-April), smaller yet sometimes substantial numbers of Snow Geese (primarily April) and American Black Ducks, and good numbers of Mallards (particularly in fall), Northern Pintails (particularly in fall, when they are early migrants), Green-winged and Blue-winged teal (the latter most common in late spring and early fall), Wood and Ring-necked ducks, Greater and Lesser scaup, Common Goldeneyes, Buffleheads, Common Mergansers, and to a lesser extent, Red-breasted Mergansers. American Wigeons and Hooded Mergansers are regular in small numbers. Rare migrants have included Tundra Swan, Fulvous Whistling-Duck, Gadwall, Eurasian Wigeon, Northern Shoveler, Redhead, Canvas-back, and Ruddy Duck. Also seen on the bay at times, especially in shallow waters close to shore, are Pied-billed Grebes, Common Moorhens, and American Coot.

Spring migration on Merrymeeting Bay begins as soon as the ice starts to break up (anywhere from early to late March, depending on the year) and continues through April. Although many birds have left the bay by late April, this period is often the best time to find rare and uncommon species. Fall migration begins in August when the first Blue-winged Teal begin passing through. The numbers and variety of birds increase through September and October. Because Merrymeeting Bay is a well-known and popular hunting spot in fall, we generally enjoy spring birding around the bay much more than fall (see the section entitled "Hunting" in the Introduction). We'd rather see the birds on the water than in a game pouch.

Most of the property that surrounds Merrymeeting Bay is privately owned. There is no shortage of No Trespassing signs, and these should be observed. The best way to bird the bay is to drive a loop around it, up the west side from Brunswick to Richmond, where you cross the Kennebec, and then down the east side to Bath. The west side is usually more productive. You will see most of the bay this way, including some of the primary feeding areas, and at a few spots you will get good overviews of large portions of the bay. This loop also leads you through a variety of wetland-associated and upland habitats, including coniferous (mostly White Pine) and deciduous woods, alder swales, fields, scrub, and small marshes. Some of the breeding species regularly seen or heard in these habitats include Osprey, American Kestrel, Ruffed Grouse, Great Horned Owl, Whippoor-will, Pileated Woodpecker, Great Crested Flycatcher, Eastern

Phoebe, Eastern Wood-Pewee, Cliff, Tree, Bank, Barn, and Northern Rough-winged swallows, Veery, Hermit and Wood thrushes, Gray Catbird, Brown Thrasher, Cedar Waxwing, Red-eyed Vireo, Pine, Yellow, Canada, and Chestnut-sided warblers, Ovenbird, American Redstart, Baltimore Oriole, Scarlet Tanager, Rose-breasted Grosbeak, Purple Finch, Eastern Towhee, Indigo Bunting, Field, Chipping, Savannah, and Song sparrows, and Bobolink.

Driving around the bay in April and September, you have a good chance of seeing migrating hawks. In winter check the fields for a Snowy or Short-eared Owl and the field borders for a Northern Goshawk, Barred Owl, or Northern Shrike. Also look and listen for such winter visitors as Pine and Evening grosbeaks, Pine Siskin, Common Redpoll, Red and White-winged crossbills, and Tree Sparrow. Most of these winter species are uncommon and irregular, but at one time or another we have seen them all in this area. If there is any open water, look for locally wintering ducks such as American Black Ducks, Common Goldeneyes, and Common Mergansers and for the occasional Great Cormorant.

At any time of year look for Bald Eagles on the bay. Especially between late September and March, you have an excellent chance of seeing several of these magnificent birds on a drive around the bay. A Maine Audubon boat trip on the bay in October 1995 recorded more than 30 Bald Eagles in one afternoon. Many of these "wintering" birds are subadults, but sometimes you will also see a few adults.

Finally, Merrymeeting Bay also has significant shorebird potential, although to date this has not been fully explored. If you have reports of interesting shorebird observations, we would appreciate hearing from you.

The loop that we describe below begins in Brunswick and ends in Bath. If you are not familiar with the area, by all means bring a good map. It is difficult to give concise directions around the bay, but as you drive this loop, you will see that these directions really are not as complicated as they might seem.

Brunswick to Bowdoinham.

Traveling from the north or south, take Route 1 into Brunswick and follow signs for Topsham. Once you cross the Brunswick-Topsham bridge (over the Androscoggin River), continue 0.3 mile to the stoplight and fork right onto Route 24 (Elm Street). Proceed 0.7 mile and fork right again onto Foreside Road; in another 3.9 miles turn right onto Pleasant Point Road. You can drive 1.2 miles down this road, but after this the road is private and you must turn around.

Pleasant Point Road runs right along the shore and affords a wonderful overview of the southwesternmost section of Merrymeeting Bay. At low tide you can often see large numbers of Canada Geese, American Black Ducks, Common Goldeneyes, and other ducks feeding near the shore. In the spring of 1995 we noticed an active Bald Eagle nest in a tall White Pine on the shore across the bay. It is difficult to see the nest, but keep your eyes open for the adults flying along the shore.

Coming back up Pleasant Point Road, turn right onto Foreside Road and continue north. In 1.2 miles the road crosses the appropriately named Muddy River. During the breeding season, Northern Rough-winged and Barn swallows nest under the bridge, and Yellow Warblers, Common Yellowthroats, and Swamp Sparrows nest in the wet thickets nearby. Continue another 0.3 mile to the stop sign and turn right onto Route 24. From here continue 3.4 miles, driving along a hilltop with a distant but sweeping view of the bay and passing through the community of Bowdoinham. Then look for an inlet and mudflat on the left side of the road, across from the railroad track. This area is generally most interesting at half tide or lower and is a good place to look for geese and other waterfowl. If it looks as though it might be worth stopping, continue just a short way up the road, pull off and park on the right, and then walk back to scan this spot.

Bowdoinham to Richmond.   Continue north on Route 24 and in 0.4 mile, at the top of the hill, turn right onto Brown's Point Road. (This road rejoins Route 24 in 4.4 miles, but it's called Pork Point Road at that end.) In 1.7 miles the road crosses the Abagadasset River; this is a good place to stop and scan for waterfowl. Also look for American Coot, which are fairly regular in this area. Bald Eagles often perch along this section of the bay, so take the time to scan treetops and other open perches around the shore.

In another 0.4 mile you will see an unmarked gravel road that forks off to the right, paralleling the high power lines. Follow this road 1 mile to its end, scanning the bay en route. Be sure to check the agricultural fields, too. Between November and March you can often find Snow Buntings and Horned Larks here, and occasionally there are a few Lapland Longspurs or American Pipits (the latter on migration only) mixed in among them.

Return to Brown's Point Road and turn right, continue 2.3 miles to the intersection with Route 24, and turn right again. In 4 miles, in the town of Richmond (*Maine Atlas* map 12, E-5), you will see the town landing, which looks out at Swan Island.

Swan Island. Swan Island is a state-owned wildlife management area administered by the Maine Department of Inland Fisheries and Wildlife (MDIFW). The area is officially known as the Steve Powell Wildlife Management Area. Measuring about 4 miles long and less than 1 mile wide, this lovely small island is a well-known nesting site for Bald Eagles. In fact, the island's name presumably derives from an Indian word for eagle, *sowangan*. Although the area where the eagles nest is restricted, you can see it during the breeding season on a special tour given by MDIFW. At the very least, you should get superb looks at the birds on the wing.

Habitats on Swan Island consist primarily of extensive hayfields and mixed woods. Between May and September you can usually find a wide variety of common breeders. Overnight visitors (camping is permitted; see below) have an excellent chance of hearing three species of nesting owls: Great Horned, Barred, and Northern Saw-whet. Wild Turkeys are common and relatively easy to see, making this one of the best places in Maine to observe this species. Other breeding species to look and listen for include Wood Duck, Common Goldeneye, Hooded Merganser (all three ducks breed in the many nest boxes that have been erected), Northern Harrier, Northern Goshawk, American Kestrel, Ruffed Grouse, Whip-poor-will, Eastern Bluebird, several species of warblers (including Blackburnian), and Bobolink.

White-tailed Deer are abundant on the island and provide wonderful photo opportunities, especially in June when you can often observe newborn fawns at very close range. Red Fox, Raccoon, and Porcupine are also common.

Swan Island is open daily for day or overnight visits from May 1 until mid-September, by reservation only. A small fee is charged. Camping facilities include 10 lean-tos (each with a view of the Kennebec), fire pits, picnic tables, and an outhouse. Ferry service is provided from the Richmond town landing (see above, "Bowdoinham to Richmond"). For more information or to make a reservation to visit the island, write or call the Maine Department of Inland Fisheries and Wildlife, RFD 1 Box 6378, Waterville, ME 04901, telephone 207-547-4167.

Shore Road, Gardiner. From the town landing in Richmond, continue north on Route 24. In 5.3 miles, at the Sagadahoc-Kennebec county line, fork right onto an unmarked, wide dirt road that parallels the railroad tracks and the Kennebec River. This is Shore Road. In 0.5 mile, where the road crosses the railroad tracks, stop and scan the river. In spring this is often one of the first places on the bay to have open water.

From March into May and from October through December, scope the large mudflat across the river for waterfowl. Snow Geese and Barrow's Goldeneyes are occasional among the more regular (and numerous) Canada Geese, American Black Ducks, Northern Pintails, Green-winged and Blue-winged teal, Common Goldeneyes, and Common Mergansers. Greater and Lesser scaup are irregular in fall. Great Black-backed and Herring gulls are almost always present (typically 100 to 200 birds), and small numbers of Glaucous and Iceland gulls are quite regular among them in winter and early spring. A few Common Ravens often can be heard or seen soaring overhead, and Bald Eagles sometimes create bedlam by flying along the river. Drive another 0.3 mile to the next railroad crossing to check the small mudflat there for additional waterfowl. Return south to the junction of Routes 24 and 197 (4.8 miles south of the intersection of Route 24 and Shore Road).

Dresden to Bath.   At the intersection of Routes 24 and 197, take Route 197 across the Kennebec River into Dresden. In another 0.6 mile turn right onto Route 128 and begin heading south down the east side of the bay. This stretch of road takes you past extensive agricultural fields, and in spring they often attract Canada Geese, Horned Larks, Snow Buntings, and occasionally Lapland Longspurs and American Pipits. Killdeer and American Woodcock also occur here (the latter typically visible only at dawn and dusk, in display). Northern Goshawks nest nearby and can sometimes be seen perched along the border of the woods. On two occasions we have also seen single Sandhill Cranes here.

In 2.3 miles, where the road crosses the Eastern River, pull over and scan. This is another good spot to look for waterfowl in spring and fall, and in summer for Northern Rough-winged Swallows, which nest under the bridge. You can often see a Belted Kingfisher here, too.

In another 9.3 miles, at the intersection of Routes 128 and 127 in Days Ferry, turn right onto Route 127. The pond at the corner here is worth a look in spring and fall, particularly for Ring-necked Ducks. Continue 2 miles to the junction with Route 1 in Woolwich, and turn right. The city of Bath lies just over the Kennebec River.

Merrymeeting Bay is a wildlife management area administered by MDIFW. You can drive around the bay at any time of year, but in fall bear in mind that this is a popular duck-hunting area. There are no facilities.

For information on local accommodations and services, write or call the Bath-Brunswick Region Chamber of Commerce, 45 Front St., Bath, ME 04530, telephone 207-443-9751, or 59 Pleasant St., Brunswick, ME 04011, telephone 725-8797.

Popham Beach State Park
(*MAINE ATLAS* map 6, E-5)

On a late summer day in 1607, the English explorer Sir George Popham landed with about 100 men near the mouth of the Kennebec River, at what is now the village of Phippsburg, and attempted to establish one of the first British colonies in the New World. Popham's experiment ended in disaster (the victim of a cold and brutal winter), but almost 400 years later, his name is still intimately associated with this area. Birders, like many others, know the area primarily for Popham Beach State Park, which offers some of the best year-round birding in midcoast Maine. Popham is an excellent place to see a good variety of seabirds and waterbirds year-round, wading birds in summer, and shorebirds, hawks, and landbirds on spring and fall migration. Highlights include nesting Piping Plovers and Least, Common, Arctic (uncommon), and Roseate terns in summer; good numbers of Bonaparte's Gulls in spring and from midsummer well into fall; and in winter a better-than-average chance of seeing such specialties as a King Eider, Razorbill, or Thick-billed Murre. Popham has also produced its share of rarities, among them Western Grebe, Wilson's Plover, Common Black-headed and Little gulls, Royal, Caspian, and Sandwich terns, Black Skimmer, and Brewer's Blackbird. Whatever the season, plan to spend at least a few hours to cover the park thoroughly. In summer it is usually very crowded, especially on weekends, but from fall through spring you will find it delightfully uncrowded. There are also three other spots worth checking in this area (two of them en route to the park), which we describe after Popham Beach.

With an estimated 618 acres of supratidal sand, Popham Beach is one of the largest and most complex beach systems in Maine. Fortunately, it is also one of the best protected. It is bounded on the west by the Morse River (a tidal inlet) and on the east by the Kennebec River. Popham Beach State Park comprises only the western half of this sys-

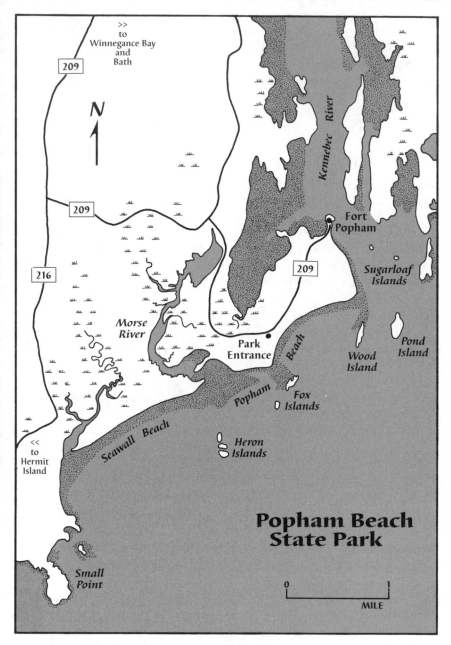

tem; Hunnewell Beach and Coast Guard Beach comprise the eastern half. Within the state park's 554 acres are more than a mile of wide beach face, a large barrier dune field and associated salt marsh, a spit and tidal inlet, a small freshwater pond, and dense shrub thickets.

Botanically the park supports unusually large stands of Beach Heather, the largest stands of American Beach Grass in Maine, and the largest mature Pitch Pine forest on sandy dunes in Maine. At low tide extensive sandflats are exposed. Offshore lie the five Heron Islands (which are a Nature Conservancy preserve), two Fox islands, two Wood islands, and at the mouth of the Kennebec, tiny Upper and Lower Sugarloaf islands. In short, this is a remarkably diverse area. The lighthouse you see offshore is 180-foot-high Seguin Light, built in 1795 and rebuilt in the late 1800s.

The best way to bird Popham Beach State Park is to park in the main parking lot (or if the gate is closed, along Route 209) and simply walk the beach. Scan the beach and tide pools below the parking lot, walk or scan Hunnewell Beach to the east (quite developed and usually not too productive), and then walk west down Popham Beach to the Morse River. This tidal inlet is usually one of the most productive spots in the park, especially at high tide when impressive numbers of terns, gulls, and shorebirds (depending on the season) roost along the beach. From here you can also scan the salt marsh behind the river. When you get back to the parking lot, bird the Pitch Pine forest in the backdune and the shrubs around the foredunes and parking lot. It is also worth walking the main road back to the west, scanning the marsh on either side of the road as you go. A half mile down the road, on the left, is a small freshwater pond bordered by dense thickets, which you can bird from the roadside.

In summer, small numbers of Piping Plovers and Least Terns usually nest along Popham Beach. As elsewhere in Maine, their nesting sites are carefully monitored by the Maine Audubon Society. Please observe any fencing or signs you see, pass as far away from the birds as possible, and do not linger. (If you don't see the birds on Popham, try scanning across the Morse River to Seawall Beach; both species often nest there, too.) Great Blue Herons and Snowy Egrets are regular around the salt marsh. Less regular but certainly not rare are American Bitterns, Green Herons, Black-crowned Night-Herons, Great and Cattle egrets, and Little Blue and Tricolored herons. In the Pitch Pines around the backdune area, look for nesting Pine Warblers, and around the pond west of the park entrance, look for nesting Yellow Warblers, Common Yellowthroats, and Song and Swamp sparrows.

Around the salt marsh look for nesting Savannah Sparrows and for both species of salt-marsh sparrows: Saltmarsh Sharp-tailed Sparrow and Nelson's Sharp-tailed Sparrow. Formerly considered a subspecies of the Sharp-tailed Sparrow complex, Nelson's Sharp-tailed Sparrow has recently been classified as a distinct species (*Ammodramus nelsoni).* Saltmarsh Sharp-tailed Sparrow *(Ammodramus caudacutus)* has a bright orange cheek triangle and dark ear patch. "Nelson's" is much duller and has a more washed-out facial pattern. "Nelson's" also has two distinct trills, whereas "Saltmarsh" delivers a complex whisper song. Interestingly, the area between Scarborough Marsh and Popham Beach appears to be the primary contact zone for these two species. Birds south of Scarborough Marsh are primarily Saltmarsh Sharp-tailed Sparrows; those north of Popham are primarily Nelson's Sharp-tailed Sparrows. For a detailed discussion of the research that formed the basis for this taxonomic split, see the 1993 paper by Jon S. Greenlaw in the *Auk* (110: 286–303).

Offshore in summer look for Common, Arctic (uncommon), and Roseate terns, all of which nest nearby. Roseates are not always easy to identify, but with their shallow, rapid wingbeats, long, flowing tail, silvery upperparts, and harsh *ka-rick* call note, they should soon be apparent. Double-crested Cormorants and Herring and Great Black-backed gulls nest on the Heron Islands, and Common Eiders, Black Guillemots, and Ospreys also nest nearby and are seen regularly in summer. Look for Bonaparte's Gulls around the Morse River in spring and from midsummer well into fall and for Laughing Gulls through-out the summer. Popham is also a good place to look for summering Red-throated Loons, King Eiders (rare), all three scoters, and Red-breasted Mergansers. The Popham area is one of Maine's southern-most breeding sites for the merganser, which occurs here year-round.

The birdlife at Popham, as at most places, is generally at its most diverse on migration, especially on fall migration when numbers of birds are augmented by the young of the year. One of the highlights of migration at Popham is shorebirds, which feed on the sandflats along the beach and Morse River and roost on the beach at high tide. Although neither the diversity nor the number of shorebirds is impressive here, you can often find something out of the ordinary. Regularly seen species include Black-bellied, Semipalmated, and Piping plovers, Killdeer, Greater and Lesser yellowlegs, Ruddy Turnstone, Spotted Sandpiper (often nesting by the Morse River), Sanderling, Semipalmated and Least sandpipers, Dunlin (primarily in fall), and Short-billed Dowitcher. You are also likely to see a few Willets or Whimbrels and occasionally a Hudsonian Godwit or Western, White-rumped, Pectoral, or Stilt sandpiper. Scan carefully for rarer species such as American Golden-Plover, Marbled Godwit, Red Knot, Baird's Sandpiper, and Long-billed Dowitcher. We have even seen a Wilson's Plover and Red-necked Stint here. Except for Willet and Pectoral

Sandpiper, the less common species are seen almost exclusively in fall. Please be careful not to disturb roosting birds.

Look offshore during migration for Northern Gannets, waterfowl, and Black-legged Kittiwakes (particularly in fall), and keep your eyes open for migrating hawks. On the right day, especially in September or October, the hawk migration can be excellent, with good numbers of Northern Harriers, Sharp-shinned Hawks, American Kestrels, and Merlins lingering to chase beleaguered shorebirds. Peregrine Falcons are uncommon but surprisingly regular. The marsh and backdune habitats behind the Morse River, and the roadside pond, are often good places to look for migrating passerines, especially warblers and sparrows. Dabbling ducks (including an occasional Gadwall) can sometimes be found on the pond. In fall, Yellow-rumped Warblers are usually by far the most abundant birds in the surrounding shrubs, and it is an impressive sight to watch hundreds of these birds devour the Bayberry crop.

From November through April, Popham Beach still offers good and diverse birding (and even if you don't see many birds, the winter beach is spectacular). Species regularly seen offshore include Red-throated and Common loons (the former less common in midwinter), Horned and Red-necked grebes, Great Cormorant, American Black Duck, Common Eider, Oldsquaw, all three scoters, Bufflehead, Common Goldeneye, Red-breasted Merganser, and Black Guillemot. Northern Pintails are occasional. Look for an occasional King Eider among the large rafts of Common Eiders, and particularly after a storm or a good blow from the east, for a Northern Gannet, Black-legged Kittiwake, Razorbill, Thick-billed Murre, or Dovekie. Sanderlings are usually common along the beach through December, and Purple Sandpipers often feed on the Fox islands (connected to the beach at low tide), sometimes lingering as late as May. From late February into May, look for Brant, which often rest on the Heron Islands as they migrate north to their arctic nesting grounds.

Don't forget to explore the upper beach and backdune area in fall and winter, too. "Ipswich" Savannah Sparrows (*Passerculus sandwichensis princeps;* formerly considered a separate species, Ipswich Sparrow) are fairly regular in October and November (sometimes overwintering with flocks of Savannah Sparrows), and a few Lapland Longspurs sometimes flock among the more regular Horned Larks and Snow Buntings. Other species to look for on the beach or around the marsh include Rough-legged Hawk, Snowy and Short-eared owls, Northern Shrike, and Common Redpoll; all are uncommon and irregular but certainly possible. Check the Pitch Pine for Golden-crowned Kinglet and for irregular winter visitors such as Pine Grosbeak, Pine Siskin, and Red and White-winged crossbills. Often lingering in the shrubs through December are Hermit Thrushes, American Robins, and Yellow-rumped Warblers. It is always worth looking for the odd landbird that winters over.

Popham Beach State Park is open year-round, from 9:00 a.m. to sunset from mid-May to Labor Day, and from 9:00 a.m. to 5:00 p.m. the rest of the year. A small entry fee is charged between mid-May and Labor Day. Facilities include a bathhouse (seasonal), outhouses, grills, and picnic tables. If you arrive early in the day (or anytime in the off-season) and find the gate closed, you are welcome to park along the side of Route 209 (not along the park entrance road) and walk in.

DIRECTIONS

The park is almost 15 miles south of the city of Bath on Rt. 209 and is well marked by signs along the way.

FROM THE SOUTH: Get off Rt. 1 in Bath at the High St./Phippsburg exit and turn right onto Rt. 209.

FROM THE NORTH: Cross the Kennebec River in Bath on Rt. 1 and take the Bath/Phippsburg/Rt. 209 exit. Immediately turn left at the stop sign, and in 0.2 mile (at the stoplight), turn left onto Washington St. Continue 2 miles and turn left onto Rt. 209.

Winnegance Bay

Winnegance Bay is just south of the city of Bath, where a short causeway separates a narrow freshwater creek on the south from a tidally influenced inlet in the Kennebec River to the north. From early spring through late fall, it is well worth stopping to scan this small area, preferably about two hours either side of high tide. (At low tide the birds are too dispersed to see well, and at high tide no flats are exposed.) The extensive mudflats here are frequented by ducks, herons, and shorebirds, and you can often find something of interest. We have seen unusually large flocks of Least Sandpipers here (1,000+), for example, and it is a good spot to look for less common peep. We were also surprised when we stopped here one day in late August and found a flock of about 350 Blue-winged Teal on the flats.

Winnegance Bay lies along Route 209. Coming from the south, it is 2.4 miles down Route 209, and coming from the north, it is 0.5 mile down Route 209 (see "Directions," above). Route 209 takes a sharp left (where you see the Winnegance General Store off to the right), and the causeway is just ahead. Park along the shoulder on the north side of the causeway and scan the flats on either side. Check a tide table to see when high and low tide are in Bath; it is admittedly a bit tricky to get here at just the right time, as we know all too well from experience.

Fort Popham

Fort Popham, owned and managed by Popham Beach State Park, commands a fine overview of the mouth of the Kennebec River. In summer this is an excellent vantage point (better than Popham Beach) from which to scan for terns; in winter you can scan for seabirds and waterbirds. The large granite fort was built during the Civil War to protect the Kennebec's flourishing shipbuilding industry. Although the fort was never completed, it was still used during the Civil and Spanish-American wars as well as during World War I. The fort itself is open only seasonally, but the road and surrounding property are accessible year-round, free of charge. Turn right onto Route 209 when you come out of the main parking lot at Popham Beach and continue 1.4 miles to the fort.

Hermit Island

Hermit Island, at the southwest end of the Phippsburg peninsula, pro vides another good vantage point from which to scan for seabirds and waterbirds. With its mixture of dense spruce-fir woods, shrubs, and open areas, this can also be a good place to look for landbirds. Many trails crisscross through the campground on the island. You are not likely to turn up anything of interest in summer, but in winter this area is well worth a check. We cover it on the Christmas Bird Count and often find a surprise bird or two. Look offshore for the same species that you would at Popham Beach State Park, and scan carefully for less common species, including Razorbill. In open areas Horned Larks and Snow Buntings are regular, and occasionally you can find some Lapland Longspurs among them or a Northern Shrike. One winter we turned up a Northern Hawk Owl.

Hermit Island is privately owned, but the campground at the south end provides public access to the shore and woods. In the off-season the campground is open during daylight hours, free of charge. At the intersection of Routes 209 and 216 south of Phipps-burg, follow Route 216 south, and in 2.9 miles turn right at the campground entrance. Park in the designated area, proceed through the gate straight ahead, and explore the shore and the many campground trails.

LOCAL ACCOMMODATIONS

For information on local accommodations and services, write or call the Bath-Brunswick Region Chamber of Commerce, 45 Front St., Bath, ME 04530, telephone 207-443-9751, or 59 Pleasant St., Brunswick, ME 04011, telephone 725-8797.

Reid State Park   (*MAINE ATLAS* map 7, D-1)

Reid State Park lies on the southeast end of Georgetown Island, which flanks the Kennebec River across from Popham Beach State Park. Like Popham Beach, Reid offers diverse and consistently good year-round birding. To many people, natives and visitors alike, this lovely park is the quintessence of coastal Maine: nearly 800 acres that include coniferous and mixed-deciduous woods, an extensive salt marsh and tidal lagoon, rocky headlands and tide pools, and more than 1.5 miles of sandy beach. The park is named for wealthy financier and Georgetown resident Walter E. Reid, who donated the land to the state in the late 1940s. Maine birders probably know the park best for the pair of Western Grebes that were found here on the 1977 Christmas Bird Count (for a first state record)—and for the fact that a lone individual continued to appear offshore every winter until 1994–1995. There is a lot more to Reid State Park than aberrant Western Grebes, however. Small numbers of Piping Plovers and Least Terns nest along the beach in summer; shorebirds, hawks, and landbirds pass through on spring and fall migration; and a good variety of seabirds and waterbirds can be seen year-round. At any time of year, you can easily spend a few hours exploring this diverse spot. On beautiful summer days the beach is full of people, but the rest of the year it is usually delightfully quiet and unpopulated.

The two most prominent features of Reid State Park are Mile Beach and Half Mile Beach. Mile Beach is a closed barrier beach that stretches from Griffith Head—the bold, rocky headland that dominates the park's northeast shore—southwest to Todd's Point. Behind it is a large salt marsh and saltwater lagoon. Half Mile Beach is an open barrier spit that runs from Todd's Point west to a tidal inlet called the Little River; it also protects a substantial salt marsh. Together these

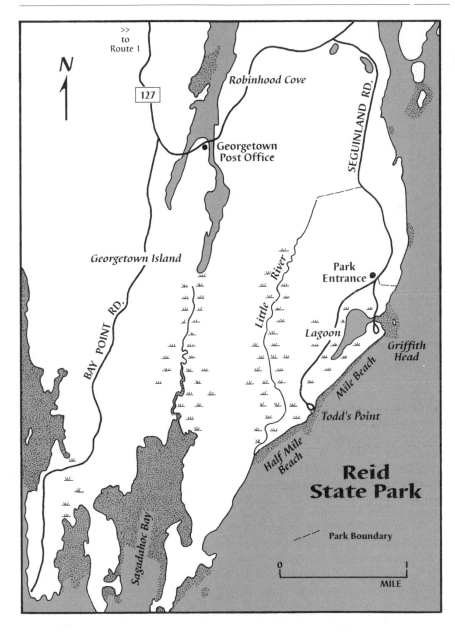

to
Route 1

N

127

Robinhood Cove

Georgetown
Post Office

SEGUINLAND RD.

Georgetown Island

Little River

Park
Entrance

BAY POINT RD.

Lagoon

Griffith
Head

Mile Beach

Todd's Point

Half Mile
Beach

Reid
State Park

Sagadahoc Bay

Park Boundary

0   1

MILE

two beaches comprise Maine's northernmost large beach system, with
an estimated 35 acres of beach and 26.5 acres of backdune habitat.

To reach the two beaches, take either of the park roads that fork
just beyond the entrance gate. Bearing left takes you to the parking
lot at Griffith Head, with access to Mile Beach; going straight takes

you to the parking lot at Todd's Point, with access to both beaches. From either parking lot, walk a loop around the beaches and the Todd's Point road. Griffith Head and Todd's Point are excellent vantage points from which to scan the water. The Todd's Point road affords good overviews of the beach systems, including the marshes and lagoon. This road is also lined with coniferous and mixed-deciduous woods that offer the most productive forest birding in the park. Check the lagoon and surrounding picnic area and the thickets around the parking lots.

In summer Reid State Park marks Maine's northernmost nesting site for Piping Plovers and Least Terns. Their nesting sites along the beach (usually Half Mile Beach) are carefully monitored by the Maine Audubon Society. Please observe any fencing or signs you see, pass as far away from the birds as possible, and do not linger. Double-crested Cormorants, Common Eiders, summering scoters, and Black Guillemots are regular offshore. Common, Arctic (irregular in small numbers), and Roseate terns—all of which nest near the mouth of the Kennebec River—can sometimes be seen, too. A pair of Ospreys nests just a few miles away at Robinhood Cove, and the birds are often seen and heard overheard.

Behind the beaches, a few Nelson's Sharp-tailed Sparrows and possibly Saltmarsh Sharp-tailed Sparrows nest in the *Spartina* grass in the salt marsh, and Savannah Sparrows nest along the edges of the marsh. You can also see waders here, with Great Blue Herons and Snowy Egrets being regular and American Bitterns, Black-crowned Night-Herons, Green, Little Blue, and Tricolored herons, and Cattle and Great egrets being occasional. Bonaparte's Gulls generally are common in spring and from midsummer well into fall, and small numbers of Laughing Gulls are regular in summer. The best place to look for gulls is at the mouth of the Little River. In the woods along the Todd's Point road, look and listen for such nesting species as Ruffed Grouse, Pileated Woodpecker, Olive-sided, Least, and Great Crested flycatchers, Red-breasted Nuthatch, Brown Creeper, Hermit Thrush, Gray Catbird, Brown Thrasher, Cedar Waxwing, Red-eyed Vireo, Nashville, Northern Parula, Yellow, Magnolia, Yellow-rumped, Black-throated Green, Chestnut-sided, and Black-and-white warblers, Common Yellowthroat, Rose-breasted Grosbeak, and Chipping and White-throated sparrows. American Black Ducks sometimes nest around the lagoon, and Belted Kingfishers can be seen here, too. You may well hear a Common Raven at any time of year. White-winged Crossbills are usually present in years with a good cone crop.

Spring and fall migration often yield some interesting birds in the park. In May and early June, and again from late August into October, the extensive thickets around the parking lots and the assortment of trees (spruces, firs, maples, birches, and alders) attract a wide variety of migrants, especially some of the softwood species such as Blackpoll, Cape May, and Bay-breasted warblers. From mid-September through November, sparrows frequent the edges of the parking lots and the openings around picnic tables, and Swamp and Lincoln's sparrows are regular among the more common Savannah, Chipping, Song, and White-throated sparrows. The Little River is always worth checking for migrant shorebirds, as are the pools and mudflats in the salt marsh behind the dunes. The species diversity usually isn't great, nor are sheer numbers, but you never know what might turn up. Black-bellied, Semipalmated, and Piping plovers, Killdeer, Greater and Lesser yellowlegs, Spotted Sandpiper (often nesting by the Little River), Ruddy Turnstone, Sanderling, Semipalmated and Least sandpipers, Dunlin (primarily in fall), and Short-billed Dowitcher are all regular. Look also for the occasional Willet, Hudsonian Godwit, Whimbrel, or White-rumped or Pectoral sandpiper, and scan carefully for such rarities as American Golden-Plover, Marbled Godwit, Red Knot, Western, Baird's, and Buff-breasted sandpipers, and Long-billed Dowitcher. Except for Willet and Pectoral Sandpiper, the less common species are seen primarily in fall. In spring and fall Reid is also a good place to look for migrating Northern Gannets offshore (especially between October and December) and for migrating hawks. The most commonly seen hawks are Northern Harriers, Ospreys, Sharp-shinned Hawks, American Kestrels, and Merlins; even Peregrine Falcons are regular in small numbers. In fall you can often see an impressive passage of waterfowl offshore. In spring as well as fall you may see some interesting ducks on the lagoon behind Mile Beach (this is visible from the road to Todd's Point, as well as from the bridge on the road to Griffith Head).

From November through March, when Maine birding becomes a bit more challenging, Reid State Park is a better place than most to see a good variety of species. Scan from Griffith Head and Todd's Point. The common species you are likely to see include Red-throated and Common loons, Horned and Red-necked grebes (the latter being particularly abundant here most winters, with as many as 185 having been recorded once), Great Cormorant, American Black Duck, Common Eider, Oldsquaw, all three scoters, Bufflehead, Common Goldeneye, Red-breasted Merganser, and Black Guillemot.

Northern Pintails and Greater Scaup are occasional. This is also a good place to look for a King Eider or Harlequin Duck and for the more unusual alcids (Common and Thick-billed murres and Dovekies have all been recorded) and after a good easterly storm, for Black-legged Kittiwakes. Purple Sandpipers are regular on the rocks all winter (sometimes lingering into May), and Sanderlings are usually common along the beaches through December. Look for dabbling ducks on the lagoon and for "Ipswich" Savannah Sparrows in the dune grass. Lapland Longspurs sometimes flock among the Horned Larks and Snow Buntings on the beach, and occasionally a Snowy or Short-eared Owl is seen on the marsh. Look for Common Redpolls feeding on the ground or on birch catkins.

In the woods along the Todd's Point road from November through March, look for Golden-crowned Kinglets and for such irregular winter visitors as Evening and Pine grosbeaks, Pine Siskins, and Red and White-winged crossbills. A Northern Shrike sometimes perches on a snag along the road or on the edge of the marsh. Boreal Chickadees are usually regular in small numbers each winter, and with a good Northern Saw-whet Owl imitation and some spishing, you may be able to call up a few. Other unusual boreal species that have been seen in the park on rare occasions include Black-backed and Three-toed woodpeckers and Gray Jay. Often lingering through December are Hermit Thrushes, American Robins, and Yellow-rumped Warblers. It is always worth checking the shrubs around the dunes and parking lots for the odd landbird that winters over.

Finally, there are two spots worth checking en route to the park. The first is the area around the Georgetown Post Office on Route 127 (see "Directions," below), where Hooded Mergansers are sometimes seen in early and late winter on a small inlet of Robinhood Cove. Park by the tiny post office and scan the inlet from the bridge. Be sure to check the feeder at the post office, too; this is a spot where we have had some nice surprises, among them Red-bellied Woodpecker, a wintering Indigo Bunting, and Lesser Goldfinch (really!). If you don't see the mergansers here, check the inlet 0.1 mile farther down the road.

The other spot worth checking is a small pond 1.7 miles south of the Georgetown Post Office on Route 127, on the right and just before you turn right onto Seguinland Road. Ring-necked Ducks are regular here in spring and fall. If you don't see the birds here, try the next pond, 1.4 miles farther down Seguinland Road.

Reid State Park is open year-round from 9:00 a.m. to sunset, and a small fee is charged. Facilities include bathhouses and snack bars (seasonal), grills, and picnic tables. The Griffith Head parking lot is open year-round, and an outhouse is available there in winter months. If you arrive when the entrance gate is closed during daylight hours (after sunrise but before 9:00 a.m.), you are welcome to park outside the entrance gate and walk in, provided that your vehicle does not block the road or gate.

DIRECTIONS

FROM THE SOUTH: Take Rt. 1 across the Kennebec River in Bath and immediately turn right onto Rt. 127 South. In 0.1 mile, at the stop sign, Rt. 127 South turns left. Follow it 8.7 miles to the Georgetown Post Office. In another 1.7 miles turn right onto Seguinland Rd. (unmarked). The park entrance is 2.2 miles ahead.

FROM THE NORTH: In Woolwich, 0.2 mile south of the blinking light that marks the intersection of Rts. 1 and 127 North, bear right onto Rt. 127 South. Continue 9 miles to the Georgetown Post Office, then proceed as from the south.

LOCAL ACCOMMODATIONS

For information on local accommodations and services, write or call the Bath-Brunswick Region Chamber of Commerce, 45 Front St., Bath, ME 04530, telephone 207-443-9751, or 59 Pleasant St., Brunswick, ME 04011, telephone 725-8797.

Damariscotta Area

Sherman Lake
Salt Bay
Pemaquid Point

The town of Damariscotta lies along the Damariscotta River, midway between Bath and Rockland. Many people probably drive through this historic and picturesque area without realizing that it has considerable ornithological potential. Three sites are of particular interest. Sherman Lake is a good place to see nesting freshwater marsh birds and migratory waterfowl. Salt Bay is good for waterfowl and nesting Bald Eagles. And Pemaquid Point is an excellent spot to look for seabirds (including some hard-to-find species) year-round and for landbirds on migration. The area is well worth a visit at any time of year. You can cover all three sites in a half day or so.

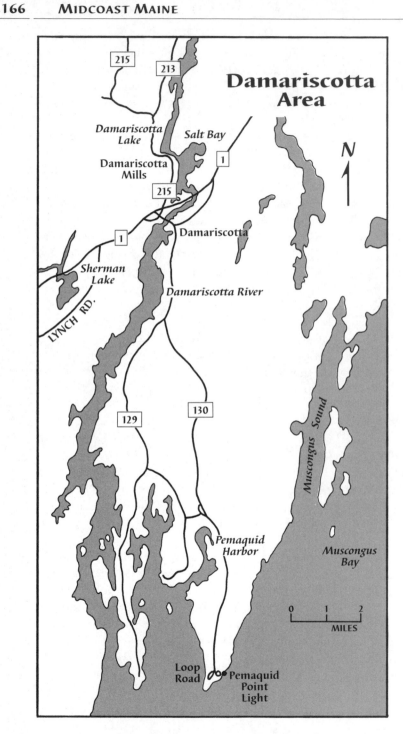

215

213

Damariscotta Area

Damariscotta Lake

Salt Bay

1

Damariscotta Mills

215

N

1

Damariscotta

Sherman Lake

Damariscotta River

LYNCH RD.

130

129

Muscongus Sound

Pemaquid Harbor

Muscongus Bay

0   1   2
MILES

Loop Road

Pemaquid Point Light

Sherman Lake (MAINE ATLAS map 7, A-2)

Sherman Lake, midway between Wiscasset and Damariscotta on Route 1, is always worth at least a quick stop. It is also a good spot to explore more leisurely by canoe. Measuring about 1 mile by 0.3 mile and bordered by an extensive cattail marsh, the lake is conveniently accessible from a highway rest stop (which includes a boat launch) and from two side roads that run along the eastern and western shores. In spring and fall the lush vegetation along the lake margin supports Mallards, American Black Ducks, Blue-winged and Green-winged teal, American Wigeons (uncommon), Northern Shovelers (rare), Wood and Ring-necked ducks, Common Goldeneyes, Buffleheads, Hooded Mergansers, and Ruddy Ducks (rare). In October and November this is an excellent place to see Lesser Scaup and American Coots.

Some of the more interesting nesting species to look for on or around Sherman Lake include Pied-billed Grebe, American Bittern, Green Heron (uncommon), Ring-necked Duck, Osprey, Marsh Wren, Warbling Vireo (in the deciduous trees around the parking lot), and Swamp Sparrow. This is also a good place to hear and possibly see two particularly reclusive species, Least Bittern and Virginia Rail. From late May through early August, Virginia Rails can often be heard and sometimes seen in the early morning, usually before sunrise. At least one pair of Least Bitterns has also nested in this area for many years, but given their secretive nature, they are easy to miss. Listen carefully for their soft, low coo-coo-coo-coo-coo-coo in spring.

Ducks often congregate on the southern end of the lake, which is visible from the access road along the east shore. If you have the time, bird along this road as visibility and respect for private property permit. You can also investigate this portion of the lake by canoe. An inconspicuous dirt road on the west shore of the lake (see "Directions," below) is a nice area to explore, too; the woods along this road can be especially good for spring migrants.

Sherman Lake is accessible year-round, free of charge. There are seasonal outhouses, picnic tables, and a boat launch at the rest stop.

DIRECTIONS

Sherman Lake is on the south side of Rt. 1, 3.2 miles east of the Wiscasset bridge and 3 miles west of Damariscotta. The rest stop is conspicuously marked. The access road that runs along the east shore of the lake (called "Dodge Rd." in the *Maine Atlas* but "Lynch Rd." on the road sign) turns south off Rt. 1, 0.6 mile east of the rest stop. The dirt road that runs along the west shore turns south off Rt. 1 immediately west of the bridge over the Sherman Lake inlet.

Salt Bay (*MAINE ATLAS* map 7, A-3)

Salt Bay, due north of Damariscotta, is a large (125+ acres), shallow, tidal portion of the Damariscotta River. This spot is worth checking at any time of year. Good numbers of waterfowl stop over on spring and fall migration, Barrow's Goldeneyes and Hooded Mergansers are regular in winter, and Bald Eagles nest nearby. Salt Bay is only a five-minute detour off Route 1, so at the very least, it is certainly convenient.

In March and April, Salt Bay can be full of waterfowl, particularly Canada Geese, Ring-necked Ducks, and Greater Scaup, along with smaller numbers of American Wigeons and Common Goldeneyes. Small numbers of Eurasian Wigeons (1 or 2) have been recorded on several occasions. A few Canvasbacks and Redheads are seen on the bay some years (usually between October and December), and Pied-billed Grebes and American Coots are occasional.

From November through March, as long as there is open water, Salt Bay is a reliable place to look for Barrow's Goldeneyes and Common and Hooded mergansers. As many as 100 Hoodeds are occasionally seen here at one time. The area you especially want to check is a small bridge across from a railroad embankment, where there is usually open water most of the winter (see "Directions," below). If you don't see the birds here, drive north a short way on Route 215 to another narrow bridge and look there. In most years, one or two Gadwalls also overwinter on the bay. Gulls roost out on the ice in winter, and you should take the time to scan them for a Glaucous or an Iceland Gull.

For as long as anyone can remember, a pair of Bald Eagles has nested nearby in Damariscotta Mills on the southern end of Damariscotta Lake. The birds are generally on the nest by mid-February, and they can sometimes be seen fishing over Salt Bay. By mid-April the locally nesting Ospreys are usually back, too; a pair nests atop a power-line pole on an island in the center of the bay, and you can get excellent looks at them as they go about the business of rearing their young.

Less majestic than eagles and Ospreys but also interesting are the birds that breed around the marshy borders of the bay. These include Least Bittern (regular in small numbers but easily missed), Wood Duck (nesting in open tree cavities), Virginia Rail, Sora, Willow and Alder flycatchers, and Swamp Sparrow.

Finally, it is also worth exploring Salt Bay for shorebirds, primarily in late summer and fall when these long-distance migrants sometimes stop over to feed on the exposed mudflats. A good spot to check is the southern end of the bay, at the intersection of Routes 1 and 215.

DIRECTIONS

FROM THE SOUTH: Take Rt. 1 to the Damariscotta-Newcastle exit, follow the exit ramp down to the stop sign at Main St., and go straight through the intersection onto Rt. 215 North. In 0.7 mile you will see the edge of Salt Bay; in another 0.5 mile is a spot on the right where you can pull off and scan (there's a good view of the Osprey nest from this stop). In another 0.7 mile is a narrow bridge and, on the right, a railroad embankment. This last spot is the best place to look for winter ducks, including Barrow's Goldeneyes and Hooded Mergansers. If you continue another 0.4 mile on Rt. 215 North, you will see another narrow bridge where you can scan; this is also a good spot to look for Hooded Mergansers.

FROM THE NORTH: Take Rt. 1 to the Newcastle/Damariscotta/ Damariscotta Mills exit and turn right onto Rt. 215 at the head of the exit. Continue 0.2 mile to the edge of Salt Bay and proceed as above.

Pemaquid Point (MAINE ATLAS map 7, C-3)

Fifteen miles south of Damariscotta, at the end of Pemaquid Neck, is a lovely promontory that is best known for its lighthouse and its vast expanse of rocks running toward the sea. As local birders well know, however, there is more to Pemaquid Point than its vistas. Like many other long peninsulas extending into open ocean, this is a fine spot to look for seabirds, waterfowl, and windblown vagrants year-round and for a good mix of landbirds on spring and fall migration. Although you are likely to see something of interest at Pemaquid Point at any time of year, it is an especially good spot to check after a strong easterly storm. Sooty, Royal, and Sandwich terns and Black Skimmer have all been recorded in this area as storm-swept vagrants. This is also one of the most reliable places south of Mount Desert Island to look for alcids in fall and winter. At any season, you can bird the point in a few hours or less.

Park by the lighthouse at the very end of the peninsula. Once you have satisfied yourself with the views, you can start looking for birds. Scan the water from the lighthouse, then walk back up the road to the north, investigating the trees and shrubs for landbirds. Don't neglect the grounds right around the lighthouse. During spring and fall migra-

tion, disoriented and windblown nocturnal migrants frequently concentrate on peninsulas such as Pemaquid. If you are here at dawn, it
can be very exciting to watch birds flying in from the ocean; they typically are exhausted and can be easily observed at close range.

Seabirds and waterfowl usually are highlights here at any time of
year. A scope will undoubtedly enhance your day's species list. Look
year-round for Red-throated and Common loons (the former rare in
summer), Northern Gannets (most common on spring and fall
migration and usually absent in midwinter), Common Eiders, all
three scoters, Great Black-backed and Herring gulls, Atlantic Puffins
(uncommon), and Black Guillemots. From spring through summer
you should also be able to see Double-crested Cormorants, Brant
(occasional from February into April), Bonaparte's and Laughing
gulls, and Common, Arctic, and Roseate terns. With a scope and
careful, persistent scanning during this season, you may also be able
to see Northern Fulmars (absent some years), Greater, Sooty, and
Manx shearwaters, Wilson's Storm-Petrels, Red-necked Phalaropes
(primarily in late summer and fall), a Parasitic or Pomarine Jaeger,
and Black-legged Kittiwakes.

In winter Pemaquid Point is a better place than most to look for
some hard-to-find species. Large numbers of Common Eiders raft offshore, and sometimes you can find a King Eider among them.
Harlequin Ducks are occasional, and Black-legged Kittiwakes are regular (although as our friend Mark Libby says, "You'll have to spend
more than ten minutes looking for them."). You can often see alcids
here, too, especially on a calm day when they don't disappear among
the waves. In fact, Pemaquid Point is one of the most reliable spots on
the Maine coast to look for alcids in fall and winter, with all six
species that occur in the Gulf of Maine being a distinct possibility
(although not in the same day!). Northeast storms in November and
December sometimes produce large flights of Dovekies and Razorbills and an occasional Atlantic Puffin. The point is also a good place
to look for Purple Sandpipers. Small numbers of Iceland and Glaucous gulls are usually reported each winter, and in some years a few
Common Black-headed Gulls are reported. Regular winter species
you can expect to see include Horned and Red-necked grebes, Great
Cormorant, and several species of common sea ducks.

Just north of the lighthouse is a 1-mile loop road that is lined
with coniferous trees and shrubs and that affords more good
overviews of open ocean. This is a good spot to look for migrating
landbirds, particularly warblers and sparrows (the latter primarily in
fall). As with all migrant traps, here it is possible to see just about all

of northern New England's regularly occurring passerines, if you hit the right day. Bear in mind that these outer peninsulas are notable haunts for Orange-crowned Warblers and Yellow-breasted Chats; look for them in dense thickets.

The loop road is also worth investigating for nesting birds. Common Ravens nest nearby, and in some years a few Boreal Chickadees and Red Crossbills do, too. Look and listen for such potential breeders as Olive-sided Flycatcher, Red-breasted Nuthatch, Brown Creeper, Winter Wren, Golden-crowned Kinglet, and several species of warblers. In winter look for crossbills and other winter finches.

One other spot on Pemaquid Neck that is worth checking, especially in winter, is Pemaquid Harbor (see "Directions," below). When the fishing boats come in, they attract large numbers of gulls, including an occasional Glaucous or Iceland Gull.

At any time of year, it is worth following Route 32 back to Route 1 and checking the east side of the Pemaquid peninsula, which overlooks Muscongus Bay and the Medomak River. Look for essentially the same species as you would from Pemaquid Point.

Pemaquid Point is accessible year-round. There is no fee, except at the lighthouse where a small fee is charged in summer. The only facilities are a few picnic tables at the lighthouse.

DIRECTIONS

FROM THE SOUTH: Take Rt. 1 to the Damariscotta-Newcastle exit, follow the exit ramp down to the stop sign, and turn right onto Main St. In 0.4 mile fork right onto Rt. 129 South, and in 2.9 miles fork left onto Rt. 130 South. The lighthouse is 11.9 miles south.

FROM THE NORTH: Take Rt. 1 to the Newcastle/Damariscotta/ Damariscotta Mills exit and at the head of the exit turn left onto Rt. 215. Continue 0.5 mile to the stop sign, turn left onto Main St., and then proceed as above.

FROM THE LIGHTHOUSE PARKING LOT TO THE HARBOR: Turn left almost immediately onto the paved loop road, which rejoins Rt. 130 in 1 mile. Continue 2.4 miles north on Rt. 130 and turn left, following signs for Pemaquid Beach. In 1.2 miles go straight through a confusing four-corner intersection and take the first right at Fort William Henry. The road leads down to the harbor.

LOCAL ACCOMMODATIONS

For information on local accommodations and services, write or call the Damariscotta Region Chamber of Commerce, P.O. Box 13, Damariscotta, ME 04543, telephone 207-563-8340.

Eastern Egg Rock   (*MAINE ATLAS* map 7, C-5)

Eastern Egg Rock, a tiny 7-acre island in the mouth of Muscongus Bay, is well known as the most accessible of four Maine islands where Atlantic Puffins nest. The island is also synonymous with seabird restoration work. Although "sea parrots" once bred on at least six islands in the Gulf of Maine, by the end of the nineteenth century they had been decimated by hunters and egg collectors. Only two small colonies remained, at Matinicus Rock and Machias Seal Island. It was against this background that in 1973 Dr. Stephen Kress of the National Audubon Society and the Cornell Laboratory of Ornithology initiated Project Puffin and began transplanting young puffins from Witless Bay, Newfoundland, to Eastern Egg Rock, in the hopes that the puffins would return to breed in the Gulf of Maine. More than twenty years of fieldwork and research have indeed paid off; thanks to Kress and his colleagues, a small colony of Atlantic Puffins once again exists on Eastern Egg Rock. The colony currently is holding steady at 16 pairs, and Kress hopes that gradually it will increase.

The best time to visit Eastern Egg Rock is in June and July when nesting activity is at its peak. Depending on your departure point (see the list of trips, below), it takes about 30 to 60 minutes to reach the island, which lies about 6 miles east of Pemaquid Point. Landing on the island is not permitted; the boats circle it slowly, and you can see the birds from the water. (To ensure the best view if you arrive in your own boat, take care to approach the birds slowly.) Although this is a small colony, and some of the birds will inevitably be away at sea feeding or hiding in their burrows, you do have a good chance of seeing small numbers of puffins here. And with a good look at even one bird, you will quickly appreciate why the birds have endeared themselves to so many people. With their striking plumage, bright red legs and feet, brightly colored bill, and comical stance, Atlantic Puffins are indeed enchanting.

The puffins may be the highlight of this trip, but they won't be all you see. Eastern Egg Rock is also one of Maine's largest Arctic, Common, and Roseate tern colonies and currently supports more than 1,000 pairs of these three species. Terns also suffered dramatically from unrestricted hunting and egg-collecting a century ago and, like the puffins, were extirpated as breeders on Eastern Egg Rock. In

1980, however—in apparent response to the elimination of nesting gulls on the island, the use of tern decoys, and playback of tern vocalizations—terns returned to Eastern Egg Rock. Since they are very effective at keeping away predatory gulls, the terns may well help secure the puffins' future.

Other species you are likely to see going to and from Eastern Egg Rock include Common Loon, Double-crested and possibly a few Great cormorants, Great Blue Heron, Common Eider, Osprey, Herring, Great Black-backed, and Laughing gulls (the last species nests on Eastern Egg Rock), and Black Guillemot. You may also see several Harbor Seals.

A trip to Eastern Egg Rock is inevitably fun and exciting as well as educational. Bring warm clothes (even in midsummer), rain gear, lip screen and sunscreen, a hat, seasickness medication (if you need it), sunglasses, and a few plastic bags to protect your binoculars and camera from spray on the boat. Call any of the following to arrange a trip.

- HARDY BOAT CRUISES—P.O. Box 326, New Harbor, ME 04554, telephone 800-278-3346. Daily trips from New Harbor. Also offers trips from Monhegan.
- CAP'N FISH—Pier One, Boothbay Harbor, ME 04538, telephone 207-633-3244 or 633-2626. Regular trips from Boothbay Harbor.
- MAINE AUDUBON SOCIETY—P.O. Box 6009, Falmouth, ME 04105, telephone 207-781-2330. At least one field trip in June and July.

Thomaston–Rockland Area

Weskeag Marsh
Owls Head State Park
Rockland Harbor

Situated at the head of the St. George River is the small, historic town of Thomaston—known for its lovely nineteenth-century homes but more conspicuously marked by the Maine State Prison at the western end of town and by the Dragon Cement factory and limestone quarry at the eastern end. Just north of Thomaston, at the southwest entrance to Penobscot Bay, is the city of Rockland, a busy fishing port and the world's largest lobster distribution center. Three sites in the Thomaston-Rockland area are of particular interest to birders and are conveniently located within about an 8-mile radius. You can visit all three in a half day or so.

Weskeag Marsh (*MAINE ATLAS* map 8, A-3)

Weskeag Marsh in South Thomaston is a large saltwater, brackish, and freshwater marsh system that is traversed by the Weskeag River and bordered by extensive hayfields and woodlots. It is a delightful area to bird, partly because it is the only good-sized marsh along this portion of the coast and partly because it is such a peaceful, little-used site. About half of the marsh and a portion of the adjoining uplands are owned by the state and make up a 537-acre tract officially known as the R. Waldo Tyler Wildlife Management Area. The Maine Department of Inland Fisheries and Wildlife manages the area, primarily for migrant and nesting waterfowl. Like other Maine marshes, Weskeag supports the greatest variety of birds between late March and early October, with the highlights being migrant waterfowl and shorebirds, nesting marsh birds (including Nelson's Sharp-tailed Sparrow), and feeding and roosting wading birds. It takes a bit of walking or canoeing to get into the heart of the marsh where you see the most birds, but the effort usually results in a broad variety of species. You will also want to check two nearby spots: a large cattail marsh just north of Weskeag Marsh and, to the south, the South Thomaston town landing on the Weskeag River. You can cover the entire Weskeag area thoroughly in two to three hours, although you will probably want to allow a bit longer if you plan to canoe through the marsh. The best time to bird the marsh is at high tide.

Weskeag Marsh is strongly tidal and includes a combination of tidal flats and pools, regularly flooded salt marsh and salt meadows, and shallow freshwater marshes with extensive cattail stands. These wetlands are accessible from Buttermilk Lane, a town road that crosses and then parallels (mostly from a distance of several hundred yards) the Weskeag River. There are no formal trails through the marsh, but you are welcome to park along the roadside and walk across any of the state-owned property. Wear boots, come well armed with mosquito repellent (especially on a windless day), and be prepared to walk at least a half mile or so across the salt meadows to get the best views of the birds. This can be tough going by midsummer when the grasses are high; be sure to keep your eyes open for potholes and ditches. (Some of these ditches were dug almost 200 years ago, when Weskeag was farmed for salt hay.) You will usually see the most shorebirds in the series of interconnected salt pans and pools on the west side of the marsh (several hundred yards from the road), where as many as 5,000 birds sometimes gather at high tide.

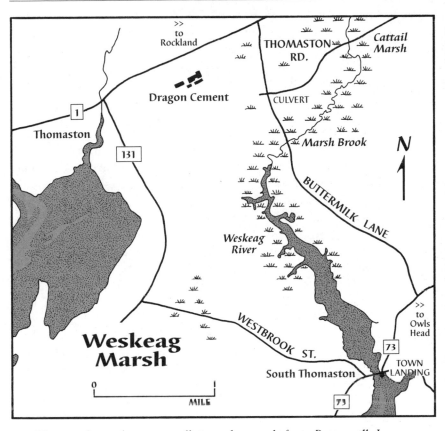

The two best places to walk into the marsh from Buttermilk Lane are 1 mile down the road from Route 1 (at the small parking area by the culvert, where the road crosses the Weskeag River; see "Directions," below) and 0.4 mile farther down the road (at the ridgetop). At either spot park along the roadside and walk into the marsh to the west, aiming for the series of interconnected pools on the west side of the river. If you are birding from the roadside with a scope, these two spots will also provide the best overviews of the marsh. Just off the road by the culvert is a densely vegetated pan that often harbors (especially on fall migration) unseen peep, Short-billed Dowitchers, and Common Snipe; check this area carefully before proceeding out into the marsh.

You can also canoe through the marsh. If you put in at the culvert on Buttermilk Lane at high tide, you can make it down to the town landing and back before low tide. One word of caution, though: there is a tricky riptide at the bridge in South Thomaston, so it is best not to go quite that far. Check a local newspaper for a tide table, noting that the tide on the river is usually at least 30 to 60 minutes later than that given for the Camden/Rockland area. Whichever way you decide to bird the marsh, please make every effort not to disturb nesting or roosting birds.

The birding is best at Weskeag Marsh between early May and late September, with late May to mid-July being the best time to find nesting species. The marsh begins to come alive by mid- to late March when the river is free of ice and the first migrant waterfowl begin stopping over to feed and rest. Regular spring and fall migrants include Canada Geese, Mallards, Wood, American Black, and Ring-necked ducks, Blue-winged and Green-winged teal, Northern Pintails, Buffleheads, American Wigeons, and all three mergansers. Snow Geese, Northern Shovelers, and Gadwalls are occasional. Once in a while you will also see a Pied-billed Grebe or Common Moorhen.

Common shorebirds to look for on spring and fall migration at Weskeag include Black-bellied and Semipalmated plovers, Killdeer, Greater and Lesser yellowlegs, Semipalmated and Least sandpipers, Ruddy Turnstones, Dunlin (in fall), and Short-billed Dowitchers. Look also for small but regular numbers of Red Knots and White-rumped (September), Pectoral, Solitary, Spotted, and Stilt sandpipers, and for an occasional American Golden-Plover, Willet, Whimbrel, Western Sandpiper, Long-billed Dowitcher, or Wilson's Phalarope. American Avocet has also been seen here on a few occasions. Most of these less common species are seen only during fall migration. In spring look for Common Snipe and American Woodcock displaying over the fields adjacent to the marsh and for an occasional Upland Sandpiper passing through. Northern Harriers are common migrants in both spring and fall.

In spring and summer look for feeding and roosting wading birds, among them Great Blue Herons, Snowy Egrets, small numbers of Glossy Ibis, and an occasional Green or Little Blue Heron, Black-crowned Night-Heron, or Great or Cattle Egret. Singing Nelson's Sharp-tailed Sparrows are usually quite easy to see perched in the tall grass along the stream; listen for their soft but distinctive two-noted song. Savannah and Swamp sparrows also nest in or around the marsh, and Northern Harriers, Ospreys, Bald Eagles (occasional), American Kestrels, Common Terns, and Belted Kingfishers hunt or feed in the area. Look around any cattails for nesting American Bitterns, Soras, Virginia Rails, and Marsh Wrens (there is a cattail pond right along Buttermilk Lane just north of the culvert). Sedge Wren has also nested in this area, although very sporadically. A pair of Red-tailed Hawks is probably nesting nearby and can be seen at almost any time of year. Also keep your eyes open for a Turkey Vulture soaring overhead; this species is now an established nester in the Camden Hills area to the north.

In the uplands around the marsh, look and listen for such characteristic nesters as Broad-winged Hawk, Barred Owl, Ruffed Grouse, Hairy and Downy woodpeckers, Eastern Kingbird, Great Crested and Alder flycatchers, Eastern Wood-Pewee, Black-capped Chickadee, Veery, Wood Thrush, Red-eyed Vireo, Chestnut-sided, Yellow, and Black-and-white warblers, Rose-breasted Grosbeak, Baltimore Oriole, Song Sparrow, Eastern Meadowlark, and Bobolink. An early morning walk at the height of the breeding season will often yield a wide variety of species.

Like any extensive open area, Weskeag is also a good place to look in winter for hawks and owls, particularly Rough-legged Hawk and Snowy and Short-eared owls, and for Northern Shrikes and Common Redpolls. Most days you probably won't see any of these hard-to-find species, but occasionally you will get lucky. You are more likely to find mixed flocks of Horned Larks, Snow Buntings, and occasionally Lapland Longspurs.

Two spots right near the marsh are also worth checking (see "Directions," below). The first is a large cattail marsh on the Thomaston Road. Check this spot in spring and summer for nesting species, particularly American Bittern, Sora, Virginia Rail, and Marsh Wren. It is private property, but you can scan it from the roadside. The other spot is the town landing on the Weskeag River in South Thomaston. Look for gulls year-round (Bonaparte's Gulls are usually regular in late summer and early fall), for Common Terns in spring and summer, and for common sea ducks (primarily Buffleheads, Common Goldeneyes, and Red-breasted Mergansers) from fall through spring. At any time of year it is worth scanning for a Bald Eagle.

Weskeag Marsh is open year-round, free of charge, from sunrise to sunset. There are no facilities. Please remember that this is a wildlife management area, not a refuge, and thus is open to hunting and trapping in season. If you are unfamiliar with what precautions should be taken during this season in Maine, please see the section entitled "Hunting" in the Introduction.

DIRECTIONS

Take Rt. 1 into Thomaston, and just east of the huge Dragon Cement plant turn south onto Buttermilk Lane (you will see a small sign "To So. Thomaston"). In 0.9 mile you will see a good-sized cattail pond on the left side of the road. In another 0.1 mile, where the road dips, you will see the culvert and, on both sides of the road (but primarily to the right), Weskeag Marsh. If you continue another 0.4 mile south, you will be atop the ridge that overlooks the marsh.

To reach the cattail marsh on Thomaston Rd., drive south down Buttermilk Lane 0.5 mile from Rt. 1 and turn left onto Thomaston Rd. (unmarked). In 0.8 mile you will see a large cattail marsh on either side of the road.

To reach the town landing in South Thomaston, continue 1.7 miles south from the culvert on Buttermilk Lane, turn right onto Rt. 73, and in 0.7 mile, where Rt. 73 takes a sharp right, you will see the town landing directly ahead.

Owls Head State Park (*MAINE ATLAS* map 14, E-4)

Owls Head State Park sits at the tip of the Owls Head peninsula and overlooks the southwestern entrance to Penobscot Bay. Included in this small but attractive state park are Owls Head Light, which was built in 1825, and the grounds surrounding it. As the only major land mass protruding from the western shore of Penobscot Bay, Owls Head can often be a good place to look for migrants. The park is primarily wooded—with a good mixture of spruces and firs, scattered birches, low deciduous trees, and raspberry thicket—and is attractive to a wide variety of birds. At almost any time of year, it is worth a quick stop to see if there is something of interest around. Look for migrant landbirds in spring and fall and for waterbirds and seabirds year-round. This is not an extensive area, so you can cover it quickly (a half hour or so). Even if you don't see many birds, you will enjoy the views.

Park in the designated lot by the shore, then walk the dirt road up to the lighthouse. Early on a clear morning at the height of spring or fall migration, the mixed habitat in the park can be productive for migrants. A good morning should yield a cross section of such common species as Northern Flicker, Alder and Least flycatchers, Blue Jay, Black-capped Chickadee, Red-breasted Nuthatch, Veery, Swainson's and Hermit thrushes, American Robin, Gray Catbird, Red-eyed Vireo, several species of warblers (look for Bay-breasted atop the spruces), Baltimore Oriole, several species of sparrows (look for Lincoln's in the low scrub), and Purple Finch. For a beautiful view of open ocean to the north and east and of the Camden Hills to the west, walk the boardwalk up to the lighthouse. Also walk the path down to the beach.

At any time of year you can see waterbirds and seabirds from Owls Head. Just remember that although the view is expansive, much of the water is a long way off, so a scope will come in handy. This is a good place to see Common Eiders and Black Guillemots year-round and Common Loons, common sea ducks, and occasionally Razorbills and Dovekies in winter. It is undoubtedly an excellent place to bird after a hurricane, but unfortunately we haven't had a chance to put it to the test yet!

Owls Head State Park is open year-round, free of charge, from 9:00 a.m. to sunset. Facilities include picnic tables and an outhouse.

DIRECTIONS

The access road to Owls Head State Park intersects Rt. 73 midway between Rockland and South Thomaston and is well marked. Turn east off Rt. 73 at the park sign and continue 3.6 miles to the park. Coming from Weskeag Marsh, turn left at the south end of Buttermilk Lane onto Rt. 73 and continue 1.3 miles to the access road.

Rockland Harbor (*MAINE ATLAS* map 14, E-4)

The city of Rockland overlooks Penobscot Bay, and its busy industrial waterfront—home port to fishing and lobster boats, ferries, and windjammers—has long been known among birders as a good spot to look for gulls, especially in winter. Like most good "gull spots," this won't be the most scenic place you've ever birded, but don't let that discourage you. If your idea of fun is looking over hundreds of gulls in the hopes of finding just a few oddballs, you will like Rockland Harbor just fine. Although you are most likely to find something unusual between late November and late March, it is worth checking the harbor at any time of year. It also attracts a good variety of ducks and other waterbirds. You should be able to cover the entire waterfront within a few hours.

At any time of year you can see large numbers of Great Black-backed, Herring, and Ring-billed gulls, and from November through March you can often find small numbers of Glaucous and Iceland gulls among them. At least a few Common Black-headed Gulls are usually recorded each year, too. Bonaparte's Gulls can be seen year-round but are usually most common in spring and from mid-July into fall. Laughing Gulls are regular in small numbers throughout the summer. Remember that sorting through large numbers of gulls takes patience and experience, and that familiarity with the various plumages of the common species will enable you to pick out something different.

In winter, also look for Common Loons, Horned and Red-necked grebes, Great Cormorants, Canada Geese, American Black Ducks,

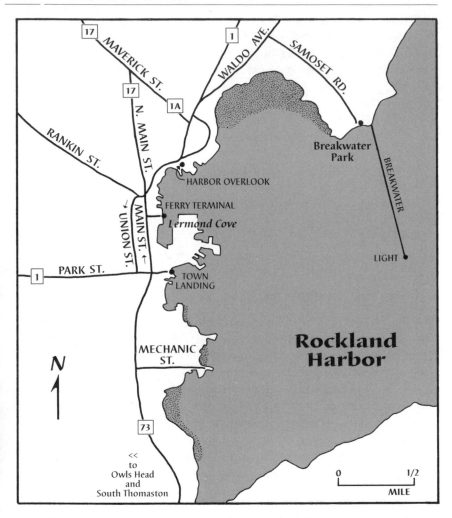

Common Eiders, Oldsquaws, White-winged Scoters, Greater Scaup, Common Goldeneyes, Buffleheads, Red-breasted Mergansers, and Black Guillemots. King Eiders and Barrow's Goldeneyes are occasional. One winter a pair of Canvasbacks lingered along the waterfront through January.

There are several spots along the Rockland waterfront from which you can scan the harbor, and any of them are worth checking. The five spots we mention below are the most accessible and usually the most productive. Each offers a different perspective on the harbor. The directions below may seem confusing if you just read them, but they are easy to follow. They take you from south to north, beginning on Route 73 on the south side of Rockland and ending at Breakwater Park on the north side.

Mechanic Street.   From Route 73 at the south end of Rockland, turn east onto Mechanic Street. Check the town park and public boat landing, which are 0.3 mile down the road on the right. Check the weedy field along the road, which can be good for sparrows. (Coming from Owls Head State Park, Mechanic Street is 1.2 miles north on Route 73; coming from Route 1 in Rockland, it is 0.6 mile south on Route 73.)

Town Landing.   Come back to Route 73, turn right, and go 0.6 mile north to the stoplight at the intersection of Routes 73 and 1. You are now facing the south end of Main Street (also Route 1), which is one-way going north. Instead of heading up Main Street, however, turn right here and go down Park Street to scan the water from the town landing.

Ferry Terminal.   Turn around, come back up Park Street, and turn right onto Main Street. In 0.3 mile you will see the Vinalhaven/North Haven ferry terminal on the right. This overlooks Lermond Cove. Pull into the parking lot and scan from both sides of the wharf.

Harbor Overlook.   Continue north on Main Street, and in 0.4 mile look for a narrow, unmarked dirt road on the right (just across the street from the Knox County Federal Credit Union). Drive a short way down here, to where you can overlook the harbor.

Breakwater Park.   Come back to Main Street and continue north. In 0.1 mile bear left with Route 1, and in 0.5 mile turn right at the stoplight onto Waldo Avenue. In another 0.5 mile turn right onto Samoset Road. In 0.6 mile, at the end of the road, you will see Breakwater Park directly ahead of you. Park and walk through the opening in the fence and out onto the breakwater. This beautiful granite structure extends almost a mile into Rockland Harbor and ends at the picturesque Rockland Breakwater Light, built in 1888. You aren't likely to see many gulls at this last stop, but you may get great looks at some other common (and not so common) waterbirds. Purple Sandpipers sometimes roost on the breakwater in winter, and King Eiders are occasional.

In fall, you should also take the time to scan the golf course that overlooks the breakwater. This is an excellent spot to look for American Golden-Plovers and Baird's, Pectoral, and Buff-breasted sandpipers.

If you happen to be taking one of the three ferries that depart from Rockland (to North Haven, Vinalhaven, or Matinicus Island), you will have the chance to see additional species. In summer look for Great and Double-crested cormorants (the latter far more common), Great Blue Herons, Ospreys, Laughing Gulls, and Common Terns. In winter look for loons, grebes, Brant (primarily March and April), sea ducks, and alcids (particularly Thick-billed Murres, Razorbills, and Dovekies). Year-round look for Common Loons, Bald Eagles, Common Eiders (often with ducklings in summer), and Black Guillemots.

DIRECTIONS

Take Rt. 1 into Rockland. From the south, Rt. 1 brings you into town on Park St. From the north, Rt. 1 intersects Park St., where you turn left.

LOCAL ACCOMMODATIONS

For information on local accommodations and services, write or call the Rockland-Thomaston Chamber of Commerce, P.O. Box 508, Rockland, ME 04841, telephone 207-596-0376.

Monhegan Island (*MAINE ATLAS* map 8, D-1)

Twelve miles offshore and well beyond the fringes of Muscongus Bay lies one of Maine's most enchanting offshore islands—Monhegan. Called *Monahigan* by the Indians, meaning "island of the sea," Monhegan was a well-established settlement as long ago as 1622, and through the years it has held a special charm for people who have come to know it. For nearly a century it has been a favorite haunt of birders, and anyone who has birded here knows why: Monhegan has a well-deserved reputation as Maine's finest migrant trap and annually attracts an astonishing variety of rare and uncommon species. Few if any other spots along the Maine coast can claim such a consistent list of rarities, among them Magnificent Frigatebird, Ivory Gull, Bridled Tern, Gyrfalcon, American Swallow-tailed Kite, Band-tailed Pigeon, White-winged Dove, Rufous Hummingbird, Say's Phoebe, Northern Wheatear, Lazuli, Painted, and Lark buntings, and Le Conte's and

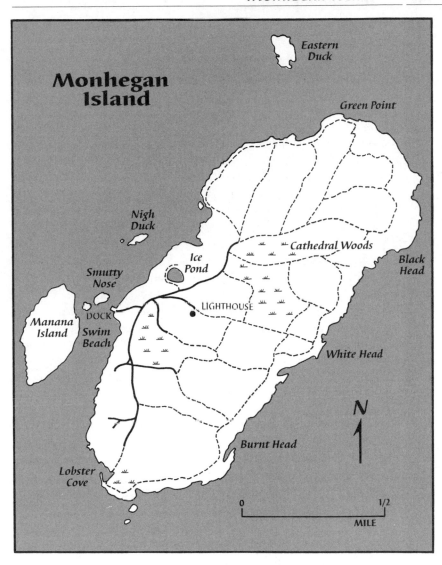

Henslow's sparrows, to name only some. Just as importantly, however, Monhegan can also be a wonderful place to see an outstanding variety of more common migrants, particularly breeding-plumage warblers in spring and sparrows and falcons (including Peregrines) in fall. Depending on the weather, you can often see impressive concentrations of birds. The best times to visit are the latter half of May and from early September through early October. By all means, though, visit Monhegan anytime you have the opportunity; it almost always has something interesting to offer. Although it is possible to make a day trip, this allows you only a few hours on the island at midday. Plan instead to spend at least one night and preferably two or three.

For a small, oval island that measures only 1.7 miles by 0.5 mile, Monhegan supports a surprising variety of habitats. A small fishing community encompasses about a third of the island; the rest has been preserved in its natural state. The island is bounded on the north and east by rocky headlands that rise to 160 feet, on the south by shallow, boulder-strewn coves, and on the west by the low-lying village. White and Red spruces and Balsam Firs blanket much of the interior, espe-cially on the northern half of the island. The southern end, which used to be farmed, is overgrown with Trailing Yew, alder swales, Shadbush, Chokecherry, and Rugosa Rose. There is a 2-acre ice pond at the north end of the village and a 9-acre swampy meadow (the island's pri-mary water source) in the village center. A mile or so of dirt roads run through the village, but the only traffic consists of a few old trucks that carry gear to and from the dock. Seventeen miles of trails wind across the island, and visitors enjoy remarkable freedom to roam at will. Be sure to get a copy of the island's trail map (available at the Monhegan Store and probably at all accommodations). Although most of the trails are marked with small signs or numbers on the trees, it is surprisingly easy to get lost or be misled by a deer trail.

Because of its offshore location, isolation (which means there are no other nearby islands on which birds can land), and small size (which means birds are more concentrated than they would be on a larger island), Monhegan is a particularly exciting place to be during migration. Spring migration usually peaks about the third week in May, and at its height it is not uncommon to see 75 to 100 species in a day. The highlight typically is the variety of warblers (as many as 20 species in a day). Fall migration is far more protracted and is usually best from early September through mid-October. It offers an excellent opportunity to study immature and fall-plumage passerines and the best chance of seeing uncommon migrants and vagrants. Although the more "regular" uncommon species vary from year to year, some of those to look for on Monhegan include Yellow-crowned Night-Heron, Yellow-billed Cuckoo, Western Kingbird, Philadelphia, White-eyed, and Yellow-throated vireos, Blue-winged and Orange-crowned war-blers, Yellow-breasted Chat, Yellow-headed Blackbird, Orchard Ori-ole, Blue Grosbeak, Dickcissel, and Clay-colored and Lark sparrows. You can often see a good variety of hawks, with Sharp-shinned Hawks, American Kestrels, and Merlins being especially numerous and a Peregrine Falcon or two being a solid possibility.

The most productive place to look for passerines is around the ice pond and along the village road from the ice pond south to Lobster Cove. It really doesn't matter where you start or which direction you go; just work your way along the roadside and stop wherever you see birds (or birders).

At the ice pond be sure to scan the north end of the pond. This is often a good spot to see a few species you won't find elsewhere on the island. Possibilities include Great Blue and Green herons, Black-crowned and Yellow-crowned night-herons, American Bittern, ducks (Mallard, American Black Duck, and Blue-winged or Green-winged teal are the most likely), Sora (uncommon), Common Snipe, Spotted and Solitary sandpipers, Greater and Lesser yellowlegs, and Belted Kingfisher. Heading south along the road, check the wet meadow, which often is a good place to see blackbirds (including Rusty) and sparrows (and also White-tailed Deer, especially at dusk). The dense vegetation around the edges attracts many species, notably Mourning Warbler and Lincoln's and Swamp sparrows. A little farther south, on the west side of the road, is tiny Swim Beach. Exhausted warblers sometimes feed on the beach fleas here and can be approached very closely. One May we actually hand-fed a few tired warblers here.

Just south of Swim Beach, next to the Careless Navigator restaurant, is a small building on the east side of the road with a steep ramp leading up to the second story. If New Yorkers—and indefatigable bird feeders—Tom and Josephine Martin are in residence (as they are every May and September), the yard will be full of birdseed, oranges, and who knows what else. On our most recent visit, Josephine was cooking squash for the birds. "I put it in the empty orange halves after the orioles clean them out," she said. Not surprisingly, the Martins' yard has become a regular stop with birders. Baltimore Orioles, Bobolinks, Rusty Blackbirds, Indigo Buntings, Purple Finches, Rose-breasted Grosbeaks, and a good variety of sparrows are often numerous here. Be sure to scan the lobster traps in the yard. Tom fills these with seed, too, and they often harbor sparrows. Any other feeding stations you encounter on the island also deserve a careful look.

Lobster Cove is an open, grassy area and can be a good place to see migrating hawks, waterfowl, seabirds, and occasionally a few shorebirds. On one of our more memorable visits to the cove, we watched a Peregrine Falcon stoop again and again on a flock of Common Eiders, and on many occasions we have watched Northern Gannets feeding offshore. This is a good place to use a scope. Other species to look for offshore include Common Loon, Greater and

Sooty shearwaters, Common Eider, scoters, Red-necked Phalarope, Black-legged Kittiwake (primarily September through March), Laughing Gull (May through September), Atlantic Puffin (occasional), and Black Guillemot. Look for landbirds on the rocks and in the short vegetation at Lobster Cove; this is another spot where we have often seen exhausted migrants, among them Common Moorhen (walking around at our feet!), Sedge Wren, Northern Wheatear, and Seaside Sparrow.

From Lobster Cove you can make your way back to the village the same way you came, or you can hike the Cliff Trail up the east side of the island and cut back to the village along one of the headland trails. We usually opt for the latter, if for no other reason than to enjoy the ocean views. This is also a good place to see a migrating Peregrine Falcon roosting on the cliffs, to watch Common Ravens at play, and to scan for seabirds. Three main trails will take you back to the village: Burnt Head, White Head, and Black Head. Look on these or any of the island's interior trails for spruce-fir inhabitants such as Red-breasted Nuthatch, Brown Creeper, Winter Wren, Golden-crowned and Ruby-crowned kinglets, Red and White-winged crossbills (uncommon), and White-throated Sparrow. If you are really ambitious and elect to hike all the way around the island (about a half-day expedition), Green Point on the north end is an excellent vantage point from which to scan, especially in the early morning at the height of fall migration, when you may be able to watch birds fly in across the water.

No one should miss a visit to Monhegan's lighthouse. This spectacular site overlooks the meadow and village, Manana Island just across the harbor, and a broad expanse of open ocean. In fall this can be an excellent place to watch migrating hawks, especially Merlins and Sharpies, which often chase prey in the brushy borders of the cemetery below. This is also a good place to look for one of Monhegan's rarest flowers, Fringed Gentian, which blooms from late August into September. If the lighthouse museum is open, be sure to visit it. You will find displays on fishing, lobstering, and island life and history, as well as an excellent photographic exhibit of the island's plants and birds. On a clear night, it is worth coming back to the lighthouse after dark to see and hear the many nocturnal migrants that often are attracted to the powerful light.

Behind the lighthouse is the ball field, which is bordered by brambles and fruiting shrubs that are attractive to Mourning Warblers, Yellow-breasted Chats, and Lincoln's Sparrows. Occasionally you will find a Clay-colored Sparrow or even an Upland Sandpiper here. In spring you can watch American Woodcock display at dawn and dusk; in fall, hawks are common overhead.

A few other spots on Monhegan also warrant mention. At Cathedral Woods you will find a beautiful old-growth Red Spruce forest where most of the trees are between 85 and 165 years old. The best birding here is often near the eastern end of the trail where the habitat is quite damp. Other productive trails include Underhill, Long Swamp, Red Ribbon, and Alder (all especially good for warblers).

In summer Monhegan can be a good place to see seabirds. Double-crested and sometimes a few Great cormorants, Common Eiders, Herring and Great Black-backed gulls, and Black Guillemots nest on three nearby rocks off the western and northern shores: Nigh Duck, Smutty Nose, and Eastern Duck. Other species you might see from the island or from the ferry anytime between May and September include Common Loon, Northern Fulmar, Greater, Sooty, and possibly Manx shearwaters, Wilson's Storm-Petrel (all tubenoses primarily from mid-June through July, and most likely if it is foggy or there is a strong easterly wind), Northern Gannet, Osprey, Laughing Gull, Common and Arctic terns, Atlantic Puffin, and Northern Phalarope (primarily August and early September). Look also for an occasional Parasitic or Pomarine Jaeger, Black-legged Kittiwake, or Razorbill. In general, you are not likely to see any landbirds of special interest on the island in summer. What you are likely to see, especially in July and August, are hundreds of day-visitors; this is the one season we avoid on the island.

Coming out to Monhegan in winter will require digging through your closet for the very warmest clothing you own, but it can be a lot of fun. From November through March look from the island (particularly from Lobster Cove or any of the three headlands) and from the ferry for Red-throated and Common loons, Horned and Red-necked grebes, Northern Gannets (with careful scanning sometimes seen in every month except January and February), Great Cormorants, and several common sea ducks. The ferry usually passes through huge flocks of Common Eiders (sometimes numbering 2,000 or more birds), and occasionally you can find a King Eider among them. You should also see large numbers of Herring and Great Black-backed gulls, smaller numbers of Black-legged Kittiwakes, and possibly a few Iceland and Glaucous gulls. This is also a good opportunity to look for winter alcids, especially from the ferry. You will undoubtedly see Black Guillemots, and the chance of seeing Razorbills is excellent and of seeing Dovekies quite good. Atlantic Puffins, Thick-billed and Common murres, and small numbers of Harlequin Ducks are irregular. On Monhegan itself look especially for Purple Sandpipers along the rocky shores; for such uncommon species as Snowy Owl, Northern Shrike, Common Redpoll, Red and White-winged crossbills (sometimes abundant), and Lapland Longspur; and for the odd passerine that winters over. Some of the unexpected species that Christmas Bird Count participants have turned up on the island include Common Black-headed and Ivory gulls, Eastern Meadowlark, Blue Grosbeak, and Lincoln's Sparrow.

As if a preponderance of birds weren't enough, there is more to Monhegan's charm. The island offers quiet and lovely vistas, a long and fascinating history, a delightful simplicity of life, and comfortable accommodations. If the birding is slow—and there certainly are times when it is—you can drop by artists' galleries and studios and the lighthouse museum. A single visit simply cannot do justice to Monhegan or its birds.

WHAT TO BRING TO MONHEGAN

Bring warm clothes for the ferry crossing and for cool nights (even in summer), good ankle-supportive shoes for hiking over rocks and trails, rain gear (even in fine weather, for the boat), and a good flashlight for walking after dark. Groceries, beer, and wine are available on the island, but they are often more expensive and the selection may be limited. There is no bank on the island. Please *do not* bring bikes or pets with you.

SERVICES AND ACCOMMODATIONS

There are three inns on Monhegan, several bed-and-breakfasts, and many rental cottages. There is also a post office and a few restaurants. Although you may be able to get a last-minute reservation for a room, particularly in May, September, or October, it is advisable to make your reservations several months in advance. Camping is not allowed on the island, so if you arrive without a reservation and can't get a room, you won't be staying long.

Below is a partial listing of accommodations. You can write any of them at Monhegan, ME 04852, or call them at the numbers listed.

- **SHINING SAILS GUEST HOUSE** (year-round), 800-606-9497, fax 207-596-7166. Also handles cottage rentals.
- **THE ISLAND INN** (mid-June to mid-September), 207-596-0371.
- **HITCHCOCK HOUSE** (year-round), 207-594-8137.
- **TRIBLER COTTAGE** (year-round), 207-594-2445.
- **MONHEGAN HOUSE** (mid-May to mid-October), 207-594-7983.
- **THE TRAILING YEW** (mid-May to mid-October), 207-596-0440.

FERRY SERVICE

Monhegan is served by passenger ferry year-round from Port Clyde and seasonally from Boothbay Harbor and New Harbor. Reservations are recommended. You must leave your car on the mainland, where parking is available for a small fee. For schedules, fares, and directions to the boat, contact the following.

- **FROM PORT CLYDE: MONHEGAN-THOMASTON BOAT LINE**—P.O. Box 238, Port Clyde, ME 04855, telephone 207-372-8848. A 70-minute trip via the *Laura B.* or *Elizabeth Ann*, which also provide year-round mail and freight service to Monhegan residents. In case of bad weather, the *Laura B.* and *Elizabeth Ann*, provide the most reliable service.

  As you head south toward Port Clyde on Rt. 131, allow a few minutes to stop along the road and scan Mosquito Harbor just south of Martinsville. This small cove, which opens to the left, is often good for waterfowl, shorebirds, and terns. American Oystercatcher, Marbled and Hudsonian godwits, and Royal Tern have occurred here in summer, Gyrfalcon and Northern Shrike in winter, and Fork-tailed Flycatcher in fall. The harbor definitely has more going for it than mosquitoes.

- **FROM BOOTHBAY HARBOR: CAPTS. BOB AND BILL CAMPBELL**—Boothbay Harbor, ME 04538, telephone 800-298-2284. A 90-minute trip via the *Balmy Days II.*

- **FROM NEW HARBOR: HARDY BOAT CRUISES**—P.O. Box 326, New Harbor, ME 04554, telephone 800-278-3346. A 60-minute trip via the *Hardy III.* Also makes trips from Monhegan to Eastern Egg Rock (see that chapter) to see nesting Atlantic Puffins.

Matinicus Rock & Matinicus Island

Matinicus Rock and Matinicus Island lie as far offshore as any islands along the Maine coast. Not surprisingly, both have long been of interest to birders. If you are especially keen to see nesting seabirds, including Atlantic Puffins and Razorbills, by all means consider a visit to Matinicus Rock. Five miles north is Matinicus Island, which can be

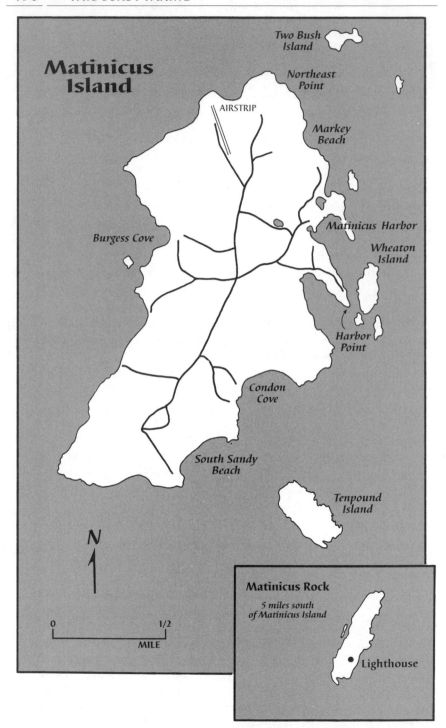

Matinicus
Island

Two Bush
Island

Northeast
Point

AIRSTRIP

Markey
Beach

Burgess Cove

Matinicus Harbor

Wheaton
Island

Harbor
Point

Condon
Cove

South Sandy
Beach

Tenpound
Island

N

0   1/2
MILE

Matinicus Rock

5 miles south
of Matinicus Island

Lighthouse

a particularly exciting place to bird on spring and fall migration. Neither of these islands is readily accessible, but with a little advance planning you can easily arrange trips to both.

Matinicus Rock (*MAINE ATLAS* map 9, D-1)

About 24 miles southeast of Rockland lies tiny Matinicus Rock—a piece of barren and windswept granite rising only 60 feet above the open ocean. For more than a century this has been one of Maine's most famous and most important seabird-nesting islands, and fortunately its isolation has largely protected it. Although seabird populations have declined on many Maine islands, here you can still find healthy nesting populations of 10 offshore species: Leach's Storm-Petrel, Common Eider, Herring, Great Black-backed, and Laughing gulls, Arctic and Common terns, Atlantic Puffin, Razorbill, and Black Guillemot. Since 1992 efforts have also been under way by the National Audubon Society to establish another breeding species: Common Murre.

Our favorite time to visit Matinicus Rock is between early June and mid-July, when nesting activity is at its peak. Depending on your departure point (see the list of trips, below), getting to the rock usually takes two to two and a half hours. Excitement inevitably builds the farther seaward you go, as does your chance of seeing pelagic species. Possibilities include Northern Fulmar (absent some years), Greater, Sooty, and occasionally Manx shearwaters, Wilson's Storm-Petrel, Northern Gannet, Red-necked Phalarope, Black-legged Kittiwake, Pomarine Jaeger (uncommon), and Common Murre, as well as any of the breeding species mentioned above. Also look for whales, particularly Harbor Porpoise and Minke Whales, and around Matinicus Rock for Harbor and, less commonly, Gray seals.

Boats are not allowed to land on Matinicus Rock, but they circle it at leisure, and you can get excellent looks at all of the birds (except the Leach's Storm-Petrels, which normally come and go from their nesting colonies only after dark). In addition to the nesting species, you should see Double-crested and a few Great cormorants and small numbers of Common Murres. You may have to look carefully at the murres to see if you are looking at real birds or at the decoys that are part of the restoration project.

Ask your boat operator if it is also possible to go around Seal Island National Wildlife Refuge to the northeast. Since 1984 the National Audubon Society, U.S. Fish and Wildlife Service, and Canadian Wildlife Service have successfully worked to restore Atlantic

Puffins and Arctic and Common terns to this island. A few pairs of Great Cormorants also nest here, and efforts are under way to attract nesting Razorbills. Although Seal Island is off-limits to the public (partly because of the nesting birds and partly because live ammunition remains on the island from former military training), you can get a good look at the birds from the water.

Any trip that goes as far offshore as Matinicus Rock requires a healthy sense of adventure. Even on a beautiful summer day, be prepared for the possibility of large swells, wind, and spray. Pack whatever food and drink you will need, rain gear, warm clothes, sunscreen and lip screen, sunglasses, seasickness medication (if you need it), and a few plastic bags to protect your binoculars and camera. As one boat operator says, "This is a trip for those who are serious about wanting to see seabirds in their habitat."

To arrange a trip to Matinicus Rock, write or call any of the following. Trips are, of course, weather dependent.

- ATLANTIC EXPEDITIONS—HC 35 Box 290, St. George, ME 04857, telephone 207-372-8621. Regular trips from Rockland.
- HARDY BOAT CRUISES—P.O. Box 326, New Harbor, ME 04554, telephone 800-278-3346. Occasional trips from New Harbor.
- MAINE AUDUBON SOCIETY—P.O. Box 6009, Falmouth, ME 04105, telephone 207-781-2330. At least one trip in June or July.
- ON MATINICUS ISLAND—contact Dick Moody (207-366-3700 days, 366-3926 evenings) or Albert Bunker (366-3737).

Matinicus Island (*MAINE ATLAS* map 9, C-1)

Five miles north of Matinicus Rock is Matinicus Island, the largest of the eight islands that make up the Matinicus Archipelago. If you love islands and offshore birding, consider a visit to this beautiful, isolated island. The birding is at its best during spring and fall migration, when Matinicus may well rival Monhegan as Maine's best migrant trap. Unlike Monhegan, however, Matinicus has never attracted many birders, primarily because the island is not as readily accessible and because for many years no regular overnight accommodations were available. We are happy to report that today Matinicus is more accessible than ever and that there are indeed overnight accommodations. The best times to visit are in the latter half of May and anytime between early September and early October. Plan to spend at least two or three nights on the island.

Matinicus is a low-lying island that measures only 2 miles long and 1 mile wide—big enough to support a nice variety of habitats and small enough to be easily covered on foot. Broad rocky shores border the northern, eastern, and western sides of the island; on the southern side is a large meadow that slopes down to a sand beach. Tall spruces and firs are distributed across the island in small, dense stands, especially on the eastern and western sides. The interior is more open; here, grassy fields and low deciduous shrubs—particularly alders, elders, and shadbush—are the dominant vegetation. There is a sizable cattail marsh on the northeast shore (just below Markey Beach) and a small freshwater pond and alder swale in the interior near the village store. One dirt road (the northern end of which is an airstrip) runs the length of the island; another extends east to the harbor and village center. The permanent population on Matinicus numbers fewer than 100, but summer residents and visitors can triple or quadruple that.

Birding is at its best on Matinicus during spring and fall migration when, depending on the weather, both the numbers and variety of birds passing through can be impressive. If the weather is at all cooperative, you should have an excellent chance of seeing a rich cross section of common migrants (75+ species in a day is not unusual) and quite likely a surprise bird or two as well. Spring migration usually peaks about the third week in May; fall migration can be good anytime from the end of August until at least mid-October. Each season has its highlights: most years, spring offers a dazzling array of breeding-plumage warblers, whereas fall offers excellent looks at southbound hawks (particularly falcons and accipiters) and immature and fall-plumage passerines (especially sparrows). Late summer and fall are also the best times to look for uncommon migrants and vagrants. Among the more intriguing records in that category from Matinicus are Gyrfalcon, Red-headed Woodpecker, Western Kingbird, Scissor-tailed Flycatcher, White-eyed and Yellow-throated vireos, Yellow-breasted Chat, Orchard Oriole, Dickcissel, and Lark Sparrow.

You can find birds just about anywhere on Matinicus, but a few consistently good spots merit special mention. The first of these is the airstrip on the north end of the island, which is bordered by a combination of low shrubs and tall conifers. During migration look for Horned Larks on the runway and for warblers (including Tennessee, Bay-breasted, Cape May, and Blackpoll) and spruce-fir residents in the tall conifers. This is also a good area to look for Red and White-winged crossbills, both of which are highly irregular. As you work your way south down the road, you are likely to see or hear such species as Olive-sided and Yellow-bellied flycatchers, Blue Jay, American Crow, Black-capped Chickadee, Red-breasted Nuthatch, Winter

Wren, Ruby-crowned and Golden-crowned kinglets, Hermit and Swainson's thrushes, Solitary and Red-eyed vireos, Northern Parula, Yellow-rumped, Black-throated Green, and Bay-breasted warblers, White-throated Sparrow, and Purple Finch.

Check the pond and alder swale in the village center for migrating warblers and sparrows (including Lincoln's Sparrow) and for nesting Green Herons, and check the cattail marsh just south of Markey Beach for freshwater species such as Swamp Sparrow. Harbor Point on the eastern shore is a good early morning stop on migration. Condon Cove, a little farther south, is a reliable spot to see Common Eiders rafting and a few shorebirds. Like most offshore islands, Matinicus does not attract much in the way of shorebirds, but Black-bellied Plover, Greater and Lesser yellowlegs, Spotted Sandpiper, and Ruddy Turnstone are all solid possibilities. Finally, check the cemetery and meadow at the south end of the island. These and other open areas on the island often host an excellent variety of species, among them Northern Flicker, Eastern Kingbird, Tree and Barn swallows, Eastern Bluebird, Cedar Waxwing, Baltimore Oriole, Rose-breasted Grosbeak, Indigo Bunting, Scarlet Tanager, Savannah and Song sparrows, and Bobolink. On a clear fall day with northwest winds, this is also an ideal place to watch accipiters and falcons—especially Sharp-shinned Hawks, Merlins, and occasionally Peregrines—chase prey. Also scan from the southern end of the island for pelagics, looking for the same species you would expect to see on or around Matinicus Rock. These same species may also be seen on the boat trip to and from the island.

Wherever you are on the island, you are likely to see and hear Common Ravens overhead and at least hear Ring-necked Pheasants.

Birders who have visited some of Maine's other offshore islands will find Matinicus to be distinctly different. The feeling of isolation, the notoriously tight-knit fishing community, and the lack of any trappings for tourists give Matinicus a rugged flavor all its own. With its combination of great natural beauty and its potential for outstanding birding, it also has all the makings for a wonderful birding adventure.

WHAT TO BRING TO MATINICUS

Bring warm clothes for the boat crossing and for cool nights (even in summer), sturdy walking shoes, rain gear, and a good flashlight for walking after dark. There is no store on the island, so if you are renting a cottage, you will also need to bring groceries.

SERVICES AND ACCOMMODATIONS

Matinicus has a post office, one seasonal restaurant, one bed-and-

breakfast, and several rental cottages. For more information, write the following at Matinicus, ME 04851, or call them at the numbers listed.
- TUCKANUCK LODGE—a bed-and-breakfast (May 1 to late October), 207-366-3830. Bike rentals available.
- FOR A LIST OF COTTAGE RENTALS—write or call the Matinicus Chamber of Commerce, 207-366-3868.

PASSENGER SERVICE
There are three main ways to get to and from Matinicus.
- CAPTAIN RICHARD MOODY—takes passengers between Matinicus and Rockland in his 40-foot boat Mary and Donna. To make a reservation, write or call Dick at Matinicus Island, ME 04851, telephone 207-366-3700 (daytime) or 366-3926 (evenings). Dick also makes trips to Matinicus Rock.
- THE NORTH HAVEN, A STATE FERRY—makes a trip to Matinicus about once a month from Rockland. For reservations, write or call the Maine State Ferry Service, P.O. Box 645, Rockland, ME 04841, telephone 207-596-2202.
- PENOBSCOT AIR SERVICE—makes daily flights to Matinicus, weather permitting, from Owls Head. It is a 12-minute flight (and not as expensive as you might think). Write or call Penobscot Air Service, P.O. Box 1286, Rockland, ME 04841, telephone 207-596-6211.

Camden Hills State Park
(MAINE ATLAS map 14, D-4)

Camden Hills State Park, in the towns of Camden and Lincolnville, provides convenient access to 5,500 acres of continuous mixed woods. It also provides access to several peaks that offer beautiful overviews of Camden Harbor and Penobscot Bay to the east and of Megunticook Lake and several ponds to the west. Birders know the park primarily as a good hawk-watching site (especially in fall) and as the spot where Turkey Vultures were first confirmed nesting in Maine, in 1982. You can see far more than hawks, however, in the Camden Hills; the area may not offer any "specialties," but it does offer a lovely and extensive stand of forested habitat in which you can find a good mix of migrant and breeding landbirds. There are 25 miles of hiking trails in the park, so you can certainly cover plenty of territory, ranging from lowland deciduous woods to mixed softwoods, sheer cliffs, and open ledges. The birding is most interesting between late April, when the first good

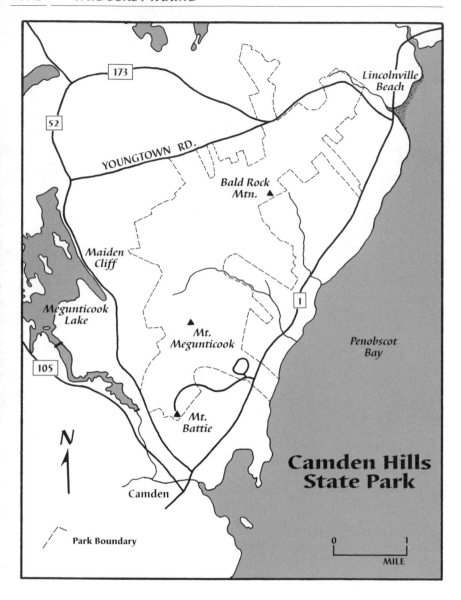

waves of passerines start moving through in earnest, through October and early November, when the last of the hawks move through. At any time during these months, you can easily spend the better part of a day hiking and birding in this lovely area. Be sure to get a trail map at the park gate.

Rising prominently from an otherwise low-lying stretch of coast, the Camden Hills consist of a small range running southwest–north-

east. The highest summit in the group is 1,380-foot-high Mt. Megunticook—hardly a mountain by many people's standards but nonetheless Maine's second-highest coastal peak. Smaller peaks in the
range include, among others, Ragged Mountain (1,300 feet), Bald
Mountain (1,272 feet), Bald Rock Mountain (1,100 feet), Mt. Battie
(800 feet), and Maiden Cliff (800 feet). You will find a good description of the park and its many trails in the AMC *Maine Mountain Guide*
(see Appendix D), which we recommend consulting if you plan to do
much hiking here.

The easiest way to bird the park is from the park headquarters on
Route 1 in Camden. From here you can drive (or walk) 1.6 miles to
the summit of Mt. Battie, which offers a stunning overview of Camden Harbor and the islands of Penobscot Bay. During migration this
is a convenient and productive spot from which to look for hawks,
and the low scrub around the parking lot can be good for landbirds.
At the edge of the parking lot, the Tablelands Trail leads 1.5 miles to
Ocean Lookout on Mt. Megunticook. This pleasant hike can be productive for both migrant and breeding species.

Although small numbers of hawks can be seen moving north over
the Camden Hills in spring (some as early as late March), the fall
migration usually is much more pronounced. On a clear day with
northwest winds, primarily between mid-September and late October, you can often see a good variety of species. You need to be on
one of the peaks, of course, to see much. The summit of Mt. Battie is
certainly convenient and popular with many birders, but it can also
be fun to hike to one of the other summits. The Maiden Cliff Trail
(off Route 52) and Bald Rock Mountain (in Lincolnville) are also popular with hawk-watchers (see "Directions," below). Common migrants
over the Camden Hills include Turkey Vultures, Northern Harriers,
Ospreys, Sharp-shinned, Red-tailed, and Broad-winged hawks, American Kestrels, and Merlins. Less regular but by no means rare are Bald
Eagles, Cooper's and Red-shouldered hawks, Northern Goshawks,
and Peregrine Falcons. The "best" migrant we have ever seen in this
area was unquestionably a Black Vulture, which we looked *down* on in
stunned surprise from atop Mt. Battie in early September one year.

You can also see a wide variety of migrant landbirds and breeding
birds in the park. Some of the more interesting species to look for during the breeding season (many of them characteristic of more
southerly areas) include Turkey Vulture, Northern Goshawk, Broad-
winged Hawk, Ruffed Grouse, Great Horned and Barred owls, Pileated
Woodpecker, Great Crested and Least flycatchers, Veery, Wood and
Hermit thrushes, Black-throated Blue, Yellow-rumped, Black-throated

Green, and Blackburnian warblers, Ovenbird, Scarlet Tanager, Rose-breasted Grosbeak, and Eastern Towhee.

The Mt. Battie Road is open from May 1 to October 31 from 9:00 a.m. to sunset, and a small fee is charged. In the off-season, you are welcome to park outside the gate (as long as your vehicle does not obstruct the gate or road) and walk into the park.

The campground is open from May 15 to October 15 and includes campsites, rest rooms, and showers. A small fee is charged. For more information, write or call Camden Hills State Park, Belfast Road, Camden, ME 04843, telephone 207-236-3109 or 236-0849.

DIRECTIONS

The entrance to the park headquarters is on the west side of Rt. 1 north of Camden and is prominently marked with a large sign.

The Bald Rock Mountain Trail (0.8 mile long) begins in Lincolnville, 1.3 miles down the Ski Shelter Trail. Turn west off Rt. 1 in Lincolnville onto Rt. 173, continue 2.3 miles, and turn left onto Youngtown Rd. Immediately ahead on the left you will see the Ski Shelter Trail parking area, well marked with a park sign (see *Maine Atlas* map 14, C-4).

The Maiden Cliff Trail (1 mile long) starts on the east side of Rt. 52 (you will see the parking area on the side of the road), 2.9 miles north of the intersection of Rts. 1 and 52.

LOCAL ACCOMMODATIONS

For information on local accommodations and services, write or call the Rockport-Camden-Lincolnville Chamber of Commerce, P.O. Box 919, Camden, ME 04843, telephone 207-236-4404.

Additional Sites of Interest

Maquoit Bay (*MAINE ATLAS* map 6, C-3)

Maquoit Bay in Brunswick is a good area to investigate for shorebirds and waterfowl. You won't find exceptional numbers of birds here, but oftentimes you will find a surprisingly good variety. This large, shallow bay is especially productive for waterfowl in spring (March through May), when hundreds of American Black Ducks congregate at the head of the bay along with smaller numbers of Mallards, Northern Pintails, Blue-winged and Green-winged teal, and American

Wigeons. A few Northern Shovelers and Gadwalls, both scarce in Maine, often appear annually, too.

By the time the ducks have dispersed from the bay, the shore-birds are moving through; except for a few weeks in early July, you can continue to see them well into October. In spring, Black-bellied and Semipalmated plovers, Greater and Lesser yellowlegs, Dunlin, Red Knots (a few), and Pectoral, Least, and Semipalmated sandpipers all occur regularly. In addition to these migrants, rarities have included Whimbrel, Hudsonian Godwit, Ruff, and all three phalaropes. In fall (which for shorebirds means primarily from mid-July through October), numbers of birds are much higher. Red Knots, White-rumped and Western sandpipers, and a few Long-billed Dowitchers can sometimes be found among the more regular migrants.

There are other birds to enjoy as well. In summer, Great Blue Herons and Snowy Egrets feed in the shallow waters; Saltmarsh Sharp-tailed, Nelson's Sharp-tailed, and Savannah sparrows can be heard singing from the salt marsh to the east, and Eastern Meadow-larks and Bobolinks breed in the large field to the west (the salt marsh and field are both private property). In fall, the bay's location makes it a good site to watch for migrant hawks, including Ospreys, Northern Harriers, Sharp-shinned Hawks, American Kestrels, Merlins, and Peregrine Falcons (the last in small numbers). In spring, one or two Common Black-headed Gulls sometime occur among the large flocks of Ring-billed Gulls.

The bay is very shallow, so it is imperative to be on hand some two and a half to three hours before or after high tide, when the shorebirds and ducks are concentrated on the mudflats.

From the center of Brunswick, follow Maine Street south, passing Bowdoin College on the left and, in another mile, Parkview Memorial Hospital, also on the left. When the road forks, 0.3 mile south of the hospital, bear right onto Maquoit Road. In 1.9 miles, where the road takes a sharp right, you will see a dirt parking area at the head of the bay directly ahead. This is a public boat landing, and most of the bay and part of the marsh can be observed from it.

Bath Waterfront (MAINE ATLAS map 6, B-5)

The historic city of Bath lies on the Kennebec River, and on the north side of the city is a public boat landing that provides an ideal spot from which to scan the river. From November through at least early April, this is an excellent place to see, at very close range, good numbers of Common and Red-breasted mergansers and Common Goldeneyes. Occasionally you can also find a few Barrow's Goldeneyes. In midwinter hundreds of gulls usually roost on the ice offshore (the amount of ice can vary dramatically with the tide), and Iceland and Glaucous gulls are regular among the more abundant Herring, Great Black-backed, and Ring-billed gulls. Many of the gulls are attracted by a fish-canning factory at the Stinson Seafood Company just south of the boat landing. Look carefully for Bald Eagles (both adults and subadults), which sometimes roost on the ice or perch across the shore in the pines. If the gulls suddenly take off, there is probably an eagle overhead.

Between April and September, you should also keep an eye out for a Peregrine Falcon along the waterfront. Since the spring of 1992, an adult bird has been spotted regularly during the breeding season in the vicinity of the Carleton Bridge over the Kennebec, where it feeds on the plentiful supply of pigeons.

The public boat landing is accessible year-round, free of charge.

Coming into Bath from the south on Route 1, take the Historic Bath exit. At the stoplight at the bottom of the hill, turn left onto Washington Street; in 0.4 mile turn right onto Linden Street; and in another 0.1 mile turn left onto Front Street, which parallels the river. In 0.5 mile Front Street merges into Bower Street. Go straight here, and in 0.1 mile fork right at the public boat landing sign. You will see the waterfront directly ahead, with ample parking.

Coming into Bath from the north on Route 1, cross the Kennebec River, and on the south side of the bridge, take the Bath/Front Street exit. Bear right onto Front Street and follow it 0.9 mile to its merger with Bower Street. Proceed as from the south.

Clarry Hill (*MAINE ATLAS* map 14, D-1)

In the small town of Union, about 10 miles due west of Camden, is a lovely blueberry barren atop Clarry Hill. Local birders know this as a delightful place to observe the spring and fall hawk migration and as a reliable spot to look for small numbers of nesting Upland Sandpipers, Eastern Bluebirds, and Vesper and Savannah sparrows. Also nesting here are Northern Goshawks, American Kestrels, Barred Owls, and Common Ravens. Red-shouldered Hawks probably nest nearby, too, as a pair can often be seen here. Turkey Vultures, which nest just to the east in the Camden Hills, are also seen regularly in summer. Small numbers of American Golden-Plovers and Whimbrels are regular southbound migrants in late summer and early fall.

Clarry Hill is private property, but a dirt road that leads to the top is used regularly by local people. There is a small dirt parking area at the top. Please do not venture into the blueberries, and do not pick them (besides belonging to someone else, they are sprayed with herbicides).

Clarry Hill Road turns south off Route 17, 0.7 mile west of the intersection of Routes 17 and 131 in Union. Proceed 1.9 miles down the road, then turn right onto the dirt road that leads to the top of Clarry Hill.

Stockton Springs (*MAINE ATLAS* map 15, A-1)

For Maine birders, Stockton Springs is synonymous with Ruddy Ducks. Ever since small numbers of these delightful birds were found wintering off Cape Jellison in the mouth of the Penobscot River some years ago, birders have come to realize that this area is particularly rich in waterfowl. From mid-October through at least early December, some 30 to 50 Ruddy Ducks can usually be found here, along with larger numbers of Mallards, American Black Ducks, Greater Scaup, Common Goldeneyes, and Buffleheads. Occasionally you can also find a few Barrow's Goldeneyes. Red-throated Loons and Red-necked Grebes are regular in fall, and there are usually good numbers of Bonaparte's and Ring-billed gulls then, too. Iceland and Glaucous gulls are occasional among the Herring and Great Black-backed gulls in winter, and from late July through winter, Little and Common Black-headed gulls are also possible. Bald Eagle is a solid possibility at any time of year.

There are three main areas to check on Cape Jellison: Fort Point Cove on the east side of the peninsula, Stockton Harbor on the west side, and Fort Point State Park on the easternmost tip. The state park is a small area of mixed woods and shrubs, and in spring and fall it can often be productive for migrants.

Turn south off Route 1 in Stockton Springs, following signs for Fort Point State Park, and in 0.7 mile (just after the railroad tracks) fork left onto East Cape Road. In 1.3 miles you will see Fort Point Cove. Park along the road beyond the houses and scan. A telescope is almost essential here, as many of the ducks may be well offshore. Continue another 1.2 miles down East Cape Road and turn left onto the park road. Bird the shrubby areas near the Coast Guard station and along the road. In winter, check the ledges offshore; King Eiders are occasional here. Walk the short trail that circles the park, and be sure to bird around the picnic area.

Return to the fork by the railroad tracks, turn left, and in 0.2 mile you will see Stockton Harbor. From late July through October, you can sometimes see hundreds of shorebirds here at low tide, and in winter you can sometimes find a Glaucous or an Iceland Gull.

Fort Point State Park is open year-round from 9:00 a.m. to sunset. A small fee is charged in summer. Facilities include a 200-foot pier, boat launch, picnic tables, grills, and toilets.

Belfast, Bucksport, & Barrow's Goldeneyes

There are two particularly reliable places in the midcoast area to look for Barrow's Goldeneyes between November and March. One is Belfast Bay, where Route 1 crosses the mouth of the Passagassawakeag River (see *Maine Atlas* map 14, A-5). Just south of Route 1 is an old bridge over the river, and this is often a good spot from which to scan. The other location is the Penobscot River in Bucksport, where Route 1 crosses the Eastern Channel of the Penobscot between Bucksport and the northern tip of Verona Island (see *Maine Atlas* map 23, E-2). Just south of the bridge, turn west and almost immediately take the second right down to the public boat landing on the river.

Although Bucksport has traditionally been the more reliable of these two sites, in recent years we have been seeing more Barrow's Goldeneyes at Belfast Bay. One day last March we counted 20-plus birds here—a treat by just about anyone's standards.

MOUNT DESERT REGION

The narrow coastal corridor bounded on the west by Penobscot Bay and on the east by Frenchman Bay is one of Maine's smallest yet most distinctive natural areas: the Mount Desert region. Even in a state that has long been famous for its beautiful and varied landscapes, this area is exceptional. Here you will find a unique mix of mountains, sea, and domed granitic islands—a combination that occurs nowhere else along the Maine coast. The islands are larger and more numerous than farther south, the bays are broader, and the water is colder (which means you will encounter more fog). Almost everywhere you look is evidence of glacial scouring, from kettle-hole ponds to U-shaped valleys and huge erratic boulders. The topography—unusually hilly for the Maine coast—includes Cadillac Mountain, at 1,530 feet the highest point on the eastern United States seaboard.

Not surprisingly, the birding in this region is also remarkably varied. Of the nearly 420 species of birds that have been recorded in Maine, at least 320 have been seen just on Mount Desert Island. Highlights include boreal landbirds and an excellent variety of waterbirds year-round, nesting Peregrine Falcons and at least 21 species of nesting warblers, good numbers of migrant landbirds in spring and fall, the highest concentration of wintering Harlequin Ducks in eastern North America, and the opportunity to do some true pelagic birding (primarily between mid-June and late September). The region is also of interest as a contact zone for many northern and southern bird species.

Although birding in the Mount Desert region can be excellent year-round, you will find the greatest diversity of species between mid-May and late September. Our favorite time to visit is in early or mid-June, when the song is at its peak, the warblers are a festival of color, and the region is not too crowded with visitors.

Isle au Haut   (*MAINE ATLAS* map 9, A-4)

When Samuel de Champlain sailed up the Maine coast in 1604, he called the outermost island in Penobscot Bay *Isle au Haut* (which in Maine is pronounced "Isle oh-ho"). Rising abruptly from the sea, the "high island" named by the famous French explorer has since come to be known as one of Maine's loveliest and most enchanting offshore islands. It is also a fine place to bird, and fortunately it is accessible year-round by mail boat from the town of Stonington on Deer Isle.

Separated from the mainland by 8 miles of island-dotted waters, Isle au Haut is an outpost of Acadia National Park, whose boundaries encompass about half of the island's 4,700 acres. Although many birders know Isle au Haut best for its high concentration of wintering Harlequin Ducks (about 150 to 200 birds as of 1995—the largest known concentration in eastern North America), it is also a wonderful migration site. You will find the greatest variety of birds in mid- to late May and from mid-August well into September, when the island can be full of migrants. The breeding season is also delightful, however, and offers the chance to see a good variety of Maine's characteristic coastal breeders (including Bald Eagle). Between May and October you will want to spend at least one night on the island, and preferably two or three, to see all that it has to offer. For one thing, you will not be able to do any early morning or evening birding unless you stay overnight. Bear in mind that you will have to do quite a bit of walking to cover the entire island; a sturdy pair of hiking boots or shoes, as well as general good fitness, is essential.

Much of Isle au Haut's charm lies in its unspoiled and quiet nature—and limited access. Acadia National Park operates a camp-

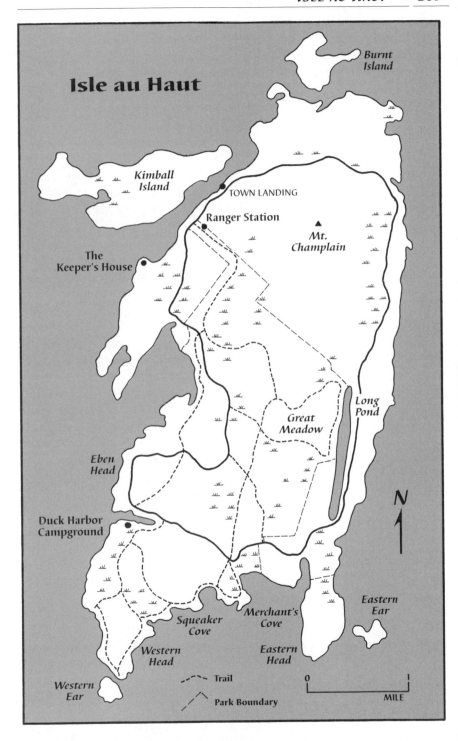

Isle au Haut

Burnt Island

Kimball Island

TOWN LANDING

Ranger Station

Mt. Champlain

The Keeper's House

Long Pond

Great Meadow

Eben Head

Duck Harbor Campground

Eastern Ear

N

Squeaker Cove

Merchant's Cove

Western Head

Eastern Head

Western Ear

- - - Trail

Park Boundary

0   1
MILE

ground with five lean-tos at Duck Harbor, and reservations must be made in advance, in writing. No other camping is allowed on the island. There is also a lovely (and expensive) inn with three guest rooms, The Keeper's House, which is a restored lighthouse station. These restrictions make the island a delightfully reclusive spot, however, and it is well worth the effort to plan ahead and obtain the necessary reservations for an overnight stay. The campground is open from May 15 to October 15 and The Keeper's House from May 1 to October 31.

Measuring about 6 miles long by 3 miles wide, Isle au Haut is among the largest of the many islands in outer Penobscot Bay. It is also one of Maine's hilliest islands, characterized by a north–south ridge of seven small mountains, the highest of which—Mt. Champlain—rises to 543 feet. The island is boreal in character and, except for small cultivated areas near habitations, is heavily forested, primarily by spruces and firs. There are several swampy and marshy areas, small sphagnum bogs, and streams; on the east side there is a large meadow (Great Meadow) and a freshwater pond (Long, or Turner, Pond). The shore is uniformly rocky and rugged, with several small coves, cobble beaches, and high promontories. A small village lies on the north and east shores, and a 12-mile road loops around the island, although only 4 miles are paved and you will rarely see a car outside the village. There are also 18 miles of trails, which are maintained by the park service. The road and the trails give visitors access to virtually the entire island. Please make every effort, however, to protect the privacy of island residents.

Although Isle au Haut's large size and proximity to so many other islands make it less of a migrant trap than Monhegan or Matinicus islands, for example, it nonetheless offers some fine birding on both spring and fall migration. During either migration you will usually find the greatest variety of landbirds around the overgrown field and apple orchard between the Duck Harbor campground and Eben Head and around Long Pond and Great Meadow. Any of the trails are worth exploring, and the mountaintops provide exquisite views. The loop road provides good edge habitat and also makes a fine birding trail. Check the good-sized cattail marsh at Merchant's Cove, where you may see a few birds you won't see elsewhere on the island, such as Great Blue Heron, Greater and Lesser yellowlegs, and Spotted Sandpiper; although the island is not particularly good for shorebirds, this is usually the best place to see any. The south end of the island is the best place from which to scan for offshore species.

Spring migration on Isle au Haut usually peaks about the third week in May, when breeding-plumage warblers are a specialty. As long as the weather cooperates, you shouldn't have much trouble seeing and hearing at least 15 species of these spring jewels—including Tennessee, Cape May, Black-throated Blue, Blackburnian, Bay-breasted, and Blackpoll—as well as a host of other landbirds. Fall migration can be good from early August through at least September and offers the best chance of seeing rarities and strays. Among the many common coastal migrants are such typical (which is not to say regular) offshore vagrants as Western Kingbird, Yellow-throated Vireo, Yellow-breasted Chat, Orchard Oriole, and Lark Sparrow. Like many other islands, Isle au Haut can also be very good for southbound hawks. Merlins can be especially numerous some days, and a Peregrine Falcon is a solid possibility.

Between mid-May and early August, you can find a wide variety of nesting species on the island. Some of the summer residents you may encounter include Bald Eagle, Osprey, Sharp-shinned and Broad-winged hawks, American Kestrel, Ring-necked Pheasant (released birds overwinter quite well on the island), Great Horned, Barred, and possibly Northern Saw-whet owls, Ruby-throated Hummingbird, Northern Flicker, Hairy and Downy woodpeckers, Eastern Kingbird, Eastern Phoebe, Olive-sided, Yellow-bellied, and Least flycatchers, Eastern Wood-Pewee, Tree and Barn swallows, Blue Jay, Common Raven, Common Crow, Boreal and Black-capped chickadees (the latter far more common), Red-breasted Nuthatch, Brown Creeper, Winter Wren, Golden-crowned and Ruby-crowned kinglets, Veery, Wood, Hermit, and Swainson's thrushes, Gray Catbird, Red-eyed Vireo, and several species of warblers, including Nashville, Northern Parula, Yellow, Magnolia, Yellow-rumped, Black-throated Green, Blackburnian, Chestnut-sided, Bay-breasted (small numbers), Black-and-white, Ovenbird, Northern Waterthrush, Wilson's (small numbers), Common Yellowthroat, and American Redstart. You may also see White-throated and Song sparrows, Dark-eyed Junco, Purple Finch, and American Goldfinch.

On the south end of the island, hike from Western Head to Eastern Head via the Cliff Trail and Goat Trail, which are spectacularly beautiful on a sunny day. Common Loons, Double-crested Cormorants, Common Eiders, Bald Eagles, Ospreys, Great Black-backed and Herring gulls, Common and Arctic terns, and Black Guillemots are all seen regularly offshore, and Great Cormorants are occasional. Look also for Northern Gannets (any time of year except midwinter, and especially after strong easterly winds), Bonaparte's and Laughing gulls, and an occasional Black-legged Kittiwake. With good winds and a little luck, you may even see a Greater or Sooty Shearwater, Atlantic Puffin, Razorbill, or jaeger. In the rocky coves along the southern shore, look particularly for Harlequin Ducks, which winter regularly off Isle au Haut and often linger into June. "Squeaker" is an old name for Harlequins, and Squeaker Cove on Western Head is a good place to look for this species. In May you might still see Purple Sandpipers in the coves.

The winter mail-boat schedule makes it impossible to spend more than four hours on Isle au Haut between mid-October and early April (unless you know an island resident who can put you up). At the very least, however, you can take the mail boat over and back, and the trip is often surprisingly productive. Just make sure you dress warmly. You are likely to see Red-throated and Common loons, Horned and Red-necked grebes, Great Cormorants, Brant (small numbers in March and April, often lingering into May), thousands of Common Eiders (high counts of 10,000+), Oldsquaws, all three scoters, hundreds of Common Goldeneyes and Buffleheads, Bald Eagles, and Great Black-backed and Herring gulls, and along rocky shorelines, Purple Sandpipers (high counts of 800). King Eiders, Barrow's Goldeneyes, Rough-legged Hawks (perched on one of the islands), and Glaucous and Iceland gulls are occasional. Unfortunately, you are almost certain not to see any Harlequin Ducks from the mail boat; the best place to see these beautiful birds is not along the mail boat's route. You can see them from the rugged south shore of the island, however (the eastern shore of Western Head is probably the best place to look) or on a special boat trip. The third Sunday in March, the Maine Audubon Society's Penobscot Valley Chapter runs an annual field trip out to Isle au Haut that typically records 100 to 150 Harlequins. For information on the trip, call or write the Maine Audubon Society, Fields Pond Nature Center, 1 Edgewood Drive, Orono, ME 04473, telephone 207-581-2900.

At any time of year look on Isle au Haut for Boreal Chickadees, which are fairly regular in small numbers, and for Common Ravens. Red and White-winged crossbills are erratic but are also possible at any time of year.

Although mammals generally are not a highlight on Isle au Haut, White-tailed Deer and Raccoons are fairly common, and since the late 1980s Coyotes have been seen or heard regularly.

Isle au Haut is accessible year-round from the town of Stonington. There is no fee for day visitors (although you of course have to buy a mail-boat ticket). A small store and post office, both with limited hours, are the only facilities available on the island.

For information about camping on Isle au Haut, write or call Acadia National Park, P.O. Box 177, Bar Harbor, ME 04609, telephone 207-288-3338. For information on The Keeper's House, write or call Jeff and Judi Burke, P.O. Box 26, Isle au Haut, ME 04645, telephone 207-367-2261.

CAMPING

Camping on Isle au Haut is on a first-come, first-served basis, so to speak, and applications must be postmarked April 1 or later. We might as well warn you that it is difficult to get a reservation simply because the demand is so high. It is always worth trying, however, especially because some people inevitably cancel. As of 1996 there is a per-visit (rather than a per-night) fee of $25 per lean-to, with visits limited to three nights.

There are five lean-tos (but no tent sites) at Duck Harbor, nicely spaced for privacy and each of which can accommodate six people. Drinking water and firewood are available at the campground. Don't forget insect repellent; the campground can be quite buggy sometimes.

Bikes are permitted (though not encouraged) on the loop road but are forbidden on the trails. The mail boat will drop off and pick up bikes only at the town landing.

MAIL-BOAT SERVICE

Isle au Haut is served by mail boat from the town of Stonington on Deer Isle, with daily service every day except Sunday. The trip takes about 40 minutes each way. A schedule is available from the Isle au Haut Company (Isle au Haut, ME 04645, telephone 207-367-5193 or 367-2355) or from Acadia National Park in Bar Harbor (see address and phone above). From mid-June through early September, the mail boat makes two trips a day directly to the campground at Duck Harbor. The rest of the year it goes only to the town landing on Isle au Haut, which is a 5-mile hike from the campground. (If you are carrying a heavy pack and time is of the essence, the road is the fastest route from the town landing to the campground.)

In summer a park ranger meets the mail boat at Duck Harbor and can give you a trail map, which is an essential item. If you disembark at the town landing and need information, ask at the store (turn left at the road and you will see it soon) or at the ranger station (turn right at the road, walk a short way, and you will see a sign and path on the left).

If you are coming out to Isle au Haut just for the day in summer, it is a good idea to take the earliest boat possible since the park service limits access to 50 visitors per day.

DIRECTIONS

To reach Stonington (*Maine Atlas* map 15, E-3 and -4), take Rt. 1 to Orland (map 23, E-3) and turn south onto Rt. 15. Follow the signs to Stonington, which is about 32 miles south. Once in Stonington, follow the road to the harbor at the bottom of the hill and turn left at the bank. Park across from the Atlantic Avenue Hardware store, then go inside to pay the proprietor for overnight parking. The mail boat leaves from the wharf below the hardware store.

LOCAL ACCOMMODATIONS

For information on local accommodations and services in the Deer Isle–Stonington area, write or call the Ellsworth Chamber of Commerce, 163 High St., Ellsworth, ME 04605, telephone 207-667-5584 or 667-2617.

Mount Desert Island
(*MAINE ATLAS* map 16)

Hulls Cove Visitor Center	Mount Desert Narrows
M.V. *Bluenose*	Bar Island Bar
Park Loop Road	Sieur de Monts Spring
Precipice Trail	Cadillac Mountain
Sewall Bog	& Other Mountains
Ship Harbor	Wonderland
Western Mountain Road	Bass Harbor Head & Marsh
Boat Trips	Lakes & Ponds

Mount Desert (pronounced "dessert") Island (MDI) offers some of the most diverse birding in eastern Maine and some of the loveliest vistas along the entire Atlantic Coast. Of the nearly 420 species of birds that have been recorded in Maine, at least 320 have been seen on MDI. Some, such as Lesser Black-backed Gull, Chuck-will's-widow, Bewick's Wren, Lazuli Bunting, and Le Conte's Sparrow, have provided first state records. Others, such as Golden Eagle, Swainson's Hawk, Purple Gallinule, Royal Tern, Ash-throated Flycatcher, Lark Bunting, and Harris' Sparrow, have embellished an already noteworthy check-

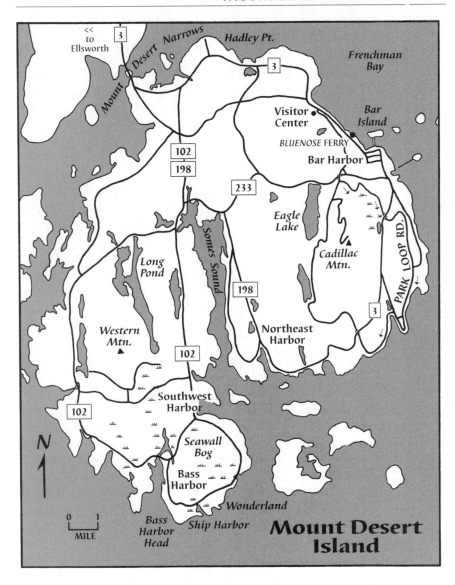

Mount Desert
Island

list. At least 21 species of warblers nest on the island, and each year a great variety of other birds are seen, too, including Bald Eagle, Peregrine Falcon (nesting since 1991), Spruce Grouse, Black-backed Woodpecker, Gray Jay, and Boreal Chickadee. MDI is also an excellent base from which to explore the offshore waters and nesting islands. Although the birding is good year-round, you will find the greatest diversity of species between mid-May and late September.

The best time to see breeding birds is in June; the best time for pelagics is mid-June through September. Plan to spend at least a few days here if you can.

MDI, which is Maine's largest island, lies 20 miles south of Ellsworth and is connected to the mainland by a causeway. Roughly heart shaped, the island measures 16 by 13 miles and is divided into east and west sides by Somes Sound. The west side of the island is flanked by Blue Hill Bay, the east side by Frenchman Bay. Bar Harbor is the only sizable town, though several smaller communities and fishing villages are scattered around the rest of the island. About half of MDI (more than 34,000 acres) lies within the boundaries of Acadia National Park. Each year about 2.5 million people visit this spectacularly beautiful park (most of them between July 4 and Labor Day), making it one of the most heavily visited national parks in the country. Most of these people, however, never make it past Bar Harbor and the Park Loop Road, which means that with a little effort you can escape the crowds. You will be most successful at this if you stay on the western side of the island and if you bird early in the day. Our favorite time to visit is in early June, when the birds have arrived but the people have not.

Named *L'Île des Monts Deserts*—"Island of Bare Mountains"—in 1604 by the famous French explorer Samuel de Champlain (and which accounts for the somewhat French pronunciation we use today), Mount Desert is remarkable for its diversity of habitats. A string of 17 mountain peaks stretches across the island from southwest to northeast, and they range in elevation from 200 feet to 1,530-foot Cadillac Mountain. Geologists believe that these granite-domed peaks may be only the remnants of a far larger mountain that was eroded by glaciers. These same glaciers left in their wake the numerous lakes and ponds that dot the island. Habitats include dense spruce-fir forests and mixed-deciduous woods, meadows and fields, heaths and bogs, freshwater and saltwater marshes, and a small (approximately 950 feet long) sand beach. Botanically the island is a contact zone for many northern and southern species, and this phenomenon is reflected in the avifauna. In general you will find birds with a southern affinity on the northeast side of the island and birds with a northern affinity on the southwest side. The abundance of "southern" species on the island has increased notably since a forest fire in October 1947 burned approximately 18,000 acres (including 10,000 acres within the park) and opened up a large new deciduous habitat.

Thanks to Acadia National Park, much of MDI is accessible to birders. There are 120 miles of hiking trails on the island; several little-traveled gravel roads; and 50 miles of carriage trails, which are closed to cars and are superb for walking, biking, snowshoeing, cross-country skiing, and horseback riding (you can rent bikes, skis, and even horses in the area).

There are so many good birding spots on Mount Desert that the island really deserves a guide of its own. We touch only on the highlights here, almost all of which lie within the park. (As you will discover for yourself, you continually pass in and out of the park as you drive around the island. Please remember to respect private property.) If you have time to bird only a few spots, the most productive are likely to be Wonderland, Ship Harbor, and Bass Harbor on the western side of the island and Sieur de Monts Spring on the eastern side.

Precise directions are not included for every stop. You will find almost all of these areas on a park map, and most are clearly marked on the park roads. For those that are not, directions are included.

Hulls Cove Visitor Center

Your first stop on MDI should be to obtain a park map so you can get yourself oriented. Acadia National Park's Hulls Cove Visitor Center is open from 8:00 a.m. to 8:00 p.m. between May 1 and October 31. You can get checklists, a schedule of park events, and park maps here (including separate maps for carriage and hiking trails) and can ask the rangers for information on recent sightings or species of interest. The visitor center also carries a good selection of books and other material geared for naturalists and outdoorspeople. See if you can get a copy of *Native Birds of Mount Desert Island and Acadia National Park* by Ralph H. Long (see Appendix D), a reasonably priced and very informative booklet.

In the off-season you can get information at park headquarters, 3 miles west of Bar Harbor on Route 233 (telephone 207-288-3338).

Now for the birds. The following sites are listed pretty much in the order you might visit them, working your way from northeast to southwest.

Mount Desert Narrows

Check the Mount Desert Narrows at the causeway that connects MDI and the mainland. In winter, as long as there is open water, this is a good place to look for ducks and other waterbirds, including an occasional Barrow's Goldeneye. Shorebirds sometimes stop here on migration. You can park at the Thompson Island Information Center, or across the road at the Thompson Island Picnic Area, and walk north or south to bird the narrows from the side of the causeway. Another spot from which to scan the narrows is Hadley Point, the northernmost tip of MDI, which is accessible from Route 3.

M.V. Bluenose

The M.V. *Bluenose* travels between Bar Harbor and Yarmouth, Nova Scotia, and provides one of the few regular opportunities for true pelagic birding in Maine. See the following chapter, "M.V. *Bluenose*," for a full description of the crossing.

Bar Island Bar

The Bar Island Bar on the north side of Bar Harbor traditionally has been a good place to see shorebirds and gulls in late summer and fall. Unfortunately, it is also a good place to see lots of people, dogs, and bikes, and the combined traffic is now so heavy (at least between mid-July and mid-August) that the birds rarely have more than a few minutes to feed at any one time before they are flushed. Still, it is worth a check. It is also worth a check in winter for ducks and other waterbirds.

From May through October, bird the bar at low to mid-tide, when it is exposed. The cobblelike substrate (actually a gravel tombolo) attracts primarily Black-bellied and Semipalmated plovers and Ruddy Turnstones, with smaller numbers of Lesser and Greater yellowlegs and Semipalmated and Least sandpipers. Ruddy Turnstones occasionally can be abundant, with high counts of 200 in late August. This is also a reliable spot to see small numbers of Red Knots. Throughout the summer look for Bonaparte's and Laughing gulls and Common Terns. Keep your eyes open for Bald Eagles, too, as there is an active nest nearby. In the summer of 1995, a Lesser Black-backed Gull was an exciting find here.

In winter the sheltered waters around Bar Island offer refuge to many waterbirds, and the bar can be a good place from which to scan them. This area is heavily hunted into December, however, so it is usually best later in the winter. Look for such common species as Red-throated and Common loons, Horned and Red-necked grebes, Great Cormorant, American Black Duck, Common Eider, Oldsquaw, all three scoters, Common Goldeneye, and Bufflehead and for the occasional Glaucous or Iceland Gull. Even Little Gull is seen here in winter on rare occasion. Purple Sandpipers sometimes can be seen, too, and may linger into May.

To reach the Bar Island Bar, follow Route 3 into Bar Harbor and turn left onto West Street (which is 2.2 miles south of the Hulls Cove Visitor Center). In 0.3 mile turn left onto Bridge Street, and at low or mid-tide you will see the bar directly ahead of you. (The park or local newspaper can provide tide information.)

Park Loop Road

If you have never been to MDI before, by all means drive the park's 20-mile Loop Road, which offers outstanding vistas of Frenchman Bay and the Cranberry islands. We recommend this drive along the east side of the island primarily for the scenery, not the birds, although in winter this can be a fine spot from which to scan for waterbirds. At midday in July and August the traffic can be quite heavy, but if you are here before 9:00 a.m. or after about 5:00 p.m., it shouldn't be a problem. There is a per-vehicle fee of $5, which is good for one week.

The Loop Road is well marked on park maps.

Sieur de Monts Spring

Sieur de Monts Spring is one of the best places on MDI to see a wide variety of species, particularly during spring and fall migration and the nesting season. The predominantly deciduous woods here attract primarily birds of a southern affinity. Species you might see include Broad-winged Hawk, Ruffed Grouse, American Woodcock, Black-billed Cuckoo, Pileated Woodpecker, Yellow-bellied Sapsucker, Barred Owl, Common Nighthawk, Great Crested, Alder, and Least flycatchers, Eastern Wood-Pewee, Eastern Phoebe, Veery, Wood Thrush, American Robin, Red-eyed and occasionally Warbling vireos, Nashville, Black-and-white, Black-throated Green, Chestnut-sided, and Yellow warblers, American Redstart, Common Yellowthroat, Ovenbird, Scarlet Tanager, Baltimore Oriole, Rose-breasted

Grosbeak, Eastern Towhee, and Swamp Sparrow. Among the rarities that have been seen here are Yellow-throated and Golden-winged warblers.

Bird the clearing around the spring in early morning, then walk to Great Meadow, north of the spring. At the nature center by the parking lot, follow the Jesup Trail north (away from the springhouse) and through the birches. You will soon cross Hemlock Road, a carriage trail, and in a half mile or so you will intersect a much narrower trail where the habitat becomes wetter and scrubbier. Turn right and then immediately left here. The trail will bisect a wet, marshy area and then will bring you out at the edge of Great Meadow. The Beavers that have a lodge along this trail sometimes flood the area and make it impassable, so wearing boots is a good idea.

A short hike up the Dorr Mountain Trail (moderately strenuous) to where it opens up in an area of exposed ledges may provide looks at Bald Eagles, Common Ravens, Winter Wrens, and several coniferous warbler species. The trail starts just north of the springhouse and is well marked.

Also visit the Wild Gardens of Acadia at the spring, where 300 species of native plants are on display in 10 habitats that simulate the surrounding environments. Every species is labeled, so if you are not as familiar as you would like to be with Maine flora, this is a good place to study.

To reach Sieur de Monts Spring, stay on Route 3 through Bar Harbor and follow the signs for the spring. Between mid-July and late August, it is a good idea to get here before 10:00 a.m. if you want a parking space.

Precipice Trail

The Precipice Trail is the sheer vertical "ladder" trail that ascends Champlain Mountain on the eastern shore of MDI. The trail is closed during the nesting season, but birders still visit the parking lot at its base, hopefully scanning the cliffs overhead for a Peregrine Falcon. Since 1991, when Peregrine Falcons successfully nested on MDI for the first time in 35 years, at least one pair of these majestic birds has been observed regularly in the park between March and September. We are not divulging any great secret here; the birds' presence has been widely publicized by the park.

Although you may see a Peregrine anywhere on MDI, the area around the Precipice Trail is an especially good place to look for this species. Courtship and mating activities are most likely to be observed in March and April and can include spectacular aerial displays. Park rangers request that you keep well away from areas where Peregrines are assumed to be nesting and avoid observing nesting birds from locations higher than the nest site.

In years when the Precipice Trail is not closed, it is a wonderful spot to see migrants, particularly spring warblers, because you can see the birds virtually at eye level. The woods on the east side of the Park Loop Road (see above) can also be good for migrants; there are no trails, but you can bird the area from the roadside.

The Precipice Trail and parking lot are located along the Park Loop Road and are well marked. About 2 miles south of the Precipice Trail you can turn off the Loop Road by turning right onto Otter Cliffs Road, which will take you back to Route 3.

Cadillac Mountain & Other Mountains

Windswept Cadillac Mountain, 1,530 feet high and accessible by car from the Park Loop Road or by hiking trail, is the highest of MDI's 17 peaks. It is also the most crowded, with a large parking lot, rest rooms, and gift shop. Even with these amenities, however, it is hard to overstate the beauty of this spot. Rising abruptly above the sea and a host of small islands, Cadillac Mountain offers a commanding and spectacular view that no one should pass up. Visibility extends in all directions for many miles, and you can see a good deal of the surrounding coast.

You usually won't see too many birds atop Cadillac, except in spring and fall when the summit provides an excellent vantage point from which to look for migrating hawks, particularly accipiters and falcons. It is also an excellent place to observe migrating and resident Bald Eagles and to watch Common Ravens at play. Sometimes you can also see migrant landbirds at the top of Cadillac, especially if you are here early in the morning and happen upon a fallout. Between May and October, hiking up the mountain offers the chance to see some of the island's common nesting and migrant species. In the breeding season, Common Nighthawks are indeed common.

MDI's other summits, accessible by trails that range from relatively easy to quite strenuous, also offer lovely vistas (and fewer people). Acadia (681 feet), Beech (839 feet and a popular hawk-watching spot), Champlain (1,058 feet), Dorr (1,270 feet), and Sargent (1,373 feet) mountains are just a few examples. A good reference for more detailed information is the AMC *Guide to Mount Desert Island and Acadia National Park* (see Appendix D). A hike to any of the island's summits is likely to be good for migrating hawks in spring and fall and for nesting species in summer.

Ask for a map of hiking trails at the Hulls Cove Visitor Center.

Seawall Bog

Seawall Bog, or the Big Heath, is a 420-acre coastal raised peatland on the southern tip of MDI. It is a lovely area, dotted with small pools and vegetated with typical peatland species such as Black Spruce, Sheep Laurel, Leatherleaf, sphagnum mosses, sundews, Pitcher Plant, and exquisite bog orchids, including Arethusa and Calopogon. There are also scattered clumps of Baked-apple Berry, which is uncommon this far south. The ornithological highlights are nesting Yellow-bellied Flycatchers, Palm Warblers, and Lincoln's Sparrows. Bird the bog in early June if you can, as Palm Warblers are early nesters and may be feeding young by the middle of the month. Along the edges of the bog look for nesting Olive-sided Flycatchers, Boreal Chickadees, Winter Wrens, Ruby-crowned Kinglets, Tennessee, Wilson's, and Canada warblers, White-throated Sparrows (ubiquitous on the island), and Dark-eyed Juncos. Boots or a pair of old sneakers that you do not mind getting wet are essential.

Seawall Bog is on the north side of Route 102A. Park at the Wonderland parking lot and look carefully on the other side of the road for several small, unmarked trails that lead into the bog. *Please:* bird the bog from its edges and stay on the well-trodden paths; the plant life is very fragile.

Wonderland

Wonderland is another fine birding spot. Although just across the road from Seawall Bog, it offers an entirely different habitat. A wide trail leads 0.6 mile through mixed deciduous and coniferous woods, crosses a dry and open area of lichen-covered ledges and Pitch Pine, and then enters a tall grove of spruces along the shore. Like Ship Harbor just south of it, Wonderland is a particularly good place to see migrant and nesting warblers, including in some years nesting Blackpolls near the water's edge. Spruce Grouse are fairly common in the area, and reportedly increasing, and Gray Jays (uncommon) and Boreal Chickadees also occur. Occasionally you can see a Common Nighthawk roosting on the ledges.

The parking lot and trail are on the south side of Route 102A and are well marked.

Ship Harbor

Ship Harbor is one of the loveliest spots on MDI and one of our favorite birding areas. In the breeding season you can find many of the island's northern landbirds and at least 18 species of warblers, including Tennessee, Blackburnian, Bay-breasted, Cape May (the first nesting record for the United States came from Ship Harbor in 1936), and Wilson's. At the head of the harbor is a spacious, open clearing bordered by Chokecherry and alder swales, and beyond it is a figure-eight–shaped trail that leads 1.6 miles through tall spruce woods to the shore and back. In early June when the Rhodora and Bunchberry are in bloom, this is an especially pretty walk.

Look for nesting and migrant warblers at Ship Harbor and for northern breeders such as Black-backed Woodpecker (rare), Yellow-bellied, Alder, Least, and Olive-sided flycatchers, Common Raven, Gray Jay (uncommon), Boreal Chickadee (uncommon), Brown Creeper, Winter Wren, Ruby-crowned Kinglet, Solitary Vireo, Hermit and Swainson's thrushes, Red and White-winged crossbills (not every year), Purple Finch, Pine Siskin (not every year), Evening Grosbeak, and Dark-eyed Junco. A Bewick's Wren seen here in 1971 provided a first (and as of 1995, only) state record.

The Ship Harbor parking lot is on the south side of Route 102A and is well marked.

Bass Harbor Head & Marsh

Bass Harbor Head is the southernmost point on MDI. It offers an excellent vantage point over open ocean and access to an extensive stand of spruce-fir woods. This is another good spot to see migrant and nesting warblers (including in some years Bay-breasted, Blackburnian, and Cape May) and is one of the more reliable places on the island to look for boreal specialties. Common Ravens can often be heard croaking nearby, and Spruce Grouse, Black-backed Woodpeckers, Yellow-bellied Flycatchers, Boreal Chickadees, Gray Jays,

Mourning Warblers (in the brushy thickets), and Red and White-winged crossbills are occasional. This is also an excellent spot from which to scan year-round for waterfowl and seabirds and, in summer, for whales and seals. King Eiders and Harlequin Ducks are occasionally seen in winter, and Harbor Porpoises are often reported in summer.

Follow signs from Route 102A to the Bass Harbor lighthouse, where you can park. Scan from the lighthouse and then walk the half mile along the road back to Route 102A to look for landbirds.

Bass Harbor Marsh, about 2 miles north of the lighthouse, is a good place to see wading birds and nesting Nelson's Sharp-tailed Sparrows and Northern Harriers in spring and summer. You can scan the marsh from the roadside. Follow Route 102A north from the lighthouse, turn left at the intersection with Route 102, and you will soon see a narrow bridge. You can park in the small parking area on the north side of the road.

Western Mountain Road

Western Mountain Road runs between Gilly Field and Seal Cove Pond on the western side of MDI. The combination of dense woods and virtually no traffic makes this a delightful (and quiet) birding spot. Black-throated Blue and Bay-breasted warblers are locally common during the breeding season (the former primarily in birches, the latter close to Seal Cove Pond). You can see a fine variety of other birds, too, with possibilities including Sharp-shinned Hawk, Northern Goshawk, Ruffed Grouse, Great Horned Owl, Yellow-bellied Sapsucker (especially around poplar stands), Yellow-bellied Flycatcher, Ruby-crowned Kinglet, Swainson's Thrush, and Solitary Vireo. You can also scan the southern end of Seal Cove Pond, where you can put in a canoe. (If you are birding from the shore, you will get a better view of the pond from Route 102.)

Western Mountain Road is marked on the park map and by road signs.

Lakes & Ponds

MDI has nearly 30 lakes and ponds, ranging in size from 5-mile-long Long Pond on the western side of the island to tiny Beaver Dam Pond (which does have an active Beaver lodge) on the eastern side. Many of these water bodies are surrounded by marshes or cattail swamps and are good birding spots. Witch Hole, Aunt Betty, and Beaver Dam ponds on the eastern side of the island and Long, Seal Cove, and Somes ponds and Echo Lake on the western side are among the most productive. Some of the characteristic breeding species to look for on and around the ponds and lakes include Common Loon, Pied-billed Grebe (uncommon; more common as a migrant), Great Blue and occasionally Green herons, American Bittern, American Black Duck, Green-winged and Blue-winged teal, Wood and Ring-necked ducks, Hooded and Common mergansers, Virginia Rail, Sora, Spotted Sandpiper, Belted Kingfisher, Marsh Wren, Common Yellowthroat, Swamp Sparrow, and Red-winged Blackbird.

Virtually all of MDI's lakes and ponds are marked on park maps. The larger ones are also marked in the *Maine Atlas*.

Boat Trips

Throughout the summer, Acadia National Park and several private companies and individuals on MDI offer a variety of boat trips. These range from short harbor cruises to all-day whale-watching and pelagic trips. We are reluctant to print specific information here because the operators and their schedules change so much from year to year. Instead, we recommend that you call or write the Bar Harbor Chamber of Commerce (address below) for current information. Tell them you are specifically interested in birding trips and ask them which they recommend. In recent years, Bar Harbor Whale Watch Co. (on the *Friendship IV* catamaran), Acadian Whale Watcher, Frenchman Bay Co., and Seabird Watcher have been among the options most popular with serious birders.

Most of the trips leave from Bar Harbor, Northeast Harbor, Southwest Harbor, or Bass Harbor. Almost any trip should provide a good opportunity to see such characteristic offshore-island nesters as Great and Double-crested cormorants (the latter far more common), Great Blue Heron, Common Eider (often with ducklings in early summer), Bald Eagle, Osprey, Great Black-backed, Herring, and Laughing gulls, Common Tern, and Black Guillemot. Look, too, for all three scoters, Red-breasted Merganser, and Oldsquaw (occasional).

A trip to Mt. Desert Rock, about 23 miles offshore (or any other trip that gets you several miles offshore), can be particularly productive as it offers a chance to see more pelagic species (and marine mammals) than does a harbor trip. From mid-June through September you have a good chance of seeing Greater, Sooty, Manx, and possibly Cory's shearwaters (the last only in summers with unusually warm water temperatures), Wilson's and Leach's storm-petrels (the former far more common), Northern Gannet, Red-necked and Red phalaropes (primarily in late summer and fall, with Red-necked Phalarope more abundant), Black-legged Kittiwake, Arctic Tern, Atlantic Puffin, and Razorbill, and possibly Roseate Tern, Parasitic Jaeger, and Great or South Polar Skua. See the section entitled "Pelagic Birding" in the Introduction for more information. Whale-watching can also be very productive in this area. Finback, Humpback, and Minke whales are the most commonly recorded species, but Pilot and Northern Right whales, Harbor Porpoise, and Atlantic White-sided Dolphin are also possibilities. You may see Harbor Seals and, especially near Mt. Desert Rock, Gray Seals bobbing in the surf.

Mount Desert Island is accessible year-round, with a broad range of facilities available in Bar Harbor and the surrounding villages as well as in Acadia National Park. There are two campgrounds in the park, one open seasonally and one year-round. Please note that many of the park roads are closed to vehicle traffic in winter. For more information, write or call Acadia National Park, P.O. Box 177, Bar Harbor, ME 04609, telephone 207-288-3338.

DIRECTIONS

At the intersection of Rts. 1 and 3 in Ellsworth, turn south on Rt. 3. MDI is 20 miles south. Be prepared for the fact that, at least between late June and Labor Day, the traffic can be quite heavy at times.

LOCAL ACCOMMODATIONS

For information on local accommodations and services, write or call the Bar Harbor Chamber of Commerce, 93 Cottage St., Bar Harbor, ME 04609, telephone 800-288-5103 (288-5103 locally).

M.V. Bluenose

One of the great delights of birding on the Maine coast is a chance to bird from the Bluenose, the 412-foot Canadian-operated car-ferry that plies the 200-mile round-trip between Bar Harbor and Yarmouth, Nova Scotia. This is one of the oldest and best-known pelagic trips

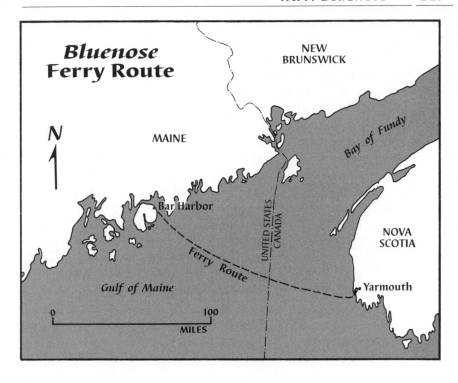

on the East Coast, and although increasing numbers of seabird and whale-watching trips are offered every year, it still provides one of the few regular opportunities for true pelagic birding in Maine. The best time to make the trip usually is between mid-June and late August, when shearwaters and petrels are most abundant. As fall pushes on and the cold begins to bite in earnest, tubenoses dwindle but the chance of seeing unusual gulls and alcids increases. To date more than 23 species of pelagic birds have been sighted from the *Bluenose,* including such rarities as Yellow-nosed Albatross, Little Shearwater, Long-tailed Jaeger, Sabine's Gull, and Royal Tern (all of which occurred in summer or early fall). In summer the *Bluenose* also provides a fine opportunity for whale-watching. Humpback, Minke, and Finback whales and Atlantic White-sided Dolphins are all seen regularly, and occasionally a Northern Right or Pilot whale is seen. Basking Shark and Ocean Sunfish are also possibilities.

Traveling almost due east from Bar Harbor to Yarmouth, the *Bluenose* crosses the northern edge of the Gulf of Maine and the mouth of the Bay of Fundy. Over much of this route, vertical circulation brings to the surface nutrient-rich bottom waters that historically have made this area renowned for its fisheries and seabird populations. Two areas along the route—the edge of the Grand Manan Bank (about 40 miles off the Maine coast and three hours out of Bar Harbor) and Lurcher Shoal (on the southwest shore of Nova Scotia and about an hour and a half out of Yarmouth)—are particularly productive and are often where you see the greatest concentrations of birds.

Although passengers generally are not permitted on the open bow of the *Bluenose*, the areas adjacent to the bridge allow good visibility forward, and from the ample deck space along the sides and stern you can scan the rest of the horizon. From mid-June through September the most commonly seen species are Greater, Sooty, and Manx shearwaters (these three in order of decreasing likelihood), Leach's and Wilson's storm-petrels (the latter far more abundant), Northern Gannet, Common Eider, Red-necked and Red phalaropes (primarily in late summer and early fall), Parasitic and Pomarine jaegers (both in small numbers), South Polar and Great skuas (also in small numbers), Great Black-backed, Herring, Laughing, and Bonaparte's gulls (the latter two primarily in Frenchman Bay), Common and Arctic terns (the former primarily in Frenchman Bay and Yarmouth Harbor), Black Guillemot (primarily in Frenchman Bay and Yarmouth Harbor), and Atlantic Puffin. Aside from Great Black-backed and Herring gulls, the most abundant species typically are Wilson's Storm-Petrel and Greater Shearwater. The more southerly Cory's Shearwater, usually rare in the Gulf of Maine, sometimes occurs in late summer when surface-water temperatures are unusually warm. Species less likely to be encountered in summer but nonetheless occasional are Razorbill, Common Murre, Ring-billed Gull (primarily in Frenchman Bay), and Black-legged Kittiwake. Sailing out of Bar Harbor, look for nesting Ospreys and Bald Eagles. In spring and fall you may see a good variety of waterfowl, and in any season it is worth scanning the flocks of Common Eiders for a King Eider.

From September through mid-October (after which the ferry currently crosses only at night), look for good numbers of Northern Fulmars, Northern Gannets, Bonaparte's Gulls, and Black-legged Kittiwakes and for smaller numbers of Greater Shearwaters and possibly Leach's Storm-Petrels, Red Phalaropes, a Pomarine or Parasitic Jaeger, and a South Polar or Great Skua. In Yarmouth Harbor look for Common Black-headed Gulls, which are sometimes seen there from fall through spring.

Birders really eager to see alcids (and brave enough to endure the cold) could once consider a *Bluenose* crossing in winter, but recent

schedule changes have eliminated that option. Call us eternal opti-
mists, but we are hopeful that perhaps the schedule will change
again. It is worth a call. If you do have a chance to make the crossing
in winter, it can be very productive. From November through March
it is possible to see all six species of alcids that occur in the Gulf of
Maine as well as Northern Fulmar, Northern Gannet (rare in midwinter), Glaucous and Iceland gulls, Black-legged Kittiwake, and possibly a skua (presumably Great, but be careful; don't rely on the calendar to identify skuas). Remember that it is a challenge to see alcids,
especially from a boat this big. Most of the time they simply sit on
the water, and they can be devilishly hard to find (let alone identify)
among the waves. Dovekies are regular and numerous—and tiny,
really tiny.

As on any pelagic trip, the success of sightings on the *Bluenose* can
vary widely. We have made crossings that were a birder's dream
(including one where we saw all five species of skuas and jaegers that
occur in the Northern Hemisphere) and others where we saw more
fog than birds. In general, however, you are likely to see more birds
on the *Bluenose*—which crosses the entire Gulf of Maine—than you
are on a chartered seabird or whale-watching trip. Also remember
that a successful pelagic trip means being on deck all the time; as
alluring as the cafeteria and warm lounges are, you won't see many
birds from them. Coming well prepared for a day on deck will
enhance your likelihood of seeing more birds and will also make the
trip a lot more fun. Warm clothing, sunscreen, and lip screen are
essential ingredients. See the section entitled "Pelagic Birding" in the
Introduction for more information.

From mid-June to mid-October, the *Bluenose* crosses daily, currently leaving Bar Harbor at 8:00 a.m. eastern daylight time (EDT)
and leaving Yarmouth at 4:30 p.m. Atlantic daylight time (ADT, one
hour ahead of EDT). The trip takes about 6 hours each way, with a
90-minute layover in Yarmouth. From mid-October to mid-March
and from early May to mid-June, the ferry crosses three times
weekly, leaving Bar Harbor at 11:00 p.m. eastern standard time
(EST) on Mondays, Wednesdays, and Fridays and leaving Yarmouth
at 4:30 p.m. Atlantic standard time (AST) on Sundays, Tuesdays, and
Thursdays. There is no ferry service from mid-March to early May. It
is *always* a good idea to call ahead and confirm the schedule in
advance; the *Bluenose* is notorious for major and unexpected schedule
changes. You don't want to drive nonstop from Iowa, eager for a
great seabird adventure, only to learn that the ferry just left.

The *Bluenose* can carry 250 cars and almost 800 passengers. Advance reservations are suggested both for cars and walk-on passengers. For further information, including schedules and fares, write or call Marine Atlantic Reservations Bureau, P.O. Box 250, North Sydney, Nova Scotia B2A-3M3, Canada, telephone 800-341-7981 or, in Bar Harbor, 288-3395.

For birders who will be spending time in Yarmouth (or elsewhere in Nova Scotia), two bird-finding guides are available: *Birding Nova Scotia* edited by Cohrs and *Birding in Atlantic Canada: Nova Scotia* by Burrows (see Appendix D). There are several spots worth checking not too far from the Marine Atlantic ferry terminal, including Cape Forchu, the Yarmouth Airport, and Pinkney's Point.

A final note: at any time of year, but especially in July and August, it is important that you make advance reservations for lodging (even camping) if you plan to spend the night in Bar Harbor.

DIRECTIONS

The Marine Atlantic ferry terminal is conspicuously located on Rt. 3 on the north side of Bar Harbor, directly across the street from the Day's Inn.

LOCAL ACCOMMODATIONS

For information on local accommodations and services in Bar Harbor, call or write the Bar Harbor Chamber of Commerce, 93 Cottage St., Bar Harbor, ME 04609, telephone 800-288-5103 (or 288-5103 locally). For information in Yarmouth, write or call the Nova Scotia Tourism Office, Suite 501, 2695 Dutch Village Rd., Halifax, NS B3L-4V2, Canada, telephone 800-341-6096.

Schoodic Peninsula
(*MAINE ATLAS* map 17, B-1)

Situated across Frenchman Bay and due east of Mount Desert Island lies another outpost of Acadia National Park: Schoodic Peninsula. The southern half of the peninsula (about 2,000 acres) comprises the only part of Acadia located on the mainland. Even on a coast legendary for its beauty, Schoodic Peninsula is an exceptionally lovely

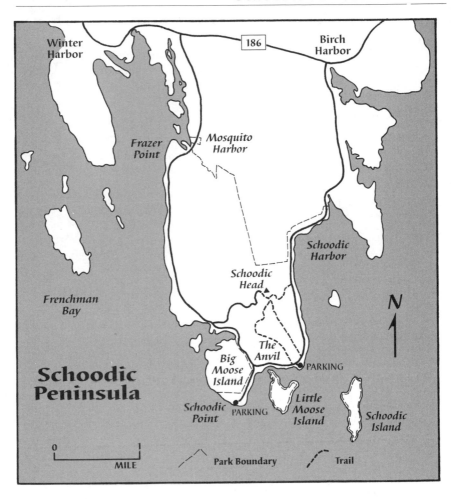

spot, whether shrouded in fog or sparkling in the sunlight. It is also a fine birding area, well worth a visit at any time of year. Highlights include Spruce Grouse and a wide variety of waterbirds year-round, good numbers of migrant landbirds in spring and fall, and several species of warblers in the nesting season. Whatever the season, plan to spend at least a few hours here. Between late June and late September you are likely to find a fair number of fellow visitors, so the earlier you get out birding, the better.

Most of Schoodic Peninsula—including 440-foot-high Schoodic Head, the highest point on the peninsula—is heavily forested, primarily with Red and White spruces, Balsam Fir, and scattered birches. Interestingly, you will also see a fair amount of Jack Pine in the park, especially on Schoodic Head. This species generally prefers more northerly and cooler climates and reaches the southern extreme of its range in central Maine. Other habitats in the park include a good-sized but sheltered open area vegetated with Rugosa Rose, goldenrods, Chokecherries, alders, and scattered pines; Schoodic Point at the southernmost end of the park; a small salt marsh; and a few small ponds. Geologically the peninsula is notable for the large black basalt dikes—some of which are several feet wide and extend north–south for several hundred feet—that are exposed in the red granite bedrock, especially at Schoodic Point. The unusual configuration of rock has also created many tide pools.

Schoodic Peninsula is accessible year-round from a two-lane, one-way park road that runs along the shore. The loop is a beautiful 9-mile drive, with lush coniferous woods on one side of the road and gently sloping rocky shore on the other. Although there are no trails along the shore, there are several places where you can park and walk down to the shore. Two trails on Schoodic Head allow you to explore the park's interior as well. There are three main areas to check, all of which are well marked by road signs.

Frazer Point & Mosquito Harbor

Your first stop will be Frazer Point, 0.2 mile south of the park boundary, where there is a large parking lot and picnic area. With its low, scrubby vegetation and sheltered location, Frazer Point is an ideal place to look for migrant landbirds in spring and fall. Check Mosquito Harbor, immediately north of the point, for waterfowl, especially those species that favor somewhat protected areas. In winter this is a good place to see Red-throated Loons, Common Eiders (year-round), Oldsquaws, Common Goldeneyes, and Buffleheads.

Schoodic Head & Vicinity

Continue south from Frazer Point, and in 2.3 miles you will see a gravel road on the left (usually closed in winter) that leads 1 mile up Schoodic Head. Drive or hike to the top of the road and then hike 0.2 mile to the summit. You will notice lots of Jack Pine, some of it quite stunted and wind flagged. A 1-mile trail descends from Schoodic Head to the Anvil, a smaller peak to the south, and ends on the park road. These trails provide a welcome opportunity to get

away from traffic and explore the woodlands. Some of the characteristic nesting species to look for between mid-May and early August
include Spruce Grouse (year-round, and seen regularly), Yellow-bellied,
Least, and Olive-sided flycatchers, Common Raven, Black-capped
and Boreal chickadees (the former far more common), Red-breasted
Nuthatch, Winter Wren, Ruby-crowned and Golden-crowned kinglets, Swainson's Thrush, Solitary Vireo, and several species of warblers, including Tennessee, Nashville, Northern Parula, Magnolia,
Cape May (a few), Black-throated Blue, Yellow-rumped, Black-
throated Green, Blackburnian, Bay-breasted, Blackpoll (a few), and
American Redstart. In winter look for Evening and Pine grosbeaks
and Pine Siskins (all quite erratic in their occurrence) and at any time
of year for Red and White-winged crossbills (also erratic). Black-
backed Woodpecker is a possibility, albeit an uncommon one, at any
time of year, and even Three-toed Woodpecker has been seen on a
few occasions.

Just beyond the bottom of the Schoodic Head road, on the left,
is a marshy pond that is worth checking, and across the road is a large
gravel bar that sometimes attracts small numbers of shorebirds. In
another 0.5 mile you will see a salt marsh on the left. Look here for
nesting Nelson's Sharp-tailed Sparrows.

Schoodic Point

To reach Schoodic Point, fork right at the triangle beyond the salt
marsh (traffic is two-way here). Schoodic Point lies at the southernmost tip of the peninsula and offers an excellent vantage point over
open ocean. In summer look for Double-crested Cormorant, Osprey,
Bonaparte's and Laughing gulls, and Common and occasionally Arctic
terns; in winter look for Red-throated Loon, Horned and Red-necked
grebes, Great Cormorant, American Black Duck, Bufflehead, Oldsquaw, Common Goldeneye, and Purple Sandpiper. Look at any time
of year for Common Loon, Common Eider (in early summer often
with ducklings), all three scoters, Red-breasted Merganser, Bald Eagle
(nesting on Schoodic Island, east of the point), Great Black-backed
and Herring gulls, and Black Guillemot. At any time of year except
midwinter scan carefully for a Northern Gannet; during migration as
many as 100-plus gannets have been seen here in a single day. This is
also a good spot in winter to look for such hard-to-find species as Barrow's Goldeneye, Harlequin Duck, King Eider, Glaucous and Iceland
gulls, Black-legged Kittiwake, and any of the alcids, especially Black

Guillemot and Razorbill. Pacific Loon (in breeding plumage in June), Eared Grebe, and Common Black-headed Gull are among the rarities that have been seen here.

Schoodic Peninsula is accessible year-round, free of charge. There are rest rooms and picnic facilities at Frazer Point.

DIRECTIONS

The park road turns south off Rt. 186 in the village of Winter Harbor. This intersection is 6.8 miles south of the intersection of Rts. 1 and 186 in West Gouldsboro and 8.9 miles south of the intersection of Rts. 1 and 186 in Gouldsboro. The road is well marked with park signs. Traffic is two-way for the first 2 miles, but just south of Frazer Point it becomes one-way.

LOCAL ACCOMMODATIONS

For information on local accommodations or services, write or call the Ellsworth Chamber of Commerce, 163 High St., Ellsworth, ME 04605, telephone 207-667-5584 or 667-2617; or the Bar Harbor Chamber of Commerce, 93 Cottage St., Bar Harbor, ME 04609, telephone 800-288-5103 (or 288-5103 in Bar Harbor).

CENTRAL MAINE

The area we refer to as central Maine includes Penobscot County and much of Piscataquis County. This is a rugged and beautiful portion of Maine, traversed by the Penobscot River and characterized by numerous lakes and ponds, mature hardwoods and often impenetrable spruce-fir woods, and several mountains. The focal point of the area is Baxter State Park, a 200,000-acre wilderness that is widely recognized as one of the most spectacular natural areas in the eastern United States. Included within the park are 46 peaks and ridges and the highest point in Maine—5,267-foot-high Katahdin. Bangor and, to its north, Orono are the only sizable population centers. Much of this part of Maine consists of privately owned (but usually publicly accessible) pulp and paper-company land.

Birders, particularly those who relish the idea of access to some true wilderness, will find much to draw them to central Maine. The highlight is the breeding season, especially June and early July, when you can find a rich assortment of boreal nesters. Spruce Grouse, Three-toed and Black-backed woodpeckers (both rare), Yellow-bellied Flycatcher, Gray Jay, Boreal Chickadee, Bicknell's (formerly Gray-cheeked) Thrush, Philadelphia Vireo, 22 species of warblers, Lincoln's and Fox sparrows, Dark-eyed Junco, and Pine Siskin all breed throughout this area. Additionally, on the Tableland in Baxter State

Park you can find one of New England's most restricted breeding species—American Pipit, which nests at only one other site in the eastern United States. Spring and fall migration bring a good variety of waterfowl to central Maine as well as many landbirds, and winter brings the chance of finding specialties such as Barrow's Goldeneyes (regular in small numbers on the Penobscot River between Bangor and Orono) and northern owls and finches.

Sebasticook Lake
(*MAINE ATLAS* map 22, A-1 & -2)

Sebasticook Lake lies about 20 miles west of Bangor and is well known as one of central Maine's most intriguing birding sites. Measuring nearly 5 miles long and about 4 miles wide, this irregularly shaped body of water provides excellent habitat for waterfowl, especially for "prairie ducks" such as Ring-necked Ducks, American Wigeons, and Greater and Lesser scaup, and occasionally Canvasbacks, Redheads, and Ruddy Ducks. If water levels are low in late summer and fall, it also provides habitat for migrating shorebirds. Common Loons, Pied-billed Grebes, Virginia Rails, American Coots, Common Moorhens, and Marsh Wrens are among the more interesting breeding birds you can find around the lake and its tributaries. The best time to bird Sebasticook Lake is between ice-out and freeze-up, which generally means between late March and late November. Allow two to four hours to drive the circuit we describe below, and if you have a telescope, by all means bring it.

Part of what makes Sebasticook Lake so interesting for waterfowl is that the soil and bedrock conditions in the Newport area are quite distinctive. Whereas much of Maine is characterized by shallow and relatively sterile soils, the Newport area is known for its deep and rich brown podzols. Sebasticook is not the stony, acidic lake that typifies much of Maine, but instead is quite alkaline. This difference in substrate is undoubtedly the reason for the different character of the aquatic vegetation at Sebasticook. Considering these differences, it is not surprising that this fertile watershed attracts a somewhat different variety of waterfowl than is typically found elsewhere in Maine. Regularly occurring species that you can expect to see on both spring and fall migration (and sometimes in summer) include Canada Goose, Mallard, Wood, American Black, and Ring-necked ducks, Northern Pintail, Green-winged and Blue-winged teal, American Wigeon,

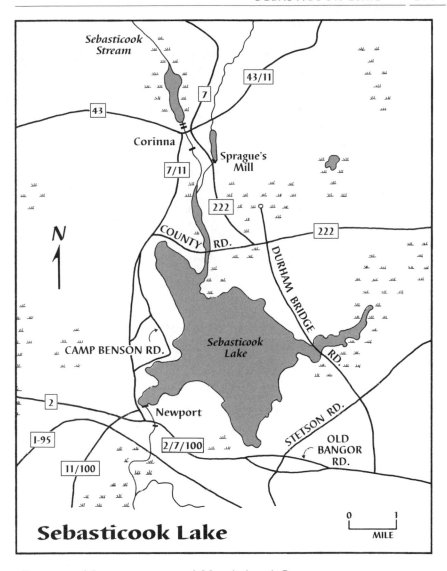

Sebasticook Lake

0   1
|_____|
MILE

Greater and Lesser scaup, and Hooded and Common mergansers. Ruddy Ducks are surprisingly regular in small numbers, and occasionally you may be fortunate enough to find a few Canvasbacks, Redheads, Northern Shovelers, or Gadwalls.

The water level at Sebasticook Lake is controlled by a dam at the southwest corner of the lake in Newport. In late summer and fall, the water level is often quite low, exposing mudflats that provide several acres of excellent shorebird habitat. Thirty to 40 Pectoral Sandpipers are not an uncommon sight here, and sometimes you can find a few American Golden-Plovers among the more abundant Black-bellied

Plovers. Careful investigation has turned up Hudsonian Godwit, Least, Semipalmated, and White-rumped sandpipers, Dunlin (sometimes lingering into November), and even Long-billed Dowitcher. Greater and Lesser yellowlegs and Common Snipe are regular along the lake. As fall pushes on in earnest, look for American Pipits, Snow Buntings, Horned Larks, and Lapland Longspurs feeding on the flats. In the fall of 1993, we even turned up a Sabine's Gull here.

The circuit we describe below is well worth doing anytime between late March and late November. For obvious reasons, you will see the most waterfowl when it is not hunting season. Maine's duck season is split into two periods with a hiatus of two weeks (usually in late October and early November), and this interlude is frequently the best period for interesting fall waterfowl. If you are not familiar with what precautions should be taken during this season in Maine, please see the section entitled "Hunting" in the Introduction.

Durham Bridge

The circuit begins at Newport, exit 39 on I-95. From the exit, drive 0.4 mile north on Route 11/100 to the first intersection and turn right (east) onto Route 2. Proceed 2.8 miles through Newport and fork left onto the lower road (this is unmarked but is Old Bangor Road). In 0.8 mile turn left at the stop sign onto Stetson Road, and in 2 miles turn left again onto Durham Bridge Road. Drive 1.3 miles to the causeway, which is known as Durham Bridge.

Park off the road (watch for soft spots) and check both sides of the causeway carefully. In spring and fall, large flocks of Hooded Mergansers are usually present in the inlet to the right. Smaller numbers of Green-winged Teal and Common Mergansers can also be found feeding in this shallow area. If any mudflats are exposed in late summer and fall, this is also an excellent area for shorebirds; Black-bellied Plovers, American Golden-Plovers, Greater and Lesser yellowlegs, Pectoral, Least, and Semipalmated sandpipers, Dunlin, and Common Snipe are all possibilities. If the water level is low enough, you can walk along the upper edge of the flats to get closer views of the shorebirds. Scan the center of Sebasticook Lake, where in fall there is invariably a large flock of Canada Geese and usually a concentration of scaup, mostly Greaters.

Sprague's Mill

Continue 2.5 miles north on Durham Bridge Road to the first intersection and turn left onto Route 222. In 2.3 miles, just after Route 222 takes a sharp left, turn right into a picnic area at the end of a small, elongated pond. This is known as Sprague's Mill, and it is an especially good place to find Wood, American Black, and Ring-necked ducks, American Wigeons, Greater and Lesser scaup, Northern Pintails, and Hooded Mergansers. In late summer, we have also seen several Pied-billed Grebes here.

To see the upper section of the pond created by Sprague's Mill, drive 0.8 mile north on Route 222 to Corinna and take a sharp right onto Route 43 East (see *Maine Atlas* map 32, E-1). In 0.6 mile stop just beyond the bridge and carefully scan both sides of the road. Many ducks frequent the pond on the right. This inconspicuous and quiet area often attracts a great many birds and is a better-than-average place to see Redheads. If the water level has been lowered, it is possible to walk along the shore to the left for a better view of the cove. Shorebirds sometimes occur in this area, but you are more likely to find Horned Larks or Snow Buntings, and possibly American Pipits and a few Lapland Longspurs. Don't neglect to scan the surrounding hayfields; a Great Gray Owl spent most of one winter sitting on nearby fence posts hunting for mice and voles.

Sebasticook Stream

Return to Corinna and continue straight through the stop sign/flashing light on Route 43. Veer right at the war memorial and flagpole onto Route 43 West, and in 0.2 mile turn right into the woolen-mill plant entrance (poorly marked) just after the third house from the corner. Stay to the left past the high-voltage enclosure as you descend into the parking lot, and just ahead you will see Sebasticook Stream. In the breeding season, American Coots and Common Moorhens can sometimes be found nearby, swimming among the reeds. In spring and fall there are usually Canada Geese, Ring-necked Ducks, American Wigeons, Blue-winged and Green-winged teal, and Hooded Mergansers out on the open part of the stream. In late fall, Swamp Sparrows, American Tree Sparrows, and late migrant warblers seem particularly attracted to the thick cattails skirting the road.

County Road & Camp Benson Road

Return to the memorial and flagpole, turn left, and immediately take the first right (unmarked) onto Route 7/11 south. In 2.2 miles take a sharp left onto County Road, and in 0.2 mile (just after you cross the railroad tracks) stop by the marsh that appears on the right. This inlet is a favorite locality for teal and occasionally for Northern Shovelers and Canvasbacks. Lesser Scaup and Ruddy Ducks can often be seen slightly farther out at the mouth of this inlet. If any mudflats are exposed, there are usually Killdeer, Pectoral Sandpipers, and Common Snipe feeding among the stumps. Marsh Wrens and Swamp Sparrows are abundant in the cattails during the breeding season, when you may also hear Virginia Rails calling. Continue along County Road another 0.9 mile to the bridge and scan this area for additional waterfowl.

Return to Route 7/11, turn left (south), and continue 2.8 miles to the southern end of Camp Benson Road. Turn left here, and in 0.5 mile (just a short way after you cross the railroad tracks) pull off and park along the roadside. The inlet and mudflats to the right are frequently good places to get close views of waterfowl and shorebirds, respectively. American Pipits, Horned Larks, Snow Buntings, and Lapland Longspurs can also be found on the flats in late fall and early spring.

Return again to Route 7/11, continue south, and take a few minutes to scan the southwestern corner of the lake. The road passes right along the shore here, and you can usually see a few Common Loons and several American Black Ducks offshore.

Continue a bit farther south on Route 7/11, and you will see exit 39 on I-95 straight ahead.

LOCAL ACCOMMODATIONS

For information on local accommodations and services in the Newport area, write or call the Bangor Area Chamber of Commerce, 519 Main St., Bangor, ME 04401, telephone 207-947-0307.

Greater Bangor Area

Penobscot River
Orrington Marsh & Fields Pond Nature Center
Bangor Airport
Mount Hope Cemetery

Even with its relatively small population of about 33,000 people, Bangor is Maine's third-largest city. Well known in the mid-1800s as the largest lumber port in the world, Bangor is better known these days as the gateway to Maine's North Woods. The city lies on the west side of the Penobscot River and is connected by three bridges to its sister city of Brewer. Whatever the season, birders can almost always find something of interest in this area.

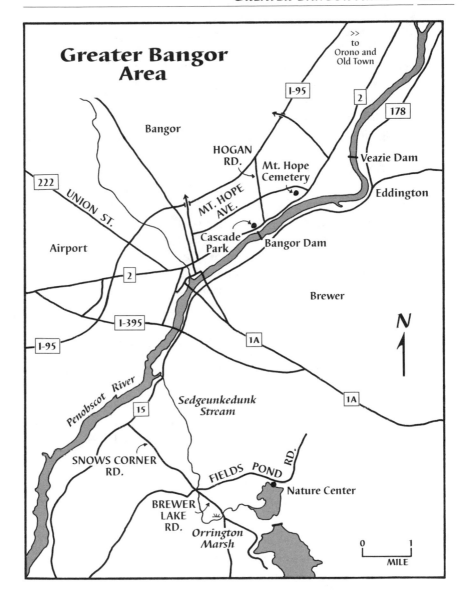

Penobscot River (*MAINE ATLAS* maps 23 & 77)

The Penobscot River is Maine's second-longest river, and birders know the 12-plus miles between Bangor and Old Town as a fine area to look for waterfowl, gulls, and occasionally migrant shorebirds. You are most likely to find something of interest between November and April. Although many birders have traditionally birded the river primarily from the Bangor and Veazie dams, we have found that the entire area between Bangor and Old Town is well worth checking. A good way to bird the river is to drive north up the west side on Route 2 (stopping at the Bangor and Veazie dams and along the roadside wherever you see birds), cross the river in Old Town, and then drive south down Route 178. With leisurely birding stops, this drive takes about an hour and a half.

This stretch of the Penobscot River was long known for the flocks of 30 to 60 Barrow's Goldeneyes that used to concentrate here each winter, but ever since the Bangor Dam was breached a few years ago, the number of birds seen in this area has dropped considerably. Smaller numbers of birds (perhaps 8 to 12) do continue to appear, however, typically arriving by early November and staying through at least March. A good place to look for them is around Eddington Bend (see *Maine Atlas* map 23, B-3), where the river takes a sharp turn and the water is quite swift. American Black Ducks, Common Goldeneyes, and Common Mergansers also occur along the river in winter, and Common Eiders, Buffleheads, and a few scoters can sometimes be found on spring and fall migration.

Each winter several Bald Eagles gather along the river to search the open water for ducks, gulls, and fish. Sometimes you can find one or two Iceland and Glaucous gulls among the flocks of Herring and Great Black-backed gulls. Common Black-headed Gulls appear irregularly in early spring, and on one occasion an Ivory Gull was seen here. The prize for the most bizarre sighting along the river, however, has to go to the Beluga Whales that appeared below the Bangor Dam one winter!

DIRECTIONS

Take I-95 to Bangor and get off at exit 49. Turn right onto Hogan Rd. and continue 1.1 miles to its intersection with Rt. 2 at the Penobscot River. Drive south on Rt. 2 to check the Bangor Dam (see below) or drive north to Orono or Old Town, stopping to check the river as birds and inclination indicate. You may want to cross the river in Old Town and come back south along Rt. 178.

TO CHECK THE BANGOR DAM: At the intersection of Hogan Rd. and Rt. 2 (see above), go south on Rt. 2. In 0.4 mile, on the right, you will see Cascade Park, the small city park located off Cascade Dr. (see *Maine Atlas* map 77, B-4). Park here, cross Rt. 2, and walk north along the railroad tracks to get a good view of the river above the dam; then walk south toward Eastern Maine Medical Center. The Bangor Dam is a good spot to look for Bald Eagles in winter, and occasionally you may see a few Barrow's Goldeneyes. The thickets bordering the railroad tracks often attract migrating passerines (especially warblers) in spring and fall, and sparrows sometimes concentrate in the weedy patches near the river.

To check the Veazie Dam: Go north on Rt. 2, and in Veazie turn right onto Main St. Cross the small railroad bridge, turn right onto Olive St., and follow it to the river and the power plant. You can often get satisfying, close views of Barrow's Goldeneyes near the shore above the power plant from mid-November until December, when ice envelops the river here.

Be sure to check below the dam, too. From the power plant, continue up the hill, turn right onto School St., and in 0.1 mile turn left onto Thompson Rd. Continue 0.4 mile and turn left onto Old County Rd. In 0.2 mile you will see Riverview Park and the Veazie Salmon Club, another good spot from which to scan the river.

Orrington Marsh & Fields Pond Nature Center

About 5 miles south of Bangor, on the east side of the Penobscot River in Orrington, is a lovely freshwater marsh that is properly known as Sedgeunkedunk Stream Marsh. Given what a mouthful that is, however, most local people refer to the spot as Orrington Marsh. Whichever name you go by, the area is known for its spring waterfowl concentrations. About 2 miles east is Fields Pond Nature Center, which was given to the Maine Audubon Society in 1994 and by the late 1990s will be home to a long-awaited environmental education center. Together these two sites can offer some very pleasant birding. Allow a few hours to check them both.

Orrington Marsh (*MAINE ATLAS* map 23, C-2). Orrington Marsh lies at the outlet of nearby Fields Pond and is one of the first places around Bangor to become free of ice in spring—often as early as March 1. Because this is about a month before open water appears anywhere else in the area, good numbers of waterfowl tend to gather here. From mid-March through April you can usually see Canada Geese, Mallards, Wood, American Black, and Ring-necked ducks, Northern Pintails, Green-winged and Blue-winged teal, American Wigeons, Common Goldeneyes, and Hooded and Common mergansers. Occasionally you can also find a small flock of Greater or Lesser Scaup and a Gadwall or two.

As spring advances, the waterfowl begin to thin out, but they are quickly replaced by a good variety of other birds. Between mid-April and mid-June, Common Snipe display and winnow over the marsh, and American Bitterns and Virginia Rails can be heard calling in the early morning. Eastern Kingbirds, Common Yellowthroats, and Swamp Sparrows remain common throughout the nesting season.

You can bird the marsh from a causeway over the Sedgeunkedunk Stream. There is virtually no walking involved, so it is a convenient (and relatively quick) birding stop.

DIRECTIONS

Take I-95 to exit 45 and follow I-395 east to exit 4 (So. Main St., Brewer). Turn south onto Rt. 15. Continue 2.2 miles, turn left onto Snow's Corner Road, and continue straight for 1.9 miles (staying left at the fork in 0.4 mile) to the Orrington Fire Department. Turn left at the yield sign, but at the stop sign 0.1 mile beyond (at the confusing 5-way intersection), turn right onto Brewer Lake Rd. Continue 0.6 mile to the small bridge that crosses Orrington Marsh, and park on the far side of the causeway.

Fields Pond Nature Center (MAINE ATLAS map 23, C-3).   In 1994, when the Maine Audubon Society received a bequest of 170 acres bordering the northern and eastern shores of Fields Pond in Orrington, the Fields Pond Nature Center became a reality. This lovely tract of land includes lakeshore, mixed-deciduous woods and mature softwoods, hayfields, and associated wetlands. An environmental education center is planned for the site (construction is scheduled to begin in 1997), and volunteers have already begun offering regular field trips and nature walks. The first trails were established in 1995, and more are planned for the future.

Birders should be able to find much of interest here. Preliminary investigations have turned up a good mix of nesting species on the property, including American Bittern, American Black Duck, Blue-winged Teal, Virginia Rail, Common Snipe, Barred Owl, Black-backed and Pileated woodpeckers, Alder Flycatcher, Winter Wren, Brown Creeper, Northern Parula, Blackburnian and Chestnut-sided warblers, Common Yellowthroat, Scarlet Tanager, Savannah Sparrow, and Bobolink. Bald Eagles and Ospreys nest nearby and are sometimes seen over the pond.

The nature center property is open every day from dawn to dusk, free of charge. There currently are no facilities for visitors, but this will change when the environmental education center is built. For more information, write or call the Maine Audubon Society at Fields

Pond Nature Center, 1 Edgewood Dr., Orono, ME 04473, telephone 207-581-2900.

DIRECTIONS

From the causeway at Orrington Marsh, follow Brewer Lake Road 0.6 mile back to the stop sign at the confusing five-way intersection. Take a sharp right onto Fields Pond Rd. In 2 miles, where you see a Maine Audubon Society sign, turn right into the nature center property.

Bangor Airport (*MAINE ATLAS* map 77, B-1)

The Bangor airport lies just west of I-95 and is bordered by open fields and grasslands that are worth checking between about mid-July and mid-March. Although this used to be one of the best birding sites in Bangor, in recent years the city has planted numerous trees in the area—reducing the expanse of open space and, with it, the variety and numbers of open-country birds the area used to attract. In July and August, however, you may still be lucky enough to see a few southbound Upland Sandpipers, and in September, American Golden-Plovers. An occasional Red-tailed or Rough-legged Hawk patrols the fields in winter, and a Snowy Owl sometimes perches atop a utility pole or fence post. Snow Buntings and Horned Larks are still quite regular in late fall and winter. In summer look for small numbers of nesting Savannah Sparrows, Eastern Meadowlarks, and Bobolinks. Two inauspicious-looking canals along Maine Avenue (see "Directions," below) are also worth checking. Look for Pied-billed Grebe, American Bittern, Blue-winged and Green-winged teal, and Common Snipe in this area.

DIRECTIONS

Take I-95 to exit 47 (Union St.) and follow signs toward the airport. In 1 mile, at the second stoplight, turn left into the airport. Scan the open areas of grassland and old tarmac on both sides of the beginning of this road and in both directions along the first crossroad, which is Maine Ave. If you turn left onto Maine Ave., you will soon see a small canal on the right, and a little farther down the road, another on the left.

Mount Hope Cemetery (*MAINE ATLAS* map 77, B-4)

Mount Hope Cemetery, encompassing 254 acres in the center of Bangor, is one of the oldest "garden" cemeteries in the country. It was designed by the well-known Maine architect Charles G. Bryant. The cemetery lies between the Penobscot River and Mount Hope Avenue and includes an attractive mix of large deciduous trees, tall conifers, ornamental shrubs, ponds, and a stream.

At the height of the spring warbler migration, which usually peaks in the second to third week in May, Mount Hope is a delightful spot to spend a few hours in the early morning. Virtually all of northern New England's regularly occurring migrant warblers pass through here, and the visibility into the trees is quite good. When you come in the main entrance, park and simply walk around, listening and looking for birds. Great Horned Owls, Pileated Woodpeckers, and Pine Warblers are among the more interesting nesting species. Christmas Bird Count participants come here in hopes of finding a Great Horned Owl or, in nearby fields, a Ring-necked Pheasant.

The cemetery is open seven days a week, free of charge, from 7:30 a.m. to 7:30 p.m. from May 1 through October 31 and from 7:30 a.m. to 4:30 p.m. from November 1 through April 30. There are no facilities for visitors.

DIRECTIONS
The main cemetery entrance is located on the west side of Rt. 2, 0.6 mile north of the intersection of Rt. 2 and Hogan Rd. (see the directions for the Penobscot River, above).

LOCAL ACCOMMODATIONS
For information on local accommodations and services, write or call the Bangor Area Chamber of Commerce, 519 Main St., Bangor, ME 04401, telephone 207-947-0307.

Orono & Surroundings

University of Maine at Orono
Demerritt (University) Forest
Hirundo Wildlife Research Area
County Road, Milford
Sunkhaze Meadows National Wildlife Refuge

Orono is 8 miles north of Bangor and is best known as the site of the University of Maine at Orono (UMO) campus. There are five good birding spots in the area, two of them on campus and three within about 5 miles of campus. You can find some very good birding in this area at just about any time of year.

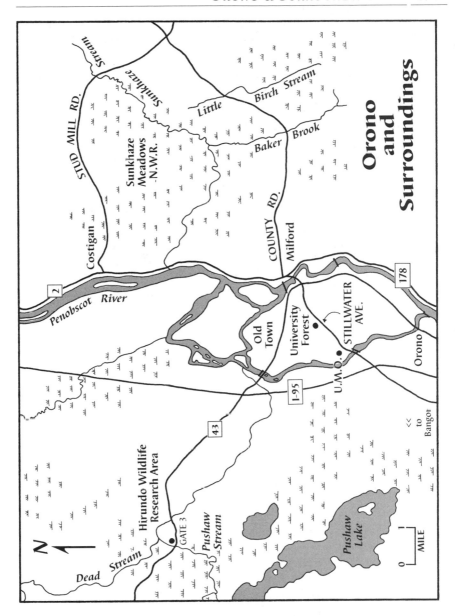

University of Maine at Orono
(*MAINE ATLAS* map 23, A-3 & -4)

The University of Maine at Orono, attractively landscaped with large deciduous trees, conifers, and many ornamental shrubs, provides a pleasant place to bird at any time of year. Winter, however, is the undeniable highlight. This is the best place in Maine, if not all New

England, to see wintering Bohemian Waxwings. These strikingly handsome birds were first observed around the university in the late 1960s, and since then they have returned almost every year (and in increasing numbers) to feed on the extensive ornamental plantings that decorate the campus. There are no guarantees, of course—birds fly! Particularly in early winter, flocks of as many as 500 to 1,000 birds are sometimes seen. The birds are very erratic, however, and even if present locally, they may not be present on campus every day. Pine Grosbeaks are also winter visitors and can often be found feeding in the crab-apple grove in the Littlefield Ornamental Garden.

The waxwings and grosbeaks typically appear by mid-November, and in a "good" winter they stay into March or early April. The best way to locate both species is to walk around the campus investigating fruited ornamental trees and shrubs. Check any large conifers; the waxwings find these especially attractive as roost sites, and oftentimes the birds' high, thin, twittering notes will reveal their presence. Begin near Memorial Union and Fogler Library, and make a loop around the campus. Be sure to include the ornamental garden. In many years White-winged Crossbills are also regular winter visitors on campus; Red Crossbills are irregular.

In fall, the open setting of the campus, and especially the large fields to the north and the expansive parking areas, usually attract good numbers of migrating American Pipits. Horned Larks and Snow Buntings are also fairly regular at this season, and a few Lapland Longspurs and Dickcissels are occasionally noted. From Memorial Union, check the large parking lot and weedy garden plots to the east. Continue east across the main access road and follow the gravel road through the deciduous trees to the large hayfields.

During the breeding season, a few pairs of Common Nighthawks usually nest on the campus, and Warbling Vireos are common in the large elms and Silver Maples. In the mixed-coniferous woodlot behind Nutting Hall and adjacent to the performing arts center parking lot, look for nesting Great Crested Flycatchers, Golden-crowned Kinglets, Veerys, Hermit and Wood thrushes, Pine, Black-throated Green, Yellow-rumped, Black-and-white, and Chestnut-sided warblers, Northern Parulas, Northern Waterthrushes, Ovenbirds, American Redstarts, and Rose-breasted Grosbeaks.

The UMO campus is accessible year-round, free of charge.

DIRECTIONS

Get off I-95 at exit 51 and follow Stillwater Ave. 0.8 mile east to College Ave. Turn right onto College Ave., and in 1.6 miles turn left onto Munson Ave. About 300 feet ahead, on the right, is an outdoor directory and map of the campus. Locate Memorial Union, Littlefield Ornamental Garden, Nutting Hall, and Demerritt (University) Forest (see below) on the map before continuing.

Demerritt (University) Forest
(*MAINE ATLAS* map 33, E-4)

Situated on the northern end of the UMO campus is the Dwight B. Demerritt Forest (better known to most people as University Forest), a large tract of agricultural fields and mixed deciduous and coniferous woods. This area is worth a visit at any time of year. The combination of many different conifer patches within the forest and its close proximity to the mature maple and oak trees that border the Penobscot River make this an excellent area to observe the spring migration. Especially in the second and third weeks in May, this is a reliable area to see virtually all of northern New England's regularly occurring migrant warblers, including softwood species such as Cape May, Blackpoll, and Bay-breasted. You can also see a good variety of other migrant passerines. Plan to spend at least two hours here.

At least 16 species of warblers remain to breed in the forest: Tennessee, Nashville, Yellow, Chestnut-sided, Magnolia, Cape May, Yellow-rumped, Black-throated Green, Blackburnian, Pine (uncommon), Bay-breasted (uncommon), Canada, Black-and-white, Northern Parula, American Redstart, and Ovenbird. A host of other birds nest in or near the edge of the forest, among them Northern Goshawk, Sharp-shinned Hawk, Ruffed Grouse, Great Horned and Barred owls, Ruby-throated Hummingbird, Northern Flicker, Pileated Woodpecker, Great Crested and Least flycatchers, Eastern Wood-Pewee, Red-breasted Nuthatch, Winter Wren, Golden-crowned and Ruby-crowned kinglets, Veery, Wood, Hermit, and Swainson's thrushes (the last uncommon), Solitary, Red-eyed, and Warbling vireos, Scarlet Tanager, Rose-breasted Grosbeak, White-throated Sparrow, Dark-eyed Junco, Purple Finch, Red and White-winged crossbills (both irregular), Pine Siskin, and Evening Grosbeak.

In winter, the variety of conifer cones that are usually available make the forest one of the best places in the region to look for White-winged and Red crossbills. And Ruffed Grouse can sometimes be found eating buds in the aspens and birches along College Avenue Extension in winter.

University Forest is accessible year-round, free of charge. There are no facilities for visitors.

DIRECTIONS

FROM I-95: Take exit 51 off I-95 and follow Stillwater Ave. 0.8 mile east. Turn left onto College Ave. Ext. and continue 1.1 miles to the Sewall Road gate (see below).

FROM THE CAMPUS: Exit the campus onto College Ave. At the stoplight at Stillwater Ave., go straight (crossing Stillwater Ave.) onto College Ave. Ext. In 1.1 miles on the right is Sewall Rd., a gated gravel road marked with a small sign. Park in the gravel pull-off on the left side of the road. We recommend the following loop: walk about 0.3 mile down Sewall Rd., take the first left onto Logan Rd., and follow it to a second gate, which comes out 0.6 mile farther north on College Ave. Ext. From here walk south (left) back to your car. This is a pleasant and easy 2-mile walk.

Hirundo Wildlife Research Area
(*MAINE ATLAS* map 33, E-2)

The Hirundo Wildlife Research Area, about 5 miles northwest of Old Town, was created by two brothers who loved the outdoors and wanted to share the pleasure they took in it with others. The Larouche brothers retired to Alton with the vision of developing this interesting property into a wildlife refuge, and they did just that. The property is now maintained as a cooperative trust with the University of Maine. The birding is most interesting during the breeding season, when you should allow at least a few hours to explore the area in any depth.

Hirundo comprises 1,500 acres of predominantly mixed deciduous and coniferous woods as well as open fields, a small pond, and two streams. The breeding-bird population here complements that of the predominantly coniferous University Forest to the southeast. Chestnut-sided Warblers, American Redstarts, Northern Waterthrushes, and other hardwood species are much more numerous at Hirundo than they are in University Forest. More than 100 nest boxes scattered across the open meadow are inhabited by Tree Swallows and are occasionally used as singing perches by nesting Savannah Sparrows. The wetland adjacent to the Pushaw and Dead streams (accessible from Gate 4; see below) also supports a pleasant variety of birds in spring and summer, among them American Bittern, Great Blue Heron, several species of ducks (Wood Duck, Blue-winged Teal, and Hooded Merganser are the most likely to be seen), Least Flycatcher, Eastern Wood-Pewee, Marsh Wren, and Swamp Sparrow. The most satisfactory way to explore this wetland is with a canoe, which we highly recommend, especially in summer. (In spring you need to be careful of fast water.)

You should also keep your eyes open for mammals at Hirundo. White-tailed Deer, Red Fox, Woodchuck, Red and Northern Flying squirrels, and Fisher are all reported commonly. Along the streams you may see Moose, Mink, Beaver, Muskrat, and River Otter.

Access into Hirundo is from four gated roads that lie within a 0.6-mile stretch along Route 43. Gate 3 is the only gate where you can park, but from here you can easily walk east or west to the other three. There is a well-marked trail system at each gate. The trail at Gate 4 (0.2 mile west of Gate 3 and just across Pushaw Stream) is generally the most interesting for birds; the gravel road parallels the stream and leads to a productive wetland area.

Hirundo is open seven days a week, from 9:00 a.m. to 5:00 p.m. in summer and from 9:00 a.m. to dusk the rest of the year. There are no facilities for visitors. There is no fee, but donations are gladly accepted.

DIRECTIONS

Take I-95 to exit 52 (Old Town, Hudson), then Rt. 43 west toward Hudson. In 5.1 miles you will see Gate 3 on the right. All visitors must register at the house at Gate 3. Please be sure to obey the few simple rules posted at each gate.

County Road, Milford (MAINE ATLAS map 33, E-5 & D-5)

A good place to see a wide mix of breeding birds and, with luck, a few boreal residents is along an 18-mile loop that we refer to as County Road. Just east of Old Town, County Road runs out of Milford and forms a loop (with the Stud Mill Road and Route 2) that circles around Sunkhaze Meadows National Wildlife Refuge (see below) and through a variety of upland-forest and wetland habitats. During the breeding season you can find Yellow-bellied Flycatchers and sometimes as many as 22 species of warblers, and at any time of year you may be lucky enough to find a Spruce Grouse, Black-backed Woodpecker, Gray Jay, or Boreal Chickadee (the woodpecker is uncommon, the others rare). The best time to drive the loop for breeding species is between mid-May and late July. Allow about two to three hours to cover the area at a leisurely pace. In June and early July be prepared for an abundance of hungry mosquitoes and black flies.

More than 120 species have been documented nesting in the County Road area, including Spruce Grouse, Black-backed Woodpecker, Yellow-bellied Flycatcher, and Mourning Warbler. This diversity is undoubtedly the result of the varied types of habitat compressed into a relatively small area. Within an approximately 3-mile radius are dense spruce-fir forests, White Pine–Eastern Hemlock stands, Atlantic White Cedar groves, northern hardwoods, deciduous wooded swamps, alder swales, streamside meadows, open Tamarack-dominated bogs, and regenerating clear-cuts.

The loop we describe below begins in Orono at exit 51 on I-95. Although we mention several specific stops, you will probably want to make many others; simply stop and bird along the road as inclination and good habitat warrant. This is a relatively quiet road (beware of logging trucks on the Stud Mill Road, however), and even from the roadside you should be able to do some fine birding. Early morning is likely to be the quietest and most productive time, especially during the breeding season.

Take I-95 to exit 51 (Stillwater Avenue) and follow signs toward Old Town and Route 2. Cross the Penobscot River on Route 2 North, and 0.1 mile north of the intersection with Route 178, turn right onto County Road (this is a total of 4 miles from I-95).

After 3.7 paved miles, County Road becomes a well-maintained gravel road. The first major birding area is 6.1 miles down the road, along Little Birch Stream (you will see a narrow, gated private road on the left). Spruce Grouse (rare) nest in this area in some years, as do Ruffed Grouse. If you are lucky enough to spot a grouse here, the two species are easy to distinguish on the basis of behavior alone: Spruce Grouse are tame and hardly ever flush, whereas Ruffed Grouse almost always flush in an explosive whir. Nesting Black-backed Woodpecker and Yellow-bellied Flycatcher have also been found in this area, and Red and White-winged crossbills are seen irregularly throughout the year.

From Little Birch Stream, County Road climbs gradually into hemlock and mixed-hardwood forests where Hermit Thrushes, Red-eyed and Solitary vireos, Black-throated Blue, Black-throated Green, Blackburnian, Bay-breasted, Cape May (uncommon), and Black-and-white warblers, American Redstarts, Scarlet Tanagers, and Rose-breasted Grosbeaks breed. Yellow-throated Vireos, rare this far north, have occurred on a few occasions in the tall Northern Red Oaks. Continuing east, be sure to check the cedar swamps for Yellow-bellied Flycatchers. If you see any extensive stands of dead trees that still have bark on them, look for Black-backed Woodpecker. This species likes to search for food on dead standing timber; recently (5 to 8 years) dead or burned trees near a stream are excellent areas to look.

Beginning about 1 mile beyond Little Birch Stream, County Road passes through a productive stretch of coniferous woods. Take the time to make frequent stops and to walk along the road. Boreal-forest warblers and Yellow-bellied Flycatchers are common, and in late June and July grouse broods (most likely Ruffed, but check adults carefully) sometimes sun themselves on the side of the road. In winter this is a good area for winter finches; the walking is easy, the traffic is minimal, visibility is unobstructed, and most importantly, winter seeds and cones are usually abundant.

Between 7.9 and 8.3 miles down County Road, take the time to walk along the edge of the Atlantic White Cedar swamp. Keep an eye out for raptors; Northern Harrier, Osprey, Northern Goshawk, Sharp-shinned, Red-shouldered, and Broad-winged hawks, and American Kestrel all nest in the vicinity. Barred and Great Horned owls also nest nearby.

Continue down County Road until it reaches the four-way stop sign at Stud Mill Road (8.4 miles from Route 2). Turn left onto Stud Mill Road (unmarked) and, if you wish, check more of the cedar swamp immediately on your left (watch out for logging trucks on this road). Continue 2.3 miles to the one-lane bridge that crosses Sunkhaze Stream. This is widely known as one of the best trout streams in central Maine. Birders can often find Alder, Yellow-bellied, and Least flycatchers, Ruby-crowned and Golden-crowned kinglets, and Bay-breasted, Blackburnian, Yellow-rumped, and Magnolia warblers, all within a few yards of the bridge.

Stud Mill Road continues past several streamside wetlands, tall woodlands, and patches of second growth, the last the result of extensive lumbering operations in the 1970s and 1980s. Any still-open, low, regenerating areas, even right along the roadside, can provide good Mourning Warbler habitat, especially if raspberries and blackberries have developed in the understory. Stop again 6.9 miles beyond the County Road intersection, where the road passes through a bog dominated by Tamarack and Black Spruce. This is another good spot to check for breeding birds, including Ruby-crowned Kinglet, Palm and Nashville warblers, and Lincoln's and White-throated sparrows.

Continue another 0.5 mile to the stop sign at the entrance to the stud mill (2-by-4s are made here, in case you were wondering). Turn right, drive 0.3 mile to Greenfield Road, turn left, and continue 0.3 mile to Route 2 in Costigan. Turn left to drive back to Old Town.

Sunkhaze Meadows National Wildlife Refuge
(*MAINE ATLAS* map 33, E-4 & -5)

Sunkhaze Meadows National Wildlife Refuge in Milford, established in 1988, consists of almost 1,000 acres of peatland, marsh, and floodplain forests. With an estimated 3,300 acres of peatland (the second-largest peatland in Maine) and 10 streams, this is a highly unusual and complex wetland ecosystem. When the snow melts in early spring and the ground is still frozen, the vast meadows for which the refuge is named look more like shallow lakes.

Birders may know Sunkhaze Meadows best for some very impressive finds, including Yellow Rail (probably breeding) and Sedge Wren (a breeder in 1991), but more common here are the birds that typify a large wetland. American Black, Wood, and Ring-necked ducks, Blue-winged Teal, and Hooded Mergansers all nest on the refuge, and several other waterfowl species stop over on spring and fall migration. American Bittern, Great Blue Heron, American Woodcock, Common Snipe, Marsh Wren, Veery, Northern Waterthrush, and Bobolink also nest here, and Nelson's Sharp-tailed Sparrow (very rare in inland Maine) is a possible nester.

Mammals seen with some regularity on the refuge include Moose, Black Bear, Porcupine, Beaver, Muskrat, Mink, and River Otter.

Access into the refuge is difficult, and the refuge office recommends that anyone planning a visit call beforehand for information. Several old logging roads provide access by foot, but the best way to bird the refuge is by canoe. Plan on a full and rigorous day for the latter, and be prepared to haul your canoe over several Beaver dams. Birder Judy Markowsky, who knows this area well, suggests that you put in at Baker Brook on County Road (see *Maine Atlas* map 33, E-5) or at Sunkhaze Stream on Stud Mill Road (*Maine Atlas* map 33, D-5), and take out at Sunkhaze Stream on Route 2 (*Maine Atlas* map 33, E-4).

The refuge is open to all legal hunting and fishing. For information on what precautions should be taken during this season in Maine, see the section entitled "Hunting" in the Introduction.

The refuge is open daily from sunrise to sunset, free of charge. There are no facilities for visitors. For more information, call or write Sunkhaze Meadows NWR, 1033 South Main Street, Old Town, ME 04468, telephone 207-827-6138. Among other things, ask them to send you a copy of Judy Markowsky's short write-up called "Birding the Sunkhaze."

Baxter State Park
(*MAINE ATLAS* maps 50, 51, 56, & 57)

> *Man is born to die. His works are short lived. Buildings crumble,*
> *monuments decay, wealth vanishes but Katahdin in all its glory*
> *forever shall remain the mountain of the people of Maine.*
> —Percival P. Baxter, 1941

Baxter State Park is a 200,000-acre wilderness in north-central Maine that is widely recognized as one of the most spectacular natural areas in New England. Although often considered to be primarily a hiker's park, this remote tract is also a favorite haunt of naturalists. For birders, Baxter State Park offers the opportunity to observe a splendid variety of breeding species—many of them of special interest—in a remarkable setting. More than 130 species nest in the park, including Northern Goshawk, Spruce Grouse, Black-backed and Three-toed woodpeckers, Yellow-bellied Flycatcher, Gray Jay, Boreal Chickadee, Bicknell's (formerly Gray-cheeked) Thrush, American Pipit, 23 species of warblers, Rusty Blackbird, and Fox Sparrow. Bird activity is at its peak between early June and early July, when breeding species are most conspicuous. Early June, when the birds are most vocal, is usually a wonderful time to bird Baxter, even with the black flies. By the first week of August, flocks of migrant warblers are already heading south, and the park can seem rather quiet. Plan to spend at least a few days here if possible. In addition to enjoying the birds, you will have the opportunity to experience a special part of Maine's wilderness where Moose, Black Bear, Mink, Coyote, Beaver, Bobcat, Fisher, Pine Marten, and River Otter also reside.

Baxter State Park was given to the people of Maine by former governor Percival P. Baxter. Recognizing the unique character of Katahdin ("the great mountain") and the land surrounding it, Baxter purchased the property in 28 parcels, which he donated to the state between 1931 and 1962 with the stipulation that the land be kept "forever wild." Today the park encompasses more than 200,000 acres of dramatic and varied terrain in the heart of Maine's northern forest. Included within it are 46 peaks and ridges (18 of them higher than 3,500 feet), numerous streams and ponds, some of Maine's oldest and most significant old-growth forests, and the state's most extensive

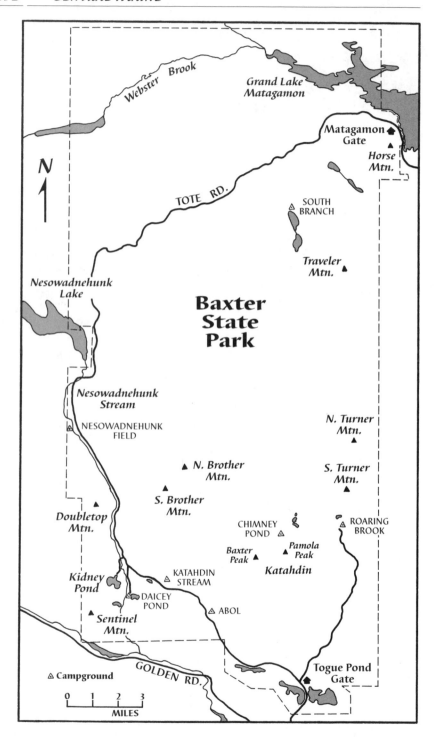

N

Webster Brook

Grand Lake
Matagamon

Matagamon
Gate

Horse
Mtn.

TOTE RD.

SOUTH
BRANCH

Traveler
Mtn.

Nesowadnehunk
Lake

**Baxter
State
Park**

Nesowadnehunk
Stream

NESOWADNEHUNK
FIELD

N. Turner
Mtn.

▲ N. Brother
Mtn.

S. Turner
Mtn.

S. Brother
Mtn.

Doubletop
Mtn.

CHIMNEY
POND

ROARING
BROOK

Baxter
Peak

Pamola
Peak

Katahdin

Kidney
Pond

KATAHDIN
STREAM

DAICEY
POND

ABOL

Sentinel
Mtn.

△ Campground

GOLDEN RD.

Togue Pond
Gate

0   1   2   3
MILES

alpine habitat. Dominating the landscape is Maine's highest and most massive mountain—and an important symbol to all Maine people—5,267-foot-high Katahdin.

Because it is a wilderness area, Baxter State Park strictly regulates access and use. Visitors can enter at two points only—Togue Pond Gate near the southeast corner and Matagamon Gate near the northeast corner—and must register with a ranger. Both gates open at 6:00 a.m.; Matagamon closes at 9:00 p.m. and Togue Pond at 10:00 p.m. Activities within the park are also strictly controlled. (For example, no oversized vehicles, motorcycles, outboard motors, or pets are permitted in the park, and no audio devices, including cellular phones and cassette players, may be operated.) Reservations are virtually essential for an overnight stay. There are motels and campgrounds outside the park, but you will undoubtedly want to be inside it for the dawn chorus. See "Camping in Baxter State Park," below, for more information.

Much of Baxter State Park is accessible to visitors, especially those willing to hike (see "Hiking in Baxter State Park," below). More than 175 miles of trails, several of them among the steepest and most demanding in New England, traverse the park. Many hikers know the park as the northern terminus of the 2,000-mile-long Appalachian Trail. One main road, the Tote Road, runs north-south along the western boundary of the park and provides access to the trails and several lowland sites. Between the roads and the trails, you can see a good deal of the park.

Anywhere you go in Baxter State Park between early June and early July, you are likely to see a wealth of birds, plants, mammals, and scenery. The birding spots we mention below are among our favorites, but they certainly are not the only good ones. Whether you are climbing Katahdin or birding primarily from the Tote Road, take the time to explore this magnificent area at a leisurely pace and to savor what it has to offer. Come well prepared for the black flies at this time of year; an ample supply of insect repellent, long pants, long-sleeved shirts, a bandanna for your neck, and a good head net (available at L.L. Bean and at many outdoor-supply stores) are all recommended.

Your first stop should be at park headquarters in Millinocket (at the intersection of Central and Sycamore streets, right next to McDonalds), where maps, checklists, and books are available for sale. It is open from 8:00 a.m. to 4:00 p.m. daily between Memorial Day and Labor Day, and Monday through Friday the rest of the year. Don't worry if you can't stop here, however; during the camping season you can get basic maps and checklists at the Togue Pond Visitor Center or from a campground ranger. It is also worth asking the rangers for information on recent sightings or species of interest.

The areas we mention below are all marked by signs in the park, so we do not give specific mileages here. We have divided the sites into two basic sections, lowland sites and higher-elevation sites.

Lowland Sites

Togue Pond Beach & Picnic Area. The Togue Pond Beach and Picnic Area lies just inside the southern entrance to Baxter State Park and overlooks Upper and Lower Togue ponds. Common Loons can be seen and heard throughout the summer, as can Belted Kingfishers. This area is of particular interest because it is one of the northernmost localities where Whip-poor-wills regularly breed. Their loud, repetitive calls can be heard in the early evening and again before dawn. Pine Warblers, also approaching their northern breeding limit, can be seen and heard in the tall White and Red pines bordering the ponds.

At Togue Pond Gate, the southern entrance to the park, the road forks right toward Roaring Brook Campground. Just beyond the fork, a small weedy pond on the left side forms the only marshy wetland habitat in this section of the park. Take the time to bird this area; American Bittern, American Black Duck, Common Nighthawk (early morning and evening), Alder Flycatcher, Wilson's, Palm, and Yellow warblers, and Swamp Sparrow all occur here.

Roaring Brook Campground & Sandy Stream Pond. Roaring Brook Campground, situated at 1,480 feet and 8.1 miles north of Togue Pond Gate, is one of the main access points for hikers interested in climbing Katahdin. For birders, the mixture of mature birch-maple forest and spruce-fir tracts makes this area an excellent introduction to the park's breeding birds. The presence of Philadelphia Vireos singing in the large birches over the parking lot should be the first clue that Baxter State Park offers a delightful birding and outdoor experience.

From the campground, hike to Sandy Stream Pond, where you should have outstanding views of Katahdin and an excellent chance of seeing Moose. This easy and fairly level hike (1.4 miles round-trip) is justifiably the most popular short hike in the park. The trail passes through stately Sugar Maples and Paper and Yellow birches before changing into a thick spruce-fir forest. The dense Moose population around the pond contributes to the sodden state of the trail, and the number of heavy, large footprints and Moose droppings reveal just how common these curiously constructed animals are here. (Rubber-bottomed boots are recommended.) Moose can often be seen plunging their heads below the surface to feed on the succulent vegetation. In fact, this is one of the best places in Maine to see these large beasts, accurately described by one naturalist as having "jack-ass ears, a punching-bag nose, an overhanging muzzle, a bell, or dewlap, that dangles from its throat, humped shoulders, a short body, long legs, and a tiny rump on which a 3½-inch tail seems pinned by mistake."

In June and early July the variety of warblers and other birds between Roaring Brook and Sandy Stream Pond can seem astonishing. First there are the deciduous-forest birds: Broad-winged Hawk, Ruffed Grouse, Hairy and Pileated woodpeckers, Yellow-bellied Sapsucker, Great Crested and Least flycatchers, Eastern Wood-Pewee, White-breasted Nuthatch, Brown Creeper, Veery, Wood Thrush, Red-eyed, Philadelphia, and Warbling vireos, Nashville, Black-throated Blue, and Black-and-white warblers, Northern Parula, Ovenbird, American Redstart, Scarlet Tanager, and Rose-breasted Grosbeak. In the mixed-transition forest listen for the exquisite song of the Winter Wren along with those of the Hermit Thrush, Solitary Vireo, and Black-throated Green, Magnolia, and Canada warblers. The spruce-fir woods support their own nesting species: Spruce Grouse, Downy and Black-backed woodpeckers, Yellow-bellied Flycatcher, Gray Jay, Boreal Chickadee, Red-breasted Nuthatch, Golden-crowned and Ruby-crowned kinglets, Swainson's Thrush, Tennessee, Cape May, Yellow-rumped, Blackburnian, and Bay-breasted warblers, Purple Finch, Pine Siskin, White-winged Crossbill, and Pine Grosbeak (the last two irregular). Finally, on or around the edge of the pond look for Ring-necked Duck, Common Merganser, Spotted Sandpiper, Belted Kingfisher, Tree Swallow, Alder and Olive-sided flycatchers, Eastern Kingbird, Cedar Waxwing, Yellow Warbler, Common Yellowthroat, Northern Waterthrush, Rusty Blackbird, and Evening Grosbeak. Not a bad collection of possibilities for a short walk. Northern Goshawks and Sharp-shinned Hawks breed in the area and are occasionally observed flying over the pond.

It is possible to make a loop around the northern end of Sandy Stream Pond to the Russell Pond Trail and back to Roaring Brook Campground (full loop 2.5 miles from Roaring Brook). This is an excellent circuit for a morning bird walk. Philadelphia Vireos are quite common along the Russell Pond Trail section of the loop.

Note that parking can be a problem at Roaring Brook. The dirt lot isn't all that big, and it is often full by 7:00 a.m., especially on weekends. Get there early in the morning or try again in the late afternoon after many of the day-hikers have left.

Tote Road. The Tote Road is the unimproved dirt road that runs primarily north-south along the western boundary of the park between Togue Pond Gate and Matagamon Gate. Seven side roads lead off it, including the road to Roaring Brook Campground and Sandy Stream Pond. It is 41 miles from Togue Pond Gate to Matagamon Gate, and although it may not sound like a very long trip, it can easily take a full day—partly because of the condition of the road and partly because you will want to stop at so many places along the way. All of the park roads are narrow and winding, and the maximum speed is 20 miles an hour.

The Tote Road passes through a variety of lowland habitats and offers excellent birding. Even casual hikers will find suitable terrain, and superb birding, in these lowland sites. We made a short trip to the park one summer with our young kids in tow, and even though we never left the lowlands, we saw all of the park's specialties except the two you really do have to climb to: Bicknell's Thrush and American Pipit.

The lowland sites that follow are all accessible from the Tote Road, proceeding from south to north.

Abol Pond. Turn left onto the Tote Road just beyond Togue Pond Gate, and in 2 miles the road will bisect Abol Pond. Surrounding the pond to the right is a boggy area with scattered, tall Tamarack and Black Spruce trees bordered by a thin strip of alders. Looming over it all is majestic Katahdin. You can scan both the pond and bog from the roadside. Look for Common Loon, Wood Duck, Common Goldeneye, Hooded Merganser, and possibly Red-breasted Merganser on the pond and for Palm and Wilson's warblers and Lincoln's Sparrow in the bog. Nashville, Magnolia, Yellow-rumped, Pine, and Canada warblers, Ovenbird, Common Yellowthroat, and American Redstart can also be seen or heard in the area. Along the road you can sometimes find a Common Nighthawk or two perching on a horizontal pine branch.

Abol Campground. Abol Campground lies in a mixed woodland where the lovely songs of Hermit and Swainson's thrushes fill the twilight forest. You will find essentially the same breeding birds here as at Roaring Brook Campground.

Beyond Abol Campground, the Tote Road passes through a long stretch of deciduous greenery where the chorus of Veerys, Wood, Swainson's, and Hermit thrushes, Black-throated Blue Warblers, Ovenbirds, Rose-breasted Grosbeaks, and Scarlet Tanagers makes for delightful birding. Although never common, Philadelphia Vireos can also be found along this stretch of road. Listen for their slightly more sluggish and less stereotyped song among the ever-abundant Red-eyed Vireos—and remember that finding Philadelphia Vireos, which tend to remain hidden in the canopy, is always a challenge.

Katahdin Stream Campground & Tracy Pond. Katahdin Stream Campground is beautifully situated around a broad meadow with a mixed forest in the background. This is a good place to see some of the park's raptors, notably Northern Goshawk (uncommon) and Sharp-shinned, Red-shouldered (uncommon), Red-tailed, and Broad-winged hawks. It is also an especially good area to hear (and sometimes see) drumming Ruffed Grouse in spring.

Just up the road from the campground is Tracy Pond, which is surrounded by dense coniferous forest and a narrow border of thick bog vegetation. Look for Common Goldeneye, Common and Red-breasted mergansers, Palm Warbler, and Swamp Sparrow on or near the pond. Walking along this stretch of the Tote Road, you may also see or hear Black-backed Woodpecker, Yellow-bellied and Olive-sided flycatchers, Boreal Chickadee, Solitary Vireo, and Tennessee, Cape May, and Bay-breasted warblers. This can also be a good area for Spruce Grouse, which sometimes dust along the road. You will find the pond 1.1 miles beyond the campground, on the left side of the road. There is a narrow unmarked path and space to park one vehicle along the roadside.

Daicey & Kidney Ponds to Ledge Falls. Daicey Pond and Kidney Pond are two of the most popular places to stay in the park. Both offer comfortable accommodations in rustic cabins, good accessibility to several trails, and for a nominal fee, canoe rentals. The birding directly around the ponds is very pleasant, though not exceptionally diverse. If you have never been awakened in the middle of the night by a yodeling Common Loon, however, you will be in for a real treat.

Just north of Kidney Pond, the Tote Road begins to parallel Nesowadnehunk (pronounced "sour-da-hunk") Stream. Rusty Blackbirds can sometimes be found in areas where spruces and firs border the streamside alders. Elsewhere in the park, look for this species in old Beaver flowages and along alder-bordered streams.

Continuing north on the Tote Road, be sure to stop at Ledge Falls, a fascinating sculptured streambed that is a favorite swimming (and sliding) spot. This is also a good place to scan for raptors soaring against the steep cliff face of Doubletop Mountain to the south. Among the species you should look for is Peregrine Falcon. In the 1980s, Horse Mountain (near the Matagamon Gate) was a hacking site for Peregrines, and since then single birds have been reported in spring and summer from many places in the park.

Nesowadnehunk Field Campground. Nesowadnehunk Field Campground marks the southern edge of what is often referred to as the Nesowadnehunk, or northwest, section of Baxter State Park. The major habitat type is mature spruce-fir forest, much of which was infested with Spruce Budworm in the early 1980s. The tall spruces you see along the Tote Road give way at higher elevations to stunted spruce forests. Other important habitat types in the area include cutover or successional forests, alder-lined stream valleys, mature beech-maple forests, and a large field. Much of this portion of the park was logged between approximately 1830 and 1965.

A combination of remoteness, excellent birding, and a variety of mammals makes the Nesowadnehunk Field Campground one of the most interesting birding and natural-history areas in north-central Maine. The ornithological attractions include Spruce Grouse, Yellow-bellied Flycatcher, Gray Jay, Boreal Chickadee, Rusty Blackbird (along streams), and breeding Pine Grosbeaks (uncommon). Black-backed and Three-toed woodpeckers are also possible (the former more likely). When the mortality of spruces and especially firs peaked with the budworm infestation in the 1980s, both of these woodpeckers were abundant in the Nesowadnehunk area, but now that many of the dead trees have fallen or have lost all of their bark, these woodpeckers have declined (with Pileated and Hairy woodpeckers now being more likely). Cape May and Bay-breasted warblers are regular in the conifers (although neither species is as abundant as it was during the peak budworm years), and Mourning Warblers are common in most forest clearings, burned areas, or cutover sites. Even Golden Eagle is a possibility here; the species apparently breeds, at least occasionally, on inaccessible mountain cliffs in this area. Any observations of this rare species should be forwarded to the Wildlife Department, University of Maine at Orono, Orono, ME 04469.

The campground itself is located in a pristine setting (formerly an old lumber camp) and includes a wide variety of habitats. On quiet mornings the drumming of Black-backed Woodpeckers, Yellow-bellied

Sapsuckers, Common Flickers, and sometimes Pileated Woodpeckers sets the mood. Intermixed is the flutelike chorus of thrushes (Veerys, Swainson's and Hermit thrushes, and American Robins) and the raucous vocalizations of Common Ravens and sometimes Gray Jays and Evening Grosbeaks. The cheery song of Mourning Warblers (in early successional habitats) and the soft, high-pitched phrases of Cape May and Bay-breasted warblers are ever present. Also breeding in or near the campground are Common Goldeneye, Common Merganser, Spotted Sandpiper, Eastern Phoebe, Alder Flycatcher, Brown Creeper, Winter Wren, Cedar Waxwing, Red-eyed, Solitary, and Philadelphia vireos (look for the last along Nesowadnehunk Stream), Tennessee, Nashville, Yellow, Magnolia, Yellow-rumped, Blackburnian, Black-and-white, and Wilson's warblers, Northern Parula, Northern Waterthrush, American Redstart, White-throated Sparrow, Dark-eyed Junco, Rusty Blackbird (uncommon), Purple Finch, Pine Siskin, and both crossbills (irregular). In the field itself look for breeding Eastern Kingbirds, Eastern Bluebirds, Eastern Meadowlarks, and Bobolinks, all of which are fairly uncommon in this part of Maine. American Woodcocks are often seen in spring in the fields and road north and south of the campground, and Lincoln's Sparrows nest along the edges of Nesowadnehunk Field, north of the campground.

The number of mammals found in the Nesowadnehunk area also warrants mention. Moose are common and likely to be seen near most lakes, ponds, and streams, or even in the campground on Nesowadnehunk Stream. Black Bears are also common but are more difficult to observe, as are White-tailed Deer and Coyotes. Coyotes can often be heard at night. Fisher, Pine Marten, Mink, and Bobcat are all permanent but secretive residents in this area, and you will be very lucky indeed if you observe one.

Nesowadnehunk Field Campground to Nesowadnehunk Lake.

Between Nesowadnehunk Field Campground and Nesowadnehunk Lake, the Tote Road passes through a long stretch of coniferous forest that provides some of the best boreal-forest birding in Maine. The habitat is primarily dense spruce-fir woods interspersed with small patches of birch and alder and here and there several good-sized blowdowns or regenerating Spruce Budworm–damaged stands. Spruce Grouse are occasionally seen along this section of the road, as are Black-backed Woodpeckers. With incredible luck you may even turn up a Three-toed Woodpecker, a much scarcer and quieter species. You may also find breeding Fox Sparrows in this area; listen for their beautiful ringing song and look for singing birds teed up atop tall spruces. This species has only recently colonized the park, and it may well be expanding.

Walk as much of this stretch of the Tote Road as time and energy permit, looking for the same breeding species as mentioned above for Nesowadnehunk Field Campground. The birding is excellent along the road and the visibility much better than in the woods. Venturing into the woods is not necessary (nor do we recommend it). Should you be so inclined, *always carry a compass, topographic map, and insect repellent.*

Most of Nesowadnehunk Lake lies outside the park, and you won't see it from the roadside. You will see a small parking area and trail, though, where you can walk out of the park along the southern boundary of the lake.

South Branch Pond Campground. South Branch Pond Campground sits on the north shore of Lower South Branch Pond at 981 feet and is bordered to the east and west by beautiful mountain scenery. This is a delightful area to canoe (rentals are available at the campground for a nominal fee) and also offers access to several good trails. The birding generally is not as diverse as it is in some other sections of the park, but the setting is spectacular. Common Loons are indeed common on both Lower and Upper South Branch pond (we once had amazing looks at one of these beautiful birds swimming underwater right next to us), and you are also likely to see Common Mergansers. Winter Wrens will serenade you from the woods, and Spruce Grouse sometimes dust along the roadside. This is also a good place to see or hear Coyotes.

Consider hiking into the Fowler Ponds from the campground. The portion of the trail between Middle and Lower Fowler ponds will take you through a pleasant wetland habitat and is a good place to look for Rusty Blackbirds. This is also an area of the park where Peregrine Falcons have been seen occasionally.

North of South Branch Pond Campground. North of South Branch Pond Campground, the habitat along the Tote Road suddenly becomes more deciduous, dominated by maple, birch, and alder. Look along this section of the road for such characteristic deciduous-forest species as Ruffed Grouse, Broad-winged Hawk, Wood and Hermit thrushes, American Robin, Chestnut-sided Warbler, Ovenbird, and Scarlet Tanager.

If you have a canoe, consider exploring Grand Lake Matagamon. A boat launch is located just below Matagamon Gate. Ospreys nest here in summer, and in fall you can usually see a good variety of waterfowl, especially in the area where Trout Brook enters the lake.

Blowdowns, Burns, & Budworm-damaged Areas. Ask the park rangers where to find accessible blowdowns, burns, or Spruce Budworm–damaged areas along the Tote Road. Especially when about five to eight years old, these sites invariably attract some interesting birds, among them several species of woodpeckers (including Black-backed and, less commonly, Three-toed), Common Nighthawk, and Mourning Warbler. You will often find the last in blackberry- or raspberry-choked areas. Other species to look for in and around such areas include Olive-sided, Alder, and Least flycatchers, Ruby-crowned Kinglet, Red-eyed Vireo, Nashville, Chestnut-sided, Magnolia, and Yellow-rumped warblers, American Redstart, White-throated Sparrow, and Dark-eyed Junco. Eastern Bluebirds occasionally nest in blowdowns in the park, and Blackpoll Warblers can often be found in some of the stunted regenerating forest.

Higher-Elevation Sites

Climbing Katahdin is a rite of passage for many Mainers and New Englanders. There are several trails up the mountain, and we leave it to you to choose your own route. We recommend that you consult a good hiking guide in making your decision. See "Hiking in Baxter State Park," below, for more information. As far as the bird species are concerned, you are likely to see essentially the same cross section whichever route you take. Given the scale of the map in this book, we have not included hiking trails on it.

Helon Taylor Trail. For birders, one of the best ascents up Katahdin is the Helon Taylor Trail, named for a longtime park superintendent. The trail leads 3.2 miles from Roaring Brook Campground directly up to Pamola Peak at 4,902 feet. Most of the trail follows the exposed Keep Ridge, and the views are spectacular. This is a fairly steep and tiring trail, and you will be exposed to the elements, so don't attempt it if the weather is questionable.

The first half mile of the trail climbs through forest before opening out to a vista known as Ed's Lookout. In addition to offering a wonderful view, this lookout is noteworthy as one of the few places we know where you can hear all six of New England's nesting thrushes. Veery, Wood, Hermit, Swainson's, and Bicknell's thrushes, and American Robin all breed within earshot of each other, and the refrain as their songs rise from different directions is beautiful. The Bicknell's Thrushes nest along the exposed open areas by the ridge; the Wood Thrushes and Veerys nest in the deciduous forest far below. The best time to hear this remarkable symphony is usually in the late afternoon and approaching darkness, or in the early morning, especially if it is foggy. The fluting songs of the Bicknell's Thrush and Veery, similar yet distinct, heard together and almost as if in chorus with each another, create a wonderfully haunting experience not to be forgotten.

From Pamola Peak the trail crosses to Baxter Peak (the highest on Katahdin) via the precipitous and very narrow Knife Edge. This difficult trail, about 1 mile long and only 2 to 3 feet wide in many places, is well named and should not be attempted in inclement weather or by inexperienced hikers. You won't see many birds above treeline, although Common Ravens and hawks like to ride the updrafts on a sunny day. If you are botanically inclined, keep an eye out for the unusual alpine flowers that grow in the crevasses along the Knife Edge. The views are, of course, breathtaking.

Hunt Trail.   The Hunt Trail begins at Katahdin Stream Campground and is perhaps the loveliest climb up Katahdin. The 5.2-mile-long trail, much of it steep and rough, to Baxter Peak crosses a suspension bridge and requires climbing over several pylon-studded boulders. Good things are never easy, though, and the views are spectacular. This trail passes through excellent spruce-fir forest, thick with Blackpoll Warblers, and then crosses a long stretch of the fascinating Tableland (see below), where American Pipits nest. In spring, the lower portion of this trail is an especially good place to hear (and sometimes see) drumming Ruffed Grouse.

Chimney Pond Trail.   The most popular trail up Katahdin is via the Chimney Pond Trail, which leads 3.3 miles from Roaring Brook Campground up to Chimney Pond Campground (see below). Even if you don't intend to hike all the way up Katahdin, consider hiking this portion of the route. It may be one of the most-traveled trails in the park, but it also offers delightful birding. If you set out at dawn (about 5:00 a.m. in June and July), you will hit the peak of the song and avoid most of the hikers who use this trail. Because of the short stature of the softwoods along this trail, and its many convenient stopping points, this an especially good trail for birders.

The trail begins in deciduous forest and parallels the south bank of Roaring Brook before climbing into thick boreal forest with dozens of singing Bay-breasted and Blackburnian warblers. At 2 miles the trail enters a scrubby clearing and then follows the southern shore of Lower Basin Pond, by which point you should be able to hear Yellow-bellied and Olive-sided flycatchers, Swainson's Thrushes, the first

Blackpoll Warblers, and Purple Finches. As you continue climbing, you will pass through a rocky glacial moraine where Blackpoll Warblers and Dark-eyed Juncos should be abundant in the woods. You may also hear the first soft notes of a Bicknell's Thrush.

If you take the North Basin Cutoff Trail off the Chimney Pond Trail, you can see one of Maine's oldest and most significant old-growth forests—a stand of Red Spruce, situated just below North Basin at 2,700 feet, where some of the trees are more than 300 years old.

Chimney Pond Campground. Chimney Pond Campground is situated at 2,910 feet beneath the magnificent 2,000-foot-high glacial cirque that forms the east side of Katahdin. In his excellent book *Katahdin: A Guide to Baxter State Park and Katahdin*, author Stephen Clark calls this "by far the most spectacular campground in the Park and, perhaps, east of the Rockies." Birders find it particularly interesting because the cirque creates a natural amphitheater that amplifies the songs of the birds nesting in the area. Nowhere will the Winter Wren's exquisite, sustained melody sound more perfect. The Yellow-bellied Flycatcher's musical *click* song can be heard within the dense forest, and Bay-breasted and Blackpoll warblers sing their simple notes from the upper limbs of spruce trees. Both Swainson's and Bicknell's thrushes occur at the campground, although the former is more numerous. (Bicknell's Thrushes predominate farther up the mountain in the stunted spruce and alder swales.) White-winged Crossbills and Pine Grosbeaks breed irregularly around the campground, with one or both species being common in some years and completely absent in others. Gray Jays are common and always eager for a handout, and you can usually spish up a Boreal Chickadee. Nesting Black-backed Woodpecker is also a possibility here.

Although it is possible to make a day hike up to Chimney Pond, see if you can get reservations for an overnight stay. It is well worth the effort.

The Tableland. The Tableland is the large alpine plateau, almost a square mile in extent, that is situated at 4,700 feet on the northwest slope of Baxter Peak. Birders know this rocky, boulder-strewn site—the largest alpine habitat in the state—as one of only two known nesting sites in New England for American Pipit. Although a fairly common and widespread migrant (primarily in fall), this nondescript, plainly colored bird breeds in the eastern United States only on Katahdin and on Mt. Washington in New Hampshire, at both sites in small numbers. Look for it on the Tableland in early June, when territorial males can be seen and heard overhead in courtship flight giving their rapid, monotonous song. As the birds flutter to the ground, they look almost like falling leaves being tossed about by the wind. The American Pipit may not be one of our most colorful or enchanting birds, but the chance to see it on its breeding grounds is a rare experience. Although the species has also been seen above treeline on some of the park's other summits (North Brother and the Travelers, for example), to date it has not been documented nesting anywhere other than the Tableland.

Common Ravens are likely to be an almost constant presence on the Tableland, and they seem to delight in performing their aerobatics in the thermals near Baxter Peak above. Curiously, the peak is also a good place to see Northern Goshawk. Although these powerful hawks breed in the forests far below, they seem to appreciate Katahdin's thermals almost as much as the ravens do. Dark-eyed Juncos often venture up to the Tableland, and a few pairs of Yellow-rumped and Blackpoll warblers sometimes nest in the patches of krummholz (literally "crooked wood"). Even at midday, you can often hear Winter Wrens singing just below treeline.

Once you have had good looks at the pipits, turn your attention to everything else there is to see on the Tableland. This site supports more than 30 species of unusual arctic-alpine plants—the greatest diversity of rare plants anywhere in Maine. Several species, such as Dwarf Birch, the dwarf willows, Alpine Bilberry, Moss Plant, and Alpine Azalea, occur nowhere else in the state.

Another thing to look for from the Tableland is the fir waves on the slopes of Owl Mountain and the Brother mountains west of Katahdin. A fir wave is an unusual phenomenon (known only in northern New England and Japan) where alternating swaths of live and dead fir trees give a mountain a striped appearance; in Maine, fir waves are known only in Baxter State Park.

HIKING IN BAXTER STATE PARK

Hiking in Baxter State Park is delightful, but it should not be undertaken casually. Hikers should be properly conditioned and equipped for moderate to strenuous exercise. Many of the trails are rocky and require hiking boots, not sneakers or other soft-soled shoes. Warm clothing, ample water, a flashlight, and a compass are essential. Don't leave the Tote Road without a detailed map of the area you intend to traverse (maps are available at the campgrounds or at Millinocket headquarters), and don't ever leave the trail. Remember that the weather can change suddenly, even in midsummer, and that you may have to turn back unexpectedly. Between late May and mid-

July, you will also want an ample supply of insect repellent. It is hard to overstate how annoying the black flies can be sometimes, especially if you have never encountered them before.

On a clear summer day several hundred people may climb Katahdin. Don't forget that many other summits in the park also provide superb hiking and birding—but with far fewer people. Some of our favorites include Doubletop, Traveler, North Traveler, South Turner, the Brothers, and Sentinel.

The park publishes maps that are adequate for short day hikes. If you plan to hike Katahdin or do any extended hiking in the park, we recommend obtaining a more detailed reference. Three that we have used and like are Stephen Clark's *Katahdin: A Guide to Baxter State Park and Katahdin*, the *AMC Maine Mountain Guide* (7th edition), and the DeLorme Mapping Company's *Map & Guide of Baxter State Park and Katahdin* (see Appendix D).

CAMPING IN BAXTER STATE PARK

Camping in Baxter State Park is for people who truly enjoy a wild, remote setting—and who are willing to accept a minimum of conveniences and certain restrictions in order to maintain that feeling of remoteness. The park operates on a total carry-in/carry-out policy. There are no electric, water, or sewer hookups and no public water sources (plan to treat your water or bring enough from home). No food or fuel (of any sort) is available in the park. The nearest places to get supplies are in Millinocket (18 miles south of Togue Pond Gate) and in Patten (26 miles southeast of Matagamon Gate). Check your gas gauge before you enter the park.

Accommodations in the park's 10 campgrounds include cabins, lean-tos, bunkhouses, tent sites, and backcountry sites. Advance reservations for an overnight stay are essential if you want to be sure of getting a space, and they are required for backcountry sites. Reservations are accepted beginning January 1 by mail or in person (not by telephone) and must be paid for in advance. For information, write or call Baxter State Park, 64 Balsam Dr., Millinocket, ME 04462, telephone 207-723-5140.

Remember that the weather can be severe, even in summer and especially above treeline. Make sure you have suitable clothing and footwear. A compass is an excellent idea, and an ample supply of insect repellent is a must. Better yet, bring head nets, especially in June.

We strongly recommend writing for a current list of park regulations before your visit. That way you will be well prepared and won't have any unpleasant surprises (unlike the Piersons, who made their first trip to the park in the 1970s on a motorcycle, only to be turned away at the gate).

Baxter State Park is open for general use from May 15 to October 15; for day use (on a day-to-day basis, depending on weather) from October 15 to December 1 and from April 1 to May 15; and for winter use (by permit only) from December 1 to April 1. A fee is charged year-round. For more information, write or call Baxter State Park at the above address.

DIRECTIONS

TO TOGUE POND GATE: The most direct route is to take I-95 to Medway (exit 56) and then Rt. 157/11 west into Millinocket. There you will see signs for the park, which is 18 miles north on Golden Rd. Coming from Greenville, take Lily Bay Rd. north to Golden Rd. This is not a direct route, but the scenery is superb, and you will go by Ripogenus Gorge, a spectacularly beautiful spot. The birding can be quite good, too.

TO MATAGAMON GATE: Take I-95 to Sherman (exit 58) and then Rt. 11 north to Patten, Rt. 159 north to the village of Shin Pond, and Grand Lake Rd. north and west to Matagamon Gate.

IN AN EFFORT TO UPDATE AND IMPROVE ITS BIRD CHECKLIST, Baxter State Park welcomes knowing of any unusual or particularly interesting bird observations in the park. Please notify a ranger of any significant sightings, or send a copy of your observations to park headquarters (address above).

LOCAL ACCOMMODATIONS

For information on local accommodations and services outside the park, write or call the Millinocket Area Chamber of Commerce, 1029 Central St., Millinocket, ME 04462, telephone 207-723-4443.

Additional Sites of Interest

Pond Farm Wildlife Management Area
(*MAINE ATLAS* map 33, A-3)

Pond Farm Wildlife Management Area in Howland is owned by the Maine Department of Inland Fisheries and Wildlife and consists of a large, shallow pond and extensive marsh that provide ideal habitat for waterfowl and migrating shorebirds. In April this wetland attracts hundreds of northbound ducks and geese, including several species that are not commonly seen inland. The list of birds seen here includes Snow Goose, Brant (rare), Canada Goose, Mallard, Wood, American Black, and Ring-necked ducks, Blue-winged and Green-winged teal, Northern Pintail, American Wigeon, Common Eider, Black Scoter, Common Goldeneye, Bufflehead, and Hooded and Common mergansers. During the breeding season you can also find such characteristic wetland birds as American Bittern, Great Blue Heron, several species of common waterfowl, Virginia Rail, Sora, Common Snipe, Marsh Wren, and Swamp Sparrow. Ospreys and Northern Harriers also nest here, and Bald Eagles can frequently be found hunting for fish.

The fall shorebird flight begins in July with the first Solitary Sandpipers, Lesser Yellowlegs, and Short-billed Dowitchers. Greater Yellowlegs become common a few weeks later, when it is also possible to find Pectoral, Least, and Semipalmated sandpipers.

The best way to explore Pond Farm is by canoe, as visibility is quite limited from the roadside.

Take I-95 to exit 54 (Howland, Lagrange) and follow Route 6/155 east. In 0.8 mile turn left onto Route 116 North (be careful: 116 bends sharply left just after the bridge). Continue on this paved road and eventually under the I-95 overpass for 3.9 miles (after the overpass you will be on North Howland Road; Route 116 bends sharply right just before the overpass and becomes gravel, although this turn is not marked). Turn right onto Seboeis Road (unmarked), and in 1.7 miles you will see a bridge and the Pond Farm WMA sign on the left. Park on the left just before the bridge. You can put in a canoe here or scan the water from the shore. There is also some good woodland birding to be had just across the bridge.

You may choose to return to points south via Route 116 on the west side of the Penobscot River. This is a quiet country road and is very pleasant.

Plymouth Pond (MAINE ATLAS map 22, B-2)

Plymouth Pond, about 20 miles west of Bangor, for many years has been a nesting site for Black Terns. You can also see a good variety of other wetland-associated species here, including Common Loon, Pied-billed Grebe, Great Blue Heron, and Marsh Wren.

At the intersection of Routes 69 and 7 in Plymouth, go south on Route 7. You will almost immediately be on a causeway that crosses the northern end of Plymouth Pond. You can scan the pond from here or, better yet, put in a canoe. If you opt for the latter, please be sure to stay a healthy distance away from the terns during the nesting season. If you continue 0.6 mile farther down the road, you will see another good spot from which to scan, and in another 0.1 mile you will see a pull-off on the right side of the road. If you park here and step down through the woods, you will see the marsh where the terns nest.

Borestone Mountain (MAINE ATLAS map 41, E-4 & -5)

Borestone Mountain lies along the Appalachian Trail in Elliotsville Township and is the site of a National Audubon Society sanctuary. This small but spectacular mountain rises to 1,947 feet and offers outstanding views from its bare summit of Lake Onawa to the east. It is a steep 1.8-mile hike to the western peak and another 0.2 mile to the eastern peak. Consult the AMC Maine Mountain Guide (see Appendix D) for hiking information.

To the best of our knowledge, Borestone Mountain has not been well explored by birders. The few birders who are aware of it probably know it for the Peregrine Falcons that have been hacked here. With luck, these birds may return to breed on the mountain's cliffs.

There is undoubtedly a great variety of other birds to see here. The habitat is a mix of deciduous and coniferous forests, and about halfway up the mountain is a series of three ponds and associated wetlands. Turkey Vultures nest on the mountain, along with a good cross section of more northern breeders, including several species of warblers.

For more information, write or call the Maine Office of the National Audubon Society, Box 524, Dover-Foxcroft, ME 04426, telephone 207-631-4050 (May through October) or 564-7946 (November through April).

To reach the mountain, take Route 15/6 north out of Monson (see Maine Atlas map 32, A-3) and bear right onto Elliotsville Road. Continue 9 miles across Wilson's Bridge and bear left. In 0.7 mile you will cross a set of railroad tracks, and 0.1 mile beyond this, on the right, is the trailhead.

WASHINGTON COUNTY

Washington County, or the Sunrise County as it is often called, is the easternmost county in the United States. It is also a remarkably lovely spot and the most unspoiled area along the Maine coast. The deeply indented and rocky coastline is marked by four large bays and headlands, and the landscape is distinguished by extensive spruce-fir forests, peatlands, and blueberry barrens (Washington County is the world's largest producer of wild blueberries). The tides, ranging from about 16 to 26 feet, are among the highest in the continental United States, and they provide a rich feast for the many shorebirds and seabirds that feed along these shores.

The birding in Washington County can be good at any time of year, and especially during the breeding season, it can be quite varied. The highlights are migrating shorebirds (primarily between mid-July and late September); gulls (year-round, but especially in August and September); nesting peatland, blueberry barren, and spruce-fir special-ties; and on the offshore islands, nesting seabirds. An added delight is that Washington County also offers a bit of solitude. Whether you are walking across the Lubec Flats in search of shorebirds, scanning for gulls off Eastport, or hiking along the shore on Great Wass Island, chances are quite good that you will be alone. Few Maine birders, and even fewer out-of-state birders, spend much time here.

We are particularly partial to Washington County in late August and early September. The birds are generally abundant (for sheer numbers and diversity, this is undeniably the best time of year), the bugs are gone, the goldenrod is at its peak, the blueberry barrens are just turning red, and the days are often crystal clear.

Petit Manan Point
(*MAINE ATLAS* map 17, A-3)

Petit Manan Point, in the town of Steuben, is a 2,166-acre peninsula situated between Dyer Bay and Pigeon Hill Bay. Connected to the mainland by a small neck, this beautiful, windswept piece of land makes up the lion's share of Petit Manan National Wildlife Refuge, which also includes property on three islands: adjacent Bois Bubert Island; Petit Manan Island, 3 miles offshore; and about 8 miles farther east, Nash Island. Petit Manan Point is the only section of the refuge that is readily accessible, although even here access is not extensive; much of the point is private property. This is a lovely and unspoiled area, however, and the birding can be excellent. You are likely to see the greatest variety of species between mid-April and late October. November can produce interesting rarities, and winter brings the possibility of a Snowy Owl, Northern Shrike, winter finches, and perhaps even a Gyrfalcon (especially in late November). Highlights include a good variety of waterbirds year-round and an excellent cross section of migrants. Many rarities have been recorded here. If you want to hike all the way to the end of the point (a beautiful but strenuous 6 miles round-trip), plan to spend close to a full day at the refuge.

Petit Manan Point includes a variety of habitats: an extensive rocky shoreline, alder thickets, small fresh- and saltwater marshes, a few brackish ponds, coastal raised peatlands (visible from the south-easternmost shore), old hayfields, more than 50 acres of blueberry barrens, and spruce-fir, Jack Pine, and mixed-deciduous woods. Two trails provide access to the shore. The Birch Point Trail, 3 miles round-trip, begins near the refuge parking area, leads northwest to a salt marsh on Dyer Bay, and takes you through blueberry barrens and mixed woods. This trail usually isn't all that productive for landbirds, although occasionally you may see a few Boreal Chickadees. A more productive trail is the Shore Trail, 1 mile round-trip, which leads to the east shore and takes you through blueberry barrens, Jack Pine and

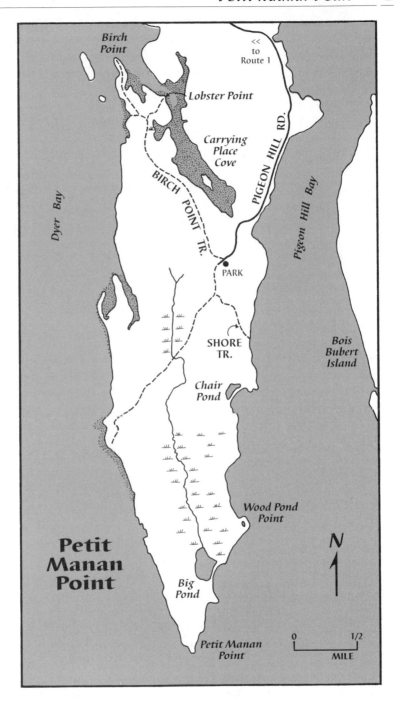

spruce-fir woods, and low shrubs. The Shore Trail begins about 0.5 mile south of the refuge parking area. From the end of this trail you can also walk another 2.5 miles along the shore to the southern end of the point. This is a beautiful walk; the south end of the point, with Big Pond and its surrounding peatlands, is especially interesting. Just be sure you have the right footwear; you will be walking over rocks the entire time. The lighthouse that you see from the peninsula is Petit Manan Light on Petit Manan Island.

Whatever the season, you are likely to see a good variety of birds along the shore at Petit Manan Point. At any time of year look for Common Loons, Common Eiders (abundant, and nesting on Bois Bubert), Surf Scoters, Bald Eagles, Great Black-backed, Herring, Ring-billed, Bonaparte's (most common in spring and again in late summer and fall), and occasionally Common Black-headed gulls, and Black Guillemots. In summer look for Double-crested Cormorants, Ospreys, Laughing Gulls, and Common and occasionally Arctic and Roseate terns (the first nesting on Bois Bubert, the other two on Petit Manan Island but usually not seen from the mainland). In winter look for Horned and Red-necked grebes, Great Cormorants, American Black Ducks, Common Goldeneyes, Buffleheads, Oldsquaws, Purple Sandpipers, Iceland Gulls (regular in small numbers), and such rarities as a Barrow's Goldeneye (try Lobster Point, on the right before you reach Birch Point), Harlequin Duck, or King Eider. Especially after a good easterly wind, look for Northern Gannets (primarily in spring and fall), Black-legged Kittiwakes (primarily in fall), and alcids. Winter is usually the best time to see alcids, although mid- to late August seems to be an especially good time to see Atlantic Puffins (as many as 50 have been seen at one time) and Razorbills from the southern tip of the island. Brant are common in March and April.

Shorebirds are often abundant on migration, especially in July, August, and September. Black-bellied and Semipalmated plovers, Greater and Lesser yellowlegs, Willets (also nesting on the point), Ruddy Turnstones, Semipalmated, Least, and White-rumped sandpipers, Dunlin (late August through October), and Short-billed Dowitchers are all regular, whereas American Golden-Plovers, Piping Plovers, Hudsonian Godwits, Red Knots (high count of 200 in August), Buff-breasted (early September), Baird's, and Western sandpipers, and Wilson's Phalaropes are occasional. An excellent place to look for shorebirds on the east shore is around the Big Pond area, which can be especially productive if storms or groundswells have washed a lot of seaweed ashore. It is also worth checking Carrying

Place Cove (this is on the right as you cross the neck of the peninsula coming south, but you can see it better by going out the Birch Point Trail and turning right).

On the southeastern end of the point, scan the coastal raised bog and Big Pond, both visible from the shore. Small numbers of Wood and American Black ducks, Hooded Mergansers, Palm Warblers, and Lincoln's Sparrows nest on this part of the island. Laughing Gulls and Common Terns, which nest on Petit Manan Island, often bathe in the fresh water.

The upland portions of Petit Manan Point are especially interesting for birders. The blueberry barrens are burned every three years to maintain habitat for American Woodcock, and the hayfields are mowed periodically for the same purpose. The best chance of seeing a woodcock is in courtship flight at dusk or dawn. Courting birds are most active from mid-April to mid-May but can usually be found into early June. Also look for Northern Harriers and for Tree, Bank, Barn, and Cliff swallows coursing over the blueberry barrens and hayfields. Look along the edges for small numbers of nesting Bobolinks and Lincoln's Sparrows. In late summer and fall, these same areas are good for Ruffed Grouse and Whimbrels (as many as 20 Whimbrels are occasionally seen in one field) and for a broad variety of migrant passerines. In fall, Sharp-shinned Hawks are abundant, American Kestrels and Merlins are common, and even Peregrine Falcons can be common on some days. Later in fall, large numbers of Horned Larks and Snow Buntings pass through, and you can often find a few Lapland Longspurs among them. Winter brings the chance of finding something decidedly uncommon—perhaps a Gyrfalcon (rare), Rough-legged Hawk, Snowy or Short-eared Owl, or Northern Shrike. Sometimes you can see Common Redpolls here, too, and on rare occasions, a Hoary Redpoll.

Spruce Grouse are rare but apparently increasing on the point, and Boreal Chickadees are present in small numbers. Common Ravens nest nearby and are usually easy to see (and hear) year-round.

Although it is certainly possible to see an impressive number of species in one day at Petit Manan Point, especially on migration, bear in mind that you will probably have to cover a good deal of territory to do so. For many birders, however, the chance to spend a day exploring such a beautiful and relatively little-visited site will be well worth it.

The national wildlife refuge property on Petit Manan Point is open year-round, free of charge, from sunrise to sunset. In summer there are outhouse facilities by the parking area.

DIRECTIONS

Turn south off Rt. 1 halfway between Steuben and Milbridge onto Pigeon Hill Rd. (*Maine Atlas* map 25, E-2 and -3). In 5.7 miles you will see the refuge boundary and, just beyond it, the parking area. Only foot traffic is allowed beyond this point.

LOCAL ACCOMMODATIONS

For information on local accommodations and services, write or call the Machias Bay Area Chamber of Commerce, P.O. Box 606, Machias, ME 04654, telephone 207-255-4402; or at the same address, the Washington County Promotions Board, telephone 800-377-9748.

Deblois Barrens & Addison Marsh

Two good birding sites lie just outside Cherryfield, a lovely old town situated on the Narraguagus River and the self-proclaimed Blueberry Capital of Maine. Just north of Cherryfield are the vast Deblois Barrens which comprise a surprisingly distinctive habitat in a state that many people know primarily for its forests and coast. Ten miles east, on the Pleasant River, is Addison Marsh, one of Washington County's few good-sized salt marshes. Especially between early spring and late fall, you can spend a delightful half day or so investigating these two sites.

Deblois Barrens
(*MAINE ATLAS* map 25, D-2, -3, & -4 and C-2 & -3)

The blueberry barrens of Washington County are a unique habitat for breeding birds in Maine, and the most extensive of these are the Deblois Barrens north of Cherryfield. In a state where some 90 percent of the land is forested, here you find thousands of acres of open, tundralike fields once scoured by glaciers and now distinguished by large boulders, scattered bogs, numerous kettle holes, outwash plains, and long sandy ridges called eskers. Lowbush Blueberry is the dominant vegetation, interspersed with Red Pine and alder thickets. If much of the land seems monocultural, it is because herbicides have been applied to the barrens since the mid-1980s to increase blueberry production. Although the birding is not diverse on the barrens, this

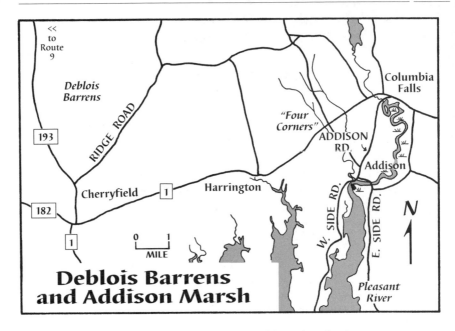

area does support an unusual assemblage of breeding birds—particularly Upland Sandpipers and Vesper Sparrows. The barrens are privately owned, but you can scan them from Route 193 (which runs 19 miles between Route 1 in Cherryfield and Route 9 to the north) as well as from the sandy "farm" roads that wind throughout the area. The best time to visit is between late May and mid-August, when the breeding species are present. You can bird the barrens quite thoroughly in a few hours.

Nesting Upland Sandpipers are a highlight of the Deblois Barrens, and with patience they are usually fairly easy to find. At least 75 pairs nest in 12-plus loose colonies between Deblois and Columbia. The birds are hard to spot unless they fly, but listen for their liquid, double note which carries remarkably well. (Early morning is often the easiest time to see these birds; the low angle of light makes them more visible on the ground, whereas overhead light later in the day seems to make them disappear.) Vesper Sparrows have declined somewhat in the area but are still quite easy to find, especially along roadsides where there is bare ground. Other species you should look for on and around the barrens during the nesting season include Northern Harrier, Ruffed Grouse, Killdeer, Common Raven, Black-billed and sometimes Yellow-billed cuckoos (especially in years of heavy tent-caterpillar infestations), Whip-poor-will, Eastern Kingbird, Yellow-bellied, Alder, and Least flycatchers, Palm and Mourning warblers, Savannah and Lincoln's sparrows, Eastern Meadowlark,

Bobolink, and Indigo Bunting. Mixed flocks of Horned Larks and Snow Buntings sometimes are abundant during migration. Although this area is a bit far from the coast, you can often see sizable flocks of Whimbrels (100+) in late July and August.

It is also worth keeping an eye out for mammals on the barrens (people aren't the only ones who like blueberries). Moose, Black Bear, Red Fox, Coyote, White-tailed Deer, Varying Hare, and Bobcat (uncommon) all occur throughout these remote lands.

With luck you can see most of the birds mentioned above from Route 193, but you will do much better by getting out into the barrens and away from the main road. As you will soon discover for yourself, there are dozens of dirt farm roads through the barrens, and although technically these are private property, people regularly drive them. It is easy to get lost anytime you get off Route 193, however, so don't venture forth without a map. Four-wheel drive is not necessary, but a little common sense is. Please remember that it is illegal to trespass on the barrens or to pick blueberries, and be on the lookout for (and yield to) commercial trucks. With patience you should be able to see all the birds from the roadsides, so please stay on them.

You should also know that the barrens are regularly sprayed with herbicides and pesticides, beginning as early as April and continuing into August. It is a good idea to stay clear of the area when it is being sprayed.

Finally, we can't resist adding a note about the sheer beauty of the Deblois Barrens. By late July the land is a sea of green and blue, dotted with hundreds of local and migrant workers who rake the berries by hand. Come September, the first frost turns the barrens an exquisite, fiery red—a sight well worth seeing in itself.

The Deblois Barrens are accessible year-round, free of charge, from Route 193. (The farm roads are not plowed in winter, and are likely to be quite muddy in early spring.) There are no facilities.

DIRECTIONS

FROM RT. 1 IN CHERRYFIELD: Take Rt. 193 north from Rt. 1 in Cherryfield, and in a few miles you will see the barrens on either side of the road. They continue for about 12 miles. The largest expanse that you can scan from the roadside lies between 9.5 and 13.5 miles north of Rt. 1.

FROM RT. 9 ("THE AIRLINE"): Take Rt. 193 south off Rt. 9 (The Airline; see "Additional Sites of Interest" at the end of the Washington County section). You will see the first extensive barrens in about 6 miles.

For a productive route through the heart of the barrens, we offer the following suggestion. From Rt. 1 in Cherryfield, take Rt. 193 north and in 1.3 miles fork right onto Ridge Rd. (unmarked). In 2.5 miles the barrens open up on either side of the road and you can start birding in earnest. In another 1.1 miles Ridge Rd. becomes dirt. Stay on this road (that is, stay right) for another 1.1 miles, then fork right onto another dirt road. This road continues 4.7 miles (and becomes paved again) to an unmarked four-way stop. Turn right here, and return to Rt. 1. You will be at the blinking light at Four Corners in Columbia, halfway between Harrington and Columbia Falls (and almost at Addison Marsh, if that's where you're headed next).

Addison Marsh (MAINE ATLAS map 25, D-5)

About 10 miles east of Cherryfield, in the village of Addison, is a good-sized salt marsh on the Pleasant River. On a part of the coast where salt marshes generally are small and few and far between, Addison Marsh is well worth checking. And it probably won't take you more than half an hour or so. You are most likely to find something of interest between April and October. Look (and listen) for Common Snipe displaying over the marsh in spring; for wading birds, primarily Great Blue Herons, Snowy Egrets, and occasionally a Great Egret or Glossy Ibis, in spring and summer; for Nelson's Sharp-tailed (now split from Saltmarsh Sharp-tailed) and Savannah sparrows nesting in the grasses; and for shorebirds and waterfowl on spring and especially fall migration. The most commonly seen shorebird species here are Black-bellied and Semipalmated plovers, Greater and Lesser yellowlegs, and Semipalmated and Least sandpipers. American Golden-Plovers, Willets, and Western, White-rumped, and Pectoral sandpipers are occasional. Northern Pintails are seen from time to time along with more common waterfowl such as Canada Geese and American Black Ducks.

Another spot worth checking is 1.2 miles south of the marsh where the East Side Road passes right next to the east shore of the Pleasant River. A few hours either side of high tide, the flats here can be good for shorebirds.

You should also check the public boat landing on the Pleasant River just west of the marsh. The river channel is almost empty at low tide, but a few hours either side of high tide it can be good for shorebirds (primarily peep, yellowlegs, and Short-billed Dowitcher), and you can often get good looks at Common Terns and a Belted Kingfisher. If you have the time and inclination, follow the West Side Road down the west side of the river, where you can scan several coves from the roadside for shorebirds.

Addison Marsh is accessible year-round, free of charge. There are no facilities.

DIRECTIONS

Turn south off Rt. 1 at the blinking light at Four Corners in Columbia (halfway between Harrington and Columbia Falls) onto an unmarked road. In 1.7 miles, bear right onto Addison Rd. (unmarked), and in 0.4 mile you will see the Addison Fire Department straight ahead. If you go right here, you will immediately see the public boat landing on the left. If you go left at the fire station, onto East Side Rd. (unmarked), you will see the marsh on either side of the road in 0.4 mile.

LOCAL ACCOMMODATIONS

For information on local accommodations and services, write or call the Machias Bay Area Chamber of Commerce, P.O. Box 606, Machias, ME 04654, telephone 207-255-4402; or at the same address, the Washington County Promotions Board, telephone 800-377-9748.

Great Wass Island
(*MAINE ATLAS* map 17, inset)

Great Wass Island is the largest island in the Great Wass Archipelago, a group of more than 50 islands lying on the edge of the Gulf of Maine just south of Jonesport. Although accessible from the mainland by bridge, Great Wass projects farther out to sea than any other land mass in Washington County, and as a result it has a specialized maritime climate and a rich diversity of unusual plants. Not surprisingly, this beautiful and unspoiled island—much of which is owned and managed by The Nature Conservancy—is also a delightful birding spot. This is a good place to look for seabirds, Spruce Grouse, and Boreal Chickadee year-round and for a fine variety of nesting landbirds, including Tennessee, Cape May, Blackburnian, Palm, Bay-breasted, and Blackpoll (local) warblers, and Lincoln's Sparrow in summer. En route to the island you can scan the blueberry barrens along Route 187 for nesting Upland Sandpipers and Vesper Sparrows and the Beals Island flats for shorebirds (these two sites are described after Great Wass Island). Although you are likely to see the greatest

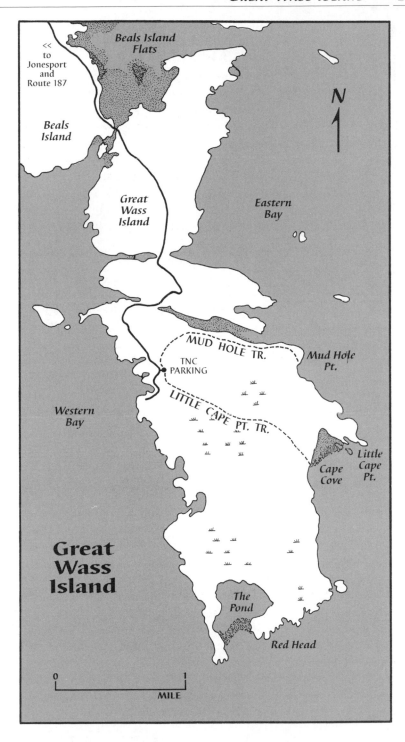

Beals Island
Flats

<< to Jonesport and Route 187

Beals Island

Great Wass Island

Eastern Bay

N

MUD HOLE TR.

TNC PARKING

Mud Hole Pt.

LITTLE CAPE PT. TR.

Western Bay

Little Cape Pt.

Cape Cove

Great Wass Island

The Pond

Red Head

0   1
MILE

variety of birds between early May and late September, Great Wass is well worth a visit at any time of year. Plan to spend close to a full day to do the island justice.

Great Wass Island measures about 5 miles long and 1 mile wide and has a relatively high, rolling topography. Spruces and firs blanket much of the island, but in the interior you will also find a 550-acre stand of Jack Pine (the second-largest stand of this tree in Maine) and extensive coastal raised peatlands. The peatlands are vegetated primarily with sphagnum moss interspersed with Black Crowberry, Bog Cranberry, Pitcher Plant, Round-leaved Sundew, and even Baked-apple Berry, a raspberry relative that is quite rare this far south. Several other subarctic species can be found closer to the shore, including Beach Head Iris, Bird's-eye Primrose (primarily at Red Head), and Marsh Felwort.

Two trails beginning at The Nature Conservancy (TNC) parking lot provide access to a good cross section of the island. The Mud Hole Trail (1.5 miles one-way) leads across the northeast end of the island and follows a long, narrow cove to Mud Hole Point (which despite its name is a beautiful spot). Little Cape Point Trail (2 miles one-way) goes across the interior of the island to Cape Cove and Little Cape Point. This trail winds through dense spruce-fir woods (we've had outstanding looks at Spruce Grouse not too far down this trail) and across open ledges of Jack Pine and offers a beautiful overview of one of the island's peatlands. For overall diversity of birds, this trail is probably your best bet. You can also walk a loop that incorporates both trails (5 miles total), and from Cape Cove you can walk south along the shore to Red Head at the southern tip of the island (another 2.5 miles one-way). Whichever route you take, be prepared for damp and rough trails and for any kind of weather (it is often very foggy here, but don't let that deter you). Also remember that walking across rocks on the shore is a lot more enjoyable with the proper footwear. If you hike south to Red Head, please return the same way you came rather than via the island's western shore, which is private property.

At least 104 species of birds have been documented breeding on the Great Wass Archipelago, and another 125 have been recorded on migration. Except for the colonially nesting seabirds, most of the archipelago's birds can be seen on Great Wass Island. As at most places, you will find the greatest diversity of birds on spring and fall migration, and you will have the best luck with breeding species in June and July. Nesting species are the highlight and include several that are uncommon or hard to find. Before leaving the TNC parking lot, check the registration box for recent sightings (and also take a trail map).

Some of the more interesting breeding species to look for in wooded sections of the island include Sharp-shinned Hawk, Spruce and Ruffed grouse (both species are regular in small numbers), Great Horned and Barred owls, Olive-sided and Yellow-bellied flycatchers, Common Raven, Boreal Chickadee (regular), Brown Creeper, Winter Wren, Ruby-crowned and Golden-crowned kinglets, Veery, Hermit and Swainson's thrushes, Solitary Vireo, Dark-eyed Junco, Red and White-winged crossbills (both irregular), and Pine Siskin. You can also see and hear several species of nesting warblers. Nashville, Northern Parula, Magnolia, Yellow-rumped, Black-throated Green, Black-and-white, American Redstart, and Common Yellowthroat are all common, whereas Tennessee, Cape May, Blackburnian, Bay-breasted, Blackpoll (generally at the southernmost tip of the island and right near the shoreline), Wilson's, and Canada nest in small numbers or only occasionally. Palm Warblers and Lincoln's Sparrows are common nesters on or around the peatlands. Osprey nest on the island, and Bald Eagles, which nest on some of the nearby islands, often feed and roost on Great Wass. Interestingly, Bicknell's (formerly Gray-cheeked) Thrush is a possible nester. Small numbers of these birds are seen on the outer headlands of Washington County in early June, but whether they are migrants or nesters is unknown. (If you have any evidence of this species breeding, please be sure to notify someone of your observations.)

Along the shore you can see a good variety of birds at any time of year. Look year-round for Common Loons, American Black Ducks, Common Eiders (abundant), Bald Eagles, Bonaparte's Gulls (small numbers scattered among the more abundant Herring and Great Black-backed gulls), Black-legged Kittiwakes (primarily in fall and winter), and Black Guillemots. During the nesting season look for Double-crested Cormorants, Great Blue Herons, Spotted Sandpipers, Laughing Gulls, and Common and Arctic terns. From about November through March look for Red-throated Loons, Red-necked and Horned grebes, Great Cormorants, Oldsquaws, all three scoters, Common Goldeneyes, Buffleheads, Red-breasted Mergansers, and Purple Sandpipers. If you are brave enough to hike out to the shore in midwinter (it's a long hike for a lot of wind!), Great Wass can be a good place to find the occasional King Eider, small raft of Harlequin Ducks, Iceland or Glaucous Gull, Thick-billed Murre, Razorbill, Atlantic Puffin, or Dovekie. The best time to look for Razorbills and puffins, however, is usually in late August, from the southeast end of the island.

After good easterly winds at almost any time of year except the dead of winter, look for a Northern Gannet offshore, and in late winter and spring look for Brant (sometimes present into mid-May). Several species of shorebirds stop over on spring and fall migration. The most common species are Black-bellied and Semipalmated plovers, Greater and Lesser yellowlegs, Ruddy Turnstone, Semipalmated and Least sandpipers, and Short-billed Dowitcher.

TNC's Great Wass Island Preserve is open to the public year-round, free of charge, from sunrise to sunset. There are no facilities. Please stay on the trails.

Route 187 Blueberry Barrens
(MAINE ATLAS map 26, D-1 to E-1)

Traveling Route 187 between Jonesboro and Jonesport, you will see a large stretch of blueberry barrens along both sides of the road. Although they are private property, you can easily scan them from the roadside. Small numbers of Upland Sandpipers and Vesper Sparrows nest on these barrens, and occasionally you will see a Northern Harrier hunting over them. Other species you might see here during the nesting season include Killdeer, Eastern Kingbird, Savannah and Lincoln's sparrows, Eastern Meadowlark (a few), Bobolink, and Indigo Bunting. In late summer and early fall this can also be a good place to see migrating Whimbrels and, later, Horned Larks and Snow Buntings. In winter it is worth looking for a Rough-legged Hawk, Snowy Owl, or Northern Shrike. In fall and winter, scan Englishman Bay and Mason Bay for ducks.

Beals Island Flats (MAINE ATLAS map 26, E-1)

The second spot to check en route to Great Wass Island is the flats along the east side of the small causeway between Beals and Great Wass islands. A few hours either side of high tide, particularly between mid-July and late September, this can be an excellent place to see good numbers and a good variety of shorebirds.

DIRECTIONS
From Rt. 1 in Addison or Jonesboro, take Rt. 187 south to the village of Jonesport and cross the bridge to Beals Island (bearing left at the T). Go across Beals Island, over the causeway to Great Wass, and bear right. In 0.6 mile the road turns to dirt, and in another 2 miles you will see a parking lot and small "Preserve" sign (with the TNC oak

leaf) on the left. If you find the parking lot full, TNC asks that you please come back another time rather than park on the main road.

LOCAL ACCOMMODATIONS

For information on local accommodations and services, write or call the Machias Bay Area Chamber of Commerce, P.O. Box 606, Machias, ME 04654, telephone 207-255-4402; or at the same address, the Washington County Promotions Board, telephone 800-377-9748.

Machias Seal Island & Machias Bay Area

Anyone interested in seabirds will want to make a trip to Machias Seal Island, for even along a coast famous for its enchanting seabird islands, Machias Seal is something special. Serving as a Canadian lighthouse outpost since 1832, the island lies in the Bay of Fundy 10 miles southeast of Cutler and boasts nesting colonies of Common Eiders, Arctic and Common terns, Atlantic Puffins, Razorbills, and Leach's Storm-Petrels. A few pairs of Black Guillemots also nest on the island, and in 1994 Common Murres were documented nesting for the first time. Fortunately, Machias Seal is one of the most accessible as well as one of the most delightful of the Gulf of Maine's seabird islands, with regular trips offered in summer from Cutler and Jonesport and also from Grand Manan, New Brunswick. You can see all of the nesting species, and a good variety of other seabirds en route, anytime between late May and mid-August. We like to visit between mid-June and mid-July, when nesting activity is at its peak. Count on devoting a full day to the trip.

Although a trip to Machias Seal is a highlight along this part of the coast, the mainland around Machias Bay also offers some outstanding birding. Route 191 from East Machias to Cutler and West Lubec traverses a strikingly beautiful and unspoiled stretch of coast and is an excellent area to look for waterfowl, seabirds, raptors, and boreal specialties year-round and for shorebirds on spring and fall migration. At least 190 species have been recorded on or adjacent to the Bureau of Public Lands property in Cutler (see "Cutler Coast Unit," below). At any time of year you can spend the better part of a day exploring the Machias Bay area.

Machias Seal Island (MAINE ATLAS map 27, E-2)

Machias Seal is a low-lying, 15-acre treeless island vegetated primarily by asters, wild parsleys, docks, grasses, sedges, and herbs. The lighthouse and two keepers' houses stand on the highest ground, and boardwalks and paths lead out to the nesting colonies. The terns and Common Eiders nest over a large portion of the island on high, grassy areas, and the alcids nest among the rocks and ledges on the southwest shore. Two blinds enable you to watch and photograph the terns and alcids from just a few feet away, and it is a thrilling experience. The terns' nesting activities are well under way by late May, and by mid-July most of the young are on the wing. The alcids' nesting activities peak about mid-June, when most of the young hatch. Adults and young of all the nesting species are usually present on the island until at least mid-August.

In the summer of 1994, surveys by the Canadian Wildlife Service found an estimated 30 pairs of Leach's Storm-Petrels nesting on Machias Seal, 50 pairs of Common Eiders, 2,400 pairs of Arctic Terns, 150 pairs of Common Terns, 1,100 pairs of Atlantic Puffins, and 100 pairs of Razorbills. This has long been the Gulf of Maine's largest colony for Atlantic Puffins and Razorbills, and it is encouraging that population numbers have increased or at least held steady for all of the above species since the early 1980s. A few pairs of Black Guillemots usually nest on the island each year, too, and in 1994 two Common Murre eggs were found—the first nesting record for the island since this species began appearing regularly here in the late 1960s. You can often see several dozen of these murres sitting on the water or standing on the shore among the Razorbills and puffins.

A visit to Machias Seal at the peak of the nesting season is an experience you will never forget. Even if you arrive in dense fog, you will hear the strident clamor of the terns well before you get off the boat. And once ashore, you will quickly appreciate the need for a hat. The terns are fiercely protective of their nests and young, and they will dive at you repeatedly and sometimes try to strike you with their bills. A hat will protect you from assault and also from the "guano bombs." At the very least, you will have an unparalleled opportunity to observe the subtle differences between Arctic and Common terns. Look carefully for a few Roseate Terns, too; in some years a few pairs are present in the melee. This species is best distinguished from Arctic and Common terns by its noticeably paler

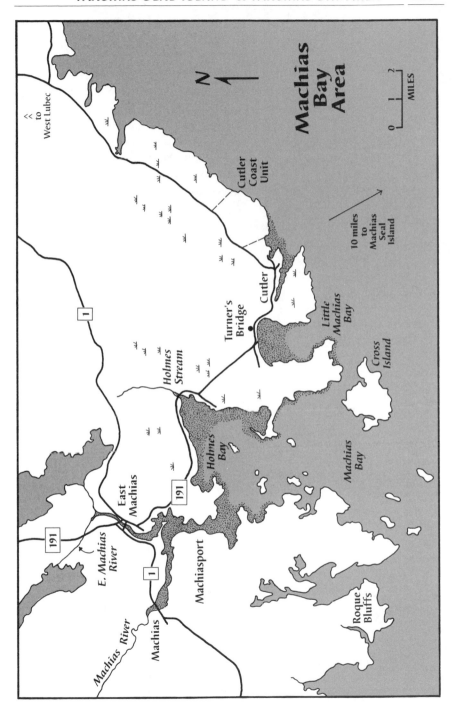

Machias Bay Area

N

MILES
0   1   2

Cutler Coast Unit

<< to West Lubec

10 miles to Machias Seal Island

1

Cutler

Turner's Bridge

Little Machias Bay

Holmes Stream

Cross Island

East Machias

Holmes Bay

Machias Bay

191

191

E. Machias River

Machiasport

1

Roque Bluffs

Machias River

Machias

plumage (the upperparts appearing almost all white in bright sunlight) and long, deeply forked tail.

Once in the blinds you will have the opportunity to watch and photograph the terns and alcids from just a few feet away. If you open the sliding windows on one side of the blind only, rather than on both sides, the birds are likely to come much closer. It is particularly delightful to observe the puffins and Razorbills at such close range as they go about their daily routine—scurrying in and out of their nests, vocalizing, preening, and just "loafing." You will get superb looks at the adults, but you probably won't see their young, which stay hidden in their burrows during the day. Several Common Murres may be perched on shore, too. Notice how much thinner the bill is, and how much browner the plumage is, than on a Razorbill. If you don't see the murres from the blinds (they aren't always visible on this part of the island), be sure to ask your captain to circle the island.

In the case of the Leach's Storm-Petrels, you are unlikely to see even an adult. These diminutive seabirds nest in underground burrows on the northeast side of the island and are rarely seen because they come and go from their nesting colonies only after dark. Like other Procellariiformes, or "tubenoses," this species has a strong and very distinctive musky odor. Even on a newly hatched chick you can see the tubenose and delicate webbed feet.

You will also find a few other birds nesting on the island, among them Spotted Sandpipers, Tree and Barn swallows, and Savannah Sparrows. In late May and again in late summer, keep your eyes open for migrants or storm-tossed vagrants; more than 100 species, including some that are rare or unusual, have been recorded here. The Canadian Wildlife Service caretaker can tell you about any recent unusual sightings.

En route to and from Machias Seal, look for a Bald Eagle (near the mainland), Greater, Sooty, and Manx shearwaters (we've sometimes seen as many as 100 Manx), Wilson's and occasionally Leach's storm-petrels, Great Cormorants, Northern Gannets, Parasitic and occasionally Pomarine jaegers, and Black-legged Kittiwakes. Look for whales, too, and ask your captain if it is possible to go around North Rock, near Machias Seal, where you can usually see a few Gray Seals, or "horseheads," among the many Harbor Seals. Your captain may also be willing to cruise by Cross Island National Wildlife Refuge, which consists of six small islands at the mouth of Machias Bay. Look for nesting Ospreys and Bald Eagles and, on Old Man Island, for nesting Razorbills.

The trip out to Machias Seal takes about an hour to an hour and a half. Depending on weather and tide conditions, you usually have anywhere from one to three hours on the island. Landing is a bit of a trick (and is at your own risk) because of the strong currents and surf and is possible only on a calm day. Your captain will anchor offshore and take you ashore in a small dory from which you scramble across the rocks to dry ground. In the event that you cannot land, the trip still provides a fine opportunity to see the birds at close range. To protect the birds, the Canadian Wildlife Service strictly controls the number of visitors per day, so make your reservations as early as possible.

Two people in Maine (and one on Grand Manan, New Brunswick) currently make regular trips to Machias Seal between late May and September 1. To make arrangements, call or write one of the following. (Whether you depart from Maine or New Brunswick, you needn't worry about border crossings; there are no Customs officials at either end of the trip.)

- **CAPT. ANDREW PATTERSON,** Bold Coast Charter Co., P.O. Box 364, Cutler, ME 04626, telephone 207-259-4484.
- **CAPTS. BARNA & JOHN NORTON,** RR 1-990, Jonesport, ME 04649, telephone 207-497-5933.
- **CAPT. PRESTON WILCOX,** Seal Cove, Grand Manan, NB, Canada E0G-3B0, telephone 506-662-8296.

Pack whatever food and drink you will need, a hat to protect you from the terns, rain gear, warm clothing (even in midsummer), lip screen and sunscreen, sunglasses, seasickness medicine (if you need it), and plastic bags to protect your camera and binoculars from spray on the boat.

Machias Bay Area
(*MAINE ATLAS* map 26, C-4 & -5, and map 27)

The mainland around Machias Bay is well worth exploring at any time of year, and Route 191—stretching almost 30 miles from East Machias to West Lubec—offers an ideal route. Starting in East Machias at the East Machias River, the road winds south along Holmes Bay to the village of Cutler and then turns north to follow the rugged "Bold Coast" up to the town of West Lubec. Habitats along the way include rivers and bays, mudflats and gravel bars, alder swales, spruce-fir and mixed-deciduous woods, peatlands, and extensive blueberry barrens and open fields. Although most of the surrounding land is private property, it is sparsely settled and undeveloped, and you can do some fine birding from the roadside. In Cutler you can also investigate a spectacular parcel of public land, the 2,200-acre Cutler Coast Unit, which is owned and managed by the Maine Bureau of Public Lands. Highlights along Route 191 include a good variety of hawks and owls year-round; the possibility of boreal residents such as Spruce Grouse, Common Raven, Gray Jay, Black-backed Woodpecker (uncommon), and Boreal Chickadee; and good numbers of shorebirds in August and September. The following areas are especially worth checking. If you plan to hike the 5.4-mile trail in the Cutler Coast Unit (which we strongly recommend), you should count on the better part of a day to explore this entire route.

Machias River.   Starting on Route 1 in Machias, stop first at the Machias River where Route 1 crosses it. This is a good place to see waterfowl in winter, Ospreys in summer, and a Bald Eagle at any time of year. The public parking lot beside the river—on the east side of Route 1, right in the center of town—is an ideal spot from which to scan. Another good spot is the public landing 0.4 mile farther north on Route 1, just past Helen's Restaurant.

Holmes Bay.   In East Machias turn south onto Route 191. In 5.9 miles you will see the first extensive flats along Holmes Bay, and in another 0.8 mile you will see the bridge over Holmes Stream, where you can pull over and scan. The flats here are a significant stopover point for migrant shorebirds, particularly between mid-July and late September. At least 19 species of shorebirds have been recorded in Holmes Bay, with Semipalmated Sandpipers and Short-billed Dowitchers being especially numerous. Good numbers of Black-bellied Plovers, Greater and Lesser yellowlegs, and Ruddy Turnstones also stop over. Red Knots and Pectoral and White-rumped sandpipers are occasional, and Hudsonian and Marbled godwits, Willets, Western, Buff-breasted, and Baird's sandpipers, and Long-billed Dowitchers are rare. The best shorebirding here is about two hours before or one hour after high tide; at low tide the birds are too dispersed to be seen well, and at high tide they roost elsewhere. In the salt marsh that borders Holmes Stream, look and listen for nesting Nelson's Sharp-tailed (now split from Saltmarsh Sharp-tailed) Sparrows.

Holmes Bay also attracts good numbers of waterfowl, especially Canada Geese and American Black Ducks. The combined concentration of waterbirds and shorebirds sometimes attracts avian predators: look in fall for such species as Bald Eagle, Peregrine Falcon, and Merlin. In 1988 a pair of Merlins nested on nearby Sprague Neck, which was New England's first confirmed nesting record for this species. (Sprague Neck is the long cobble beach that projects into the southern end of Holmes Bay. Local birders know it for the thousands of shorebirds that sometimes gather here each fall. Although managed in conjunction with The Nature Conservancy, the property belongs to the U.S. Navy and, for security reasons, is inaccessible to the public.)

Little Machias Bay & Cutler Harbor. Continue south on Route 191, and 0.6 mile after the road turns sharply to the left (3.4 miles south of the Holmes Stream bridge) stop at Turner's Bridge on Little Machias Bay. The flats here are another spot worth checking at midtide for migrant shorebirds. This is a particularly reliable place to see good numbers of Whimbrels on fall migration. Cutler Harbor, 2.5 miles farther south, is worth checking year-round for waterfowl, seabirds (especially gulls), and Bald Eagles.

If you are wondering about all those radio towers rising higher than 800 feet across Little Machias Bay in North Cutler, they are part of the U.S. Navy's Cutler Naval Computer and Telecommunication Station, which operates the most powerful radio station in the world. The unit has a transmitting power of 2 million watts and coordinates communication with navy ships, submarines, and planes operating throughout the Atlantic Ocean.

Cutler Coast Unit. In the summer of 1994, the Maine Bureau of Public Lands opened up access to a magnificent piece of property just east of Route 191. Encompassing almost 2,200 acres, the Cutler Coast Unit includes a 5.4-mile loop trail that begins at a large open meadow along Route 191, leads down to the shore and across several headlands and cliffs, and then passes through lovely stands of spruce-fir and mixed woods, a Black Spruce bog, streamside wetlands and thickets, and grassland barrens. Between the superb ocean views (when it isn't foggy) and the unusual variety of habitats it traverses, this trail is a welcome boon to Washington County birders. At least 190 species have been recorded on or adjacent to the property, including Bald Eagle, Merlin (probable breeder), Peregrine Falcon, and at least six species of owls: Long-eared, Great Horned, Snowy, Barred, Short-eared, and Northern Saw-whet. Yellow Rail and Sedge Wren may possibly breed in the wet grasslands, but as yet neither species has been confirmed.

The unsheltered and steep stretch of coast between Cutler and Lubec is often called Maine's "Bold Coast." It is appropriately named, being characterized by 200-foot-high cliffs and a high-energy shoreline of cobble beaches and tide pools. The birdlife is rich, and the trail and headlands in the Cutler Coast Unit provide ideal vantage points from which to scan. In summer, Common Ravens and probably Black Guillemots nest on the cliffs, and Common Eiders, Ospreys, and Arctic and Common terns often feed offshore. Especially after strong easterly winds, it is worth looking for some of the more common pelagic species such as Greater and Sooty shearwaters, Northern Gannet, Black-legged Kittiwake, and Atlantic Puffin. Look, too, for Razorbills, which nest not too far south on Old Man Island at the entrance to Little Machias Bay. The Bold Coast is also an excellent spot to look for whales in mid- to late summer; the most likely species are Finback and Minke whales, but Humpback Whale and Harbor Porpoise are also possibilities.

With its unusual mix of habitats, the inland portion of the Cutler Coast Unit also supports a rich assemblage of species. Some of the more interesting breeders to look for are American Bittern, Northern Harrier, Sharp-shinned Hawk, Northern Goshawk, Merlin (probable breeder), Ruffed Grouse, Virginia Rail, Sora, Killdeer, Spotted Sandpiper, Common Snipe, American Woodcock, Great Horned, Barred, Northern Saw-Whet, and (possibly) Short-eared owls, Whip-poorwill, Yellow-bellied Sapsucker, Pileated Woodpecker, Olive-sided, Yellow-bellied, Least, and Alder flycatchers, Brown Creeper, Sedge Wren (a possible breeder—check Schooner Brook Meadow, the large meadow along Route 191), Winter Wren, Ruby-crowned and Golden-crowned kinglets, Veery, Swainson's, Hermit, and Wood thrushes, Solitary and Red-eyed vireos, at least 21 species of warblers (including Tennessee, Cape May, Blackburnian, Palm, Bay-breasted, Blackpoll, and Wilson's), Vesper, Savannah, Lincoln's, and Swamp sparrows, Dark-eyed Junco, Bobolink, Red and White-winged crossbills (irregular), Pine Siskin, and Evening Grosbeak. Interestingly, Bicknell's (formerly Gray-cheeked) Thrush is a possible breeder; small numbers of these birds are seen on the outer headlands of Washington County in early June, but whether they are migrants or nesters is unknown. (If you have any evidence of this species breeding, please be sure to notify someone of your observations.) Boreal residents include Spruce Grouse, Black-backed woodpecker (uncommon), Gray Jay, Common Raven, and Boreal Chickadee.

On migration, the headlands can be particularly productive, with large numbers of thrushes, sparrows, and other passerines stopping to feed and rest as they journey south. Sharp-shinned Hawks, American Kestrels, Merlins, and Peregrine Falcons are also regular migrants, and you can often get excellent looks at them. Bald Eagles are regular year-round.

A visit to the Cutler Coast Unit in winter is cold business indeed, but the rewards can be worth it. Look for boreal residents and, offshore, for loons and grebes, Great Cormorants, a good variety of waterfowl (including Harlequin Ducks), Black-legged Kittiwakes, alcids, and Purple Sandpipers.

Rarities (primarily migrants) sighted on or near the Cutler Coast Unit include Yellow Rail, Long-eared Owl, Blue Grosbeak, Painted Bunting, and Clay-colored and Grasshopper sparrows.

Large mammals that have been seen on the property include Moose, Coyote, Varying Hare, and Bobcat. You can also see several species of unusual plants, including Beach Head Iris, Pearlwort, Arethusa, Baked-apple Berry, and Northern Yarrow.

The Cutler Coast Unit is open year-round, free of charge, from sunrise to sunset. A small (currently two car) and inconspicuous parking area is located on the east side of Route 191 by the large open meadow where Schooner Brook crosses the road; it is 3.8 miles north of the dock in Cutler village (where Route 191 makes a sharp turn) and 10.2 miles south of the intersection of Routes 189 and 191 in West Lubec. Look for a small brown sign by the meadow. There are no facilities at the Cutler Coast Unit, but there are three primitive walk-in campsites along the shore.

For information about camping at the Cutler Coast Unit, write or call the Maine Bureau of Public Lands, Eastern Regional Office, Airport Road, Box 415, Old Town, ME 04468, telephone 207-827-5936.

To West Lubec.   In Cutler, Route 191 turns north and continues almost 11 miles to West Lubec. Along most of the way you will see extensive blueberry barrens interspersed with open fields and alder swales. In summer this stretch of road can be a good place to look for nesting Northern Harriers and Vesper Sparrows (fields); Yellow-bellied Flycatchers, Palm Warblers, and Lincoln's Sparrows (boggy areas); and Alder Flycatchers and Wilson's Warblers (alder swales). Short-eared Owl and Sedge Wren are possible nesters in the area, and American Kestrels are often seen hunting over the fields or teed up on the telephone wires. During migration look for Whimbrels (southbound birds are sometimes seen as early as July 1) and for hawks, particularly accipiters and falcons. Sharp-shinned Hawks, American Kestrels, Merlins, and Peregrine Falcons are all regular migrants. In fall, when the blueberry barrens turn a blaze of red, this is a beautiful drive.

From November through March this section of Route 191 has traditionally been a good area to look for raptors, which occur some years in unusually high numbers. It tends to be a hit-or-miss area, but species you should look for include Northern Harrier (occasional), Northern Goshawk, Sharp-shinned, Red-tailed, and Rough-legged hawks, and Great Horned, Snowy, Northern Saw-whet, Barred, and Short-eared owls. Horned Larks and Snow Buntings sometimes are abundant, especially on migration; it is worth scanning them for Lapland Longspurs. This portion of Route 191 also tends to be a good area to see Northern Shrikes and Common Redpolls. Look for other wintering finches, too. Red Foxes and Coyotes can also be seen on occasion.

LOCAL ACCOMMODATIONS

For information on local accommodations and services, write or call the Machias Bay Area Chamber of Commerce, P.O. Box 606, Machias, ME 04654, telephone 207-255-4402; or at the same address, the Washington County Promotions Board, telephone 800-377-9748.

Lubec

Lubec Flats   Quoddy Head State Park

The small town of Lubec, on lower Passamaquoddy Bay, was once famous for its thriving sardine industry. Today, with the sardine industry having crashed and only a few of Lubec's 20-plus canneries still operating, this quiet town is but a shadow of its former self. Although most people visiting Lubec nowadays are simply passing through, among those who do stop and explore, more than a few are surely birders. Lubec is well known primarily as a shorebirding area, but it can also be a good place to see seabirds (including an excellent variety of gulls) year-round, nesting warblers (including Blackpoll), and boreal residents such as Spruce Grouse, Gray Jay, Common Raven, and Boreal Chickadee. There are two areas of special interest: the Lubec Flats, which offer some of the best shorebirding in Maine, and Quoddy Head State Park, a superb vantage point from which to scan for seabirds and a good place to look for boreal specialties.

Lubec Flats (MAINE ATLAS map 27, B-4)

The Lubec Flats lie on the northern side of West Quoddy Head, a narrow arm of land extending 2 miles east into Grand Manan Channel. The tides in this region range from 16 to 26 feet, and the mudflats they expose twice daily provide a feast of insects, worms, and other invertebrates for migrant shorebirds. The mudflats extend all the way from West Quoddy Head to Lubec Neck, 3 miles north; in some areas they extend as far as 1 mile east. The Lubec Flats attract some of the

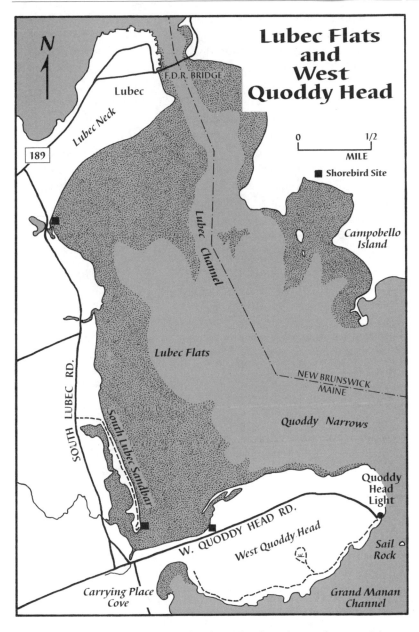

Lubec Flats and West Quoddy Head

N

Lubec

Lubec Neck

189

F.D.R. BRIDGE

Lubec Channel

0   1/2
MILE

■ Shorebird Site

Campobello Island

SOUTH LUBEC RD.

Lubec Flats

South Lubec Sandbar

NEW BRUNSWICK
MAINE

Quoddy Narrows

Quoddy Head Light

W. QUODDY HEAD RD.

West Quoddy Head

Sail ○ Rock

Carrying Place Cove

Grand Manan Channel

largest concentrations of shorebirds to be found anywhere in Maine and are an internationally important staging area for these long-distance migrants. As elsewhere, fall migration is far more pronounced than spring; it generally begins here by mid-July, peaks in mid-August, and continues into late October. When the flats are flooded at high tide, this is also a good place to see large flocks of roosting gulls. Between the shorebirds and the gulls, you can easily spend a half day looking over the birds here.

Each fall thousands of shorebirds stop to feed and rest on the Lubec Flats. Unfortunately, as at many traditional staging areas in eastrnmost Maine and Atlantic Canada, the numbers of birds have dropped notably since the late 1970s—a phenomenon that has not been fully explained. Yet even though many of us remember a time when shorebirds were more abundant in Lubec than they now are, it still remains a very impressive area. The most common species are Black-bellied and Semipalmated plovers, Greater and Lesser yellowlegs, Red Knot, Ruddy Turnstone, White-rumped, Least, and Semipalmated sandpipers, Dunlin, and Sanderling. The area is particularly good for Semipalmated Sandpipers; counts of up to 5,000 of these peep are not uncommon from late July through August. Black-bellied Plovers appear in large numbers in early August and peak in late August and September. Look for smaller though regular flocks of Semipalmated Plovers, White-rumped Sandpipers (this is one of the best places in Maine for this species), Ruddy Turnstones, and Short-billed Dowitchers; Sanderlings and Dunlin follow later in the season. Greater and Lesser yellowlegs are regular but rarely abundant, as is true of Red Knots.

Species that are seen less commonly include American Golden-Plover, Killdeer, Whimbrel, Willet, and Solitary, Spotted, and Western sandpipers. American Avocet, Marbled and Hudsonian godwits, and Baird's, Buff-breasted, and Stilt sandpipers are rare, but a few are seen from year to year. In short, keep your eyes open and examine flocks carefully; sheer numbers make anything a possibility here. This is one of the few places in Maine where Curlew Sandpiper has been seen.

At high tide when the Lubec Flats are flooded, hundreds and sometimes thousands of gulls roost on the water, and at any time of year they merit scanning. Herring and Great Black-backed gulls are abundant year-round, and small numbers of Ring-billed Gulls are regular. Bonaparte's Gulls can usually be found year-round, too, and are especially numerous in August and September, when you can sometimes see flocks of several thousand in lower Passamaquoddy Bay. This is also a good time of year to look for something more unusual; Common Black-headed and Little gulls are reported annually, and even Sabine's and Franklin's gulls have been seen here. Black-legged Kittiwakes occur just offshore in winter, and Glaucous and Iceland gulls are usually reported every winter, too.

In March and April the Lubec shore is one of the better spots in eastern Maine to see large numbers of Brant (high counts of up to 2,000), which sometimes linger into May.

There are three especially good spots from which to scan the Lubec Flats. The first is from South Lubec Road (see "Directions," below), 0.4 mile south of Route 189, where there is a small freshwater pond on the west side of the road and a small brackish pond on the east side. Scan the broad gravel beach (in both directions) below the road and, just beyond it, the flats. At high tide you can sometimes see large mixed flocks of Semipalmated Plovers and Semipalmated, Least, and White-rumped sandpipers roosting right next to the road; 2,000 to 4,000 birds are not uncommon here on fall migration. This is also a good place to see roosting gulls. Check the pond and cattails across the road, where you can often see such species as American Bittern, Wood and American Black ducks, and Green-winged Teal.

Continue another 1.4 miles south on South Lubec Road and turn left onto an unmarked gravel road (just before utility pole #68). This road takes you out onto the South Lubec Sandbar, a 3,500-foot-long sand and gravel spit running parallel to the shore and protecting a stream and good-sized salt marsh. This property is owned by the Maine Department of Inland Fisheries and Wildlife; although not marked with any signs, it is open to the public. As our friend Charlie Duncan, director of the Institute for Field Ornithology in nearby Machias, says, "This is the spot. Be here—not anywhere else—on the falling tide." Drive or walk the dirt road to the end of the spit (1 mile), scanning the flocks along the beach and flats as you go (if you are driving, be careful not to get stuck in the sand). The best shorebirding is usually at the south end of the beach. We do not recommend walking along the beach, as this is more likely to disturb birds. Be sure to check the extensive salt marsh, too. This is a wonderful place to get good looks at Nelson's Sharp-tailed (now split from Saltmarsh Sharp-tailed) Sparrow, a relatively common—but notoriously elusive—nester in the wetter portions of salt marshes. Savannah Sparrows and Bobolinks can usually be seen here as well. In winter, this beach can be a good area to look for such open-country species as Rough-legged Hawk, Snowy and Short-eared owls, Northern Shrike, Horned Lark, Snow Bunting, and Lapland Longspur.

The third spot to check for shorebirds is on West Quoddy Head. Come back up the South Lubec Sandbar, turn left (south) onto South Lubec Road, continue 1 mile, and bear left onto West Quoddy Head (there is a good overview of the salt marsh just before this turn). In 0.6 mile you will see an informal parking place on the left, and from here there is another good overview of the flats. Off to the right is a long cobble spit (almost covered on extreme high tides) which is anchored to West Quoddy Head. Large numbers of birds often congregate here, especially near the western tip of the spit. The property between the road and shoreline is private, but you can scan the flats from the roadside. The birds are usually most concentrated and most visible one to two hours after high tide.

Remember as you explore these areas that tides are everything with shorebirds. The best time to bird the Lubec Flats is on a midtide, two to three hours before or after high tide (the timing varies a bit from day to day, depending on tidal amplitude). At high tide you run the risk of disturbing roosting birds, and at low tide the birds are too widely dispersed to be studied closely. Remember, too, that the tide rises very quickly here—1 vertical foot every 15 minutes; you must take care not to get stranded on a rising tide. "Just one more look" can lead to real problems.

As at any shorebird site, please be extremely careful not to disturb feeding or roosting birds; this is especially important at Lubec because of the large numbers of birds that gather here.

The Lubec Flats are accessible year-round, free of charge. There are no facilities.

Quoddy Head State Park (*MAINE ATLAS* map 27, B-4)

Quoddy Head State Park, on the southeastern shore of West Quoddy Head, rises a dramatic 200 feet above a spectacular surf-bound coast. Many people visit the park to see adjacent red-and-white-striped Quoddy Head Light—built in 1858 and one of the most photographed lighthouses on the East Coast—but birders come for more than just the view. In addition to offering an outstanding vantage point from which to scan for seabirds and waterbirds year-round, this 481-acre park offers extensive stands of dense spruce-fir forest, a 7-acre open peatland accessible by boardwalk, and 43-acre Carrying Place Bog. Four trails provide access to the shore, cliffs (which are fenced off), forest, and peatlands. You are likely to find something of interest here at any time of year, with late May through July being the best time to see breeding species, especially warblers. Spruce Grouse, Gray Jay, Common Raven, and Boreal Chickadee are permanent residents. If you intend to hike the trails, plan to spend at least a few hours here.

The obvious place to begin birding is right at the parking lot, where you look out across the Grand Manan Channel toward Grand Manan and Campobello islands. The big rock straight out from the parking lot is Sail Rock, the easternmost point of land in the United States. On a clear day the view is spectacular, but we might as well warn you that you shouldn't count on this. West Quoddy Head is billed as the foggiest place in the United States; it is wrapped in fog an average of 59 days a year (many of them in summer). But even on a foggy day, it is worth trying to scan offshore. Scan from the picnic area and from the lighthouse, just to the east. Regular summer sightings include Double-crested and Great cormorants (the latter often on Sail Rock), Common Eiders, Black Guillemots, Ospreys, Herring, Great Black-backed, Ring-billed, and Bonaparte's gulls (the last more common in mid- and late summer), Black-legged Kittiwakes (primarily after early July), and Common and Arctic terns. Red-breasted Mergansers, all three scoters, and Bald Eagles are occasional. Especially after strong easterly winds, it is also worth looking for some of the more common pelagic species such as Greater and Sooty shearwaters, Northern Gannet, Razorbill, and Atlantic Puffin (rare). In August and September you can often see large concentrations of Bonaparte's Gulls offshore, and these are always worth scanning for something unusual; Common Black-headed and Little gulls are annual in lower Passamaquoddy Bay. This is also one of the best places along the Maine coast to see whales from shore. The most likely species are Harbor Porpoise and Finback and Minke whales. You are also likely to see Harbor Seals bobbing in the surf.

From mid- or late November through at least March, the diversity of offshore birds is greater, as is the likelihood of seeing something unusual. Red-throated and Common loons, Horned and Red-necked grebes, Great Cormorants, Common Eiders, all three scoters, Oldsquaws, Common Goldeneyes, Red-breasted Mergansers, Herring and Great Black-backed gulls, and Black Guillemots are all regular; Black-legged Kittiwakes, Razorbills, Thick-billed Murres, and Dovekies are occasional. Look, too, for Purple Sandpipers on the rocks and for an occasional Northern Gannet (any time of year except the dead of winter), Harlequin Duck, and Iceland, Glaucous, or even Common Black-headed Gull. Brant are regular in March and April and sometimes linger into May.

Signs at the parking lot will direct you to the trails. A good "loop" is to walk west along the Coastal Trail to Carrying Place Cove, being sure to veer off to the Bog Trail (which goes through the 7-acre unnamed peatland; see below), and then to walk back along West Quoddy Head Road to the park entrance. This approximately 4.5-mile walk provides an opportunity to explore most of the park. It is also worth walking the short Inland Trail near the parking lot.

From late May through July, look and listen in the spruce-fir woods for a variety of nesters, among them Winter Wren, Golden-crowned and Ruby-crowned kinglets, Swainson's and Hermit thrushes, and Tennessee, Magnolia, Yellow-rumped, Cape May (uncommon), Blackpoll, and Bay-breasted warblers. Nestled in the middle of these damp woods is a beautiful small peatland, which is accessible from the Bog Trail. This especially pleasant trail, with excellent interpretive signs along the boardwalk, is a good place to look for Boreal Chickadee, Olive-sided and Yellow-bellied flycatchers, Palm Warbler, White-throated and Lincoln's sparrows, and Dark-eyed Junco. If you continue on to Carrying Place Cove, you will find a broad, shallow inlet where the 16- to 26-foot tides of this region expose an extensive intertidal zone; here you can look in late summer and fall for migrant shorebirds and roosting gulls. You can also scan the southern side of Carrying Place Bog from here. This 43-acre peatland is an excellent example of a raised coastal peatland. What is most unusual about it is the manner in which it is being eroded by tidewater, exposing a 10- to 15-foot vertical cliff of peat and underlying sediments. For many years there has been an active Bank Swallow colony here.

A trail at the head of Carrying Place Cove leads across a grassy field up to West Quoddy Head Road; from here you can walk back to the park entrance, scanning Carrying Place Bog from the roadside along the way. There are no trails into the bog (you should not walk into it because the plant life is very fragile), but you can bird it from the roadside. Look along the grassy and shrubby edges for such characteristic nesters as Alder Flycatcher, Veery, Yellow Warbler, Common Yellowthroat, and Savannah Sparrow. Small groups of shorebirds sometimes roost along the stream on spring and fall migration. Carrying Place Bog also supports several plant species typically found farther north, including Baked-apple Berry and reindeer mosses. (If you are driving down West Quoddy Head Road, there is a good overview of the bog 0.3 mile east of South Lubec Road.)

Year-round specialties to look for in the park include Spruce Grouse (fairly regular and usually easiest to see in mid- or late summer, when the birds are in family groups), Black-backed Woodpecker (uncommon), Common Raven, Boreal Chickadee, and Red and White-winged crossbills (both species irregular in range and abundance).

Quoddy Head State Park is open daily from May 15 to October 15, from 9:00 a.m. to sunset, and has toilet and picnic facilities. There is a small admission fee. If you arrive before 9:00 a.m. or in the off-season and find the park gate closed, you are welcome to park outside and walk in (0.2 mile), provided that your vehicle does not block the road or gate. The Bureau of Parks and Recreation asks that you show caution on the trails in winter, when the footing is often very slippery. Adjacent Quoddy Head Light is not open to the public, but the grounds are open from 9:00 a.m. to sunset from May 15 to October 15 (admission is included in the park fee). You may walk the lighthouse grounds in the off-season.

DIRECTIONS

In Lubec, turn south off Rt. 189 onto South Lubec Rd. The road is not marked, but there is a sign for Quoddy Head State Park. You will see the first shorebird stop we mention in 0.4 mile, the access road to the South Lubec Sandbar in another 1.4 miles, and West Quoddy Head Rd. in another mile. The entrance road to the park is 1.8 miles down West Quoddy Head Rd., on the right, and is well marked.

LOCAL ACCOMMODATIONS

For information on local accommodations and services, write or call the Lubec Chamber of Commerce, P.O. Box 123, Lubec, ME 04652, telephone 207-733-4522; or the Washington County Promotions Board, P.O. Box 606, Machias, ME 04654, telephone 800-377-9748.

Campobello Island, New Brunswick (*MAINE ATLAS* map 27, A-4)

Campobello Island, New Brunswick, is connected to Lubec, Maine, by bridge and is well known as the beloved summer home of Franklin and Eleanor Roosevelt. If it seems like a stretch to include this beautiful Canadian island in a book about Maine, it may help to know that the island is home to the Roosevelt-Campobello International Park, which is jointly administered by the U.S. and Canadian governments. More importantly, from our perspective, it is an island full of good birding. Campobello is an excellent place to see a wide variety of seabirds and waterfowl year-round, breeding landbirds between late May and early August, and shorebirds, hawks, and landbirds on spring and fall migration. Highlights include unusually large numbers of gulls, especially in late summer and winter; at least 20 species of nesting warblers; resident boreal species such as Spruce Grouse, Gray Jay, and Boreal Chickadee; and in winter, a better-than-average chance of seeing such hard-to-find species as Glaucous and Iceland gulls, Razorbill, Thick-billed Murre, and Dovekie. In winter you can bird Campobello in half a day, but anytime between mid-May and late September you can easily spend two to three days here. Whatever the time of year, you are likely to find this rugged and scenic island delightfully uncrowded.

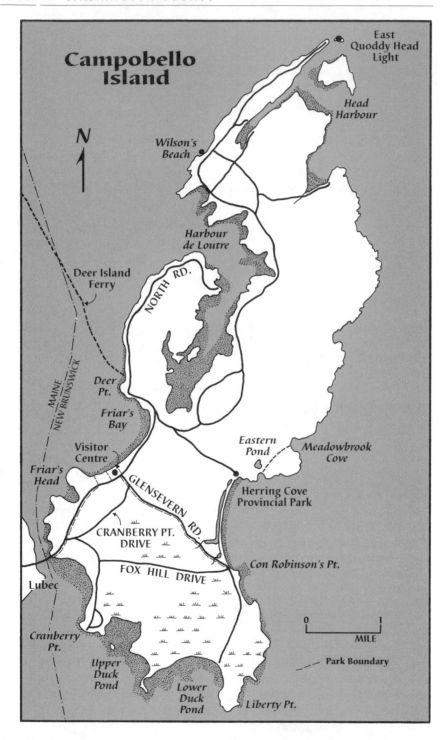

Campobello
Island

East
Quoddy Head
Light

Head
Harbour

N

Wilson's
Beach

Harbour
de Loutre

NORTH RD.

Deer Island
Ferry

MAINE
NEW BRUNSWICK

Deer
Pt.

Friar's
Bay

Eastern
Pond

Meadowbrook
Cove

Visitor
Centre

Friar's
Head

GLENSEVERN RD.

Herring Cove
Provincial Park

CRANBERRY PT.
DRIVE

FOX HILL DRIVE

Con Robinson's Pt.

Lubec

0   1
MILE

Cranberry
Pt.

Park Boundary

Upper
Duck
Pond

Lower
Duck
Pond

Liberty Pt.

Campobello is situated in lower Passamaquoddy Bay and measures about 10 miles long by 3 miles wide. Much of what makes the island so attractive to birds—and birders—is its variety of habitats. Between East Quoddy Head at the northern end of the island and Cranberry Point at the southern end, you will find coniferous, deciduous, and mixed woods, cobblestone and sand beaches, salt- and freshwater marshes, peatlands, brushy and open fields, ponds, thickets, and several spectacular headlands. Crossing the border at Lubec is a simple formality (no passport is necessary for U.S. citizens), and finding your way around is easy. Just remember that Campobello is on Atlantic time (one hour ahead of eastern time) and that all prices are of course in Canadian dollars (although U.S. currency is readily accepted).

The following are some of the island's best birding spots. Your first stop should be the information center on your right just after you cross the FDR Memorial Bridge (a reliable nesting site for Cliff Swallows), where you can get a map and other material. Since you will find all the areas we mention on an island or park map, we do not include precise directions to each stop.

Roosevelt-Campobello International Park

Roosevelt-Campobello International Park was established in 1964 as a joint memorial by Canada and the United States to Franklin Delano Roosevelt, who spent more than half the summers of his life here. The park comprises 2,800 acres (essentially the southern quarter of Campobello) and is divided into two distinct sections: the Visitor Centre and four Roosevelt cottages on the west side of Campobello's main road, and the Natural Area on the east side. Within the Natural Area you can explore extensive peatlands (they include about a third of the park), spruce-fir and mixed woods, fields and thickets, and several miles of shoreline. There are more than 8 miles of gravel or dirt roads in the park and another 8 miles of hiking trails, all well maintained and well marked.

A logical place to begin your investigation of the park is at the **Visitor Centre**, where you can get maps, bird lists, and other material. The area surrounding the Visitor Centre and cottages is surprisingly good for birding, with nicely spaced trees and extensive flower beds. Boreal Chickadees are quite regular in the spruces, and in summer the flowers attract many Ruby-throated Hummingbirds. Even if you have come just to bird, take the time to visit the 34-room Roosevelt "cottage." It is a fascinating place, filled with the memory of

FDR and his presidency and family. Among other things, you can see the telescope that FDR used to look at birds. Just across the main road from the cottages is Campobello's **Fire Pond** (where the fire engines fill up), a good spot to check during the breeding season as well as during migration.

Just west of the Visitor Centre is **Friar's Head**, a picnic area with a spectacular view of Passamaquoddy Bay and the surrounding islands. The thickets and brambles here afford cover for many birds, especially on migration. This is one of the best places on the island to look for Mourning Warblers (uncommon), with early June usually being the best bet. A short trail (about 0.3 mile) loops around the head. Breeding birds are not especially numerous, but Black-billed Cuckoos, Yellow and Chestnut-sided warblers, Common Yellowthroats, American Redstarts, and Song Sparrows are all regular, and Indigo Buntings are possible. Even if there weren't a bird in sight, though, you'd be hard pressed to find a lovelier picnic site.

Directly opposite the Visitor Centre is **Glensevern Road** (it is not marked as such, but there is a park sign), which will take you into the Natural Area. Stop first at the **Eagle Hill Bog**, where there is an attractive boardwalk with interpretive signs. Yellow-bellied Flycatchers, Palm, Canada, and Wilson's warblers, and Lincoln's and White-throated sparrows are among the characteristic nesting species to look for in and around this and other peatlands in the park.

Continue to **Con Robinson's Point**, a fine spot from which to scan the shoreline and see Grand Manan, another New Brunswick island, rising majestically some 10 miles to the southeast. Common Eiders, Common and Arctic terns, and Black Guillemots are all regular offshore, and Bank Swallows and a few Belted Kingfishers nest in the bank to the north. This point is a good place to park and walk along the road to Liberty Point, 2.3 miles south. This walk takes you through a pleasant stretch of deciduous and coniferous woods, and in the early morning during the breeding season you can hear, and often see, a good variety of species. Winter Wrens, Swainson's Thrushes, Solitary Vireos, and several species of warblers—among them Tennessee, Nashville, Northern Parula, Magnolia, Cape May (small numbers), Yellow-rumped, Black-throated Green, Blackburnian, Bay-breasted, Black-and-white, Ovenbird, Canada, and American Redstart—are all regular. Gray Jays and Boreal Chickadees are possible year-round, and Common Ravens can often be heard "croaking" overhead or in the distance. With luck, you may even see a Spruce Grouse, although a Ruffed Grouse is more likely. From the cliffs at **Liberty Point** look for seabirds and waterfowl year-round (Black

Guillemots breed in the rocks here); for Ospreys and an occasional Bald Eagle in summer; and for migrating hawks, particularly falcons, in fall. The view is stupendous, with Grand Manan looming in the distance and West Quoddy Head Light in Lubec visible across the Quoddy Narrows.

From Liberty Point, **Lower Duck Pond and Bog** are worth checking for breeding species and migrants. A cobblestone barrier beach separates the ocean and a brackish pond, with the latter surrounded by the largest peatland in the park. During the breeding season look for characteristic bog nesters and for Killdeer, Spotted Sandpipers, and Savannah Sparrows; on migration look for occasional flocks of shorebirds. To protect both the bird- and plant life, please be sure to bird the bog from its edges instead of walking into it. Even from the edges, you will find that walking is wet business, so wear sneakers or boots. The well-protected cove is a favorite stopping point for waterfowl in spring and fall, and even in winter you may find ducks rafted up here. In summer look for Harbor Seals hauled out on the ledges offshore at low tide.

Fox Hill Drive, a 2.2-mile walk or drive, also offers a variety of habitats, including dense spruce-fir woods and scattered peatlands, birches, maples, and Mountain Ash. This road is probably the best place on the island to look for boreal residents such as Spruce Grouse, Black-backed Woodpecker (uncommon), Gray Jay, and Boreal Chickadee. We had a wonderful look at a female Spruce Grouse and three young here in late August one year as they fed on Tamarack needles just a few feet away from us.

Upper Duck Pond and Bog, though smaller than their counterparts to the east, are likewise worth checking for breeding species and migrants. As at Lower Duck, there is a well-protected cove here, as well as mudflats.

Finally, walk or drive at least the upper portion of **Cranberry Point Drive**. Although this road generally is not as interesting for birds as the other roads in the park, there is a good-sized stand of dead spruce-fir—the result of a severe Spruce Budworm infestation—near the Glensevern Road. This area will eventually regenerate, but until it does, it is a good place to look for Mourning Warblers and Black-backed Woodpeckers (uncommon).

The park's grounds and trails are open year-round, free of charge, and include picnic and outhouse facilities. The Visitor Centre and cottages are open daily from Memorial Day weekend through mid-October, free of charge, from 9:00 a.m. to 5:00 p.m. eastern daylight time (10:00 a.m. to 6:00 p.m. Atlantic daylight time).

Friar's Bay

Friar's Bay lies between Friar's Head to the south and Deer Point to the north and is a good spot to scan at any time of year. The best vantage point is from the left-hand side of Campobello's main road, 0.8 mile north of the entrance to Roosevelt-Campobello International Park and near Friar's Bay Motel. There is plenty of space to pull over and park. Scan for gulls year-round (there are often hundreds, and sometimes thousands, roosting on the beach or water); for shorebirds in late summer and fall (at high tide they often feed in the wrack along the beach and can be seen at very close range); and for loons, grebes, waterfowl, and alcids and other seabirds from November through March. Be sure to check the north end of the beach behind the restaurant.

Large numbers of gulls can be seen off Campobello at any time of year; August and September are especially good months to find something unusual. Bonaparte's Gulls are usually abundant at this time of year, with flocks of several thousand sometimes occurring in lower Passamaquoddy Bay. Look for Common Black-headed and Little gulls among them. In winter look offshore for Black-legged Kittiwakes (abundant) and for Bonaparte's (uncommon) and Common Black-headed (rare) gulls. A few Glaucous and Iceland gulls often roost among the Great Black-backed and Herring gulls in winter. Small numbers of Ring-billed Gulls are regular year-round, and Laughing Gulls are occasional in summer.

North Road

North Road offers lovely views to Eastport and Indian Island and has several spots where you can pull over and scan. This is typically a good place to see gulls year-round and Great Cormorants and other winter seabirds from November through March. North Road terminates at Harbour de Loutre, a protected inlet where you can often find several species of ducks; this is private property, so please ask permission before trespassing.

Deer Island Ferry

The small ferry that operates between Campobello and Deer Island (and between Deer Island and Eastport, Maine) in June, July, and August provides a fine opportunity to look for unusual gulls, especially in August, and to explore Deer Island. See the chapter "Eastport" for a full description of the ferry trip and Deer Island. The crossing between Campobello and Deer Island takes about 45 minutes; there are seven departures a day. There is no need to take your car, and the fee is nominal. Double-check the return schedule so you don't find yourself stranded on Deer Island. (And remember that the ferry operates on Atlantic time!)

To reach the ferry, turn left at the T intersection just north of Friar's Bay onto North Road. In 0.7 mile you will see the narrow road down to the ferry landing on the left. You can park here free of charge.

Herring Cove Provincial Park

This attractive park overlooks a long (nearly 1.5 miles) sand and gravel beach and, behind it, a freshwater pond—Lake Glensevern. Birds on and near the beach generally are not numerous, but you can usually find Common Eiders and Black Guillemots year-round and a few Red-throated or Common loons, Horned or Red-necked grebes, Oldsquaws, and Black-legged Kittiwakes in winter. Common Ravens and Bald Eagles often soar in the updrafts produced by Herring Cove Head, the large headland to the north. In the breeding season, Savannah, Swamp, and Song sparrows are regular in the grass and along the edge of the pond, and on a fall day with northwest winds the hawk migration can be impressive. Northern Harriers, Ospreys, Sharp-shinned Hawks, and American Kestrels are the most common migrants, and they often swoop low over the pond.

During the breeding season and migration, the trail from Herring Cove Beach to Meadowbrook Cove is often productive. At the parking lot at the northern end of the beach, you will see a road ascending a small rise. Follow this road (there may be a chain across it, but this is to stop vehicles, not people), staying to the right, and you will soon see the trail. This walk offers a wide variety of northern breeding species, and in migration the area can be loaded with birds. The trail borders Eastern Pond, an especially interesting area. This small body of water was formed by heavy ocean waves pounding the stones to create a barrier stone beach, called a barachois. This barachois and the brackish pond created by it are an impressive example of how the ocean's tremendous force helps shape the land.

If you spend the night at the park campground, be sure to walk along the edge of the golf course, especially in the early morning. The progression from coniferous to deciduous woods usually guarantees several woodland species. From late May through early July the number of singing birds is impressive. Ask at the park office for directions to the sewage pond, where you can often find a few species of ducks.

The park is open from approximately June 1 (the exact date varies from year to year) through September and has camping, picnic, and outhouse facilities. For more information, write or call the Campobello Island Chamber of Commerce (see below), or in summer, call the park directly at 506-752-2396.

Wilson's Beach Pier

The pier at Wilson's Beach is always worth a stop to look for gulls year-round and for other seabirds, especially alcids, in winter. From late November through March, look for such characteristic species as Red-throated and Common loons, Horned and Red-necked grebes, Great Cormorant, and Black-legged Kittiwake. In flight years, Razorbills, Thick-billed Murres, and Dovekies can be seen from the dock. South of Wilson's Beach, be sure to check the many small coves that border the road; they often contain small gulls.

East Quoddy Head

East Quoddy Head, or North Head, is one of our favorite places on Campobello. This narrow spit of land marks the entrance to Head Harbour and provides a spectacular vantage point from which to look for seabirds at any time of year and for whales in summer. It can also be a great "fall-out" spot in early morning on spring or fall migration. Across the narrow channel is East Quoddy Head Light.

East Quoddy Head offers spectacular views in nearly all directions (at least if it isn't foggy). Early mornings in spring and fall often find this point alive with migrant passerines. Check the thickets on either side of the parking area, then wander back down the road. In migration it is not difficult to find most of the following: Northern Flicker, Yellow-bellied Sapsucker, Hairy and Downy woodpeckers, Least Flycatcher, Eastern Wood-Pewee, Tree, Bank, Barn, and Cliff swallows, Blue Jay, Black-capped Chickadee, Red-breasted Nuthatch, Winter Wren, Ruby-crowned and Golden-crowned kinglets, Cedar Waxwing, Veery, Hermit and Swainson's thrushes, Gray Catbird, American Robin, Solitary and Red-eyed vireos, Tennessee, Nashville, Yellow, Northern Parula, Magnolia, Cape May, Black-throated Blue (uncommon), Yellow-rumped, Black-throated Green, Blackburnian, Chestnut-sided, Bay-breasted, Blackpoll, Palm, Wilson's, Canada, Black-and-white, and Mourning (uncommon) warblers, Ovenbird, Northern Waterthrush, and Common Yellowthroat. Chipping, White-throated, White-crowned, Fox, Lincoln's, Swamp, and Song sparrows, Baltimore Oriole, Rose-breasted Grosbeak, and Dark-eyed

Junco are all seen regularly. Sometimes you can also see hawks migrating over this point.

In summer this is a wonderful place to look for seabirds. Black-legged Kittiwakes and Black Guillemots are regular; interestingly, the kittiwakes breed on North Wolf Island, visible out to sea from East Quoddy Head Light. Occasionally (particularly during extended periods of foggy weather) you can see a Wilson's Storm-Petrel, Greater, Sooty, or Manx Shearwater, or Northern Gannet offshore. Bonaparte's Gulls are often abundant in August and September, and it is worth checking them carefully for something unusual such as a Common Black-headed or Little Gull. Since the early 1990s Merlins have been seen here regularly in summer and are probably breeding nearby. With luck, you will see a few whales, too. In the late afternoon or evening, especially in August, whales sometimes pass close at hand, and oftentimes you will hear them (as they exhale) before you see them. Harbor Porpoise and Finback and Minke whales are the most likely species, but Humpback, Pilot, and Northern Right whales and Atlantic White-sided Dolphin are also possible. On more than one occasion we have picnicked here in August twilight and watched Finback Whales feeding just offshore as shearwaters and Northern Gannets flew by in the distance.

Coming out to East Quoddy Head in winter requires being dressed for some serious cold weather, but the birds are often worth it. This is an excellent place to see Black-legged Kittiwakes, Iceland Gulls (sometimes as many as 15), and alcids, particularly Razorbills.

Boat Trips

Campobello is a delightful spot from which to take an offshore boat trip. The one company currently offering commercial trips specializes in whale-watching, but like most whale watches, these trips also provide a wonderful opportunity to see seabirds. Because the whales in this area often feed close to shore, you may not go all that far offshore, but you should have excellent looks at many common inshore species (essentially the same species listed above for East Quoddy Head).

Cline Marine, Inc., operates scheduled trips out of Campobello in July, August, and September and charter cruises in other months. For more information, write or call Cline Marine at Leonardville, Deer Island, New Brunswick, Canada E0G-2G0, telephone 506-529-4188 (Campobello) or 747-2287 (off-season).

Campobello is accessible year-round from Lubec via the FDR Memorial Bridge (no fee), or from Eastport and the New Brunswick mainland in June, July, and August via the Deer Island ferry (small fee).

DIRECTIONS
At the intersection of Rts. 1 and 189 in Whiting (or at the inter-section of Rts. 189 and 191 in West Lubec), take Rt. 189 east toward Lubec. Once in Lubec, you will see signs for the FDR Memorial Bridge and Campobello Island.

LOCAL ACCOMMODATIONS
For information on local accommodations and services, write or call the Campobello Island Chamber of Commerce, Campobello Island, New Brunswick, Canada E0G-3H0, telephone 506-752-2233 or 752-2513; or the Lubec Chamber of Commerce, P.O. Box 123, Lubec, ME 04652, telephone 207-733-4522. For a free copy of the *New Brunswick Travel Guide* (and other information on New Brunswick), call 800-561-0123.

Cobscook Bay State Park
(*MAINE ATLAS* map 27, A-2)

Cobscook Bay State Park is part of the 7,189-acre Edmunds Unit of Moosehorn National Wildlife Refuge, which was established in 1937 as the northeasternmost of a chain of migratory bird refuges stretch-ing from Florida to Maine (see the chapter "Moosehorn National Wildlife Refuge, Baring Unit"). Since the early 1960s, 888 acres of the Edmunds Unit have been operated as Cobscook Bay State Park, which sits on a lovely peninsula in a finger of Cobscook Bay. *Cob-scook*, an Indian word meaning "boiling tides," is an apt name for a place where the tides average 24 feet. Birders know this scenic and secluded park as an excellent spot to look for nesting and wintering Bald Eagles and for a good variety of coniferous-nesting species, especially warblers. What many birders may not know, however, is that from the park they can also bird a substantial amount of the rest of the Edmunds Unit located on the west side of Route 1. With more than 4 miles of dirt roads and trails, the Edmunds Unit provides access to a variety of open, wooded, and wetland habitats (including several small ponds and Beaver flowages) and offers the chance to see a fine cross section of birds, especially during the breeding sea-son. Bald Eagle, Merlin, Spruce Grouse, Gray Jay, Boreal Chickadee, and 23 species of warblers are among the 140 species that have been documented breeding in the Edmunds Unit (including Cobscook

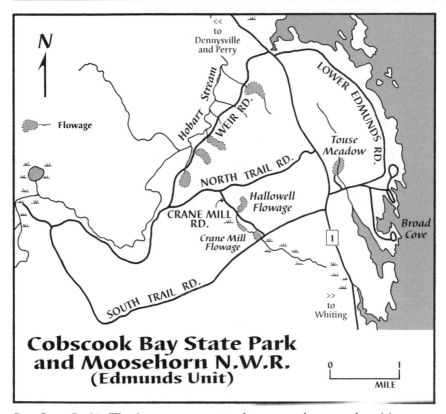

N

<< to Dennysville and Perry

Flowage

Hobart Stream

WEIR RD.

NORTH TRAIL RD.

CRANE MILL RD.

Crane Mill Flowage

Hallowell Flowage

Touse Meadow

LOWER EDMUNDS RD.

Broad Cove

1

>> to Whiting

SOUTH TRAIL RD.

Cobscook Bay State Park and Moosehorn N.W.R.
(Edmunds Unit)

0   1
MILE

Bay State Park). The best time to visit this area is between late May and early or mid-August, when the nesting species are present. You can easily spend a half day exploring the state park and adjacent portions of the refuge. The park is also a delightful place to base yourself while exploring other areas in eastern Washington County. The campsites, many of them situated right on the shore, are unusually spacious and attractive, and even in July and August you won't find all that many people here.

Habitats at Cobscook Bay State Park include second-growth coniferous and deciduous woods, open fields, a rocky shoreline with extensive tidal flats, and a managed flowage. The best way to bird the grounds—which are dominated by beautiful, tall conifers—is simply to walk the park road. When the song is at its peak in June, an early morning or evening walk usually yields many birds. Some of the more interesting species to look for include Northern Goshawk, Broad-winged Hawk, Merlin (at least one pair has nested since the early 1990s near the boat ramp at the edge of Broad Cove), American Kestrel, Great Horned and Barred owls, Pileated and Black-backed woodpeckers (the latter is uncommon but occasionally nests right in the campground), Yellow-bellied Sapsucker, Yellow-bellied and Alder flycatchers, Common Raven, Winter Wren, Golden-crowned and Ruby-crowned kinglets, Veery, Hermit and Swainson's thrushes, Solitary Vireo, and several species of warblers, including Tennessee, Northern Parula, Yellow, Cape May, Black-throated Green, Blackburnian, Chestnut-sided, Bay-breasted, American Redstart, and occasionally Blackpoll.

Species regularly sighted along the shore in summer include Common Loon, Double-crested Cormorant, Great Blue Heron, Osprey, Spotted Sandpiper, Great Black-backed, Herring, Ring-billed, and Bonaparte's gulls (the last primarily in late summer and fall), and Common Tern. From mid-July through at least September you can also see shorebirds feeding on the flats. Black-bellied and Semipalmated plovers, Greater and Lesser yellowlegs, and Least and Semipalmated sandpipers are usually the most abundant species. At any time of year this is an excellent place to look for Bald Eagles. Cobscook Bay supports one of Maine's densest and most consistently productive breeding populations of Bald Eagles and is also one of the state's four major wintering areas for this species. In 1995 at least two pairs of eagles nested here.

Be sure to check Tousse Meadow, the managed flowage located behind the park's maintenance garage. A variety of nesting waterfowl is usually present here, as well as Pied-billed Grebe, American Bittern, Belted Kingfisher, and Common Nighthawk.

In the Edmunds Unit on the west side of Route 1, you can find a good cross section of both wetland and upland breeding birds. The habitat here is primarily wooded (spruce-fir with some mixed hardwoods), with 5-acre block openings and 100-foot-wide strip cuts scattered throughout. Two wetland areas, Crane Mill and Hallowell flowages, are accessible from the Crane Mill and North Trail roads between early May and late November. Five other flowages are accessible by foot from the Weir Road. Look for such species as Pied-billed Grebe, American Bittern, Canada Goose (small numbers), Wood, American Black, and Ring-necked ducks, Green-winged and Blue-winged teal, Hooded and Common mergansers, American Kestrel, Ruffed and occasionally Spruce grouse (your best bet for the latter is along the Crane Mill or North Trail road), Killdeer, American Woodcock, Common Snipe, Black-billed and occasionally Yellow-billed cuckoos (both rare in years when there are few Gypsy Moth caterpillars), Common Nighthawk, Belted Kingfisher, Eastern Kingbird, Least, Alder, and Olive-sided flycatchers, Gray Jay (uncommon), Black-capped and Boreal chickadees (both common; a good place to look for the latter is the Route 1 end of North Trail Road), several species of warblers (including Black-throated Blue, Mourning, Wilson's, and Canada), several species of sparrows (Savannah, Chipping, White-throated, Lincoln's, Swamp, and Song), and Rusty Blackbird (uncommon).

In winter, Cobscook Bay State Park is an especially good place to see large numbers of American Black Ducks. It is estimated that at least 25 percent of Maine's wintering American Black Duck population occurs offshore here; counts of several hundred birds are not uncommon. A flock of 75 to 200 Canada Geese usually winters in this area, too. Also look for loons, grebes, and sea ducks such as Greater and Lesser scaup (mixed flocks of 10 to 100 are sometimes seen on the Christmas Bird Count), Common Eider, Oldsquaw, all three scoters, Common Goldeneye, Bufflehead, and Red-breasted Merganser. Brant are regular in March and April, and Snow Geese are occasional. In fall, an extensive stand of Wild Rice in the Tousse Meadow area usually attracts many Wood and American Black ducks.

At any time of year keep an eye out for finches. Pine (winter only) and Evening grosbeaks, Purple Finch, Red and White-winged crossbills, Pine Siskin, and American Goldfinch are all possibilities, but their numbers vary by season and year.

This can also be a good area to look for large mammals. In summer you can often see Harbor Seals bobbing in the water or basking on the ledges at the park. In the Edmunds Unit you might see a Black Bear (especially in spring or late summer), White-tailed Deer, Coyote, Moose, Red Fox, Varying Hare, Beaver, River Otter, Porcupine, Muskrat, or Bobcat.

Cobscook Bay State Park is open year-round, and a small fee is charged. The campground is open from May 15 to October 15 and includes campsites, bathrooms, a picnic area, and a boat launch. If you arrive outside the camping season and find the park gate closed, you are welcome to park outside it and walk in, provided that your vehicle does not block the road or gate. For information about camping at the park, write or call Cobscook Bay State Park, P.O. Box 51, Dennysville, ME 04628, telephone 207-726-4412.

The Edmunds Unit on the west side of Route 1 is open to foot traffic year-round during daylight hours (it is a wonderful place to ski or snowshoe in winter) and to vehicle traffic between early May and late November. There are no facilities or fees. There is a bulletin board at the Route 1 end of the North Trail Road. Note that the Edmunds Unit (with the exception of Cobscook Bay State Park) is open to deer hunting in fall. If you are unfamiliar with what precautions you should observe during this season in Maine, please see the section entitled "Hunting" in the Introduction.

DIRECTIONS

Cobscook Bay State Park is located off Rt. 1 between Whiting and Dennysville. The well-marked access road is 4.3 miles north of the intersection of Rts. 1 and 189 in Whiting and 16.3 miles south of the intersection of Rts. 1 and 190 in Perry. The park is 0.5 mile down this road.

LOCAL ACCOMMODATIONS

For information on local accommodations and services, write or call the Machias Bay Area Chamber of Commerce, P.O. Box 606, Machias, ME 04654, telephone 207-255-4402; or at the same address, the Washington County Promotions Board, telephone 800-377-9748.

Eastport   (MAINE ATLAS map 27, A-4, & map 37, E-3)

Deer Island Ferry & Deer Island
Eastport Flats
Eastport Waterfront

Separated from Lubec, across Cobscook Bay, by less than 3 miles of water (but more than 40 miles of road) is the easternmost city in the United States—Eastport. The city sits on Moose Island in lower Passamaquoddy Bay overlooking Deer and Campobello islands, New Brunswick. Like Lubec, Eastport was also a major sardine producer at one time (the canning process is said to have been invented here in 1875), but today this once-bustling city is relatively quiet. From a birder's perspective, however, Eastport has much to offer. The highlights are the Deer Island ferry, from which you can sometimes see impressive numbers of gulls (with rarities among them) in late summer and fall, and Deer Island. The Eastport Flats can offer shorebirding in late summer and fall, and the Eastport waterfront is a good place to look for unusual gulls and alcids, especially in winter. In August and September, when the abundance and diversity of birds are greatest, you can spend several hours exploring the Eastport area.

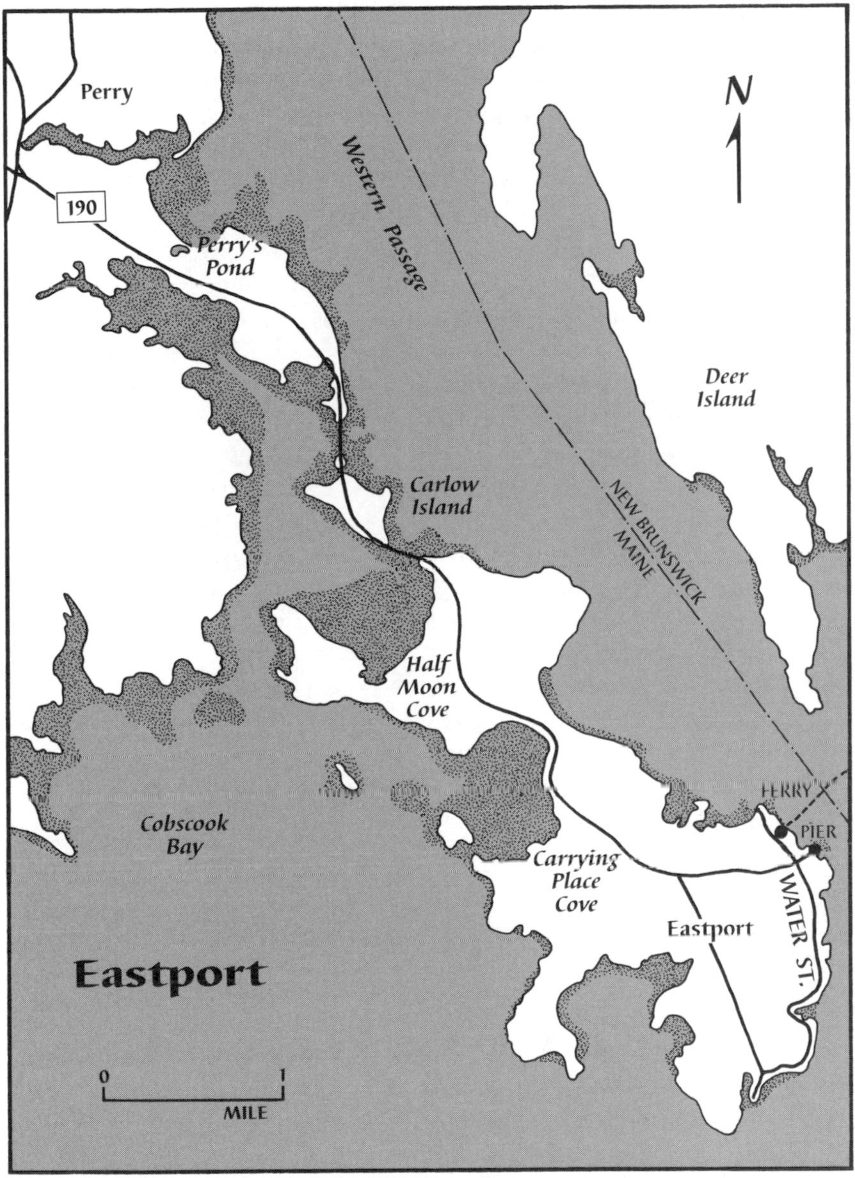
Perry
190
Perry's Pond
Western Passage
N
Deer Island
Carlow Island
NEW BRUNSWICK
MAINE
Half Moon Cove
FERRY
PIER
Cobscook Bay
Carrying Place Cove
Eastport
WATER ST.
Eastport
0
1
MILE

Deer Island Ferry & Deer Island

The passages among the islands in Passamaquoddy Bay offer some fine birding. Fortunately, two small ferries run between them in June, July, and August—one between Eastport and Deer Island and the other between Deer and Campobello islands (also see the chapter

"Campobello Island, New Brunswick"). Both ferries provide an excellent opportunity to look for unusual gulls, especially in August, and to explore Deer Island. The crossing between Eastport and Deer Island takes about 25 minutes, with hourly departures from each side throughout the day. The fee is nominal, and there is no need to take your car, even if you intend to stay a few hours and explore the island (a bike is perfect, however, if you have one with you). This is almost guaranteed to be the smallest ferry you have ever been on—and also the most fun. It is a good idea to double-check the return schedule, or you will be spending the night at the Deer Island campground (which, if you plan ahead, is very pleasant). Remember that Deer Island is in New Brunswick and thus is on Atlantic time, one hour ahead of eastern time in Eastport.

The best time to take the ferry is in late August, when large numbers of gulls are attracted to the passages in Passamaquoddy Bay and in particular to the Old Sow. The Old Sow is a massive upwelling whirlpool created between Eastport and Deer Island by the movements of the tide and the configuration of the bottom of the bay. It is named for the low, snorting sound that emanates from its gyre. Widely reputed to be one of the largest whirlpools in the world, the Old Sow brings a rich supply of small crustacea (euphausiids and copepods) to the surface twice a day. The largest numbers of birds are usually seen around the Old Sow about two hours before high tide (they tend to disappear quickly at high tide). You can scan the birds from the ferry and also from the southern end of Deer Island. We like to do both and then explore for warblers and other landbirds on Deer Island. After you go through Customs on the island (a simple formality for U.S. citizens, but it's a good idea to have a driver's license or other form of identification), head left to the southern tip of the island, which looks straight across to Eastport. This is an ideal place from which to scan. A scope is not essential, but you will certainly find one useful.

As recently as the early 1980s, the Deer Island ferries and the southern tip of Deer Island offered the opportunity to witness a truly staggering concentration of birds—20,000 or more Bonaparte's Gulls and more than a million Red-necked Phalaropes. Like many Maine birders, we vividly remember when phalaropes used to spread like a slick across the water and when the ferries seemed to ply their way through the Bonies. Today, though, for reasons that are not entirely clear but that are probably linked to changes in the food resource, this phenomenon no longer exists. Impressive numbers of Bonaparte's Gulls still occur in August and September (occasionally 10,000-plus), but they don't begin to approach historical numbers, nor are the birds as densely concentrated. Sadly, no Red-necked Phalaropes have been seen here in several years, and this species is now listed as threatened in Maine.

Having said all this, we hasten to add that it is still well worth looking for gulls in this area. After all, a few thousand Bonaparte's Gulls are not an everyday occurrence, and the less-common gull species have shown virtually no decline. The trick to finding rarities is to pick out and identify any odd-looking gulls from the large numbers of Bonies and smaller numbers of Herring, Great Black-backed, and Ring-billed gulls. The concentration of Bonies develops in early August and remains through September and sometimes through October. If you are patient, you may well find something unusual among them. Black-legged Kittiwakes are regular in small numbers, for example, and Common Black-headed and Little gulls are annual (two or three, and occasionally more, of each of the last two species are sometimes present). Laughing Gulls are rare. Sabine's Gulls have been seen at least twice in recent years, and at least four Franklin's Gulls have been recorded. Keep your eyes on the birds around the Old Sow, which is still one of the best places to look for rarities.

If you get tired of scanning gulls or feel the need the stretch your legs, there is usually a good mix of warblers and other passerines on Deer Island. This lovely island measures about 9 miles by 3 miles and offers plenty of good birding. (It is also a delightful island to bird by bicycle.) You are likely to hear the nasal notes of Boreal Chickadees, and you may see Gray Jays robbing unsuspecting campers of their sandwiches. Spish in the chickadees, and scatter some bread for the jays; you may get robbed, too.

From the southern tip of the island, take the left side of the loop through the woods and past the Customs house to the shore. The island is usually full of migrant warblers by mid-August, with Cape May Warblers being regular and Tennessee, Yellow, Magnolia, Yellow-rumped, Blackburnian, Chestnut-sided, Bay-breasted, Black-and-white, Palm, Wilson's, and Canada warblers, Ovenbirds, Northern Waterthrushes, Common Yellowthroats, and American Redstarts usually present as well. Other species that are often seen here include Common Raven, Red-breasted Nuthatch, Winter Wren, Ruby-crowned Kinglet, Cedar Waxwing, Gray Catbird, Solitary and Red-eyed vireos, Rose-breasted and Evening grosbeaks, Chipping, White-throated, and Song sparrows, Dark-eyed Junco, Purple Finch, and American Goldfinch. Red and White-winged crossbills are occasional, as are Lincoln's and Swamp sparrows. Even Western Tanager and White-winged Dove have been recorded here. If time permits, bird the main road. Don't forget the ferry, and don't forget Atlantic time!

Deer Island is accessible year-round by ferry, from Eastport in June, July, and August, and from Letete, New Brunswick, all year. There are camping, motel, and picnic facilities on the island.

Another option for exploring the waters around Eastport and Deer Island is to take a whale watch with Capt. George Harris, who operates out of Eastport. Write or call Capt. Harris at 24 Harris Point Road, Eastport, ME 04631, telephone 207-853-4303 or 853-4859.

Eastport Flats

The Eastport Flats used to offer some of the best shorebirding in Maine, but since the late 1980s the numbers of birds seen here have declined dramatically, as they have at many other traditional staging areas in easternmost Maine and Atlantic Canada. If you are driving down to Eastport anyway, however, it is still worth checking this area for shorebirds; access is easy, and you won't lose much time stopping at a few traditionally good areas to take a quick scan. Perhaps someday the birds will return.

All along Route 190 from Perry into Eastport you will see extensive mudflats and gravel bars which still attract small numbers of migrant shorebirds, primarily between mid-July and early October. You can bird the area easily from the roadside; the best time to do it is at midtide. We recommend stopping to scan at what have traditionally been the four most productive spots along Route 190: Perry's Pond (1 mile south of Route 1, at the far side of a field on the north side of Route 190; this is private property, but you can scan it from the roadside); the causeway just after the Pleasant Point Passamaquoddy Indian reservation (2.4 miles south of Route 1, and just north of Carlow Island); Half Moon Cove (3.5 miles south of Route 1); and Carrying Place Cove (5 miles south of Route 1).

The Eastport Flats are accessible year-round, free of charge. There are no facilities.

Eastport Waterfront

The Eastport waterfront is worth scanning at any time of year—for small gulls year-round (particularly in late summer and fall) and for white-winged gulls, alcids, and other seabirds in winter. The town pier and factory wharves along Water Street offer excellent views of the bay, and the rooftops provide convenient perches for the gulls. In August and September, look for the same species as you would from the Deer Island ferry (see above).

Few birders will venture to a place as remote as Eastport in the bleak winter months, but if you dress warmly it can be fun—honestly. And the Eastport waterfront is a better bet than many places for seeing some of Maine's hard-to-find winter specialties. Black-legged Kittiwakes often are abundant offshore. They are joined by several more widespread species, among them Common Loon, Horned and Red-necked grebes, Great Cormorant, Common Eider, Herring and Great Black-backed gulls, and Black Guillemot. In good flight years you can see Thick-billed Murres and Dovekies and occasionally a few Razorbills. This is an excellent place to look for Glaucous and Iceland gulls, and sometimes you can find a Common Black-headed Gull. Little Gull has been seen here in winter (and summer), and this is one of the few places in Maine where Ivory Gull has been seen. Sometimes you can see Purple Sandpipers along the rocky shore, and at any time of year you might see a Bald Eagle. On your way down to Eastport from Perry, take the time to scan the coves en route for waterfowl.

We can't resist adding one of Eastport's most unusual bird sightings—the adult Northern Gannet that "nested" here a few years ago. The "nest" was a little-used dory that was moored in a cove along the waterfront, and the "eggs" were white plastic floats nestled atop a pile of fishing nets.

The waterfront is accessible year-round, free of charge.

DIRECTIONS

At the intersection of Rts. 1 and 190 in Perry, turn south onto Rt. 190 and continue 7.1 miles to Water St. Turn left, go 0.1 mile, and you will see the town pier almost immediately on the right. Go 0.2 mile farther and you will see a narrow road on the right and a small sign that reads "Ferry to Canada." Turn right here. From the ferry landing, turn around and come back down Water St. to investigate the waterfront.

LOCAL ACCOMMODATIONS

For information on local accommodations and services, write or call the Eastport Area Chamber of Commerce, P.O. Box 254, Eastport, ME 04631, telephone 207-853-4644; the Washington County Promotions Board, P.O. Box 606, Machias, ME 04654, telephone 800-377-9748; or (especially for Deer Island) the Quoddy Loop Regional Tourism Office, Box 688, Calais, ME 04619, telephone 207-454-2597. For a free copy of the *New Brunswick Travel Guide* (and other information on New Brunswick), call 800-561-0123.

Moosehorn National Wildlife Refuge, Baring Unit

(*MAINE ATLAS* map 36, C-5)

Moosehorn National Wildlife Refuge—notable for its waterfowl, nesting woodcock, and Bald Eagles—is situated just south of the New Brunswick border and was established in 1937 as the northeastern-most of a chain of migratory bird refuges stretching from Florida to Maine. Today the refuge consists of two units located about 20 miles apart: the 17,257-acre Baring Unit on the St. Croix River in Calais and the 7,189-acre Edmunds Unit on Cobscook Bay in Robbinston (see the chapter "Cobscook Bay State Park"). The Baring Unit of the refuge is managed intensively for American Woodcock and water-fowl, but you can see a great variety of other birds as well. More than 200 species have been recorded, and almost 140 have been found nesting, including Spruce Grouse, Black-backed Woodpecker, Gray Jay, and 23 species of warblers. For many years this has also been one of the most reliable places we know to see nesting Bald Eagles. The best time to visit is between mid-April and mid- to late Novem-ber. You can bird the refuge by car from the Charlotte Road (the paved road that runs between Routes 1 and 214, and the primary access to the refuge) and by walking some of the 50-plus miles of dirt side roads. Virtually all of these side roads are gated off to traffic, and they make wonderful hiking trails. Plan on at least a full day to bird the refuge thoroughly.

The Baring Unit is essentially an upland area. The highly glaciated terrain is characterized by rolling hills, large ledge outcrops, extensive fields, a few lakes and bogs, and many ponds, marshes, and streams. The U.S. Fish and Wildlife Service has altered virtually the entire natural drainage system of the area to increase habitat for waterfowl, and former meadows and wooded swamps have been flooded to form a myriad of small and large ponds. The largest of these is Magurrewock Marsh on the northern end of the refuge. Woodlands consist primarily of second-growth stands of aspen, beech, birch, maple, spruce, fir, and pine. Signs of woodcock manage-ment are everywhere, with small clear-cuts—in various stages of regeneration—distributed throughout the refuge.

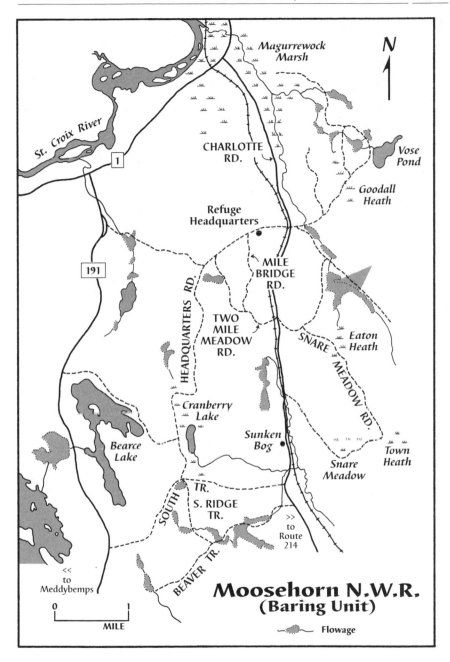

N

Magurrewock Marsh

St. Croix River

1

CHARLOTTE RD.

Vose Pond

Goodall Heath

Refuge Headquarters

191

MILE BRIDGE RD.

HEADQUARTERS RD.

TWO MILE MEADOW RD.

SNARE MEADOW RD.

Eaton Heath

Cranberry Lake

Sunken Bog

Town Heath

Bearce Lake

Snare Meadow

SOUTH

TR.

S. RIDGE TR.

>> to Route 214

<< to Meddybemps

BEAVER TR.

Moosehorn N.W.R.
(Baring Unit)

0   1
MILE

Flowage

Moosehorn may not feel like a wilderness area, owing to its many signs of management, but it is a delightfully rich and diverse birding spot—and you can often get unusually good looks at many of the birds. Late May through mid- or late July is the best time to see breeding species. A good place to begin your investigations is along the Charlotte Road at Magurrewock Marsh. This is probably the best place in the refuge to look for waterfowl and other wetland-associated breeders. It is easily scanned from Route 1, the Charlotte Road, and an observation blind near the southern end of the marsh (the parking area is on the east side of the Charlotte Road, 1.3 miles south of Route 1). Canada Geese, Mallards, Wood, American Black, and Ring-necked ducks, Green-winged and Blue-winged teal, and Hooded and Common mergansers are all regular breeders, as are Common Loons, Pied-billed Grebes, American Bitterns, Ospreys, Virginia Rails, Soras, Killdeer, Spotted Sandpipers, Common Snipe, Belted Kingfishers, Eastern Kingbirds, Marsh Wrens, Swamp Sparrows, and Red-winged Blackbirds. Green Herons are occasional nesters, Yellow Rails have been heard on several occasions, and Least Bitterns have been seen a few times.

Magurrewock Marsh is also a reliable place to see Bald Eagles. For several years a pair has nested just south of Route 1 on a former Osprey platform, and they can be observed at almost any time of year with minimal disturbance. A favorite perch (for the Ospreys, too) is one of the large dead elms between the northern edge of the marsh and Route 1. At least one other pair of eagles is thought to be nesting in the Baring Unit. Many of the eagles seen here are immatures, providing an unusual opportunity to examine the plumage variations exhibited in these young birds.

From the marsh, continue south down the Charlotte Road, stopping as habitat and birds indicate. The side roads provide access to much of the refuge and a variety of habitats, ensuring a good cross section of birds. The northern section of the Headquarters Road, Two-mile Meadow Road, and Mile Bridge Road traverse a mixture of Red and White pines, spruce and Balsam Fir, and birch, aspen, beech, and maple. Characteristic breeders in this part of the refuge include Northern Goshawk, Sharp-shinned, Cooper's (rare), and Broad-winged hawks, Ruffed and Spruce grouse, Black-billed Cuckoo, Great Horned, Barred, and Northern Saw-whet owls, Ruby-throated Hummingbird, Yellow-bellied Sapsucker, Pileated, Hairy, Downy, and Black-backed (uncommon) woodpeckers, Great Crested (uncommon) and Least flycatchers, Eastern Wood-Pewee, Common Raven, American Crow, Black-capped and Boreal chickadees, Red-breasted Nuthatch, Brown Creeper, Winter Wren, Golden-crowned and Ruby-crowned kinglets, Swainson's, Hermit, and Wood thrushes, Solitary and Red-eyed vireos, Nashville, Northern Parula,

Magnolia, Yellow-rumped, Black-throated Green, Black-and-white, Mourning (in raspberry thickets), and Canada warblers, Ovenbird, Rose-breasted Grosbeak, White-throated Sparrow, Dark-eyed Junco, and Purple Finch.

The southwestern portion of the refuge, accessible from the South Trail, South Ridge Road, and Beaver Trail, offers more extensive stands of second-growth coniferous woods (primarily spruces and firs). To the east, the Snare Meadow Road also provides access to spruce-fir habitat, though much of the area here has been cut close to the road. These two areas offer the best opportunities to see permanent residents such as Spruce Grouse (during the breeding season, ask at the refuge office where family groups are currently being seen), Black-backed Woodpecker (uncommon), Gray Jay, and Boreal Chickadee (common). Olive-sided Flycatcher and Cape May (scarce some years), Blackburnian, and Bay-breasted warblers also nest here, as do many of the species mentioned above.

The many ponds, wooded swamps, and streams scattered throughout the refuge offer extensive edge habitats, many of them overgrown with dense alder stands. These wet thickets and borders are good places to look for several species, among them Yellow-bellied and Alder flycatchers, Veery, Gray Catbird, Tennessee, Chestnut-sided, and Yellow warblers, American Redstart, and Rusty Blackbird (uncommon). Wherever you find extensive stands of dead trees that still have bark on them, look for Black-backed Woodpecker, a species that likes to search for food on dead standing timber; recently (5 to 8 years) dead or burned trees near a stream are excellent areas to look.

True bog habitat is not extensive at Moosehorn, but areas such as the Goodall, Eaton, and Town heaths are all worth checking for Palm Warbler and Lincoln's Sparrow; both species nest here in small numbers. Around Goodall Heath and Vose Pond, check the birch/aspen stands for nesting Black-throated Blue Warblers. In drier and more open upland areas, look for such nesting species as Northern Harrier, American Kestrel, Indigo Bunting, Vesper and Savannah sparrows, and Bobolink.

Research and management programs at Moosehorn for the past three decades have yielded valuable information on the American Woodcock, and you shouldn't have too much trouble flushing one. Present at the refuge from late March well into November, this shy upland shorebird dwells in alders by day and in clearings by night. The best chance of seeing a woodcock is in courtship flight at dusk or dawn. If you have never seen this delightful spring ritual, ask at refuge headquarters for directions to a display area. Courting birds are most active at dusk from mid-April to mid-May but can usually be found into early June.

Spring and fall migration also offer a variety of birds at Moosehorn. Spring migration begins in late March or early April when the first good-sized patches of open water appear and several species of waterfowl stop to rest and feed in Magurrewock Marsh. The diversity of migrant waterfowl usually peaks about mid-April. In addition to the nesting species mentioned earlier, look for Buffleheads and Red-breasted Mergansers and, less commonly, for Snow Geese, Northern Pintails, Gadwalls, American Wigeons, and small numbers of Lesser Scaup. Northern Shovelers, Barrow's Goldeneyes, and Ruddy Ducks are rare, and even Tundra Swan has been seen a few times. By mid- to late May many landbirds are also moving through. At the peak of the migration it shouldn't be any great chore to see or hear at least 18 species of warblers.

Fall migration is under way by mid- to late August when small groups of shorebirds stop to feed in the marsh, among them Semipalmated Plovers, Greater and Lesser yellowlegs, Least, Semipalmated, Solitary, and Pectoral sandpipers, and Short-billed Dowitchers. Landbirds also start moving south by mid- or late August, and warblers and sparrows are often abundant. Among the latter, Lincoln's Sparrow is a common migrant. The fall waterfowl migration is usually at its best between late September and late November, with many birds remaining as long as there is open water, sometimes into mid-December.

At any time of year, keep your ears and eyes open for finches. Purple Finches and American Goldfinches are permanent residents; Pine and Evening grosbeaks (the former primarily in winter), Red and White-winged crossbills, and Pine Siskin are all irregular possibilities.

Moosehorn is also an excellent place to see large mammals. At least 35 species of mammals have been recorded by refuge personnel. Black Bears are abundant and can often be seen along the roads in spring, in blueberry fields in August, and foraging for apples in fall. Beaver are also abundant, and their work is visible on nearly every pond and stream. White-tailed Deer are sometimes seen feeding in clearings or crossing the roads, and occasionally you will see a Moose, Porcupine, Red Fox, Coyote, Mink, Varying Hare, Woodchuck, Striped Skunk, Raccoon, or even River Otter. Bobcat has also been seen, primarily in remote and rocky areas of the refuge.

The refuge is open to trapping and deer hunting in fall. If you are unfamiliar with what precautions you should observe during this season in Maine, please see the section entitled "Hunting" in the Introduction.

Moosehorn National Wildlife Refuge is open daily year-round from dawn to dusk, free of charge. Except for year-round outhouse facilities at the headquarters, there are no facilities in the refuge. Be sure to stop at the headquarters (see "Directions," below) when you arrive, where you can get a map and checklist of refuge birds and can inquire if anything unusual has been seen recently. The refuge manager can also direct you to the best places to see certain species of interest. The office is open Monday through Friday from 7:30 a.m. to 4:00 p.m. Visitors are also invited to accompany wildlife biologists on waterfowl- and woodcock-banding operations and should call ahead to arrange this. For more information, write or call Moosehorn NWR, P.O. Box 1077, Calais, ME 04619-1077, telephone 207-454-7161.

DIRECTIONS

Access to the Baring Unit is from the Charlotte Rd., which is accessible from the north via Rt. 1 and from the south via Rt. 214. The refuge entrance at Rt. 1 is prominently marked. To reach refuge headquarters from the intersection of Rt. 1 and the Charlotte Rd., continue down the Charlotte Rd. 2.4 miles and turn right. The office is 0.5 mile ahead.

LOCAL ACCOMMODATIONS

For information on local accommodations and services, write or call the Greater Calais Area Chamber of Commerce, 235 Main St., Calais, ME, 04619, telephone 207-454-2308; or the Washington County Promotions Board, P.O. Box 606, Machias, ME 04654, telephone 800-377-9748.

Additional Sites of Interest

Roque Bluffs State Park (*MAINE ATLAS* map 26, D-3)

Roque Bluffs State Park lies at the end of a lovely point overlooking Englishman Bay and is worth a quick check at any time of year. The 274-acre park is easily accessible (it is right along the roadside), and there is very little walking involved. On the ocean side of the road is a half-mile-long sand and cobble beach, and on the other side is a shallow freshwater lake—making for the unusual combination of salt- and freshwater habitats side by side. American Beachgrass, Seabeach Sandwort, and Beach Pea are abundant on the dunes, and Rugosa Rose and Evening Primrose are abundant in the backdunes. Roque Bluffs is a fairly reliable site for Bald Eagles year-round, for common sea ducks and the occasional Barrow's Goldeneye in winter, and for a good variety of migrants in spring and fall. Redhead and Gadwall have both been seen on the pond in addition to more common migrant waterfowl, and Hooded Mergansers are sometimes seen in summer. If the birds fail you, the bloom of the roses and Beach Pea in summer is reason enough for the trip.

The park is open from May 15 to September 30, from sunrise to sunset, but you are welcome to park and explore the grounds at any time of year. A small fee is charged in summer. Facilities include toilets and, in summer, picnic tables and a bathhouse.

On Route 1 in Jonesboro, turn south onto Roque Bluffs Road and continue 5.5 miles to a T intersection. Turn right here, and you will see the park in 1.7 miles. You can also reach the park by turning off Route 1 in Machias onto Roque Bluffs Road.

The Great Heath (*MAINE ATLAS* map 25, C-3)

Located in Columbia just east of the Deblois Barrens and bisected by the Pleasant River is Maine's largest open peatland—the Great Heath. If you have a canoe, this is a delightful area to spend a day birding and botanizing, especially between late May and mid-August. You will have the chance to see many common and unusual peatland plants and a mix of peatland-associated breeding birds, including Ring-necked Duck, Yellow-bellied Flycatcher, Palm Warbler, and Lincoln's Sparrow. Some of the other species you might see or hear include American Bittern, Great Blue Heron, Mallard, American Black Duck, Northern Harrier, Osprey, Red-tailed and Broad-winged hawks, Solitary Sandpiper, and Great Horned Owl.

The Great Heath comprises more than 4,000 acres and is vegetated primarily with sphagnum mosses and low shrubs such as Leatherleaf, Labrador Tea, Bog Rosemary, and Sheep Laurel. Formed by the coalescing of several smaller raised peatlands, the heath is notable for its extensive dwarf shrub community, many ponds and ridges, and scattered islands of trees. It supports several orchid species, including unusually large numbers of Arethusa, and a small population of Bakedapple Berry, which is rare in Maine. The southern third of the heath is privately owned, but the northern two-thirds is owned by the Maine Bureau of Public Lands and managed primarily for research.

The Pleasant River (distinct from the Pleasant River that is a tributary of the Piscataquis River) meanders through about 14 miles of the Great Heath and provides an ideal avenue for exploration. It takes a full day to canoe the entire length of the heath. For details, consult the *AMC River Guide: Maine* by Yates and Phillips (see Appendix D).

Please remember that all peatlands are fragile and should be treated with the utmost care. The best policy is to confine your exploration to the riverside. If you do go onto the heath, step carefully and on the firmest ground, and do not pick up or uproot any plants. Bring an ample supply of insect repellent for the hungry black flies, mosquitoes, and deer flies.

Most birders will probably want to put in their canoe at the southern end of the Great Heath, off the Ridge Road. From Route 1 in Cherryfield, take Route 193 north and in 1.3 miles fork right onto the Ridge Road (unmarked). In 3.6 miles the road becomes dirt. Stay on this "main" road (that is, stay right) for another 1.1 miles, and then fork right onto another dirt road. The first major dirt road off to the left will lead to the Pleasant River. (Note: In dry summers, when pumps here are used to irrigate nearby fields, this is a very noisy spot; you may want to put in farther north.)

The Great Heath is accessible year-round, free of charge, from dawn to dusk.

The Airline, or Route 9
(MAINE ATLAS maps 23, 24, 25, 35, & 36)

Chances are good that if you spend much time in eastern Maine, you will eventually find yourself on the Airline, the main highway that runs east-west across central Washington and Hancock counties. Officially known as Route 9, the Airline is a 98-mile-long straight shot connecting Bangor and Calais. The road dates back to the mid-1800s when a dirt trail was built to improve mail service from Bangor to Calais; later it was upgraded for stagecoach travel.

Today the Airline is basically a fast route across eastern Maine, but birders can find many places to stop along the way. Between Bangor and Calais, the Airline goes through dense spruce-fir woods, scattered birches and alder swales, small peatlands and blowdowns, and as you go farther east, across several blueberry barrens. The birding is best during the nesting season (between mid-May and mid-August); highlights to look for include nesting warblers and spruce-fir residents. You will have the best luck early in the morning when birds are vocalizing and the traffic is lightest.

We do not recommend stopping along the Airline itself—it's just too dangerous—but we do recommend investigating the many narrow dirt roads that run off it. If you go down these roads just a short way, you will avoid the roar of the traffic and can get out and stretch your legs and look for a few birds. (Be on the lookout for logging trucks, don't block any roads, and take care not to get lost on the endless and poorly mapped side roads.) You may not see all that much at any one stop, but several stops over the course of a morning can lead to a surprisingly good variety of birds. Possibilities include Black-backed Woodpecker (uncommon), Yellow-bellied and Olive-sided flycatchers, Gray Jay, Boreal Chickadee, Winter Wren, both kinglets, Swainson's and Hermit thrushes, Solitary Vireo, several species of warblers, including Tennessee, Nashville, Cape May, Black-burnian, Bay-breasted, Blackpoll, and Mourning (in raspberry thickets), Lincoln's Sparrow, Rusty Blackbird, Purple Finch, Evening Gros-beak, Pine Siskin, and both crossbills. On the blueberry barrens look for Northern Harriers and Savannah and Vesper sparrows.

If you turn south off the Airline just west of Beddington, onto Route 193, you can explore the largest expanse of blueberry barrens in Maine; see the chapter "Deblois Barrens and Addison Marsh." The Airline also has several access roads leading to small lakes and ponds, and these can be fun to explore if you have the time and inclination.

There are very few places to stop for food or gas along the Airline, so you might want to start with a full tank and stomach.

AROOSTOOK COUNTY

With an area of nearly 6,500 square miles, Aroostook County is the largest county east of the Mississippi River—and one of the most sparsely populated. Although many people think of "The County," as it is called in Maine, as one large commercial forest, it is also an area of lakes and rivers, low rolling hills, isolated mountaintops, and rich agricultural fields. Still, there is no denying that this is primarily logging country; more than 4 million acres of Aroostook County are commercial forestland, whereas less than 1 million acres are farmed, mostly for potatoes.

The best birding in Aroostook County generally is between about late April and early October, when you can find a wide cross section of boreal nesters and migrants. You can also find an excellent variety of nesting waterfowl (among them small numbers of Northern Shovelers, Northern Pintails, American Wigeons, and Gadwalls) and, in appropriate habitats, several species that many birders may not associate with Aroostook County. Least Bittern, Northern Harrier, Upland Sandpiper, American Coot, Common Moorhen, Bonaparte's and Ring-billed gulls, Common Tern, Marsh Wren, Eastern Meadowlark, and Bobolink all occur in this region. Shorebirds stop over on their fall migrations, and waterfowl (including Snow Geese, Common Eiders, Bufflehead, and all three scoters) stop over in spring as well as fall. In short, there is far more to Aroostook County than Spruce Grouse and Boreal Chickadees.

It may seem ironic that in a section of this book that covers so much territory, we single out so few sites. This is partly because much of the landscape is so similar ecologically. But it is also because much of Aroostook County, particularly the northwestern section, has not been well explored by birders. The flip side of this last coin, of course, is that many wonderful opportunities still exist for birders in Aroostook County. Especially if you relish the idea of a remote birding trip combined with some true wilderness camping, much awaits you here.

The North Maine Woods
(*MAINE ATLAS* maps 54 through 70)

The region we call the North Maine Woods is a vast area of nearly 3 million acres that encompasses virtually all of western Aroostook County and northernmost Piscataquis and Somerset counties. Included within this remote and largely uninhabited area are two of the most famous wild rivers in the Northeast—the Allagash and the St. John—and a good deal of unspoiled and beautiful land. Habitats range from dense spruce-fir forests and northern hardwoods to blowdowns and second growth, from large lakes and white-water river rapids to meandering streams, quiet ponds, and boggy and marshy areas. This is not a wilderness, however. Far from it. About 95 percent of this land is privately owned commercial forestland, and more than 2,000 miles of permanently maintained logging roads and several thousand miles of temporary, unmaintained roads traverse it.

As managed as the North Maine Woods is, however, you can still find within it many beautiful areas and many patches of boreal habitat. The birding is generally at its best from mid-May through late July or early August, when you can see a broad cross section of northern Maine's breeding birds. If you can, plan to spend several days in the region, preferably with a canoe.

Wherever you find good-sized patches of spruce-fir forest and northern hardwoods (and there are many), look and listen for boreal forest specialties. Nesting warblers are a highlight; without too much effort you should be able to find 20 species, including Tennessee, Nashville, Magnolia, Cape May, Black-throated Blue, Yellow-rumped, Black-throated Green, American Redstart, Blackburnian, Bay-breasted,

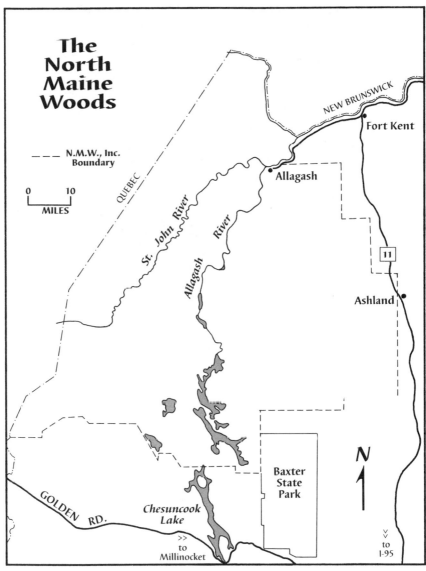

The North Maine Woods

- - - N.M.W., Inc. Boundary

0   10
MILES

QUEBEC

NEW BRUNSWICK

Fort Kent

St. John River

Allagash River

Allagash

11

Ashland

Baxter State Park

GOLDEN RD.

Chesuncook Lake

>>
to Millinocket

N

to I-95

Blackpoll (generally high-elevation or stunted spruce flats), Northern Waterthrush, Mourning (common in blowdowns, regenerating clear-cuts, and raspberry thickets), Wilson's, and Canada. Spruce Grouse are present and delightfully approachable when found, as are Gray Jays and Boreal Chickadees. Black-backed Woodpeckers (uncommon) and Three-toed Woodpeckers (rare) both occur in the area; the best way to find them is usually to listen for their quiet tapping. Neither of these species is as numerous now as at the peak of the Spruce Budworm outbreak in the 1980s. The loud "croaking" of Common Ravens is a characteristic sound of these woods, as are the beautiful songs of Winter Wrens, Veerys, and Swainson's and Hermit thrushes. Olive-sided and Yellow-bellied flycatchers, Golden-crowned and Ruby-crowned kinglets, and Dark-eyed Juncos are all common. The northern finches are typically irregular both in range and numbers, but Evening and Pine grosbeaks, Pine Siskins, and Red and White-winged crossbills are all solid possibilities. Fox Sparrow has recently been documented breeding in the region; although uncommon, it seems to be increasing. Listen for its loud, sweet song. Boreal Owl has also been recorded in this part of Maine, albeit rarely.

Other characteristic forest breeders include Sharp-shinned, Broad-winged, and Red-tailed hawks, Northern Goshawk, American Kestrel, Ruffed Grouse, Great Horned, Barred, and Northern Saw-whet owls (all of the owls are more likely to be heard than seen), Northern Flicker, Pileated, Hairy, and Downy woodpeckers, Yellow-bellied Sapsucker, Blue Jay, Black-capped Chickadee, Red-breasted Nuthatch, Brown Creeper, Solitary and Red-eyed vireos, White-throated Sparrow, and Purple Finch.

On lakes and rivers and in their associated wetlands, you will find still more birds. Common Loons nest on many of the lakes and ponds, and in quiet backwaters you may see broods of Canada Geese, Mallards, Wood, American Black, and Ring-necked ducks, Green-winged and Blue-winged teal, Common Goldeneyes, and all three mergansers. Ospreys and Belted Kingfishers are often seen diving for fish, Tree Swallows sweep back and forth across the water, and occasionally you will see a Bald Eagle. On the islands in Allagash Lake are nesting Herring and Bonaparte's gulls (this is one of Maine's few nesting sites for Bonies) and Common Terns. Great Blue Herons are silent but conspicuous along shorelines, and American Bitterns call noisily in late May and early June. Spotted Sandpipers and Common Snipe are regular nesters, and from early to late August small numbers of Greater and Lesser yellowlegs and Least Sandpipers sometimes stop to feed and rest along the lakeshores. Occasional nesters include Pied-billed Grebes, Double-crested Cormorants, Black-crowned Night-Herons, Green Herons, and Rusty Blackbirds. In adjacent uplands, look for Swamp and Lincoln's sparrows. The latter typically are quite shy, but in the breeding season you can often attract them by squeaking or spishing.

The North Maine Woods is also a wonderful place to look for mammals. Moose may well top your list for sheer numbers, but other common species you might see include White-tailed Deer, Muskrat,

Raccoon, Woodchuck, Beaver, Porcupine, and Varying Hare. Less commonly seen but also present are Black Bear, Red Fox, Coyote, River Otter, Mink, Pine Marten, Bobcat, and even Lynx.

In an area this large and diverse, and where habitats can change suddenly when commercial land is clear-cut, it is difficult to single out specific birding sites. The best approach is to look for areas of undisturbed habitat, such as along the Allagash Wilderness Waterway or St. John River, or in the state-owned Maine Public Reserve lots. A canoe trip is certainly a delightful way to explore the area, but you can also see a good deal by camping on one of the many lakes or ponds and by exploring the roadsides. There are few developed hiking trails, but many of the abandoned or temporary logging roads are suitable for walking. *Remember that at all times logging trucks have the right of way!* We cannot emphasize this strongly enough. These are private roads, and normal load and speed limits do not apply. Yield and get as far off the road as you possibly can, and never block any road, active or abandoned. Also, remember that for cars, at least, these are not high-speed roads; if you value your car's suspension, you should plan on averaging about 20 miles an hour on the logging roads.

A few practical suggestions will make your visit to the North Maine Woods more enjoyable. First and foremost, be prepared for hordes of black flies anytime between late May and late July. We recommend head nets (available at many hardware and outdoor-supply stores in Maine, as well as at L.L. Bean) in addition to an ample supply of insect repellent (which we prefer to put on our clothes instead of our skin, though it's not beneficial to either). A compass and good topographic maps are musts if you intend to venture off the roadsides, which you invariably will do (even if you don't intend to). And finally, a sturdy pair of hiking boots will ensure dry feet even after a day of tramping through damp woods.

The North Maine Woods is accessible year-round, with access into it controlled by North Maine Woods, Inc., a nonprofit organization of private landowners (primarily timber and paper companies) and state government agencies. All recreationists must enter through one of NMW's several checkpoints, where a small daily fee is charged. There are about 300 primitive individual camping sites within the area, and there are several well-known sporting camps, some of which are accessible only by air. Unless you are at a sporting camp, you will not find any facilities (including gas stations, tow trucks, grocery stores, or restaurants) in the North Maine Woods. In case of emergency, help is available at all NMW checkpoints and at several points along the Allagash Wilderness Waterway.

Allagash Wilderness Waterway & St. John River

A canoe trip down the Allagash Wilderness Waterway or St. John River offers a spectacular opportunity to explore an extended section of the North Maine Woods. You will need far more information than we can provide here to plan your trip, but what follows should at least get you pointed in the right direction.

Allagash Wilderness Waterway. The Allagash River flows more than 100 miles from its headwaters west of Allagash Mountain north to its confluence with the St. John River. Ninety-two of these miles are within the state-owned Allagash Wilderness Waterway (AWW). Established in 1966, the AWW protects both sides of the river and all of its lakes, ponds, and streams for 500 feet beyond the high-water mark. As Maine naturalist Dean Bennett wrote in his 1994 book *Allagash: Maine's Wild and Scenic River,* "Today, surrounded by land managed for its timber resources, this narrow strip of waterway still provides a sense of the northern forest of an earlier day." It also provides a unique way to bird this region. Several birders have commented on how dense the birdlife is along the river—undoubtedly because it comprises a narrow corridor of forestland in the midst of a managed timber forest.

The Allagash has long been known as one of the most hydrologically (and thus biologically) diverse of Maine's rivers, primarily because of its many large lakes and ponds and associated wetlands. If you start at Telos Landing just west of Baxter State Park, take the side trip to Allagash Lake, and paddle all the way north to the St. John, you will cover almost 97 miles and see much that the river has to offer. Depending on water levels, the full trip takes about 9 to 10 days and consists of a mix of flat water and white water, with the most difficult rapids rated Class III. The river is busiest in July and August. You will find fewer people and more birds in June, but you will find more black flies then, too. If you get to Allagash Lake, be sure to hike up Allagash Mountain, from which you can see almost the entire watershed of the river.

St. John River. The St. John River rises from a series of small ponds in northwestern Maine and flows north and then east to form part of Maine's northern boundary. For canoeists, Fourth St. John Pond is the highest practical point from which to start a journey;

from here it is 132 miles to the village of Allagash just below the New Brunswick border.

In general, the habitat through which the St. John flows is not as diverse as that around the Allagash; the St. John has much less flat water and many more rapids, so you probably will not see as many wetland-associated birds. But as Yates and Phillips say in the *AMC River Guide: Maine*, the St. John is "a semiwilderness area that has no equal east of the Mississippi." Although virtually all of the land on either side of the river is privately owned, and much of it is managed for timber, you will still pass through a great deal of unspoiled and beautiful forestland. In mid- and late May, a trip down the St. John is a festival of arriving warblers, all easily seen before the trees have leafed out to hide them.

Because the St. John has few large lakes or ponds near its headwaters, the water level is very sensitive to rainfall (or the lack of it) and can sometimes change significantly in just a few hours. After snowmelt in mid- to late May is usually the best time to run the river. With high water, the entire 132-mile trip usually takes five to seven days. The most difficult rapids are rated as Class III, although weather conditions can sometimes up them suddenly to Class IV.

In late July look for Furbish's Lousewort and other rare plants in flower.

Anyone planning to canoe the AWW or St. John should write or call the Maine Bureau of Parks and Recreation, State House Station #22, Augusta, ME 04333, telephone 207-287-3821. You should also get a copy of the *AMC River Guide: Maine* by Yates and Phillips, or DeLorme's *Allagash & St. John Map and Guide* (see Appendix D).

If you are not an expert canoeist, bear in mind that guided canoe trips are a time-honored tradition in Maine. You can choose among several outfitters, some of them specializing in the history of these waterways, for example, or in fishing or wildlife. All reputable trips are led by registered Maine Guides. For information on outfitters, write or call North Maine Woods, Inc. (see below).

Maine Public Reserve Lands

The Maine Bureau of Public Lands manages several thousand acres in the North Maine Woods. Most of these Public Reserve Lands, such as the 15,000-acre Deboullie Mountain and Pond tract just south of the New Brunswick border and east of the Allagash (*Maine Atlas* map 63, A-1), or the 11,000-acre Squa Pan tract east of Ashland (*Maine Atlas* map 64, E-4), are located in exceptionally beautiful areas and have been little explored by birders. For information on visiting one of these sites, call or write the Maine Bureau of Public Lands, State House Station #22, Augusta, ME 04333, telephone 207-289-3061.

ADDITIONAL INFORMATION

North Maine Woods, Inc., publishes an annual guide map and brochure, which is a must if you are planning to visit this area. For information, write or call NMW, P.O. Box 421, Ashland, ME 04732, telephone 207-435-6213 (8:30 to 11:30 a.m. and 1:00 to 4:30 p.m. Monday through Friday). Be sure to ask if there are any special restrictions in the area you intend to visit. (For example, on roads owned by Great Northern Paper Company, no bicycles—including those attached to a bike rack on your vehicle—are permitted.)

For information on sporting camps, write the Maine Sporting Camp Association, P.O. Box 89, Jay, ME 04239 (no telephone).

Route 11, Knowles Corner to Masardis (MAINE ATLAS map 58, E-2 to A-2)

Route 11 runs the length of Aroostook County, from Sherman Mills to the Canadian border. If you drive a good portion of it, you can see that it essentially divides the county into two distinct parts. To the west of the highway lie the vast commercial forestlands of the timber and paper companies; to the east lie the fields and farms of the fertile Aroostook Valley. The northern half of Route 11 has been designated a Scenic Highway, and deservedly so, but it is the southern half that birders are likely to find most interesting—especially the 20-some miles between Knowles Corner and Masardis. This beautiful stretch of road is well worth driving anytime between about mid-May and late August, when you can see a broad cross section of distinctly boreal landbirds. You can bird this portion of Route 11 leisurely in a few hours or less.

The Knowles Corner–Masardis section of Route 11 traverses a lovely stretch of varied and mostly undisturbed boreal habitat. On both sides of the road are spruce-fir and mixed woods interspersed with streams, swampy and boggy areas, and even a few small ponds (although the last are not really visible from the roadside). Otter Pond and Matherson Pond lie along the west side of the road a little

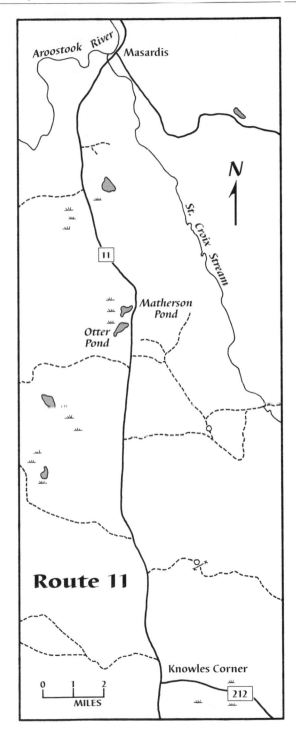

more than halfway along this portion. Three picnic sites provide ideal places to stop and bird along the roadside, and you can also explore the various logging roads that intersect the highway. We want to emphasize here that Route 11 is known for its high accident rate. Please show extreme caution when birding along it. The road is heavily traveled by logging trucks, which drive very fast and cannot slow down or stop easily. Always be on the lookout for—and yield to—logging trucks (and Moose). If you stop along the roadside, make sure that you pull well off the road, even if you are staying in your vehicle, and do not block any side roads. We like to bird Route 11 at dawn, when the song is at its peak and the traffic is usually lightest. Saturday and Sunday mornings are usually ideal.

Among the highlights on Route 11 are nesting warblers, with 12-plus species being a good possibility. Look especially for Tennessee, Nashville, Magnolia, Cape May (uncommon except during Spruce Budworm outbreaks), Yellow-rumped, Black-throated Green, Blackburnian, Bay-breasted, Blackpoll (scarce), Northern Waterthrush, Wilson's, and Canada. Other species you are likely to see or hear include most of the typical boreal breeders, among them Spruce Grouse (the turnout near Otter and Matherson ponds is one of the best places to look), Olive-sided and Yellow-bellied flycatchers, Gray Jay, Common Raven, Boreal Chickadee, Winter Wren, Golden-crowned and Ruby-crowned kinglets, Veery, Swainson's Thrush, Solitary Vireo, White-throated and Lincoln's sparrows, Dark-eyed Junco, Rusty Blackbird (around ponds and streams), Purple Finch, and Pine Siskin. Species such as Evening and Pine grosbeaks and Red and White-winged crossbills are irregular but always possible. Listen, too, for Black-backed and Three-toed woodpeckers, both of which are elusive boreal residents. Even Boreal Owl is a possibility, albeit a remote one.

We do not recommend making a special trip to Route 11 in winter, but if you are traveling this way anyway, it is worth keeping your eyes open for spruce-fir residents such as Boreal Chickadee, Gray Jay, Black-backed and Three-toed woodpeckers, and Northern Hawk Owl (rare). This can also be a very good area to see winter finches. Red and White-winged crossbills, Pine and Evening grosbeaks, and Common Redpoll are all seen fairly regularly, and occasionally a few Hoary Redpolls are found. Bohemian Waxwing is also seen along this road fairly often.

Route 11 is a state highway, accessible year-round. Except for the picnic sites mentioned above, there are no facilities between Knowles Corner and Masardis.

DIRECTIONS

FROM THE SOUTH: Take I-95 north to exit 58 in Sherman and follow signs to Rt. 11 North.

FROM THE NORTH: Follow Rt. 163 west out of Presque Isle or Rt. 212 north out of Smyrna Mills; both lead directly to Rt. 11.

LOCAL ACCOMMODATIONS

For information on local accommodations and services, write or call the Presque Isle Area Chamber of Commerce, P.O. Box 672, Presque Isle, ME 04769, telephone 207-764-6561.

Christina Reservoir & Lake Josephine (*MAINE ATLAS* map 65, D-3)

Christina Reservoir and Lake Josephine, about 6 miles due east of Presque Isle, have become well known in recent years for their superlative waterfowl diversity. Since 1990, when Presque Isle birder Bill Sheehan started checking this area regularly and spreading the word about it to others, at least 28 species of waterfowl have been sighted here, including several uncommon or rare species. This is Maine's only documented breeding site for Northern Shoveler and Northern Pintail and is one of only four known breeding sites in the state for American Wigeon. In 1993 it also provided the first recent state record for nesting Short-eared Owl. Add to this a fine variety of wetland-associated and upland breeders, migrant passerines and shorebirds, and the possibility of Snowy and Short-eared owls and other open-country species in winter, and you have a superb birding site indeed. In all, more than 180 species have been recorded in and around Christina Reservoir and Lake Josephine. As Bill Sheehan says, "Not bad for an unmanaged, inland location that is birded by only a few folks." The area is worth a visit at any time of year, especially between late April and (depending on freeze-up) early to late December. Especially at the height of the breeding season, plan on at least a few hours to do the site justice.

Christina Reservoir is a large, shallow impoundment that was created at the head of the Prestile Stream in the 1960s to provide a

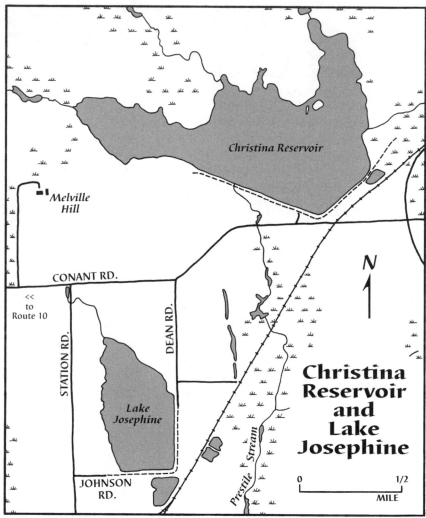

Christina Reservoir

Melville Hill

CONANT RD.

<<
to
Route 10

STATION RD.

DEAN RD.

Lake Josephine

JOHNSON RD.

Prestile Stream

N

Christina
Reservoir
and
Lake
Josephine

0   1/2
MILE

steady water supply to what are now the McCain Food company's food-processing factories downstream. The reservoir is bounded to the south by a mile-long dike, to the north by hayfields and agricultural lands, and to the east and west by spruce-fir and mixed-deciduous woods. About a mile south of the reservoir is what local people call Lake Josephine, or Lake Jo, and what the *Maine Atlas* calls Industrial Waste Pond. Whichever name you go by, there is no getting around the fact that this is a large potato-processing wastewater lagoon—and depending on the day and season, it can stink to high heaven. Fortunately, the birding compensates for the odor. Public roads traverse three sides of Lake Jo, and on the southeast corner is a high dike that overlooks the lake and several smaller (discontinued) sludge ponds that are slowly filling in with cattails. Both Lake Jo and Christina Reservoir are characterized by good-sized patches of dri-ki (standing or floating deadwood). Although the reservoir, lake, and most of the surrounding land are owned and maintained by McCain Food, the company allows nearly unrestricted access to the area.

The best way to bird Christina Reservoir is to walk the mile-long dike that runs along its southern border. Both this dike and the one at Lake Jo are about 30 feet high and provide excellent vantage points. Walk the dike at Christina in both directions, scanning the reservoir itself (it measures about 1.5 miles by 0.5 mile) and the cattail and sedge thickets along the shore. Lake Jo is quite a bit smaller than Christina Reservoir and does not have the sedge and cattail habitats, but be sure to check it, too. Public roads border the western, southern, and eastern sides of the lake and provide good vantage points, particularly from the southeast corner, where you can scan from atop a dike. You can bird from your car, or you can stop and walk the roadside. At the southeast corner of the lake, be sure to check the large cattail stands and sludge ponds on the south side of Johnson Road. Also check the small pond at the intersection of Conant and Station roads (see "Directions," below, and the site map).

From ice-out through freeze-up (typically late April until early or late December), Christina Reservoir and Lake Jo support a remarkable array of migrant and breeding waterfowl. Numbers of birds sometimes reach several hundred. The first waterfowl start arriving in early April, as soon as puddle-sized patches of open water appear in the Prestile Stream. Even in mid- to late December you can still find birds wherever there is open water. Late June through July, when broods are visible, typically yields the highest counts of birds, whereas late spring and fall bring the greatest diversity in species. Snow Geese, Common Eiders, Oldsquaws, Buffleheads, and all three scoters are regular on spring and fall migration (the eiders and scoters are more common in fall, the Oldsquaws in spring). Ruddy Ducks, Gadwalls, Barrow's Goldeneyes, and Lesser and Greater scaup (the latter more regular) are uncommon. For four consecutive springs, late April to early May of 1985 through 1988, a Eurasian Wigeon was also seen here. Common breeding species on the reservoir and lake include Canada Goose, Mallard, Wood, American Black, and Ring-necked ducks, Green-winged and Blue-winged teal, Common Goldeneye, and Common and Hooded mergansers. Additionally, small numbers of Northern Shovelers, Northern Pintails, American Wigeons, and Gadwalls also nest.

As impressive as the waterfowl diversity is, there is much else to see around Christina Reservoir and Lake Jo. Least Bitterns (western shore of Christina), American Coots, Common Moorhens, and Marsh Wrens (northern shore of Christina) all reach or approach the northern extreme of their breeding ranges here. Several more common wetland-associated breeders can also be found, among them Common Loon, Pied-billed Grebe, Double-crested Cormorant, Great Blue Heron, American Bittern, Bald Eagle (probably nesting just north of Christina), Osprey, Virginia Rail, Sora, Spotted Sandpiper, Common Snipe, Great Black-backed, Herring, Ring-billed, and Bonaparte's gulls, Common Tern, Belted Kingfisher, Veery, and Swamp Sparrow. Uncommon species include Black Tern, Green Heron, and Black-crowned Night-Heron.

In summer and fall, the water is drawn down on Lake Jo as wastewater is used to irrigate crops. This exposes some productive "mudflats" along the southwestern and northeastern shores, which attract good numbers of shorebirds. Killdeer, Greater and Lesser yellowlegs, Solitary, Pectoral, Semipalmated, and Least sandpipers, and Short-billed Dowitchers are all regular. Semipalmated and Black-bellied plovers, Ruddy Turnstones, Whimbrels, White-rumped Sandpipers, Dunlin, Sanderlings, and Wilson's Phalaropes are occasional. American Golden-Plovers also occur in good numbers some years. Merlins and occasionally Peregrine Falcons are in turn attracted by the shorebirds. A Peregrine was seen here regularly in the summer and fall of 1994, feeding on the ducks and shorebirds.

This area also supports a good variety of landbirds. One of the most distinguished sightings in recent years was the pair of Short-eared Owls that nested near the western side of Christina Reservoir in 1993. The birds were not seen again in 1994, but you can be sure that birders will continue to look for them in this area. More regular species to look for around the hay- and agricultural fields include Northern Harrier, Upland Sandpiper (small numbers), American Kestrel, Tree Swallow, Horned Lark, Savannah and Vesper sparrows (the latter uncommon), Eastern Meadowlark, and Bobolink. Spring and fall migration bring a good variety of warblers and other passerines through the mixed woods and scrubby areas. Walking along the dike at Christina Reservoir on a good spring morning, it is possible see 20-plus species of warblers in the tall trees behind the dike; best of all, you can see them at eye level.

The weedy and brushy edges of the dikes and the hay- and agricultural fields are good for sparrows and other ground feeders year-round. From late fall through winter look for the occasional Rough-legged Hawk and Snowy or Short-eared Owl (all three have been seen on the elevated irrigation pipes) and for Horned Larks, Lapland Longspurs (uncommon), American Pipits (regular between late September and late October), and Snow Buntings. When there is open water in winter, Great Cormorants, Horned Grebes, and Iceland Gulls have been found.

It is also worth keeping your eyes open for mammals in this area. Some of the larger species that are seen with some regularity include Moose, Black Bear, White-tailed Deer, River Otter, Muskrat, Mink, Beaver, Porcupine, and Woodchuck.

Christina Reservoir and Lake Josephine are accessible year-round, free of charge, from sunrise to sunset. There are no facilities. McCain Food generously allows public access to both sites, although seasonal agricultural practices occasionally limit access. Please respect this private property, and do not block access roads or gates. McCain Food also asks birders not to drive the length of the dike at Christina, but instead to park in the small clearing provided (see "Directions," below).

You should also know that in October this is a popular duck-hunting spot. If you are unfamiliar with what precautions you should take during this season in Maine, see the section entitled "Hunting" in the Introduction.

DIRECTIONS

TO LAKE JOSEPHINE: At the intersection of Rts. 1 and 10 (Academy St.) in the center of Presque Isle, turn east onto Rt. 10. Go 1.4 miles, and where Rt. 10 takes a sharp turn to the right, go straight onto Conant Rd. In 3.7 miles turn right onto Station Rd. You are now near the northwest corner of Lake Josephine. In 0.9 mile turn left onto Johnson Rd., and in 0.5 mile turn left again onto Dean Rd.

TO CHRISTINA RESERVOIR: At the intersection of Dean Rd. and Conant Rd., turn right onto Conant Rd., and in 0.8 mile turn left onto an inconspicuous, unmarked dirt road. You will see the dike along the southern end of Christina Reservoir just ahead. You can drive up to it and park in the small clearing provided by McCain Food. (If you are coming from Rt. 1A, this dirt road is 0.5 mile west of the intersection of Rt. 1A and Conant Rd.)

LOCAL ACCOMMODATIONS

For information on local accommodations and services, write or call the Presque Isle Area Chamber of Commerce, P.O. Box 672, Presque Isle, ME 04769, telephone 207-764-6561.

Additional Sites of Interest

All of the "Additional Sites" in Aroostook County are underbirded and may well be worthy of more coverage than we give them. We hope that listing them here will encourage birders to investigate them more thoroughly.

Gordon Manuel Wildlife Management Area
(MAINE ATLAS map 53, B-3)

The Gordon Manuel Wildlife Management Area, which is owned and managed by the Maine Department of Inland Fisheries and Wildlife, consists of approximately 6,500 acres just south of Hodgdon that are bisected by the south branch of the Meduxnekeag River. Habitats include the river, wetlands, agricultural fields, and upland forests. This area has not been birded very thoroughly or consistently, but it is well worth a stop. Great Blue Heron, several species of waterfowl, Osprey, American Woodcock, and Ruffed Grouse are among the many species that have been recorded. There is almost certainly a good assemblage of wetland-associated breeding species waiting to be discovered. About 8 miles of trails are open to foot and all-terrain vehicle (ATV) traffic.

The area is open daily from sunrise to sunset, free of charge. There are no facilities. As at most wildlife management areas in Maine, hunting is allowed in season.

Access is from the Horseback or Town Line roads.

Aroostook State Park (MAINE ATLAS map 65, E-1)

Aroostook State Park, on the shore of Echo Lake just south of Presque Isle, offers a pleasant place to hike, fish, and bird. During the nesting season, scan the lake for Common Loons, Ospreys, and waterfowl, then hike the 2 miles up Quaggy Joe Mountain. Although the summit is only 1,213 feet, it provides some lovely views. Along the way you can see a pleasant variety of birds, including Common Ravens, several species of nesting warblers, and Dark-eyed Juncos.

The park is open from May 15 to October 15; a small fee is charged for day as well as overnight use. For information about camping, write or call the park at 87 State Park Road, Presque Isle, ME 04769, telephone 207-768-8341 (in season) or 764-2040 (off-season).

The park is about 4 miles south of Presque Isle on the west side of Route 1. The entrance is well marked with a sign.

Haystack Mountain (MAINE ATLAS map 64, D-4)

Haystack Mountain is on the north side of Route 163 halfway between Ashland and Presque Isle. It is an easy 1-mile climb to the summit, and the view—of Squa Pan Lake and, beyond it, Katahdin—is lovely. You can see and hear a good cross section of birds during the breeding season, including Swainson's Thrush and Philadelphia Vireo. In September and October this can be a good hawk-watching spot.

Caribou Dam (MAINE ATLAS map 65, B-1)

The Caribou Dam stretches across the Aroostook River in the city of Caribou and is a good place to look for ducks and gulls, particularly from November through April. The river flows north here, and for all but a few weeks in the coldest part of the winter (usually January and February), there is open water below the dam. Common Goldeneyes and Common Mergansers are regular, and it is not unusual to find a few Barrow's Goldeneyes and Hooded Mergansers among them. Iceland Gulls are occasional throughout the winter, and Snow Geese are regular in early spring. In August and September this is a good spot to look for Great Blue Herons and Black-crowned Night-Herons, both of which roost regularly in the conifers along the river.

At the blinking light at the intersection of Routes 1 and 161 in Caribou, go north on Route 1. Almost immediately take the first right onto Washington Street. At the end of Washington Street, turn right or left onto Lyndon Street, which parallels the river. To the right is the dam (the conifers directly across the river are where the herons roost); to the left is a public boat launch. Both are good places to park and scan.

Long Lake (MAINE ATLAS map 68, C-3 & D-3)

Long Lake is almost on the Canadian border. If you are headed up to Fort Kent or Madawaska, a scenic and potentially birdy detour anytime between about mid-April and late November is to take Route 162 north through St. Agatha to Frenchville. This will take you along the entire western shore of Long Lake, which you can bird from the roadside. Snow Geese and various sea ducks stop on the lake in spring and fall (Common Eiders, Oldsquaws, Buffleheads, and all three scoters are fairly regular). In summer Common Terns nest on two small islands along the northwestern shore. This may also be a nesting site for Bonaparte's Gulls. Interestingly, Buffleheads have been seen in summer at the northern end of the lake.

When you turn off Route 161 onto Route 162 southwest of the lake, drive to the public boat landing in the village of Sinclair and scan the southern end of the lake. Continue north another 6.5 miles, and you will see a boat launch and picnic site on the shore. This is another good point from which to scan; be sure to check the cove directly to the south (a reliable place to see Snow Geese and other waterfowl). The two tern-nesting islands are between this point and the village of St. Agatha to the north.

If you have time, you may also want to investigate Route 161 for several miles on either side of its intersection with Route 162. There are some beautiful boreal woods and boggy areas along this route; particularly during the breeding season, you may well turn up a good variety of birds. Look for essentially the same species that you would in the North Maine Woods.

APPENDIX A

Checklist of Maine Birds

By Peter D. Vickery, Jody Despres, and Jan Erik Pierson

This checklist portrays our understanding of the status, distribution, and seasonal abundance of Maine's birds. A total of 419 species of birds and one additional form, "Thayer's" Gull, have been recorded in Maine as of October 1995, excluding the extinct Labrador Duck, Great Auk, and Passenger Pigeon. No fewer than 27 species and that one form (listed below) have been added to the state list since 1978. Of these, four had occurred in Maine before but were not then recognized as full species (marked with an asterisk below). A specimen of Eurasian Siskin, collected at Kittery in 1962, had previously gone unlisted as a possible escape from captivity. Eurasian Siskins are now considered vagrants from Eurasia. In addition, two reports of Sprague's Pipit, although not thought to have been American Pipit, are now treated as Pipit sp., due to possible confusion with other species.

Additions to the Maine state list since 1978 include the following:

Black-browed Albatross (hypothetical)
Band-rumped Storm-Petrel (hypothetical)
Red-billed Tropicbird
White Ibis

Garganey
American Swallow-tailed Kite
Mississippi Kite (hypothetical)
Wild Turkey (re-introduced, now established and thriving)
Pacific Golden-Plover*
Wilson's Plover
South Polar Skua
"Thayer's" Gull
Bridled Tern
Vermilion Flycatcher (hypothetical)
Eurasian Jackdaw
Townsend's Solitaire
Bicknell's Thrush*
Townsend's Warbler
Cassin's Sparrow
Black-throated Sparrow (hypothetical)
Nelson's Sharp-tailed Sparrow*
Golden-crowned Sparrow
Boat-tailed Grackle (hypothetical)
Shiny Cowbird
Bullock's Oriole*
Common Chaffinch
Eurasian Siskin
Lesser Goldfinch

The primary goal of this checklist is to define the relative abundance of 330 species of birds and one additional form, "Thayer's" Gull, that occur regularly in Maine. Also noted for each species are its present breeding status as well as coded information about its geographic distribution or irruptive status where appropriate. An additional 89 species that have been recorded in the state but do not occur on an annual or near-annual basis are also listed in the "Vagrants & Accidentals" section at the end of this list.

We have indicated the relative abundance (for common, fairly common, and uncommon birds) or the seasonal occurrence (for rare birds). We assume that the observer is in suitable habitat at the proper season. We have used additional modifiers (primarily geographical) for species that are not evenly distributed across the state. Although many birding site-guides use bar graphs to represent the probability of seeing a species in the right habitat at the right season, such graphs are intended to represent that probability for a birder of "average" skills, a definition we find difficult to make. In order to represent the abundance of an individual species in the state, we assume that: (1) the user has a knowledge of the species' habits and its habitat preferences; (2) the user can identify species by sound as well as sight; and (3) the user has a general understanding of the distribution or movements of the species within the state.

Birders familiar with checklists that indicate the probability of an average birder seeing a species will find few differences here for most species, especially highly visible ones such as waterfowl, gulls, shorebirds, and raptors. However, for secretive or nocturnal species which are more likely to be heard than seen, the abundances presented here may seem, at first glance, to be overstated. For example, Virginia Rails are very common in most marshes in Maine, but even an experienced birder is unlikely to hear more than a few of these secretive birds on a particular day. A birder unfamiliar with this species' vocalizations is unlikely to record any individuals on a typical day, even when most marshes are full of them. However, active rail censusing with a tape recorder (used to illustrate a point here, but generally to be avoided) reveals this species' true abundance. Similarly, an "average" birder may be unlikely to hear or see more than one or two Ruffed Grouse or Great Horned Owls in a day. Yet persistent searching for these species in appropriate habitat during the time of year when they are most audible again demonstrates their actual status. Remember that time of day can make a great difference; many species are far more audible and visible early or late in the day.

It is difficult to define the status of a species when it is common at one or two sites but generally uncommon to rare elsewhere. Although it is possible to see 50 or more Glossy Ibises in spring at Scarborough Marsh, the species is uncommon elsewhere in coastal southern Maine, and it is decidedly rare northeast of Popham Beach. Several waterfowl species, particularly Barrow's Goldeneye and Harlequin and Ruddy ducks, fall into this category as well. In general, we have tried to select a reasonable middle ground that does not reflect peak abundances at a single site.

The codes used to denote abundance in this checklist are marked for 10-day periods. Note that for the sake of simplicity we have excluded the "occasional" category from this checklist. We recognize that a few species (e.g., Lark Sparrow) occur with sufficient frequency that they should be classified as occasional, but for general ease of use have placed most occasional species in the rare category. Conversely, several species are placed in the uncommon category here but possibly could be considered occasional. We believe these exceptions are too few to justify a fifth category of abundance. Abundance codes are defined as follows:

Common to abundant: usually present in moderate to large numbers, e.g., 10 or more recorded per day.

Fairly common: usually present in small numbers, e.g., 5 to 9 recorded per day.

Uncommon: usually recorded in low numbers, typically 1 to 4 per day during the period, but as low as 5 per year for a few species (e.g., Great Egret, Red-shouldered Hawk, Northern Shrike, Louisiana Waterthrush, Yellow-breasted Chat, Clay-colored Sparrow).

Rare: averaging 1 to 4 present annually in the state during the period.

The status of a very few species (e.g., Great Skua) is speculative or not well documented for certain times of the year. These species are marked with question marks (**?**) in the graphs for those periods.

Additionally, the following codes are used to indicate other information.

B Breeds annually in at least moderate numbers.
b Breeds annually in small numbers.
? Breeding suspected but not yet confirmed.
F Formerly bred in at least moderate numbers.
f Fewer than ten records of breeding.

Breeding status is indicated to the left of the graph, under the heading "**Br.**"

Most species are not distributed evenly across the state. To help define the distribution of some less-widespread species, we have divided the state into three regions (see map). If a species is limited to one or two of these regions, we have indicated the region(s) to the right of the graphs, under the heading "**Note.**" This approach has reduced, but not eliminated, some of these distributional problems. Birding in coastal Washington County may be similar but not identical to birding in Baxter State Park. We trust that visitors and local birders will forgive us for any shortcuts or generalizations that impinge upon the unique qualities of each region.

S Southern Maine, defined as the southern part of the state north to a line curving from Monhegan Island northwestward to Augusta, and thence southwestward to Brownfield.

N Northern Maine, defined as the northern part of the state south to a line curving from Mount Desert Island northwestward to Bangor and Greenville, and thence southwestward to Grafton Township.

M Mid-Maine, defined as that area between **S** and **N** as defined above.

There are several additional modifiers under "**Note.**"

   * Breeding is restricted to one or two regions (modifies **S**, **N**, or **M** as defined above). Non-breeders may occur in all three regions.

  *K Breeds only on Mt. Katahdin (American Pipit).

   C Typically found only within 10 miles of the coast. We have indicated only those species which routinely use non-coastal habitats elsewhere in eastern North America, but in Maine are almost exclusively located within 10 miles of the coast. Many species which are primarily coastal in Maine and elsewhere (e.g., Sanderling and the scoters) are not noted with a "**C.**"

   I Irruptive species, fairly common to abundant in some years, rare or absent in others.

   ? Reflects uncertain breeding status as noted under "**Br.**"

Examples of usage under "Note."

CS,CM Typically occurs only within 10 miles of the coast in Southern Maine and Mid-Maine.

  S, M Typically occurs only in Southern Maine and Mid-Maine.

   *N Breeds only in Northern Maine, though non-breeders may occur in any region.

*M,*N Breeds only in Mid-Maine and Northern Maine, though non-breeders may occur in any region.

Taxonomy

In an effort to make this checklist as accurate and up-to-date as possible, we have consulted with leading taxonomic authorities, especially Richard Banks, Chair of the American Ornithologists' Union (AOU) Committee on Taxonomy and Nomenclature. We thank Dick Banks and associates for sharing their insights and wisdom. We have included all known name changes in this checklist but recognize that change will not stop with the publication of this list. In the near future we anticipate that Solitary Vireo will be regarded as three separate species. Who knows what the eastern form will be called? Speciation and taxonomy are continuing processes. The best we can do is remain flexible and be grateful we are not struggling with the complexities of South American antbirds or flycatchers.

Four recent taxonomic changes have been adopted by the AOU and are reflected in this checklist.

1. Gray-cheeked Thrush has been separated into two species: Bicknell's Thrush (*Catharus bicknelli*), which breeds primarily on mountain slopes throughout New England and the Canadian Maritimes, and Gray-cheeked Thrush (*Catharus minimus*), now restricted in the breeding season to Newfoundland, boreal Canada, Alaska, and eastern Siberia, and occurring in Maine as a spring and fall migrant.

2. Northern Oriole has again been separated into two species, the eastern Baltimore Oriole (*Icterus galbula*) and the western Bullock's Oriole (*Icterus bullockii*). Baltimore Oriole is a common breeding bird in the state and appears in the main checklist, whereas Bullock's Oriole is a rare vagrant.

3. Rufous-sided Towhee has been separated into two species, Eastern Towhee (*Pipilo erythrophthalmus*) and the western Spotted Towhee (*Pipilo maculatus*), an occasional vagrant to eastern North America that should be watched for in Maine.

4. Sharp-tailed Sparrow has been separated into two species, Nelson's Sharp-tailed Sparrow (*Ammodramus nelsoni*) and Saltmarsh Sharp-tailed Sparrow (*Ammodramus caudacutus*). Nelson's Sharp-tailed Sparrow now comprises the three northern forms of the former Sharp-tailed Sparrow (*A. c. nelsoni, A. c. alterus*, and *A. c. subvirgatus*) and breeds from southern Maine (with Scarborough Marsh as an approximate southern limit) east through the Canadian Maritimes and west to Hudson Bay in central Canada. Saltmarsh Sharp-tailed Sparrow includes the two southern subspecies of the former Sharp-tailed Sparrow (*A. c. caudacutus* and *A. c. diversus*) and breeds from southern Maine (with Scarborough Marsh as an approximate northern limit) south along the Mid-Atlantic Coast to Virginia.

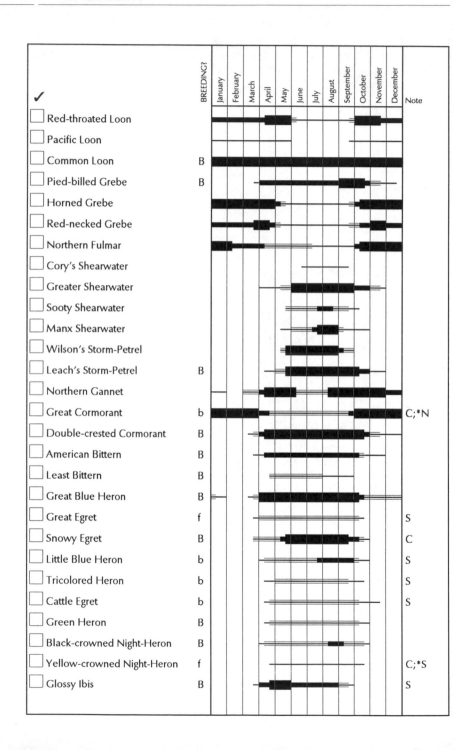

✓	BREEDING?	January	February	March	April	May	June	July	August	September	October	November	December	Note
☐ Red-throated Loon														
☐ Pacific Loon														
☐ Common Loon	B													
☐ Pied-billed Grebe	B													
☐ Horned Grebe														
☐ Red-necked Grebe														
☐ Northern Fulmar														
☐ Cory's Shearwater														
☐ Greater Shearwater														
☐ Sooty Shearwater														
☐ Manx Shearwater														
☐ Wilson's Storm-Petrel														
☐ Leach's Storm-Petrel	B													
☐ Northern Gannet														
☐ Great Cormorant	b													C;*N
☐ Double-crested Cormorant	B													
☐ American Bittern	B													
☐ Least Bittern	B													
☐ Great Blue Heron	B													
☐ Great Egret	f													S
☐ Snowy Egret	B													C
☐ Little Blue Heron	b													S
☐ Tricolored Heron	b													S
☐ Cattle Egret	b													S
☐ Green Heron	B													
☐ Black-crowned Night-Heron	B													
☐ Yellow-crowned Night-Heron	f													C;*S
☐ Glossy Ibis	B													S

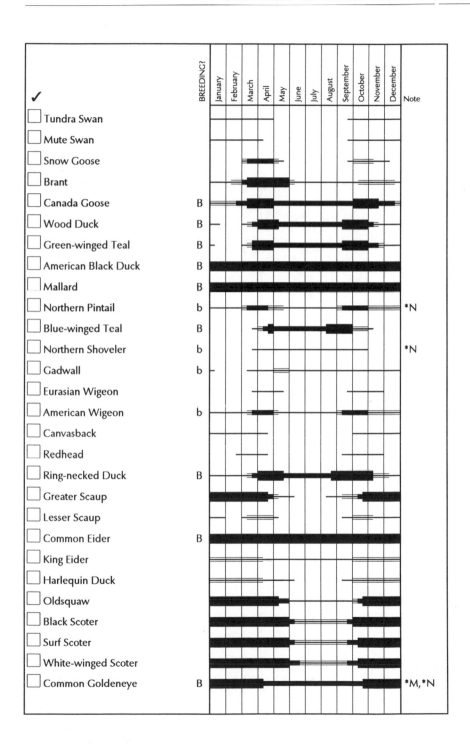

✓	BREEDING?	January	February	March	April	May	June	July	August	September	October	November	December	Note
☐ Tundra Swan														
☐ Mute Swan														
☐ Snow Goose														
☐ Brant														
☐ Canada Goose	B													
☐ Wood Duck	B													
☐ Green-winged Teal	B													
☐ American Black Duck	B													
☐ Mallard	B													
☐ Northern Pintail	b													*N
☐ Blue-winged Teal	B													
☐ Northern Shoveler	b													*N
☐ Gadwall	b													
☐ Eurasian Wigeon														
☐ American Wigeon	b													
☐ Canvasback														
☐ Redhead														
☐ Ring-necked Duck	B													
☐ Greater Scaup														
☐ Lesser Scaup														
☐ Common Eider	B													
☐ King Eider														
☐ Harlequin Duck														
☐ Oldsquaw														
☐ Black Scoter														
☐ Surf Scoter														
☐ White-winged Scoter														
☐ Common Goldeneye	B													*M,*N

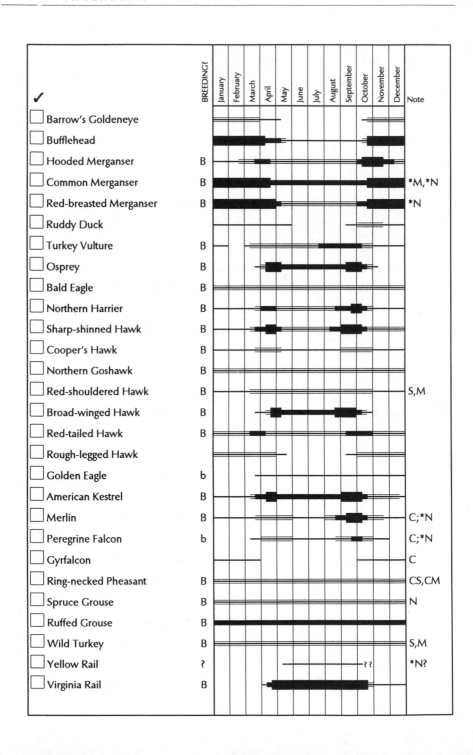

✓	BREEDING?	January	February	March	April	May	June	July	August	September	October	November	December	Note
☐ Barrow's Goldeneye														
☐ Bufflehead														
☐ Hooded Merganser	B													
☐ Common Merganser	B													*M,*N
☐ Red-breasted Merganser	B													*N
☐ Ruddy Duck														
☐ Turkey Vulture	B													
☐ Osprey	B													
☐ Bald Eagle	B													
☐ Northern Harrier	B													
☐ Sharp-shinned Hawk	B													
☐ Cooper's Hawk	B													
☐ Northern Goshawk	B													
☐ Red-shouldered Hawk	B													S,M
☐ Broad-winged Hawk	B													
☐ Red-tailed Hawk	B													
☐ Rough-legged Hawk														
☐ Golden Eagle	b													
☐ American Kestrel	B													
☐ Merlin	B													C;*N
☐ Peregrine Falcon	b													C;*N
☐ Gyrfalcon														C
☐ Ring-necked Pheasant	B													CS,CM
☐ Spruce Grouse	B													N
☐ Ruffed Grouse	B													
☐ Wild Turkey	B													S,M
☐ Yellow Rail	?										? ?			*N?
☐ Virginia Rail	B													

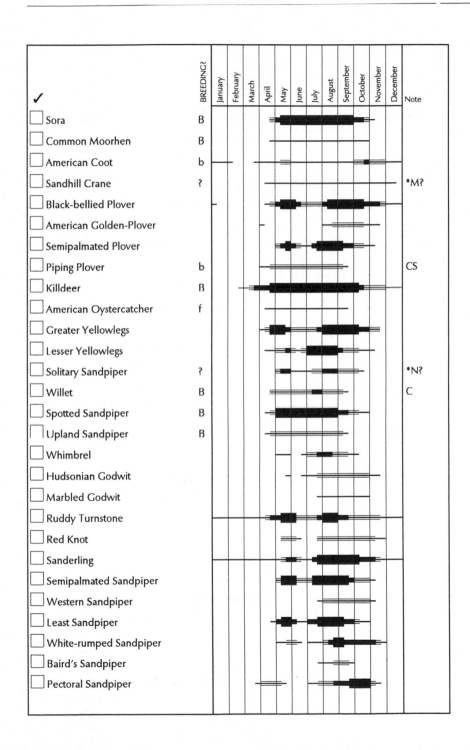

✓	BREEDING?	January	February	March	April	May	June	July	August	September	October	November	December	Note
☐ Sora	B													
☐ Common Moorhen	B													
☐ American Coot	b													
☐ Sandhill Crane	?													*M?
☐ Black-bellied Plover														
☐ American Golden-Plover														
☐ Semipalmated Plover														
☐ Piping Plover	b													CS
☐ Killdeer	B													
☐ American Oystercatcher	f													
☐ Greater Yellowlegs														
☐ Lesser Yellowlegs														
☐ Solitary Sandpiper	?													*N?
☐ Willet	B													C
☐ Spotted Sandpiper	B													
☐ Upland Sandpiper	B													
☐ Whimbrel														
☐ Hudsonian Godwit														
☐ Marbled Godwit														
☐ Ruddy Turnstone														
☐ Red Knot														
☐ Sanderling														
☐ Semipalmated Sandpiper														
☐ Western Sandpiper														
☐ Least Sandpiper														
☐ White-rumped Sandpiper														
☐ Baird's Sandpiper														
☐ Pectoral Sandpiper														

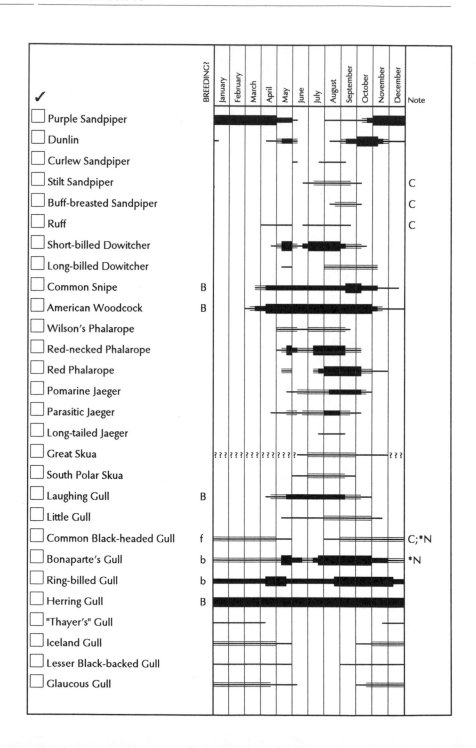

✓	BREEDING?	January	February	March	April	May	June	July	August	September	October	November	December	Note
☐ Purple Sandpiper														
☐ Dunlin														
☐ Curlew Sandpiper														
☐ Stilt Sandpiper														C
☐ Buff-breasted Sandpiper														C
☐ Ruff														C
☐ Short-billed Dowitcher														
☐ Long-billed Dowitcher														
☐ Common Snipe	B													
☐ American Woodcock	B													
☐ Wilson's Phalarope														
☐ Red-necked Phalarope														
☐ Red Phalarope														
☐ Pomarine Jaeger														
☐ Parasitic Jaeger														
☐ Long-tailed Jaeger														
☐ Great Skua		??????????????????										???		
☐ South Polar Skua														
☐ Laughing Gull	B													
☐ Little Gull														
☐ Common Black-headed Gull	f													C;*N
☐ Bonaparte's Gull	b													*N
☐ Ring-billed Gull	b													
☐ Herring Gull	B													
☐ "Thayer's" Gull														
☐ Iceland Gull														
☐ Lesser Black-backed Gull														
☐ Glaucous Gull														

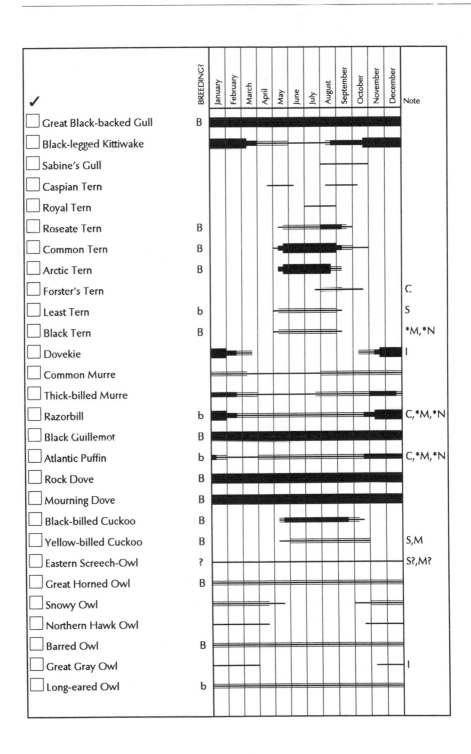

✓	BREEDING?	January	February	March	April	May	June	July	August	September	October	November	December	Note
☐ Great Black-backed Gull	B													
☐ Black-legged Kittiwake														
☐ Sabine's Gull														
☐ Caspian Tern														
☐ Royal Tern														
☐ Roseate Tern	B													
☐ Common Tern	B													
☐ Arctic Tern	B													
☐ Forster's Tern														C
☐ Least Tern	b													S
☐ Black Tern	B													*M,*N
☐ Dovekie														I
☐ Common Murre														
☐ Thick-billed Murre														
☐ Razorbill	b													C,*M,*N
☐ Black Guillemot	B													
☐ Atlantic Puffin	b													C,*M,*N
☐ Rock Dove	B													
☐ Mourning Dove	B													
☐ Black-billed Cuckoo	B													
☐ Yellow-billed Cuckoo	B													S,M
☐ Eastern Screech-Owl	?													S?,M?
☐ Great Horned Owl	B													
☐ Snowy Owl														
☐ Northern Hawk Owl														
☐ Barred Owl	B													
☐ Great Gray Owl														I
☐ Long-eared Owl	b													

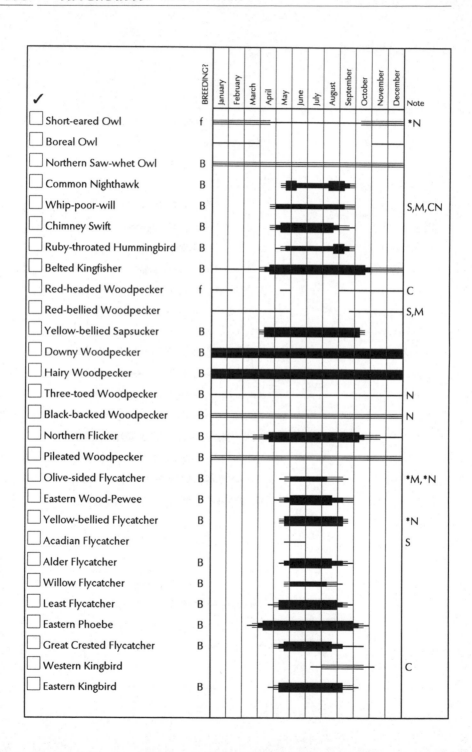

✓	BREEDING?	January	February	March	April	May	June	July	August	September	October	November	December	Note
☐ Short-eared Owl	f													*N
☐ Boreal Owl														
☐ Northern Saw-whet Owl	B													
☐ Common Nighthawk	B													
☐ Whip-poor-will	B													S,M,CN
☐ Chimney Swift	B													
☐ Ruby-throated Hummingbird	B													
☐ Belted Kingfisher	B													
☐ Red-headed Woodpecker	f													C
☐ Red-bellied Woodpecker														S,M
☐ Yellow-bellied Sapsucker	B													
☐ Downy Woodpecker	B													
☐ Hairy Woodpecker	B													
☐ Three-toed Woodpecker	B													N
☐ Black-backed Woodpecker	B													N
☐ Northern Flicker	B													
☐ Pileated Woodpecker	B													
☐ Olive-sided Flycatcher	B													*M,*N
☐ Eastern Wood-Pewee	B													
☐ Yellow-bellied Flycatcher	B													*N
☐ Acadian Flycatcher														S
☐ Alder Flycatcher	B													
☐ Willow Flycatcher	B													
☐ Least Flycatcher	B													
☐ Eastern Phoebe	B													
☐ Great Crested Flycatcher	B													
☐ Western Kingbird														C
☐ Eastern Kingbird	B													

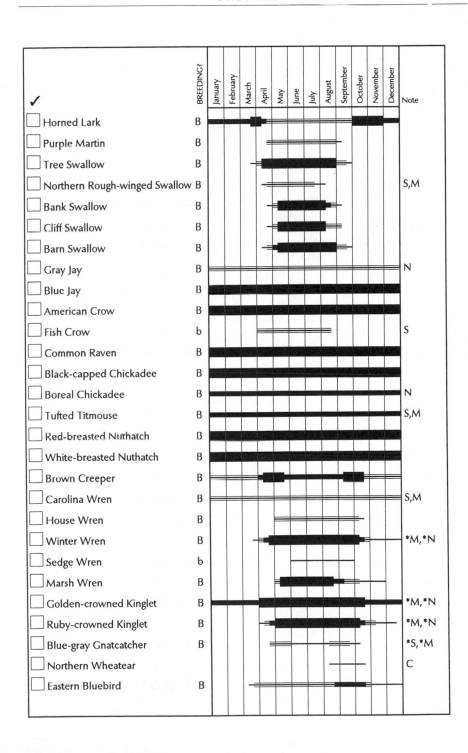

✓	BREEDING?	January	February	March	April	May	June	July	August	September	October	November	December	Note
Horned Lark	B													
Purple Martin	B													
Tree Swallow	B													
Northern Rough-winged Swallow	B													S,M
Bank Swallow	B													
Cliff Swallow	B													
Barn Swallow	B													
Gray Jay	B													N
Blue Jay	B													
American Crow	B													
Fish Crow	b													S
Common Raven	B													
Black-capped Chickadee	B													
Boreal Chickadee	B													N
Tufted Titmouse	B													S,M
Red-breasted Nuthatch	B													
White-breasted Nuthatch	B													
Brown Creeper	B													
Carolina Wren	B													S,M
House Wren	B													
Winter Wren	B													*M,*N
Sedge Wren	b													
Marsh Wren	B													
Golden-crowned Kinglet	B													*M,*N
Ruby-crowned Kinglet	B													*M,*N
Blue-gray Gnatcatcher	B													*S,*M
Northern Wheatear														C
Eastern Bluebird	B													

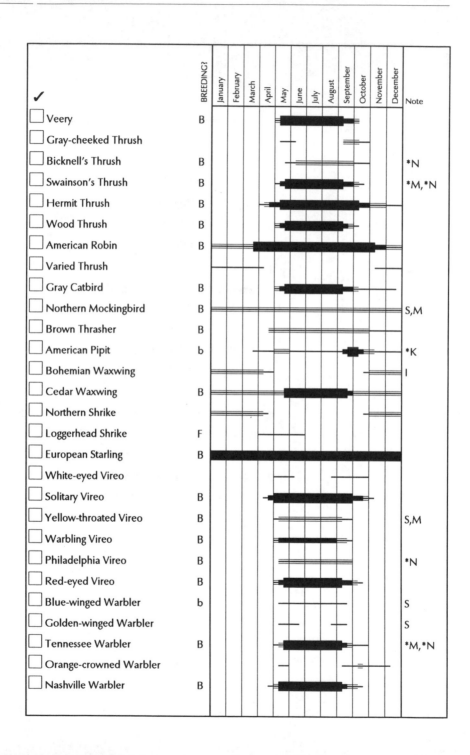

✓	BREEDING?	January	February	March	April	May	June	July	August	September	October	November	December	Note
☐ Veery	B													
☐ Gray-cheeked Thrush														
☐ Bicknell's Thrush	B													*N
☐ Swainson's Thrush	B													*M,*N
☐ Hermit Thrush	B													
☐ Wood Thrush	B													
☐ American Robin	B													
☐ Varied Thrush														
☐ Gray Catbird	B													
☐ Northern Mockingbird	B													S,M
☐ Brown Thrasher	B													
☐ American Pipit	b													*K
☐ Bohemian Waxwing														I
☐ Cedar Waxwing	B													
☐ Northern Shrike														
☐ Loggerhead Shrike	F													
☐ European Starling	B													
☐ White-eyed Vireo														
☐ Solitary Vireo	B													
☐ Yellow-throated Vireo	B													S,M
☐ Warbling Vireo	B													
☐ Philadelphia Vireo	B													*N
☐ Red-eyed Vireo	B													
☐ Blue-winged Warbler	b													S
☐ Golden-winged Warbler														S
☐ Tennessee Warbler	B													*M,*N
☐ Orange-crowned Warbler														
☐ Nashville Warbler	B													

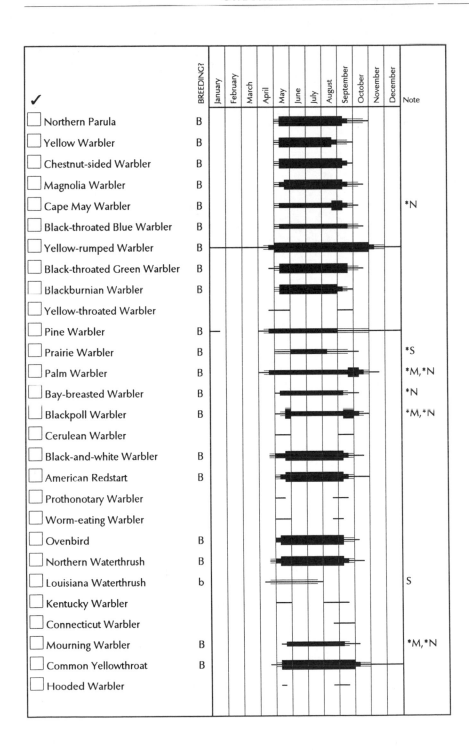

✓	BREEDING?	January	February	March	April	May	June	July	August	September	October	November	December	Note
☐ Northern Parula	B													
☐ Yellow Warbler	B													
☐ Chestnut-sided Warbler	B													
☐ Magnolia Warbler	B													
☐ Cape May Warbler	B													*N
☐ Black-throated Blue Warbler	B													
☐ Yellow-rumped Warbler	B													
☐ Black-throated Green Warbler	B													
☐ Blackburnian Warbler	B													
☐ Yellow-throated Warbler														
☐ Pine Warbler	B													
☐ Prairie Warbler	B													*S
☐ Palm Warbler	B													*M,*N
☐ Bay-breasted Warbler	B													*N
☐ Blackpoll Warbler	B													*M,*N
☐ Cerulean Warbler														
☐ Black-and-white Warbler	B													
☐ American Redstart	B													
☐ Prothonotary Warbler														
☐ Worm-eating Warbler														
☐ Ovenbird	B													
☐ Northern Waterthrush	B													
☐ Louisiana Waterthrush	b													S
☐ Kentucky Warbler														
☐ Connecticut Warbler														
☐ Mourning Warbler	B													*M,*N
☐ Common Yellowthroat	B													
☐ Hooded Warbler														

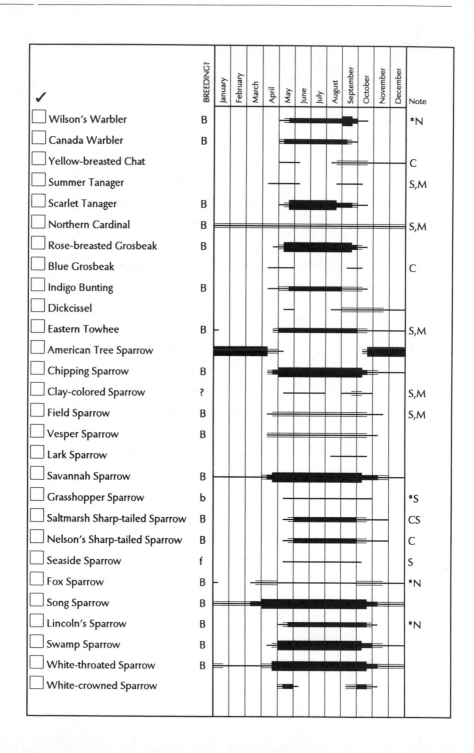

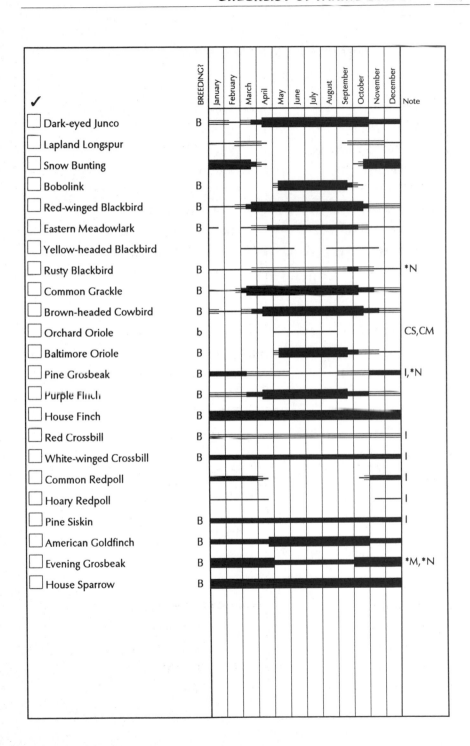

✓	BREEDING?	January	February	March	April	May	June	July	August	September	October	November	December	Note
☐ Dark-eyed Junco	B													
☐ Lapland Longspur														
☐ Snow Bunting														
☐ Bobolink	B													
☐ Red-winged Blackbird	B													
☐ Eastern Meadowlark	B													
☐ Yellow-headed Blackbird														
☐ Rusty Blackbird	B													*N
☐ Common Grackle	B													
☐ Brown-headed Cowbird	B													
☐ Orchard Oriole	b													CS,CM
☐ Baltimore Oriole	B													
☐ Pine Grosbeak	B													I,*N
☐ Purple Finch	B													
☐ House Finch	B													
☐ Red Crossbill	B													I
☐ White-winged Crossbill	B													I
☐ Common Redpoll														I
☐ Hoary Redpoll														I
☐ Pine Siskin	B													I
☐ American Goldfinch	B													
☐ Evening Grosbeak	B													*M,*N
☐ House Sparrow	B													

Vagrants & Accidentals (89 species)

* = hypothetical species

Eared Grebe *
Western Grebe
Audubon's Shearwater *
Little Shearwater *
Black-browed Albatross *
Yellow-nosed Albatross
European Storm-Petrel *
Band-rumped Storm-Petrel *
Red-billed Tropicbird
White-tailed Tropicbird
American White Pelican
Brown Pelican
Magnificent Frigatebird
Lesser Frigatebird
White Ibis
Wood Stork
Fulvous Whistling-Duck
Whooper Swan
Greater White-fronted Goose
Garganey
Steller's Eider
Black Vulture
American Swallow-tailed Kite

Mississippi Kite *
Swainson's Hawk
Willow Ptarmigan
Clapper Rail
King Rail
Corn Crake
Purple Gallinule
Northern Lapwing
Pacific Golden-Plover
Wilson's Plover
American Avocet
Black-necked Stilt
Long-billed Curlew
Eskimo Curlew
Bar-tailed Godwit
Red-necked Stint
Franklin's Gull
Mew Gull *
Ivory Gull
Gull-billed Tern
Sandwich Tern
Bridled Tern
Sooty Tern

Black Skimmer
Band-tailed Pigeon
White-winged Dove
Barn Owl
Chuck-will's-widow
Rufous Hummingbird
Say's Phoebe
Vermilion Flycatcher *
Ash-throated Flycatcher
Tropical Kingbird
Scissor-tailed Flycatcher
Fork-tailed Flycatcher
Variegated Flycatcher
Black-billed Magpie
Eurasian Jackdaw
Bewick's Wren *
Townsend's Solitaire
Pipit sp. *
Black-throated Gray Warbler
Townsend's Warbler
Western Tanager
Black-headed Grosbeak
Green-tailed Towhee

Lazuli Bunting
Painted Bunting
Black-throated Sparrow *
Cassin's Sparrow
Smith's Longspur
Chestnut-collared Longspur
Lark Bunting
Golden-crowned Sparrow
Harris' Sparrow
Le Conte's Sparrow
Henslow's Sparrow
Western Meadowlark
Shiny Cowbird
Brewer's Blackbird
Boat-tailed Grackle *
Bullock's Oriole
Common Chaffinch
Eurasian Siskin
Lesser Goldfinch
Gray-crowned Rosy-Finch

APPENDIX B

Birds of Special Interest

This appendix includes short discussions of several species deemed to be of special interest to birders in Maine. For many species, localities included in this book are listed; readers should refer to the index and from there to the appropriate chapters for more details or for directions. Although many of the best sites for a species may be listed below, the index may lead you to other sites that offer potential as well. Also check the index if you are interested in a species not listed in this appendix.

Four groups of particularly interesting birds are discussed in the Introduction under the section entitled "Migration"; these are Waterfowl, Shorebirds, Diurnal Raptors (Hawks and Others), and Landbirds. There are also sections in the Introduction entitled "Pelagic Birding" and "Winter Birding."

Red-necked Grebe. Fairly common winter visitor and common spring and fall migrant along the coast (late October–April). At some sites (e.g., East Point Sanctuary or Fortunes Rocks Beach at Biddeford Pool, Reid State Park, and on Mount Desert Island off Indian Point and along Ocean Drive between Sand Beach and Thunder Hole), sizable groups occur. Rare in summer.

Northern Fulmar. Common pelagic winter visitor (October–March); not seen from shore. Except in unusual years, typically rare from spring to early fall.

Manx Shearwater. Uncommon summer (June–September) visitor, reported in small numbers (typically 5 or fewer) from pelagic crossings (e.g., M.V. *Bluenose* and M.V. *Scotia Prince*) and on trips from Bar Harbor out to Mt. Desert Rock. Sometimes much more numerous around Machias Seal Island, with dozens of birds (sometimes 100+) present.

Wilson's Storm-Petrel. Breeds in the south Atlantic; common visitor to Maine waters from late May through August, with numbers declining in September. Infrequently seen from shore, but anywhere from dozens to several hundred are regular on pelagic crossings such as the M.V. *Bluenose* and M.V. *Scotia Prince*; smaller numbers are recorded on most trips from Bar Harbor out to Mt. Desert Rock.

Leach's Storm-Petrel. Although this species breeds on a small number of Maine's offshore islands, it is virtually never seen from shore. Most reliably found on pelagic crossings (e.g., M.V. *Bluenose* and M.V. *Scotia Prince*) from late May through September (fewer in October), with anywhere from several dozen to several hundred reported; smaller numbers are also seen on some trips from Bar Harbor out to Mt. Desert Rock.

Great Cormorant. Although small numbers have bred on several offshore islands, this species is primarily a winter visitor to coastal waters. Typically replaces Double-crested Cormorant from fall through early spring (mostly November to early April), when common; immatures are seen with migrating Double-crested Cormorants in late September and October. Sightings of summer individuals, mostly immatures, have been increasing in recent years.

King Eider. Very uncommon winter visitor (primarily mid-November to mid-March) to rocky coastal shores, with scattered individuals or small numbers reported mainly from southern and midcoast areas. Most dependably seen among rafts of Common Eiders at the Cliff House or along Marginal Way in Ogunquit, or at Cape Neddick Light (the Nubble). Other sites where you have a better-than-average chance of seeing this species include Seapoint Beach in Kittery, East Point Sanctuary at Biddeford Pool, Two Lights State Park, Reid State Park, Pemaquid Point, and Isle au Haut.

Harlequin Duck. The best place to see this uncommon winter visitor is at Cliff House or along Marginal Way in Ogunquit, where 20 to 45 birds occur annually; also found at Old Orchard Beach and Scarborough Beach Park (2–8 individuals). The largest concentration of Harlequin Ducks in the western North Atlantic occurs off Isle au Haut (150+ individuals); contact the Maine Audubon Society (see Appendix D) regarding winter trips.

Barrow's Goldeneye. Uncommon winter visitor (November–March) to harbors, bays, and ice-free patches of larger rivers; typically scattered in singles or twos and threes at several sites, but larger aggregations are regular features in most winters on the Penobscot River in Bucksport (15+), the Passagassawakeag River in Belfast (15+), the Kennebec River in Bath, and the Harraseeket River in South Freeport. Small numbers still occur along the Penobscot River between Bangor and Orono. Back Cove in Portland was for many years a good place for this species, but there have been very few sightings in recent years.

Bald Eagle. Uncommon permanent resident and migrant. Now listed as federally and state threatened after 15 years of steady recovery (and expansion across the state) through the 1980s and early 1990s. In 1994, 175 pairs nested. Reliable sites for finding this species include Merrymeeting Bay (nesting at several sites, among them Swan Island), the Bath waterfront along the Kennebec River (winter), Salt Bay (Damariscotta area), Mount Desert Island (including Bar Harbor area), Cobscook Bay State Park (two nest sites and a major wintering area), the Eastport-Lubec-Campobello Island region, the Baring Unit of Moosehorn National Wildlife Refuge (Magurrewock Marsh; a pair has nested next to Route 1 in recent years, but not in 1995), and Christina Reservoir (summer).

Northern Goshawk. Uncommon and difficult-to-see permanent resident and migrant. No site can reliably guarantee a sighting of this species. Annual spring and fall migrant in small numbers at Mt. Agamenticus, Clarry Hill (Union), and along the coast.

Peregrine Falcon. Rare resident and uncommon migrant. Since the early 1990s, five or six pairs have nested annually at scattered locations, including Precipice Trail in Acadia National Park and several sites in the western mountains. Most likely to be seen along the coast or offshore islands during spring (April–May) and particularly fall (late August–October) migration; prime sites include Mt. Agamenticus, Popham Beach State Park, Reid State Park, and Monhegan Island.

Spruce Grouse. The nemesis of many visiting birders, this species is often present but difficult to find in its typical habitat— boggy boreal forest of spruce and fir. April and early May are often the best time to see males; after early July, females (and their newly hatched young) are often more conspicuous at the edges of roads and trails. Birds sometimes dust-bathe along dirt roads. Your best bet to see this species is likely to be climbing one of the western mountains (e.g., Baldpate and Old Speck in Grafton Notch State Park, Saddleback Mountain in Rangeley, and the Bigelow Range); along quiet roads through appropriate stretches of habitat in Baxter State Park, Acadia National Park (regular at Schoodic Point and Wonderland), and the North Maine Woods; or (especially in early morning) in quiet woods such as those on Great Wass Island or at Quoddy Head State Park. These birds typically freeze upon approach and can easily go unnoticed. They also can be found high in the trees, so it pays to look up.

Piping Plover. Federally threatened and state endangered. Rare migrant. Often found at nesting sites on sandy beaches with Least Terns; 1995 population 40 pairs. Nests regularly at Popham Beach State Park and Reid State Park, also Laudholm Beach in Wells. Please use great care and do not disturb this rare bird.

Upland Sandpiper. Uncommon spring (late April–May) and fall (late July–August) migrant. Breeds regularly on the larger blueberry barrens in Washington County, on the Sidney Grasslands, and on the Kennebunk Plains. Other sites include Clarry Hill in the midcoast area and the Christina Reservoir area in Aroostook County.

Purple Sandpiper. Locally common in winter (November to mid-April, sometimes lingering into May), favoring rocky shores and islets. Feeds at the edge of the surf on seaweed-covered rocks. Reliable sites include Fort Foster in Kittery, Wells Beach and Harbor, Cape Neddick Light, Cliff House (Ogunquit), Kennebunk Beach, East Point Sanctuary and Fortunes Rocks Beach at Biddeford Pool, Two Lights State Park, Reid State Park, Pemaquid Point, and Schoodic Point. A telescope really helps with this species.

American Woodcock. One of the harbingers of spring, giving hope that winter truly will end, woodcock usually return by late March or early April and stay until early November. Difficult to find after May except by chance; males display vigorously and vocally just after sunset and before sunrise (and at other times through the night) from April typically through May. A widespread breeder, common where there are clearings close to cover. Most rural Mainers know these birds (as "timberdoodles"), so you can ask about a site. Moosehorn National Wildlife Refuge is managed for woodcock (see the chapters "Cobscook Bay State Park" and "Moosehorn National Wildlife Refuge, Baring Unit" for more information).

Red-necked Phalarope. Primarily a fall migrant offshore (mid-July to early September); regularly seen in small numbers (50+) from the M.V. *Bluenose* and on other pelagic trips. What was once a flood is now only a trickle; the hundreds of thousands to several million birds that once passed through Passamaquoddy Bay in easternmost Maine and the Bay of Fundy vanished suddenly in the late 1980s for unknown reasons, and only a small fraction of those numbers have been seen since.

Red Phalarope. Fall pelagic migrant (August–early October), regularly seen (100+) from the M.V. *Bluenose* and on other offshore boat trips.

Little Gull. Rare spring (May) and fall (August–November) migrant, usually associated with Bonaparte's Gulls. Regular off Eastport, Campobello Island, and Deer Island in August–September; otherwise irregular along the coast. In southern Maine, Pine Point Narrows in Scarborough seems to be the best site for this species. Patience and familiarity with various plumages of Bonaparte's Gulls, with which Little Gull can easily be confused, are important.

Common Black-headed Gull. Uncommon migrant. Usually associates with Bonaparte's and Ring-billed gulls. Has attempted breeding on Petit Manan Island. More numerous than Little Gull; regular off Campobello Island, Eastport, and Deer Island in fall, uncommon elsewhere along the coast. One or two birds usually overwinter in Portland (Back Cove or near the sewage treatment plant near Eastern Promenade); also check Rockland Harbor.

Iceland & Glaucous Gulls. Both of these "white-winged" gulls are regular winter visitors to the coast and, in very small numbers, to several inland sites, with Iceland Gulls usually more common than Glaucous. Immatures and adults of both species (in ones and twos) reliably seen between November and late March at Hills Beach near Biddeford Pool, Portland (Mill Creek Shop 'n Save in South Portland, Back Cove, and Portland Harbor), the Bath waterfront, Rockland Harbor, Campobello Island (East Quoddy Head), and the Eastport waterfront. These are also among the best places to see Common Black-headed Gull.

Roseate Tern. Uncommon breeding species along the Maine coast; federally endangered. Through a program controlling gulls and human presence on nesting islands, the breeding population in the state doubled in 10 years to 144 pairs in 1994. Major nesting sites are Jenny Island (Casco Bay), Eastern Egg Rock, and Petit Manan Island; also a possibility on Machias Seal Island. Colonies occasionally shift nesting islands entirely, which is likely to occur again. Regularly seen in late July through August at Pine Point Narrows in Scarborough, Popham Beach State Park, and Reid State Park. Also seen at Biddeford Pool, especially Hills Beach.

Arctic Tern. Common nesting bird on offshore islands, with favored sites being Matinicus Rock, Seal Island, Machias Seal Island, and Petit Manan Island. By controlling gulls and humans at nesting sites, population has rebounded over 10 years to more than 5,000 pairs in 1994. More pelagic than Common Tern and less likely to be observed from shore. Regularly seen on midsummer pelagic crossings on the M.V. *Bluenose* and M.V. *Scotia Prince* and on boat trips to Mt. Desert Rock.

Least Tern. Uncommon nesting bird of sand beaches, where its population has suffered greatly from the effects of development and human disturbance. With concentrated protection efforts, it has rebounded slowly and numbers have fluctuated between 80 and 120 pairs in the early 1990s. Nesting sites include Crescent Surf Beach in Wells (birds are usually visible in the inlet at the north end of Laudholm Beach at Laudholm Farm), Popham Beach State Park area, and Reid State Park.

Black Tern. Local nester on a few scattered marshy lakes in inland Maine, with fewer than 100 pairs statewide. Primary sites include Messalonskee Lake in Belgrade, Plymouth Pond in Plymouth, Great Moose Lake in Harmony, and Douglas Pond in Palmyra.

Dovekie. Tiny arctic seabird usually seen only from late October to mid-March (and irregular from year to year). Occasional "wrecks" of small numbers occur along the coast and even some miles inland after strong coastal storms with high winds from the east or northeast. Otherwise, best seen on a winter trip to Monhegan or across other offshore waters (e.g., on the Vinalhaven or North Haven ferries). (Juveniles of some larger alcids look similar—and are about as small.)

Razorbill. Most easily seen at nesting colonies on Matinicus Rock or Machias Seal Island; also nests at several other smaller and less accessible colonies on offshore islands. Regular on summer boat trips to Mt. Desert Rock. In winter, possible along much of Maine's rocky coast, but favored sites include Cape Neddick Light (the Nubble) in York, Cliff House in Ogunquit, Monhegan Island, and Head Harbour Passage off Campobello Island (especially from East Quoddy Head).

Black Guillemot. Fairly common permanent resident on rocky coast and offshore islands. Easily seen on the mail boat between Port Clyde and Monhegan Island.

Atlantic Puffin. Premier sites are nesting colonies on Machias Seal Island (carefully regulated landing and photography from blinds) and Matinicus Rock (landing not permitted). Smaller colonies include a native one on Petit Manan Island and two where puffins have been reintroduced: Eastern Egg Rock and Seal Island. Small numbers also seen on summer trips to Mt. Desert Rock and on most M.V. *Bluenose* crossings in summer and early fall; otherwise, sightings are rare. Little is known about winter habits of this species.

Northern Owls. Northern owls are an attraction in any of the states bordering Canada, and indeed, Maine has had its share (almost always in winter) of visiting Great Gray, Northern Hawk, and Boreal owls. None of these species occurs annually, however, or at predictable sites. If any northern owls are around (and in some years they are decidedly more common than in others), your best bet for finding one is to call one of Maine's bird alerts (see Appendix D) or someone you know who is knowledgeable about Maine birding. The one northern owl that is found in Maine annually is Snowy Owl (see below).

Snowy Owl. In most years single birds are scattered around the state in small numbers; more frequent along the immediate coastline. Irregular "flight years," however, bring unusually high numbers, when individuals or small numbers may be reported from 20 or more sites. These diurnal owls favor large open areas, including marshes, agricultural fields, and beaches. Locations with near-annual reports include Biddeford Pool (including Wood Island off East Point Sanctuary), Scarborough Marsh, Back Cove in Portland, and Bangor airport.

Three-toed Woodpecker. Rare inhabitant of the northern half of Maine; most birders are unlikely to see this species without concerted effort and a large dose of luck. Frequently associated with large areas of dead standing softwoods (e.g., those killed by fire, flooding, or Spruce Budworm infestation); abundance of this species rises and falls with the availability of such habitat.

Black-backed Woodpecker. More likely to be seen than Three-toed Woodpecker, but nevertheless uncommon in most areas of boreal (spruce-fir) forest along coast (east of Mount Desert Island) and inland primarily north of Waterville. Maine population may rise significantly after a massive Spruce Budworm outbreak but presently appears to be at lower levels. Like Three-toed Woodpecker, this species favors large areas of recently (5 to 8 years) dead standing softwoods, but it is regularly seen among living trees as well. Quiet and unobtrusive (unlike Downy and Hairy woodpeckers).

Yellow-bellied Flycatcher. Common nester in boreal forest and around the edges of peatlands, primarily from Mount Desert Island and Augusta north. Knowing the song and calls is key to finding this bird. Less conspicuous on migration (late May to early June; late August to mid-September).

Gray Jay. Uncommon permanent resident of boreal forest. Primarily east of Mount Desert Island along the coast (rare in recent years in coastal Washington County); elsewhere mostly north of Bangor.

Bicknell's Thrush (formerly Gray-cheeked Thrush). Generally a rare migrant (late May to early June; late September to October); breeds commonly in stunted spruce and birch-alder on mountaintops, usually above 2,800 feet, including on Old Speck and

Baldpate in Grafton Notch State Park, Mt. Blue, Saddleback, the Bigelow Range, and Katahdin. In the right habitat, often abundant. Difficult to locate as it generally sings before dawn or after dusk. Recognized by American Ornithologists' Union in 1995 as a species distinct from Gray-cheeked Thrush.

American Pipit. Uncommon spring migrant (mostly May) and fairly common to common fall migrant (September–early November); a few individuals overwinter. A small, isolated population nests on the Tableland on Katahdin in Baxter State Park; only other known nesting site in eastern United States is Mt. Washington in New Hampshire.

Bohemian Waxwing. Winter visitor (November–early April). Abundance varies greatly from year to year; rare in most years, but uncommon to fairly common every four to five years. University of Maine at Orono campus is the best-known near-annual site (flocks sometimes number 500 to 1,000 birds).

Northern Shrike. Irregular winter visitor (November– April) throughout, varying from rare to uncommon. Often perches on tops of low trees or dead snags in and around open areas.

Yellow-throated Vireo. Uncommon nester in southwestern Maine, primarily inland and south of Augusta and Rumford, reaching northeastern limit of its range. Nesting sites include Brownfield Bog and Cobbosseecontee Lake watershed.

Philadelphia Vireo. Uncommon migrant and nester, primarily north of a line from Rumford to Bangor. On nesting grounds local and often difficult to find, as song is very similar to that of Red-eyed Vireo. At many locations prefers mixed stands of mature aspens and birches. Nesting sites include Grafton Notch State Park, Mt. Blue State Park, and Baxter State Park.

Mourning Warbler. Uncommon spring and fall migrant. Fairly common nester, primarily north of Bangor, but reaching farther south in western Maine. Favors boreal habitats with regenerating clear-cuts, burns, blowdowns, or other disturbed areas with fallen logs and tangled, low deciduous growth, especially raspberries.

Vesper Sparrow. Uncommon to rare spring (April) and fall (late September–October) migrant. Breeds regularly on blueberry barrens in Kennebunk (Kennebunk Plains), Union (Clarry Hill), and Washington County (especially Deblois Barrens), and in potato fields in Aroostook County; elsewhere infrequent or uncommon in summer.

Grasshopper Sparrow. Rare spring and fall migrant. Fifteen to 20 pairs breed regularly on Kennebunk Plains, where species approaches northeastern limit of its breeding range. Declining in the Northeast and throughout range (U.S. populations declined nearly 70 percent in past 25 years).

Saltmarsh Sharp-tailed Sparrow & Nelson's Sharp-tailed Sparrow (formerly one species, Sharp-tailed Sparrow).

In 1995 the American Ornithologists' Union recognized the two populations (formerly subspecies) of Sharp-tailed Sparrow as separate species. The population found commonly in salt marshes in southern Maine north to Scarborough Marsh and Popham Beach State Park, formerly *Ammodramus caudacutus caudacutus*, is now called Saltmarsh Sharp-tailed Sparrow (not an informative name, since its new sibling species also occupies salt marsh along the northeastern coast). The population that breeds along the central and eastern portion of the coast (and very rarely inland), formerly *Ammodramus caudacutus subvirgatus*, is now called Nelson's Sharp-tailed Sparrow. Nelson's reaches its southwestern limit at Scarborough Marsh and Popham Beach, where the two species overlap. Nelson's Sharp-tailed Sparrow sings a typical "primary" song; Saltmarsh Sharp-tailed Sparrow sings a complex "whisper" song, which is a longer "variable mix of notes, syllables, and phrases" (Greenlaw 1993). See the 1993 paper by J. S. Greenlaw entitled "Behavioral and morphological diversification in Sharp-tailed Sparrows (*Ammodramus caudacutus*) of the Atlantic Coast" (*Auk* 110: 286–303) for a complete explanation and analysis.

Rusty Blackbird. Fairly common migrant (mid-March through April; mid-September to mid-November), associated with grackles and blackbirds. A few individuals overwinter along the coast. Uncommon breeder north of Bangor and in Washington County; occurs around edges of small ponds, in flooded areas of spruce and alder, and around margins of peatlands with open water.

"Winter" Finches. Maine's so-called winter finches include Pine Grosbeak, Red and White-winged crossbills, Common (and rarely Hoary) Redpoll, Pine Siskin, and Evening Grosbeak. If we only knew what made them tick, we could tell everyone else who is looking for them exactly what to do! As many a frustrated birder knows, however, these northern finches are irregular both in their ranges and numbers. One year a particular species may be widespread over the state, another year entirely absent. Your best bet for seeing any of these unpredictable species is to call one of Maine's bird alerts (see Appendix D) or to post a query with a birding friend in the state who might know what is happening this year. Remember, too, that all of these species except the redpolls breed in Maine (although some are no more predictable then than they are in winter); check the index for sites where you might find these species during the breeding season.

APPENDIX C

Algae, Lichens, Fungi, Plants, & Animals

Following are the scientific names of all algae, lichens, fungi, plants, and animals (excluding birds) mentioned in the text.

Algae

Rockweeds .... *Fucus* spp.

Lichens & Fungi

Earth Star Puffball......................... *Geaster hygrometricus*
Reindeer moss .... *Cladonia tenuis,*
                                              C. alpetris, and
                                              C. rangiferina

Plants

Alder.. *Alnus* spp.
Alpine Azalea .... *Loiseleuria procumbens*
Alpine Bilberry .... *Vaccinium uliginosum*
American Beach Grass.................... *Ammophila breviligulata*
American Beech .... *Fagus grandifolia*
Arethusa... *Arethusa bulbosa*

Aspens ....*Populus* spp.

Asters ....*Aster* spp.

Atlantic White Cedar ....*Chamaecyparis thyoides*

Baked-apple Berry ....*Rubus chamaemorus*

Balsam Fir ....*Abies balsamea*

Barberries ....*Berberis* spp.

Bayberry...*Myrica pensylvanica*

Beach Head Iris ....*Iris setosa* v. *canadensis*

Beach Heather...............................*Hudsonia tormentosa*

Beach Pea ....*Lathyrus maritimus*

Beeches...See American Beech

Bigelow's Sedge............................*Carex bigelowii*

Birches...*Betula* spp.

Bird's-eye Primrose ....*Primula laurentiana*

Blackberries ....*Rubus* spp.

Black Crowberry ....*Empetrum nigrum*

Black Grass.....................................*Juncus gerardii*

Black Spruce...................................*Picea mariana*

Bog Cranberry ....*Vaccinium macrocarpon*

Bog Rosemary...............................*Andromeda polifolia* v. *glaucophylla*

Bulrushes ....*Scirpus* spp.,
                                 Bolboschoenus spp.,
                                 Trichophorum spp., and
                                 Schoenoplectus spp.

Bunchberry ....*Cornus canadensis*

Calopogon......................................*Calopogon tuberosus*

Cattails ....*Typha* spp.

Cedars ....See Atlantic White Cedar or
                                 Northern White-Cedar

Cherries...*Prunus* spp.

Chestnut Oak.................................*Quercus prinus*

Chokecherry...................................*Prunus virginiana*

Clintonia ....*Clintonia borealis*

Common Ragweed ....*Ambrosia artemisiifolia*

Common Wood Sorrel ....*Oxalis montana*

Cotton Grass ....*Eriophorum* spp.

Crab apples ....*Malus* spp.

Diapensia ....*Diapensia lapponica*

Docks...*Rumex* spp.

Dusty Miller....................................*Artemesia stelleriana*

Dwarf Bilberry...............................*Vaccinium cespitosum*

Dwarf Birch....................................*Betula minor*

Dwarf Willow	Salix spp.
Eastern Hemlock	Tsuga canadensis
Elderberries	Sambucus spp.
Elms	Ulmus spp.
Evening Primrose	Oenothera biennis
Firs	See Balsam Fir
Flowering Dogwood	Cornus florida
Fringed Gentian	Gentianopsis crinita
Furbish's Lousewort	Pedicularis furbishiae
Glassworts	Salicornia spp.
Goldenrods	Solidago spp.
Goldthread	Coptis trifolia spp. groenlandica
Gray Birch	Betula populifolia
Hemlock	See Eastern Hemlock
Honeysuckles	Lonicera spp.
Jack Pine	Pinus banksiana
Jointweed	Polygonella articulata
Labrador Tea	Rhododendron groenlandicum
Leatherleaf	Chamaedaphne calyculata
Lowbush Blueberry	Vaccinium angustifolium
Maples	Acer spp.
Marsh Felwort	Lomatogonium rotatum
Moss Plant	Harrimanella hypnoides
Mountain Ash	Sorbus americana
Mountain Cranberry	Vaccinium vitis-idaea ssp. minus
Mountain Maple	Acer spicatum
Mountain Sandwort	Minuartia groenlandica
Northern Blazing Star	Liatris scariosa v. novae-angliae
Northern Red Oak	Quercus rubra
Northern White-Cedar	Thuja occidentalis
Northern Yarrow	Achillea millefolium borealis
Oaks	Quercus spp.
Orach	Atriplex patula
Paper Birch	Betula papyrifera
Pearlwort	Sagina nodosa
Pines	Pinus spp.
Pitcher Plant	Sarracenia purpurea
Pitch Pine	Pinus rigida
Poplars	Populus spp.
Red Maple	Acer rubrum
Red Pine	Pinus resinosa
Red Raspberry	Rubus idaeus

Red Spruce .... *Pinus rubens*
Rhodora .... *Rhododendron canadense*
Round-leaved Sundew .... *Drosera rotundifolia*
Rugosa Rose .... *Rosa rugosa*
Salt-meadow Cord Grass .... *Spartina alterniflora*
Salt-meadow Grass .... *Spartina patens*
Scrub Oak .... *Quercus ilicifolia*
Seabeach Sandwort .... *Honckenya peploides*
Sea Lavender .... *Limonium carolinianum*
Seaside Goldenrod .... *Solidago sempervirens*
Seaside Plantain .... *Plantago maritima* v. *juncoides*
Sedges .... *Carex* spp.
Shadbush .... *Amelanchier* spp.
Sheep Laurel .... *Kalmia angustifolia*
Silver Maple .... *Acer saccharinum*
Sphagnum moss .... *Sphagnum* spp.
Spike Grass .... *Distichlis spicata*
Spruces .... *Picea* spp.
Star Flower .... *Trientalis borealis*
Striped Maple .... *Acer pensylvanicum*
Sugar Maple .... *Acer saccharum*
Sundews .... *Drosera* spp.
Tall Wormwood .... *Artemisia campestris* ssp. *caudata*
Tamarack .... *Larix laricina*
Toothed White-topped Aster .... *Aster paternus*
Trailing Yew .... *Taxus canadensis*
Twinflower .... *Linnaea borealis*
Viburnums .... *Viburnum* spp.
White Ash .... *Fraxinus americana*
White Pine .... *Pinus strobus*
White Spruce .... *Picea glauca*
Wild Rice .... *Zizania aquatica*
Willows .... *Salix* spp.
Witch Hazel .... *Hamamelis viginiana*
Yarrow .... *Achillea millefolium*
Yellow Birch .... *Betula alleghaniensis*

Sources used to compile the above lists were the *Checklist of the Vascular Plants of Maine* (third revision, Josselyn Botanical Society, Bulletin 13, Maine Agricultural and Forest Experiment Station, University of Maine, Orono, ME, 1995) and *Newcomb's Wildflower Guide* (L. Newcomb, Little, Brown and Co., Boston, 1977).

Animals

INVERTEBRATES

Beach fleas .... *Orchestia* spp.
Black flies .... Simuliidae
Brittle stars .... Ophiuroidea
Deer flies .... *Chrysops* spp.
Deer Tick .... *Ixodes dammini*
Green Sea Urchin .... *Strongylocentrotus droebachiensis*
Gypsy Moth .... *Lymantria dispar*
Hermit crabs .... *Pagurus* spp.
Mosquitoes................................ Culicidae
Sea stars .... Asteroidea
Sponges .... Porifera
Spruce Budworm........................ *Choristoneura fumiferana*
Tent caterpillars......................... Lasiocampidae
Whelks .... Gastropoda

FISH

Basking Shark............................ *Cetorhinus maximus*
Landlocked Salmon..................... *Salmo salar*
Ocean Sunfish .... *Mola mola*
Trout .... *Salvelinus* spp.

REPTILES

Blanding's Turtle .... *Emydoidea blandingii*
Northern Black Racer.................. *Coluber constrictor*
Painted Turtle............................ *Chrysemys picta*
Snapping Turtle .... *Chelydra serpentina*
Spotted Turtle .... *Clemmys guttata*

MAMMALS

Atlantic White-sided Dolphin ...... *Lagenorhynchus acutus*
Beaver .... *Castor canadensis*
Beluga Whale .... *Delphinapterus leucas*
Black Bear .... *Ursus americanus*
Bobcat...................................... *Felis rufus*
Coyote...................................... *Canis latrans*
Finback Whale .... *Balaenoptera physalus*
Fisher .... *Martes pennanti*
Gray Seal .... *Halichoerus grypus*

Harbor Porpoise .... *Phocoena phocoena*
Harbor Seal .... *Phoca vitulina*
Humpback Whale .... *Megaptera novaeangliae*
Lynx .... *Felis lynx*
Mink .... *Mustela vison*
Minke Whale .... *Balaenoptera acutorostrata*
Moose .... *Alces alces*
Muskrat .... *Ondatra zibethicus*
Northern Flying Squirrel .... *Glaucomys sabrinus*
Northern Right Whale .... *Eubalaena glacialis*
Pilot Whale .... *Globicephala melaena*
Pine Marten .... *Martes americana*
Porcupine .... *Erethizon dorsatum*
Raccoon .... *Procyon lotor*
Red Fox .... *Vulpes vulpes*
Red Squirrel .... *Tamiasciurus hudsonicus*
River Otter .... *Lutra canadensis*
Snowshoe Hare .... See Varying Hare
Striped Skunk .... *Mephitis mephitis*
Varying Hare .... *Lepus americanus*
White-tailed Deer .... *Odocoileus virginianus*
Woodchuck .... *Marmota monax*

Sources used to compile the above list were *The Amphibians and Reptiles of Maine* (ed. M. L. Hunter, Jr., J. Albright, and J. Arbuckle, Maine Agricultural Experiment Station, Orono, ME, 1992), *A Field Guide to the Atlantic Seashore* (K. L. Gosner, Houghton Mifflin Co., Boston, 1978), *A Field Guide to the Insects of America North of Mexico* (D. J. Borror and R. E. White, Houghton Mifflin Co., Boston, 1970), *A Field Guide to the Moths of Eastern North America* (C. V. Covell, Jr., Houghton Mifflin Co., Boston, 1984), and *Walker's Mammals of the World* (4th ed., R. M. Nowak and J. L. Paradiso, Johns Hopkins University Press, Baltimore, MD, 1983).

APPENDIX D

Resources

Books

Adamus, P. Undated. *Atlas of Breeding Birds in Maine, 1978–1983.* Maine Dept. Inland Fisheries and Wildlife, Augusta, ME. (Out of print, but available in some Maine libraries or through interlibrary loan.)

American Ornithologists' Union. 1983. *Check-list of North American birds.* 6th ed. American Ornithologists' Union, Washington, D.C.

Appalachian Mountain Club. 1993a. *AMC Guide to Mount Desert Island and Acadia National Park.* 5th ed. Appalachian Mountain Club Books, Boston, MA.

Appalachian Mountain Club. 1993b. *AMC Maine Mountain Guide.* 7th ed. Appalachian Mountain Club Books, Boston, MA.

Bennett, D. 1988. *Maine's Natural Heritage: Rare Species and Unique Natural Features.* Down East Books, Camden, ME.

Bennett, D. 1994. *Allagash: Maine's Wild and Scenic River.* Down East Books, Camden, ME.

Burrows, R. 1988. *Birding in Atlantic Canada: Nova Scotia.* Jesperson Press, St. Johns, NF.

Calhoun, C. 1994. *Maine.* Compass American Guides, Oakland, CA.

Caputo, C. 1989. *Fifty Hikes in Northern Maine.* Countryman Press, Woodstock, VT.

Cilley, D., and S. Cilley, eds. 1993. *Appalachian Trail Guide to Maine.* 12th ed. Maine Appalachian Trail Club, Augusta, ME.

Clark, S. 1988. *Katahdin: A Guide to Baxter State Park and Katahdin.* North Country Press, Unity, ME.

Cohrs, J. S., ed. 1991. *Birding Nova Scotia.* Rev. ed. Nova Scotia Bird Society, Halifax, NS.

Curtis, W. 1995. *Maine: Off the Beaten Path.* 2d ed. Globe Pequot Press, Old Saybrook, CT.

DeLorme Mapping Co. 1989. *Allagash & St. John Map and Guide.* DeLorme Mapping Co., Freeport, ME.

DeLorme Mapping Co. 1993. *Map & Guide of Baxter State Park and Katahdin.* DeLorme Mapping Co., Freeport, ME.

DeLorme Mapping Co. 1995. *The Maine Atlas and Gazetteer.* 18th ed. DeLorme Mapping Co., Freeport, ME. (Widely available at grocery stores, bookstores, gas stations, sporting-goods outlets, etc. Revised almost annually, so get the newest edition.)

Dunne, P., D. Sibley, and C. Sutton. 1988. *Hawks in Flight.* Houghton Mifflin Co., Boston, MA.

Gibson, J. 1989. *Fifty Hikes in Southern Maine.* Backcountry Publications, Woodstock, VT.

Harrison, P. 1983. *Seabirds: An Identification Guide.* Houghton Mifflin Co., Boston, MA.

Hayman, P., J. Marchant, and T. Prater. 1986. *Shorebirds: An Identification Guide to the Waders of the World.* Houghton Mifflin Co., Boston, MA.

Hill, R. A. 1989. *Maine Forever: A Guide to Nature Conservancy Preserves in Maine.* Maine Chapter, The Nature Conservancy, Brunswick, ME.

Kane, L. J., compiler. Undated. *On Water, on Wings, in the Woods: A Guide for Maine Wildlife Watchers.* Maine Dept. Inland Fisheries and Wildlife, Augusta, ME.

Long, R. H. 1987. *Native Birds of Mount Desert Island and Acadia National Park.* 4th ed. Beech Hill Publishing Co., Mt. Desert, ME. (Available primarily at Acadia National Park headquarters and at bookstores and museums on Mount Desert Island.)

Palmer, R. S. 1949. *Maine Birds.* Museum of Comparative Zoology, Cambridge, MA. (An outstanding, but out-of-print, resource. Available in some Maine libraries and through interlibrary loan. Rarely, you can find a copy in a used-book store.)

Scott, S. L., ed. 1987. *Field Guide to the Birds of North America.* 2d ed. National Geograhic Society, Washington, D.C.

Tree, C., and E. Roundy. 1995. *Maine: An Explorer's Guide.* 7th ed. Countryman Press, Woodstock, VT. (The introductory section entitled "What's Where in Maine" is especially helpful. Revised almost annually, so get the most recent edition.)

Walton, R. K. 1988. *Bird Finding in New England.* David R. Godine, Boston, MA.

Yates, K. A., and C. R. Phillips. 1991. *AMC River Guide: Maine.* 2d ed. Appalachian Mountain Club Books, Boston, MA.

Periodicals

Birding. Bimonthly magazine of the American Birding Association. Articles on a wide variety of subjects, including field identification, bird finding, and taxonomy. Contact: American Birding Association, P.O. Box 6599, Colorado Springs, CO 80934, e-mail birding@aba.org.

Bird Observer. Bimonthly publication of Bird Observer of Eastern
Massachusetts, an organization dedicated to enhancing the
understanding, observation, and enjoyment of birds. Regularly
covers species and areas of interest to Maine birders. Contact:
Bird Observer, P.O. Box 236, Arlington, MA 02174.
The Guillemot. Amateur, bimonthly newsletter published by the
Sorrento Scientific Society. Updates on many aspects of natural
history in Maine. Contact: *The Guillemot,* 12 Spring St., Bar
Harbor, ME 04609.
Journal of Field Ornithology. Quarterly professional journal published
by the Association of Field Ornithologists. Contact: Ornitho-
logical Societies of North America, P.O. Box 1897, Lawrence,
KS 66044-8897.
Maine Bird Notes. Quarterly report on bird sightings in Maine.
Contact: *Maine Bird Notes,* Rt. 1 Box 825, Turner, ME 04282.
Maine Naturalist. Peer-reviewed quarterly published by Eagle Hill
Wildlife Research Station. Contributions deal with many aspects
of natural history in Maine and the rest of the Acadia bioregion.
Contact: *Maine Naturalist,* P.O. Box 99, Steuben, ME 04680.
Winging It. Monthly newsletter published by the American Birding
Association. Contact: *Winging It,* P.O. Box 6599, Colorado
Springs, CO 80934, e-mail birding@aba.org.

Bird Alerts

MAINE RARE BIRD ALERT: 207-781-2332. Run by the Maine Audubon
Society (P.O. Box 6009, Falmouth, ME 04105-6009). Phone
message is updated weekly.
DOWN EAST BIRDLINE: 207-244-4116. An independent bird alert run
by Ann Bacon, P.O. Box 19, Mt. Desert, ME 04660. Phone message is updated weekly.

Workshops & Courses

AUDUBON ECOLOGY CAMP. Located on Hog Island in upper Muscongus
Bay and administered by the National Audubon Society. Week-
long sessions for adults offered throughout the summer. For
more information, write or call the camp at Keene Neck Road,
Medomak, ME 04551, telephone 207-529-5880.
EAGLE HILL FIELD RESEARCH STATION. An independent, nonprofit organization in Steuben, Maine, committed to quality educational programs in natural history. Intensive week-long seminars and workshops on several subjects are offered throughout the summer in a
beautiful natural setting. For more information, contact the station at P.O. Box 9, Steuben, ME 04680-0009, telephone 207-546-
2821, fax 207-546-3042, e-mail eaglehill@maine.maine.edu.

INSTITUTE FOR FIELD ORNITHOLOGY. A nonprofit organization directed by ornithologist Charles Duncan and dedicated to increasing knowledge of birds in their natural habitats. Workshops are offered at the institute in Machias, Maine, on shorebirds, seabirds, and warblers, and at Cape May, New Jersey, on raptors. The institute also maintains a small ornithology library emphasizing distributional and identification works, the major journals, and works of particular interest to Maine and the Maritimes. For more information, contact the institute at 9 O'Brien Ave., Machias, ME 04654, telephone 207-255-3313 ext. 289, fax 207-255-4864, e-mail cduncan@acad.umm.maine.edu.

SHOALS MARINE LABORATORY. Located about 6 miles off the southern coast of Maine on Appledore Island and administered by the University of New Hampshire and Cornell University. Several science courses are offered on the island each summer, including (in most years) at least one course in ornithology. For more information, contact SML at Stimson Hall, Cornell University, Ithaca, NY 14853, telephone 607-255-3717, e-mail shoals-lab@cornell.edu, home page http://www.sml.cornell.edu.

Major Natural History & Conservation Organizations

MAINE AUDUBON SOCIETY, P.O. Box 6005, Falmouth, ME 04105-6009, telephone 207-781-2330, e-mail maineaudubon@agc.org. (An independent, statewide organization; not a chapter of the National Audubon Society.)

MAINE COAST HERITAGE TRUST, 167 Park Row, Brunswick, ME 04011, telephone 207-729-7366, e-mail mcht@biddeford.com, home page http://www.cltn.org.

NATIONAL AUDUBON SOCIETY, Maine State Office, P.O. Box 524, Dover-Foxcroft, ME 04426, telephone 207-564-7946, home page http://www.igc.org/audubon/contents/html. Additionally, there are six regional Maine chapters of NAS: York County (based in Kennebunk), Prout's Neck, Merrymeeting (based in Brunswick), Midcoast (based in Rockland), Western Maine (based in Farmington), and Central Highlands (based in Dover-Foxcroft). Call the state office in Dover-Foxcroft for information on individual chapters.

NATURAL RESOURCES COUNCIL OF MAINE, 271 State St., Augusta, ME 04330, telephone 207-622-3101, e-mail nrcme@igc.apc.org.

THE NATURE CONSERVANCY, Maine Chapter, 14 Maine St., Brunswick, ME 04011, telephone 207-729-5181, home page http://www.tnc.org.

INDEX

A Word from the
AMERICAN BIRDING ASSOCIATION,
The Organization Devoted to North American Birders

ABA is *the* organization of North American birders, and its mission is to bring all the excitement, challenge, and wonder of birding to you. As an ABA member you will get the information you need to increase your birding skills so that you can make the most of your time in the field.

Each year members receive six issues of ABA's award-winning magazine, *Birding*, and twelve issues of *Winging It*, a monthly newsletter. ABA's periodicals put you in touch with the birding scene across the continent. ABA conducts regular conferences and biennial conventions in the continent's best birding areas, publishes a yearly *Membership Directory/Yellow Pages* to help you keep in touch, offers discount prices for bird books, optical gear, and other birding equipment through ABA Sales, and compiles an annual *Directory of Volunteer Opportunities* for members. The organization's *ABA/Lane Birdfinding Guides* set the standard for accuracy and excellence.

ABA is engaged in bird conservation through such activities as Partners in Flight and the American Bird Conservancy. ABA encourages birding among young people through youth birding camps and other activities, and publishes *A Bird's-Eye View*, a quarterly newsletter by and for its younger members. The organization promotes ethical birding practices. In short, the AMERICAN BIRDING ASSOCIATION works to ensure that birds and birding have the healthy future they deserve.

"ABA is the best value in the birding community today."
Roger Tory Peterson

The AMERICAN BIRDING ASSOCIATION gives active birders what they want. Consider joining today.

For information, contact:
AMERICAN BIRDING ASSOCIATION
P.O. Box 6599
Colorado Springs, Colorado 80934
Tel.: 800-850-2473